The Great Financial Meltdown

NEW DIRECTIONS IN MODERN ECONOMICS

Series Editor: Malcolm C. Sawyer, *Professor of Economics, University of Leeds, UK*

New Directions in Modern Economics presents a challenge to orthodox economic thinking. It focuses on new ideas emanating from radical traditions including post-Keynesian, Kaleckian, neo-Ricardian and Marxian. The books in the series do not adhere rigidly to any single school of thought but attempt to present a positive alternative to the conventional wisdom.

For a full list of Edward Elgar published titles, including the titles in this series, visit our website at www.e-elgar.com.

The Great Financial Meltdown

Systemic, Conjunctural or Policy Created?

Edited by

Turan Subasat

Department of Economics, Mugla Sitki Kocman University, Turkey

NEW DIRECTIONS IN MODERN ECONOMICS

Edward Elgar PUBLISHING

Cheltenham, UK • Northampton, MA, USA

Published by
Edward Elgar Publishing Limited
The Lypiatts
15 Lansdown Road
Cheltenham
Glos GL50 2JA
UK

Edward Elgar Publishing, Inc.
William Pratt House
9 Dewey Court
Northampton
Massachusetts 01060
USA

A catalogue record for this book
is available from the British Library

Library of Congress Control Number: 2016931499

This book is available electronically in the **Elgar**online
Economics subject collection
DOI 10.4337/9781784716493

MIX
Paper from
responsible sources
FSC® C013056

ISBN 978 1 78471 648 6 (cased)
ISBN 978 1 78471 649 3 (eBook)

Typeset by Servis Filmsetting Ltd, Stockport, Cheshire
Printed and bound in Great Britain by TJ International Ltd, Padstow

To those who died for peace and democracy in Turkey

Contents

Contributors

Erdogan Bakir received his BS and MS from the Middle East Technical University in Ankara, Turkey and his PhD from the University of Utah, USA. In 2006–2007, he held a Swedish Institute postdoctoral scholarship at the Gothenburg University in Sweden. He has been teaching at the Bucknell University in Lewisburg, USA since 2008. His research, which focuses on business cycles and the neoliberal form of capitalism in the USA, has been published in political economy journals including the *Review of Radical Political Economics*, *Science and Society* and *Journal of Economic Issues*.

Riccardo Bellofiore is a professor at the University of Bergamo, Italy. He teaches advanced macroeconomics, history of economic thought, monetary economics and international monetary economics. His research interests include capitalist contemporary economy, endogenous monetary approaches, Marxian theory and the philosophy of economics. Among his recent publications are: 'Crisis Theory and the Great Recession: A Personal Journey, from Marx to Minsky' (*Research in Political Economy*, 2011); '"Two or Three Things I Know about Her": Europe in the Global Crisis, and Heterodox Economics' (*Cambridge Journal of Economics*, 2013); and with Francesco Garibaldo and Mariana Mortagua, 'A Credit-Money and Structural Perspective on the European Crisis: Why Exiting the Euro is the Answer to the Wrong Question' (*Review of Keynesian Economics*, 2015); and five co-edited books: with Giovanna Vertova, *The Great Recession and the Contradictions of Contemporary Capitalism* (Edward Elgar Publishing, 2014); with Scott Carter, *Towards a New Understanding of Piero Sraffa. Insights from Archival Research* (Palgrave Macmillan, 2014); with Guido Starosta and Peter Thomas, *In Marx's Laboratory. Critical Interpretations of the Grundrisse* (Leiden, 2013); and with Ewa Karwowska and Jan Toporowski, two volumes in honour of Tadeusz Kowalik: *The Legacy of Rosa Luxemburg, Oskar Lange and Michal Kalecki* (Palgrave Macmillan, 2014) and *Economic Crisis and Political Economy* (Palgrave Macmillan, 2013).

Al Campbell is a retired Emeritus Professor of Economics from the University of Utah, USA, currently living in Bern, Switzerland. He is a longstanding member of the Steering Committee of the Union for Radical Political Economics (URPE), a member of the Programme Committee of the International Initiative for Promoting Political Economy (IIPPE) and on the editorial board of the *International Journal of Cuban Studies*. His central research interests over his career have been the nature, structure and functioning of contemporary capitalism (neoliberalism today), theoretical issues concerning more humane socialist alternatives, and empirical considerations of contemporary national economies attempting to build such an alternative. He is the editor of *Cuban Economists on the Cuban Economy* (University Press of Florida, 2013).

Radhika Desai is a professor at the Department of Political Studies and Director, Geopolitical Economy Research Group, University of Manitoba, Winnipeg, Canada. She is the author of *Geopolitical Economy: After US Hegemony, Globalization and Empire* (Pluto Press, 2013), *Slouching Towards Ayodhya: From Congress to Hindutva in Indian Politics* (Three essays Collective, 2nd rev. edn 2004) and *Intellectuals and Socialism: 'Social Democrats' and the Labour Party* (Lawrence & Wishart, 1994), a *New Statesman and Society* Book of the Month. She is editor of *Theoretical Engagements in Geopolitical Economy* (Emerald, 2015), and *Developmental and Cultural Nationalisms* (Routledge, 2009), and co-editor with Paul Zarembka of *Revitalizing Marxist Theory for Today's Capitalism* (Emerald, 2010). She is also the author of numerous articles in *Economic and Political Weekly*, *New Left Review*, *Third World Quarterly* and other journals, and chapters in edited collections on parties, political economy, culture and nationalism. With Alan Freeman, she co-edits the Geopolitical Economy book series with Manchester University Press and the Future of Capitalism book series with Pluto Press. She serves on the editorial boards of *Canadian Political Science Review*, *E-Social Sciences, Pacific Affairs*, *Global Faultlines*, *Research in Political Economy*, *Rivista Economica Critica*, the *World Review of Political Economy* and *International Critical Thought*.

Ben Fine is Professor of Economics at the School of Oriental and African Studies (SOAS), University of London, UK and holds honorary positions at the Universities of Johannesburg (Senior Research Fellow attached to the South African Research Chair in Social Change), Rhodes University (Visiting Professor, Institute of Social and Economic Research), and Witswatersrand (Associate Researcher, Corporate Strategy and Industrial Development). His recent books include: as contributing editor, with K. Bayliss, *Privatization and Alternative Public Sector Reform in Sub-Saharan Africa: Delivering on Electricity and Water* (Palgrave Macmillan, 2008); co-edited with Alfredo Saad-Filho and Marco Boffo, *The Elgar Companion to Marxist Economics* (Edward Elgar, 2012); co-authored with

Dimitris Milonakis, *From Political Economy to Economics: Method, the Social and the Historical in the Evolution of Economic Theory* (Routledge, 2009), awarded the 2009 Gunnar Myrdal Prize; co-authored with Dimitris Milonakis, *From Economics Imperialism to Freakonomics: The Shifting Boundaries Between Economics and Other Social Sciences* (Routledge, 2009), awarded the 2009 Deutscher Prize; co-authored with Alfredo Saad-Filho, *Marx's Capital*, sixth edition (Pluto Press, forthcoming); *Theories of Social Capital: Researchers Behaving Badly* (Pluto Press, 2010); as contributing editor, with K. Bayliss and E. Van Waeyenberge, *The Political Economy of Development: The World Bank, Neoliberalism and Development Research* (Pluto Press, 2011); as contributing editor with J. Saraswati and D. Tavasci, *Beyond the Developmental State: Industrial Policy into the 21st Century* (Pluto Press, 2012); as contributing editor with Kyung-Sup Chang and Linda Weiss, *Developmental Politics in Transition: The Neoliberal Era and Beyond* (Palgrave Macmillan, 2012). He has served as an advisor to trade unions, other progressive organizations, and to international, national and local agencies and governments, and served as one of four international expert advisors on President Mandela's 1995–1996 South African Labour Market Commission. He currently sits on the Social Science Research Committee of the UK's Food Standards Agency for which he chaired the Working Group on Reform of Slaughterhouse Controls. He is Chair of the International Initiative for Promoting Political Economy (IIPPE).

Vassilis K. Fouskas is Professor of International Politics and Economics at the University of East London (UEL), UK and the Director of the Centre for the Study of States, Markets and People (STAMP) in the UEL's Royal Docks School of Business and Law. He is the founding editor of the *Journal of Balkan and Near Eastern Studies* (Routledge, six issues a year since 1998) and the co-author (with Constantine Dimoulas) of *Greece, Financialization and the EU: The Political Economy of Debt and Destruction* (Palgrave Macmillan, 2013).

Alan Freeman is a former principal economist at the Greater London Authority, UK where he was responsible for London's Economic Forecast, the Living Wage, and the Creative Economy. He retired in 2011 and lives in Winnipeg, Canada where, with Radhika Desai, he is co-director of the Geopolitical Economy Research Group. With Hasan Bakhshi and Peter Higgs he co-authored *A Dynamic Mapping of the UK's Creative Economy* (NESTA, 2014), which laid the statistical basis for the UK Department of Culture, Media and Sport's creative industry estimates from 2015 onwards. With Radhika Desai he co-edits the Future of World Capitalism book series (Pluto) and writes regularly on economics and politics. His books include *The Benn Heresy*, a biography of the UK politician Tony Benn (Pluto, 1981, rev. edn 2014), and with Boris Kagarlitsky, *The Political Economy of Empire and the Crisis of Globalisation* (Pluto, 2002). He co-edited *Marx, Ricardo, Sraffa* with Ernest Mandel (Verso, 1984), *Marx and Non-equilibrium Economics* with Guglielmo Carchedi (Edward Elgar Publishing, 1996), and *The New Value Controversy* with Andrew Kliman and Julian Wells (Edward Elgar Publishing, 2004).

David Harvey is a Distinguished Professor of Anthropology and Geography at the Graduate Center of the City University of New York, USA. He is the author of *The Limits to Capital* (Basil Blackwell, 1982), *The Condition of Postmodernity* (Blackwell, 1989), *The New Imperialism* (Oxford University Press, 2013), *A Brief History of Neoliberalism* (Oxford University Press, 2005), *The Enigma of Capital* (Profile Books, 2010) and, most recently, *Seventeen Contradictions and the End of Capitalism* (Oxford University Press, 2014). His popular video lectures on Marx's *Capital*, Volumes 1 and 2 are available free at www://DavidHarvey.org.

Annina Kaltenbrunner is a lecturer in the economics of globalization and the international economy at Leeds University Business School, UK. Her areas of research are development economics, international finance, monetary economics, international political economy, heterodox economics and methodology. She has published on emerging market currency internationalization, financial integration, external vulnerability, and the eurozone crisis and has collaborated on work for the United Nations University (UNU) and the European FP7 Project AUGUR. She is currently contributing to several projects including the European FP7 FESSUD, a two-year project on Finance and Inequality with the Foundation for European Progressive Studies (FEPS), and commissioned work on currency internationalization by the Brazilian central bank.

Elif Karacimen is an assistant professor of economics in the Department of Economics at Recep Tayyip Erdogan University, Turkey. Her research interests include the political economy of banking and credit, financialization in emerging capitalist economies and household debt. She has published articles in the *Cambridge Journal of Economics* and *Journal of Balkan and Eastern Studies*. She obtained her BS in Economics from the Middle East Technical University, Turkey, and her PhD in Economics from the School of Oriental and African Studies (SOAS), University of London, UK. She is a member of Research on Money and Finance (RMF).

David M. Kotz is a professor of economics at the University of Massachusetts Amherst, USA and Distinguished Professor in the School of Economics at the Shanghai University of Finance and Economics, China. His recent books are: *The Rise and Fall of Neoliberal Capitalism* (Harvard University Press, 2015); *Contemporary Capitalism and Its Crises* (Cambridge University Press, 2010), co-edited with Terrence McDonough and Michael Reich; and *Russia's Path from Gorbachev to Putin: The Demise of the Soviet System and the New Russia* (Routledge, 2007), co-authored with Fred Weir. He has published articles in the *Review of Radical Political Economics, Science and Society, Monthly Review, World Review of Political Economy* and *International Critical Thought*.

Stavros D. Mavroudeas studied at the Economics Department of the University of Athens, Greece (BA Economics 1985), the School of Oriental and African Studies (SOAS), University of London (MSc Economics 1986), and Birkbeck College, University of London, UK (PhD Economics 1990). He is currently working as Professor in Political Economy in the Economics Department of the University of Macedonia. He has published in many academic journals including *Science and Society, Review of Radical Political Economics, Review of Political Economy, Economie Appliquee, International Critical Thought*. His publications include *The Limits of Regulation: A Critical Analysis of Capitalist Development* (Edward Elgar, 2012), *Greek Capitalism in Crisis – Marxist Analyses* (Routledge, 2014), 'Development and Crisis: The Turbulent Course of Greek Capitalism' (*International Critical Thought*, 2013), 'Regulation Theory: The Road from Creative Marxism to Post-Modern Disintegration' (*Science and Society*, 1999), 'Periodising Capitalism: Problems and Method: The case of the Regulation Approach' (*Research in Political Economy*, 1999), 'Work More or Work Harder? The Length and the Intensity of Work in Marx's "*Capital*"' (*Science and Society*, 2010), 'Duration, Intensity and Productivity of Labour and the Distinction between Absolute and Relative Surplus-Value' (*Review of Political Economy*, 2010), 'A History of Contemporary Political Economy and Post-Modernism' (*Review of Radical Political Economics*, 2006), 'All Work and No . . . Pay? Unpaid Overtime in Greece: Determining Factors and Theoretical Explanations' (*Industrial Relations Journal*, 2014).

Simon Mohun is Emeritus Professor of Political Economy at Queen Mary University of London, UK. His research interests are primarily concerned with the theoretically informed measurement, description and explanation of trends in aggregate profitability in developed capitalist economies since the 1960s. He has written extensively on value theory, productive and unproductive labour in capitalist societies, and the rate of profit in the US economy. His most recent work is concerned with the development of long time series of quantitative measures of class in the US economy, the empirical measurement of Goodwin-type cycles in the post-war UK economy, and finance and financial crisis. He is an active member of the International Initiative for Promoting Political Economy (IIPPE).

Özgür Orhangazi is an associate professor of economics at Kadir Has University in Istanbul, Turkey. He is the author of *Financialization and the US Economy* (Edward Elgar, 2008) and numerous articles and book chapters on financialization, financial crises and alternative economic policies. He previously taught economics at Roosevelt University in Chicago, USA.

Michael Roberts is an independent researcher. He has worked in the City of London, UK as an economist for more than 30 years. He is the author of *The Great Recession: A Marxist View* (Lulu, 2009). He has a new book, *The Long Depression*, to be published by Haymarket in 2016. He has published in the *World Review of Political Economy* and *Historical Materialism* journals and presented papers at the Association of Heterodox Economists, Historical Materialism, Allied Social Sciences Association (ASSA), Society for the Advancement of Social Sciences (SASE) and International Initiative for Promoting Political Economy (IPPE) conferences. He blogs at thenextrecession.wordpress.com.

Turan Subasat is a professor at the University of Mugla. He received his BSc from the University of Istanbul, and his MSc (Birkbeck College) and PhD (SOAS) from the University of London, UK. He previously taught development studies at the University of London (School of Oriental and African Studies, SOAS), economics at the University of Bath, UK and economics at the Izmir University of Economics, Turkey. His research focuses on development economics, international trade, foreign direct investment (FDI) and Turkish economy and he has published in political economy journals including the *Review of Radical Political Economics* and *Journal of Balkan and Eastern Studies*.

Jan Toporowski is Professor of Economics and Finance at the School of Oriental and African Studies (SOAS), University of London, UK and a visiting professor at the University of Bergamo, Italy. He studied economics at Birkbeck College, University of London, UK and the University of Birmingham, UK. Jan Toporowski has worked in fund management and international banking. His most recent book is *Michal Kalecki An Intellectual Biography Volume 1 Rendezvous in Cambridge 1899–1939* (Palgrave, 2013).

John Weeks is Professor Emeritus of Development Economics, School of Oriental and African Studies (SOAS), University of London, UK, and former director and founder of the Centre for Development Policy and

Research, SOAS. He has published over 70 scholarly articles and 12 books plus several edited volumes. Since retirement he has sought to intervene in debates over current policy, especially in Britain and the eurozone. He is a founding member of the UK advocacy organization, Economists for Rational Economic Policies. His most recent book critiques neoliberal economics for non-expert readers, *Economics of the 1%: How Mainstream Economics Serves the Rich, Obscures Reality and Distorts Policy* (Anthem, 2014).

Acknowledgements

I would like to extend my sincere thanks to the Izmir University of Economics, Turkey. A special thanks goes to Professor Cemali Dincer, then the Vice Dean, for his enthusiastic support without which this book would not have been possible.

Abbreviations

ABCP	asset-backed commercial paper
BEA	Bureau of Economic Affairs
BIS	Bank for International Settlements
BRICS	Brazil, Russia, India, China, South Africa
CDOs	collateralized debt obligations
CEO	chief executive officer
EAP	Economic Adjustment Programme
ECB	European Central Bank
ECE	emerging capitalist economy
EEC	European Economic Community
EMU	European Monetary Union
EU	European Union
FCIC	Financial Crisis Inquiry Commission
FDI	foreign direct investment
Fed	Federal Reserve
FI	financial intermediation
FIH	financial instability hypothesis
FINSIM	financial intermediation services indirectly measured
FSITA	fuzzy set ideal type analysis
GDP	gross domestic product
ILO	International Labour Organization
IMF	International Monetary Fund
IS/LM	investment/saving / liquidity preference/money supply
L^{FI}	labor in financial intermediation
L^{RE}	labor in real estate; renting and business activities
MEC	marginal efficiency of capital
MEGA	Marx-Engels-Gesamtausgabe
MELT	monetary equivalent of labour time
NAICS	North American Industrial Classification System
NATO	North Atlantic Treaty Organization
NDP	net domestic product
NFC	non-financial corporation
NIA	national income accounts
OCA	optimal currency area

OCC	organic composition of capital
OECD	Organisation for Economic Co-operation and Development
PASOK	Panhellenic Socialist Movement
PASOK-ND	PASOK–New Democracy
PIGS	Portugal, Ireland, Greece, Spain
PPP	purchasing power parity
RE	real estate; renting and business activities
ROP	rate of profit
RPF	rate of profit to fall
SIC	Standard Industrial Classification
SMEs	small and medium-sized organizations
TDH	twin deficits hypothesis
TRPF	tendency of the rate of profit to fall
UK	United Kingdom
UNCTAD	United Nations Conference on Trade and Development
US	United States
$VA^{FI\&RE}$	value added in financial intermediation; real estate; renting and business activities
VA^{FI}	value added in financial intermediation
VA^{RE}	value added in real estate; renting and business activities
VCC	value composition of capital
WRA	welfare regime approach
WWII	World War II

PART I

Introduction

1. The crisis in context

Turan Subasat

PART I: INTRODUCTION

Economic crises have long occupied an important place in the political economy literature. Political economy approaches to the global crisis can roughly be divided into three. First, there are those that result from the contradictory structural characteristics of the capitalist mode of production. These explanations include theories such as the tendency of the rate of profit to fall, the profit squeeze, underconsumption, overaccumulation, disproportionality and the moral depreciation of capital. Second, many argue that crises result from the conjuncture of unanticipated events such as rapid oil price increases, rapid advances in technologies, excessive financialization, the emergence of alternative centers of capital accumulation and repositioning in the class relationships. Third, economic crisis can also result from government policies, either intentional or unintentional. This approach is prompted by the apparent increase in the frequency and economic cost of crises since the 1980s when neoliberal policies became dominant in the major capitalist countries. In this view, the crisis of 2008 was the necessary outcome of a 30-year trend in economic deregulation in the advanced capitalist economies. This policy shift represented a conscious choice by the capitalist classes in each country, just as the previous period of regulation had been a policy choice.

Most authors in this book recognize that the separation of causes along the above distinct lines may not be easy, as systemic, conjunctural and policy-driven factors often overlap and display a complex relationship. Let alone complicated issues such as financialization, seemingly straightforward conjunctural issues such as the 1973–1979 oil crisis has been considered as a crisis of accumulation linked with the contradictory nature of capital accumulation. Alan Freeman (Chapter 5) suggests that the immediate causes of crisis and systemic underlying causes, such as declining profit rates which can worsen all the other contradictions, should be separated from each other. Therefore, he argues, while financialization may seem to cause the crisis, what caused financialization requires an explanation.

Likewise, Stavros Mavroudeas (Chapter 17) considers neoliberalism and financialization as conjunctural by-products of the systemic tendencies. Turan Subasat (Chapter 10) separates policy-making from policy errors as the focus on policy errors takes an accidental view of crises and implies that crises could be prevented by circumventing mistakes. Policies, however, are social constructions influenced by complex class struggles and they cannot be treated as policy errors. Policy-making is deeply enrooted in class relations and many policy-based causes are in fact also systemic.

David Kotz (Chapter 2) addresses this issue directly and argues that although the contradictions of capitalism (-in-general) offer the best explanation of crises, ignoring policies and contingent events results in misleading conclusions. This is because capitalism-in-general cannot explain why a particular crisis occurs in a particular time and place without undertaking a more tangible analysis. The particular form of capitalism is a useful concept that helps us to avoid falling into the capitalism-in-general versus state policies dichotomy. While the fundamental characteristics of capitalism remain the same, it takes a series of distinct forms over time and space which last for an extended period of time, and identified by specific institutions, ideas and class relations. Although state policy is subject to change rapidly, a form of capitalism is a coherent entity that lasts for a significant period of time, constrains state policies and provides them with stability and coherence. Neoliberalism is the prevailing form of capitalism since the 1980s which can explain the nature of the capital accumulation process and the subsequent crisis.

This chapter aims to provide the reader with an analytical summary of the main discussions in this book which cover a wide range of issues. The collection of closely related chapters in this book reviews, advocates and critiques the three approaches to the global crisis to assess their analytical and empirical validity. The book is organized in five parts. After Part I (Introduction), Part II (Crisis and Profitability) exclusively focuses on the role of profit rate. Part III (The Crisis in Economic and Social Reproduction) involves six chapters with various theoretical and empirical perspectives. Part IV (Crisis and Finance) has a narrower focus on the role of financialization. The final part, Part V (The Crisis Unfolds), focuses on the crisis in Greece.

PART II: CRISIS AND PROFITABILITY

Marxian debates naturally involve a number of classical crisis theories that this book deals with first. Notably, there is an important debate over the role of the tendency of the rate of profit to fall (TRPF) which many of the authors either directly or indirectly address. Marx developed the TRPF theory to show that capitalist competition would necessarily lead to increase in the organic composition of capital which would reduce profit rates and lead to capitalist crisis. Even amongst the classical Marxists, however, there has been an ongoing debate over the significance of the theory as the main cause of capitalist crises. The theory has been challenged both theoretically and empirically. Testing the empirical validity of the theory is also problematic due to complex procedures developed to measure the rate of profit. The three chapters in Part II are exclusively dedicated to this debate.

David Harvey's Chapter 3 argues that Marx derived the 'law' under 'draconian' assumptions and suggests that Engels was far more enthusiastic about the TRPF than Marx, who never went back to the theory later in his life despite its evident incompleteness. Therefore, he argues, we should not take his theoretical conclusions too far. In his view, Marx perceived crises as momentary and violent eruptions that resolve the existing contradictions which can be considered as opportunities of capitalist reconstruction rather than a sign of the imminent end of capitalism.

Harvey argues that the rate of profit can be stabilized by a variety of factors such as a devaluation of the existing constant capital due to technical change, monopolization, or accelerating turnover times in both production and circulation. He argues, moreover, that a productivity increase that is not associated with job losses would not reduce surplus value production. Moreover, a fall in profit rates could result from a number of reasons rather than an increase in the organic composition of capital. For instance, the consumption level of the working classes can cause problems in two ways: too-low wages can cause low demand and realization problems, and too-high wages can cause profit squeeze.

Harvey also questions the logic of the TRPF by focusing on the form of industrial organization and argues that the level of vertical integration within a firm (or sector) would artificially change the composition of capital. This is because if a firm chooses to produce more (less) means of production within the firm, it will buy less (more) means of production from other firms which will artificially increase (decrease) its rate of profit which is calculated based on capital advanced to buy constant and variable capital.

Michael Roberts (Chapter 4) offers a comprehensive critique of Harvey and argues that Marx never abandoned the TRPF as a relevant explanation of crises. He never went back to the theory in his later years simply because he was satisfied with it. Rather than developing the theory he tried to figure out how to use it to explain the cyclical nature of capitalism as well as its transitory nature. Roberts contends that Marx's assumptions for the

TRPF are realistic and can be reduced to just two: labor power is the only source of value, and capital accumulation leads the organic composition of capital to rise. He argues against the view that each crisis has a different or 'conjunctural' origin. The recurrent nature of capitalist crises implies that they must have a common cause. 'A Marxist theory of crises must look beneath the appearance of events' to identify the underlying causes and separate them from the triggers that may take many different forms, such as collapsing housing bubbles and stock markets. Acknowledging the relevance of TRPF, therefore, does not imply that financialization has no relevance to the crash of 2008.

Regarding Harvey's accelerating turnover as a factor that can stabilize the rate of profit, Roberts argues that it can boost the rate of profit for an individual capitalist only at the expense of other 'slower' capitalists. He also argues that vertical integration would be irrelevant to the economy as a whole and would have no impact on the organic composition of capital as long as the same number of workers use the same capital equipment to perform exactly the same tasks.

Regarding the empirical evidence, he suggests that Harvey's skepticism is unfounded. There is overwhelming evidence for a secular fall in the rate of profit in the United Kingdom, the United States (US) and in many other countries across the globe which is caused by the rising organic composition of capital. He concludes his chapter by arguing that rejecting TRPF means Marx had no theory of crisis at all.

Freeman (Chapter 5) provides another vigorous defense of the TRPF and argues that the profit rate is the only credible competitor left in the contest to explain what is going wrong with capitalism. He claims that the long-run decline in the profit rate is caused by the dynamics of capitalism. To prove the relevance of profit rates he notes that there is a very close link between the variations in the rate of profit and the variations in the rate of accumulation. Regarding profit rates, he claims that its decline (rather than the lack of it) is the norm. Freeman suggests that the attempt to establish a direct link between TRPF and crisis results from a major confusion, since the TRPF worsens all the other contradictions and causes crisis indirectly. There is a need, therefore, to separate the 'immediate causes of crisis' from the TRPF as the underlying real cause. In other words, while Marx offers a theory of crisis based on the TRPF, he does not reduce a theory to a mechanism. Therefore, Freeman argues, while some conjunctural phenomenon such as financialization and neoliberalism may seem the cause of the crisis, what caused them requires an explanation. In his view, financialization and neoliberalism are not alternative causes of crisis but they themselves can be explained by the TRPF.

While they do not address the TRPF directly, other authors also join into the debate over profit rates. John Weeks (Chapter 6), for example, argues that 'the typical "falling rate of profit" mechanism fails to get out of the starting gate as a candidate for generating cross-country crises', since it requires a critical value for the organic composition to provoke crisis, and hitting this critical value for many national capitals simultaneously would be impossible (see also Subasat, Chapter 10, on this point). Moreover, lower profit rates are likely to cause a slower rate of accumulation rather than a crisis. Even when the decline in profit rates could be linked to a crisis, it could result from other causes than the increase in organic composition. Simon Mohun (Chapter 12) empirically shows that the dismantling of the structures of the 'golden age' successfully curtailed the fall in the rate of profit since the 1980s. To explain the relatively moderate recovery of the profit rates (despite a radical fall in real wages) he develops a new measure, class rate of profit, which includes not only profits but also capitalist labor income which can be treated as a form of profit. He concludes that the increase in class rate of profit makes a falling rate of profit explanation of the crisis even more implausible. Al Campbell and Erdogan Bakir (Chapter 7) also focus on the outsized upper financial sector salaries and bonuses that can actually lower a firm's rate of profit. While they argue that the fall in profit rate and the income share of the top 1 percent was the reason why US capitalists adopted neoliberal policies in the 1980s, they also recognize that those polices were effective in reversing the decline in profit rates. By focusing on the value composition of capital (rather than organic composition), Riccardo Bellofiore (Chapter 15) argues that TRPF theory downplays the impacts of technical change on constant capital which can actually increase the rate of profit. While Kotz (Chapter 2) and Özgür Orhangazi (Chapter 14) agree that the post-1980 era has witnessed strong recovery in the profit rate in the US, Mavroudeas (Chapter 17) argues that falling profitability, caused by the increase of the organic composition of capital, is one of the main contributors to the crisis in Greece. Although Radhika Desai (Chapter 8) supports TRPF in general, she develops an argument based on the lack of demand by workers (underconsumption).

PART III: THE CRISIS IN ECONOMIC AND SOCIAL REPRODUCTION

The third part of the book covers a number of alternative Marxian theories. Most of the contributions to this book agree that the profit-squeeze argument is irrelevant to the crisis since US real wages lagged behind productivity increase since the 1980s. Weeks (Chapter 6) and Harvey (Chapter 3) argue that crises often result from the failure to recapture the value of fixed means of production (premature oldness or moral depreciation of fixed capital) due to the development of new and superior machines that undermine the profitability of the old. The profitability of the firms that use the old technologies is necessarily undermined as they try to match the prices of the firms that use the new technologies. These firms, therefore, cannot recapture the full value of their fixed means of production through the sale of their output. The fall in profitability results from the failure to realize the value of fixed means of production rather than the increase in the organic composition of capital. Since capitalists finance their fixed means of production via borrowing, the failure to realize the value of fixed means of production reveal itself as financial crisis. But not all financial crises are systemic capitalist crises.

Weeks (Chapter 6) defines crisis as 'a disjuncture that prevents complete reproduction of the circuit of capital' and argues that a slower rate of accumulation does not signify a crisis. The speed of accumulation varies over time and across countries due to their historically and culturally specific circumstances. In order to distinguish systemic (or severe) crises from those that are not, he calculates the percentage deviation of the US gross domestic product (GDP) from its 85-year trend between 1929 and 2013. These figures suggest that only two episodes (the Great Depression and the current crisis) are qualified as systemic crises and three episodes (in the early 1950s, late 1950s, and late 1970s into the early 1980s) as recessions. Although during the recessions the US economy experienced rapid declines, the GDP remained above its long-term trend. Therefore, Weeks argues, if we are to call these episodes 'crisis' we need to find another word (perhaps 'catastrophe') to describe the episodes of 1930–40 and 2008–13.

Overproduction and underconsumption theories find limited support in this book. Kotz (Chapter 2) argues that neoliberalism has blocked some crisis tendencies by undermining wages and increasing profits, and nurtured others by increasing inequality. The stagnant real wages would seem to set the stage for a crisis of underconsumption. Consumer spending, however, trended upward due to excessive lending policies and increased productive capacity that 'become surplus once the asset bubble deflated and consumer spending returned to a normal relation to disposable income'. This crisis, therefore, marks the 'tendency of overaccumulation of fixed capital, one of the crisis tendencies of capitalism-in-general'.

Desai (Chapter 8) summarizes a number of alternative approaches in the classical Marxist theories of crisis and mostly focuses on the working class demand (consumption) as an explanation of both economic boom and subsequent crisis. In her view, the Great Depression resulted from the rapid expansion of consumer goods without an equivalent increase in wages and public expenditure to realize it. Similarly, the post-war 'golden age' was associated with the rises in wages due to the strength of working classes. Rapid increase in productivity allowed rapid increase in wages without reducing profits. Expanding working class consumption was tolerated because it compensated for the weak external and colonial markets. By the end of the 1960s, however, slowing productivity increases made it difficult to increase wages without eating into profits. Better-organized working classes, the increase in oil prices, the failure of the Bretton Woods system, the demands for a new international economic order by increasingly assertive developing countries and rising protectionism constituted the background against which the 'new right' won its victory, and where it would seek to resolve the crisis. While the neoliberal era inflicted great pain on the working classes and developing countries, it failed to resolve the capitalist crisis as the underlying demand problem worsened. Expanding demand among the top income earners was unable to resolve the problem of overcapacity and overproduction.

By focusing on social reproduction in the context of neoliberal social policy, Ben Fine (Chapter 9) criticizes the welfare regime approach and argues that how scholarship, ideology and policy respond to it reflects the essence of the current crisis. He argues that 'its warranted demise . . . is part and parcel and a reflection of the systemic nature of the crisis'. Fine suggests that the fundamental weakness of the welfare regime approach largely results from its failure to understand the essence of neoliberalism in general and financialization in particular. By agreeing with most of the authors in this book, Fine argues that the current global crisis is a crisis of neoliberalism which has been associated with extensive state intervention to support financial markets. The radical transformation of capitalism into neoliberalism is associated with the transformation of economic and social reproduction which is 'marked by the heavy and increasing role of finance in both economic and social restructuring'.

While Subasat (Chapter 10) does not refute the relevance of the systemic causes of the 2008 crisis, his chapter focuses exclusively on the policy-based and conjunctural causes. In his view policy-based factors are in essence also systemic, as policy-making is deeply enrooted in class relations. He argues that the 2008 international crisis was primarily caused by the simultaneous deregulation of trade and financial sectors which created large and unsustainable balance-of-payments problems in a number of major developed countries which were also aggregated by a number of conjunctural factors: the accumulation of large foreign reserves in a number of developing countries after their financial crisis since the 1980s, the rapid increase in the crude oil prices between 2002 and 2008, China's competitive exchange rate policy and its accession to the World Trade Organization (WTO) in 2001, and the introduction of the euro in 1999, have all contributed to the rapid increase in global liquidity and large current account problems in a number of developed countries. The rapidly increased foreign debt and current account deficits created overfinancialization which was evident from the emerging bubble economies that inevitably collapsed.

Based on Marx's reproduction schemes and by emphasizing the distribution of income between capitalists and workers, and the time gap between the production of means of production and consumption, Subasat (Chapter 11) develops a new theoretical model to explain the cyclical nature of capital accumulation and crisis. The model shows that even when the shares of profits and wages in total output remain the same, problems associated with insufficient demand and crisis can occur since different stages of capital accumulation require different levels of wages and profits to avoid insufficient demand. The dynamics of the capital accumulation process necessitates radical changes in income distribution to avoid sufficient demand which is near impossible to achieve. When there is a large reserve army of labor (unemployment), low wages bring about faster accumulation of capital. Once the reserve army of labor declines substantially, however, insufficient demand emerges which requires capitalists to increase radically either their consumption or wages to avoid a crisis. Both are very difficult adjustments for capitalists.

PART IV: CRISIS AND FINANCE

The fourth part of the book focuses on financialization. While most chapters touch upon it, the five chapters in Part IV focus exclusively on the role of financialization. All the authors agree that the neoliberal financial system (or financialization) is an inherent tendency within capitalism and a major source of instability which signifies a radical structural transformation from the former financial system. While financialization historically takes different forms (Orhangazi, Chapter 14; Desai, Chapter 8; Subasat, Chapter 10), it also has some common characteristics. Compared to what it was before, the neoliberal financial system has much fewer links with real production, trade and consumption (Mohun, Chapter 12). The neoliberal financial system is characterized by the domination of the 'sale and repurchase agreements' which are undertaken purely for financial reasons, where dealers intermediate risk and make most of their profits through this intermediation process. Securitization (a process that bundles loans and resells them) was the central component in this transformation (Mohun, Chapter 12).

In the past, banks made loans for business and mortgages, and profited from the difference between lending and borrowing rates. Since the 1980s, however, the financial system became a risk-seeking sector that earned large profits (Kotz, Chapter 2). Transformed by financialization, even non-financial corporations began making significant profits from financial investments. Many authors also agree that the separation of the management of firms from their ownership, which led to 'corporate capitalism', played a significant role in the financialization process (Orhangazi).

Since the neoliberal world is significantly different from the world Marx lived in, the relevance of Marxian theorization of the financial system is also questioned (Mohun, Chapter 12). In this view, Marxism lagged behind these developments due to its undeveloped monetary theory (Bellofiore, Chapter 15). Most authors also agree on the complementary and contradictory relationship between the financial and productive sectors (Orhangazi, Chapter 14; Kaltenbrunner and Karacimen, Chapter 16). Financialization can act as an accelerator and destabilizer (Orhangazi, Chapter 14).

Beyond the above common ground, the authors have produced a number of thought-provoking arguments. Mohun (Chapter 12), for example, argues that while the extraordinary pay packages in the financial sector are considered one of the main causes of inequality (which subsequently contributed to the crisis), the causality also runs the other way around: the growth in inequality is a major source of growth of the neoliberal financial system as well as its instabilities. In other words, both the rising inequality as well as crisis is the generic characteristic of neoliberalism. Since the 1980s there has been a radical increase in the 'class profit share' (normal profits and salaries of the top-income earners) which implies large sums of money seeking 'safe' assets for investment. But because financial instruments guaranteed by the US government (Treasury and agency securities) were in short supply, the only option was to invest in privately created and insured (collateralized) instruments. While the large funds generated by the class profit share created a financial bubble and only a small portion (about 2 percent) of the US GDP financed subprime mortgages, their impact was magnified due to the configuration of the financial sector. Because the location and size of subprime risks were unknown, the decline in housing prices influenced all institutions holding securitized mortgages and had an impact on interbank markets. Once money markets stopped funding capital markets, the financial system collapsed. Mohun, therefore, argues that 'unless the issue of soaring top incomes is addressed, the neoliberal financial system remains crisis-prone'.

Jan Toporowski (Chapter 13) argues that while the 2008 financial crisis has been analyzed as a crisis of deregulation, financialization, neoliberalism and speculation, it cannot be properly understood without a serious analysis of how capitalism functions in terms of production, distribution and the financing of capital accumulation. In this regard, corporate finance has played an important role in the explanation of the crisis. Business corporations have access to the full range of financial markets all around the world, which allows them to take full advantage of long-term debt markets and stabilize their financing costs. Large industrial corporations also account for the large portion of fixed investment which is critical to capital accumulation, aggregate demand, employment and the realization of value as well as boom and bust cycles. These facts provide a suitable framework to analyze the crisis in the sphere of corporate finance. As the title of the chapter suggests, the crisis was in fact a crisis of accumulation caused by the merger and acquisition activities (which accounted for 80 percent of the debt of the six largest industrial multinational companies) of the non-financial corporations which were heavily financed by short-term borrowing. Eventually, this led to the liquidity squeeze and a decline in fixed investment which, in turn, impaired their ability to support debt structures and transmitted the crisis to the rest of the economy. In other words, it was the failure of capital accumulation (upon which capitalism depends for the realization of value) rather than the failure of the financial system (that is, Lehman Brothers) that caused the crisis.

Orhangazi (Chapter 14) criticizes the Marxian narratives that consider financialization exclusively as a response to overaccumulation and declining profitability. He rejects the primacy of the real sector over the financial sector, which is no longer the case due to the structural changes that have taken place in the financial and non-financial sectors. Orhangazi argues that financialization is an inherent tendency within capitalism which historically takes different forms, and the relationship between finance and the productive sectors forms a complementary and contradictory unity. Finance can facilitate capital accumulation but also aggravate recursive turbulence that can be instigated from the financial and non-financial side of the economy. The corporate capitalism, where the owner ceases to be a direct proprietor of productive capital, was the first step towards financialization. Aspirations to avoid the risks associated with the productive capital accumulation process led to the move from direct ownership of productive capital to ownership of financial securities, and created the tendency towards financialization. The financialization of the non-financial corporations contributed to their profitability not only via financial incomes but also via providing credit to their consumers which facilitated their sales. The contradictory nature of financialization, however, led to a decline in real investment due to both the higher profitability in the financial markets and shareholder pressure to generate short-term returns. The decline in real investment and the increase in riskier financial investment prepares the ground for a bubble economy and subsequent crisis.

Bellofiore (Chapter 15) argues that financial Keynesianism should be incorporated into Marxian theory to account for the current 'great' capitalist crisis. In his view capitalism moved into a new stage from the 1970s, associated with changes in banking, finance and debt, but Marxism lagged behind these developments due to its undeveloped monetary theory. The new capitalism is novel in many aspects which requires a new interpretation. The neoliberal counter-revolution was marked by tax cuts and a rise in public debt. Contrary to the common perception, rather than abolishing the state, neoliberalism redefined its functions in favor of capitalist classes. The state was in charge of directly organizing competition and embedding the 'free' market into other social institutions. The marketization of government functions is falsely presented as rolling back the frontiers of the state, and 'regulation-in-denial' is coined to indicate this contradiction. Neoliberalism is a state-driven project and has nothing to do with laissez-faire. Bellofiore argues that: 'The system was a market-generated functional equivalent of government demand management and sustained consumption by separating purchasing power from individual labor income. Borrowing was undertaken by individuals themselves on the basis of property mortgages or credit card ratings largely divorced from the labor market situation.' In this sense neoliberalism can be defined as 'privatized Keynesianism'.

Financialization, in his view, means 'favoring financial to productive placements' and it was the result of the combination of government deficits and credit squeeze. The state was pushed into becoming a permanent debtor, forced to contain social expenditures and submit to the commands of the financial elite. The creditors required a rising value-appreciation of their assets and crisis became the key gadget for them to capture political power. In affluent times economic agents tend to invest more into riskier projects which initially nurture faster growth but eventually develop into a bubble and create the conditions for a crisis.

Chapter 16 by Kaltenbrunner and Karacimen also focuses on the contradictory role of financialization in emerging capitalist economies. It argues that while financialization creates opportunities to foster capital accumulation by increasing the availability and diversity of finance, it also leads to increasing volatility and instability by increasing speculative investments. The chapter also suggests that the 'finance' versus 'real' sector type dichotomy fails to capture dynamic interdependencies and interactions between these two sectors. This implies that the experiences of emerging capitalist economies with financialization are heterogeneous and depend on the country specific circumstances. To demonstrate the contradictory role of financialization, the chapter focuses on the changing asset and liability structures of non-financial corporations that invest more in short-term financial assets and borrow from international markets. On the positive side, financialization was pivotal in the international expansion of large non-financial corporations from the leading emerging capitalist economies, as is evident from their accelerated foreign direct investment outflows. On the negative side, however, it increased the impacts of international financial crisis through increased trade and financial integration. Increase in international operations compelled non-financial corporations to use international currencies and liquid financial assets for both speculative and hedging purposes.

Campbell and Bakir (Chapter 7) argue that a narrow focus on financialization in terms of a struggle between financial and productive capital interests is misleading. Instead, they consider financialization as an important instrument in the neoliberal aggression against workers. Financialization is not accidental, harmful to capitalism as a whole or 'driven strictly by its own interests separate from those of capital as a whole'. Financialization makes 'important contributions to neoliberalism's central goal of intensifying capital's attack on labor', through many mechanisms including personal debt.

Freeman (Chapter 5) suggests that interest and profit rates determine the distribution of surplus between financiers and industrialists, and there is an inverse relation between the growth of industry and the influence of financial capital. Crisis encourages capitalists to withdraw from production into holding money which is a very aggressive source of income. The new financial instruments are the modern form of money capital. The growth of the financial classes is a manifestation of capitalism's failure to maintain investment and production. Due to the low profit rates in the 1970s and 1980s such financial assets became an attractive alternative to productive investment. The rise of neoliberalism was not a resolution to the crisis but was the political manifestation of the interests of rentier classes.

Desai (Chapter 8) argues that understanding 'financialization' requires a geopolitical economy of the end of Western supremacy and of the US attempts at world dominance. She argues that 'financialization' (used in the singular) which applies to all times and places is misleading, and diverse national financial systems imply that financial bubbles and crises are mainly national. This also means that crisis spreads around the world via discrete trails rather than uniformly. Desai argues that the succession of discrete dollar-denominated international financializations, which are rooted in the Anglo-American financial system, since the breakdown of the Bretton Woods system, were necessary (and necessarily short-lived) requirements of maintaining the dollar's role as the world's currency. Deficits were the only way to provide international liquidity but were subject to the Triffin dilemma which 'needed to be counteracted by a series of financializations'. Each financialization temporarily prevented the dollar from declining faster by increasing the demand for dollars.

After briefly reviewing the financialization arguments, Subasat (Chapter 10) suggests that the relevant literature largely overgeneralizes financialization and fails to account for the diverse experiences of many developing and developed countries. He defines financialization broadly as the expansion of financial services as a percentage of total national income and classifies four levels of financialization which are essential to capture varying incidents of financialization and crisis. In this view, overfinancialization, which is associated with excessive financial inflows and current account deficits, is the only level of financialization that is directly associated with financial crisis. The relevant data denote that the rapid surge in financialization prior to the crisis was primarily caused by the expansion in real estate activities rather than financial intermediation, which is irreconcilable with the financialization hypothesis.

PART V: THE CRISIS UNFOLDS

The final part of the book focuses on the ongoing crisis in Greece. Mavroudeas (Chapter 17) starts his chapter by reviewing the alternative explanations of the Greek crisis from the mainstream (conjunctural or policy errors), radical (a blend of conjunctural and structural) and Marxist (systemic) perspectives. He adopts the circuit of capital perspective on the crisis and argues that while the circulation and distribution sphere are important, the production sphere is the leading domain. Neoliberalism and financialization are conjunctural by-products of the systemic tendencies. After criticizing the failure of mainstream explanations to consider the deep roots of the crisis in the production sphere, he also deals with the radical explanations which mostly focus on financialization. Mavroudeas argues that the degree of financialization and private household debt in Greece have historically been very low compared to the advanced capitalist countries. Private household debt began to rise following the accession to the European Monetary Union (EMU) and subsided with the crisis. He then develops a Marxist approach and argues that the crisis in Greece is an integral part of the 2008 global crisis resulting mainly from the TRPF which is also aggravated by Greece's subordinate place within the European Union (EU). By referring to the empirical literature, he claims that TRPF is the main cause of both the 1973 and the 2008 crises. Although the decline in profit rates since 1973 experienced a partial recovery during the neoliberal period, it was insufficient to reverse this process and resulted in low rates of investment and productivity growth. Mavroudeas claims that Greece is a middle-range capitalist country which strives to exploit other countries. But it has also been exploited by more advanced capitalist economies to an intensifying degree since its accession into the EU.

Vassilis Fouskas (Chapter 18) adopts a global fault-lines approach to analyze the crisis in Greece. He starts by questioning the reasons why Greece has not received much external help to deal with its ordeal. This is not, he argues, because Greece has lost its significance for the US, but because the US is no longer the credit power in the world. There has been a visible power-shift to China and other emerging capitalist economies as a result of neoliberal financialization policies since the 1970s. He argues that the 2008 crisis is one of neoliberal financialization as well as a perpetual power shift to Asia and other emerging capitalist economies. Fouskas suggests that the collapse of the Bretton Woods system is the key to understanding the emergence of neoliberal financialization, a process which has been driven by the financial centers of New York and London. This process, while it failed to restore profitability in the real economic sector, led to consumption and a debt-driven growth which marked the beginning of prolonged deterioration of Western economies.

In his view, regionalization was a response to the new multi-polar world and Anglo-American-led financialization. European customs and currency unions were established under the leadership of Germany. The introduction of the EMU and the German neo-mercantilist model of financialization (which was based on low inflation, low wages and high export growth), however, aggravated the gap between core and periphery by recycling German trade surplus and causing massive debts in the eurozone periphery.

Fouskas argues that Greece, with its weak industrial sector and corrupt bureaucracy, is a dependent or subaltern state which lags behind the advanced capitalist core. Financialization in Greece, therefore, was also subordinate to the interests of the core. Greece has a long history of balance-of-payments problems. While this is a structural and historical problem, an agency perspective is also relevant here. A large and persistent current account deficit indicates 'an overdeveloped layer of . . . import consortia' that has been called '*comprador bourgeoisie*' which 'has been the dominant social class in Greece'. Greece's subaltern financialization started in the second half of the 1990s as a launching pad for Germany's financial expansion to Eastern Europe. While 'Greek banks' played a major role in this region, they were largely owned by foreign financial institutions. Therefore Greek banks mostly served the banks of the core capitalist countries of Europe. The subaltern financialization and *comprador bourgeoisie* can explain large current account deficits financed by heavy external borrowing which caused high growth rates in the early 2000s but subsequently was proven to be unsustainable.

2. Roots of the current economic crisis: capitalism, forms of capitalism, policies and contingent events

David M. Kotz

That capitalism has inherent crisis tendencies is a central claim of Marxism. Since neoclassical theory views capitalism (a market economy in that framework) as internally stable and always tending toward a full employment equilibrium, a crisis must result from a development external to the fundamental processes of capitalism, either a contingent event (exogenous shock) or a mistaken state policy. The former can cause a crisis, which the presumed natural corrective mechanism of the market will quickly resolve. The latter can block the market's natural stabilizing mechanism, as in Friedman's argument that mistaken Federal Reserve policy turned a normal recession into the Great Depression.[1]

Marxists, starting with Marx himself, have portrayed the orthodox view of crisis as 'apologetic': one more way to let capitalism off the hook for the severe problems it brings. When economic crisis leads to mass unemployment, business failures, homelessness, even hunger, neoclassical economists point the finger at the state or bad luck. Marxists rightly reject this view, pointing out that crises emerge from the basic workings of capitalism.

However, this rejection of the neoclassical apologetic approach to crisis has been interpreted in problematic ways in some of the Marxist crisis literature. The defensible view that features of the economy other than the fundamental contradictions of capitalism cannot provide a satisfactory explanation of crises is extended to the belief that an adequate explanation of crises – particularly those that are large in magnitude or duration – can be found solely at the level of capitalism-in-general. Sometimes it is assumed that each individual crisis can be categorized as due either to deep contradictions of capitalism, or to policy or contingent event causes. In this approach, to explain a big crisis one must demonstrate that it falls into the 'deep contradiction' category and not the policy or contingent event category, since finding a significant role for factors other than deep capitalist contradictions in a severe crisis is regarded as contrary to Marxism.

To utilize the potential power of Marxism for explaining capitalist crises, it is necessary to take account of four different levels of abstraction at which one can analyze the capitalist system: (1) capitalism-in-general; (2) the particular form of capitalism at a given time and place; (3) state policies; and (4) contingent events. All four levels of analysis are necessary to produce an adequate account of any capitalist crisis. What distinguishes the dynamics of a severe crisis from those of a short-term business cycle recession is not the presence or absence of fundamental capitalist crisis tendencies but the way those crisis tendencies play out within a particular historical context that includes more concrete aspects of the economic system.

This chapter considers the role of each of the four levels of analysis of capitalism for Marxist crisis theory, arguing that the prevailing form of capitalism should not be overlooked in the analysis of particular economic crises. Focusing on the United States (US) where the current economic crisis originated, it offers an explanation for the crisis that began in 2008 and shows how each level of analysis contributes to a full explanation. The last section considers the advantages and possible disadvantages of this approach to economic crisis analysis.

2.1 ECONOMIC CRISIS AND THE FOUR LEVELS OF ANALYSIS OF THE CAPITALIST ECONOMY

Marxists have traditionally defined an economic crisis as an interruption in the accumulation process. Two types of interruption, or crisis, occur in capitalist economies: short-run and long-run. A short-run crisis is a downturn in production, profit and employment typically lasting six months to two years, which ends and gives way to normal accumulation through internal mechanisms of capitalism, although not before significant costs have been imposed on various segments of society.[2] While some Marxists have suggested reserving the term 'crisis' for more severe interruptions of accumulation, there are two reasons for referring to milder downturns as crises. First, the traditional Marxist crisis tendencies – falling rate of profit, underconsumption, profit squeeze, overaccumulation of fixed capital, disproportionality – play a role in causing such short-run crises. Despite their relative brevity and self-correcting character, they are manifestations of the contradictory nature of capital accumulation. Second, at the time Marx wrote, the word 'crisis' was widely applied to such short-run downturns in economic activity, perhaps inspired by the financial panic that usually accompanied an economic downturn in that era. If Marxists wish to continue the use of Marx's term 'crisis' for interruptions in the capital accumulation process due to the internal mechanisms of capitalism, then consistency dictates that the term be applied to the relatively mild and self-correcting short-term interruptions in accumulation.

However, my concern here is the analysis of long-lasting economic crises, which can be called long-run crises. A long-run crisis is a long-lasting interruption in the accumulation process, which differs from a short-run crisis in two ways besides simply the length of time it occupies. First, economic expansion can occur during some subperiods of a long-run crisis, as in 1933–37 in the US during the Great Depression of the 1930s. Thus, a long-run crisis is defined by subnormal accumulation rather than continuously decreasing production (negative accumulation). Second, a long-run crisis cannot be resolved by internal mechanisms of capitalism but requires economic restructuring if normal accumulation is to resume. For that reason, a long-term crisis can alternatively be called a structural crisis. That economic restructuring is required to resolve such a crisis is the reason it lasts a long time.

The economic crisis that began in 2008 gives every indication of being a long-run, or structural, crisis. In the US economic expansion resumed after the second quarter of 2009, but the rate of expansion has been very slow: gross domestic product (GDP) rose at 2.3 percent per year through the third quarter of 2014 (US Bureau of Economic Analysis 2015: Table 1.1.6). Capital accumulation has been lackluster, unlike the usual sharp rebound after a short-term crisis. While the official unemployment rate has declined substantially, the most meaningful indicators of the state of the labor market, such as the ratio of employment to population, have barely improved since 2009. Economic conditions have been even worse in a number of other developed economies. What kind of explanation can be provided for this type of crisis?

First one should consider the contradictions of capitalism-in-general that can give rise to economic crisis via the crisis tendencies of capitalism. However, while the fundamental crisis tendencies of capitalism-in-general represent the starting point for crisis analysis, an analysis at that level of abstraction cannot serve to explain why a particular crisis occurs in a particular place at a particular time. Which crisis tendency will cause a crisis? What determines whether a crisis will be of the short-run or long-run type? Apart from the disproportionality crisis tendency, the other crisis tendencies can each in principle be implicated in a structural crisis as well as a short-run, self-correcting crisis.[3]

To proceed any further, one must undertake a more concrete analysis than that of capitalism-in-general. However, this does not mean that the next step is to examine state policies and contingent events. There is another level of analysis that lies between that of capitalism-in-general and that of policy and contingent events. That is the level at which one identifies the particular form of capitalism in a given place at a given time.

Capitalism has existed for several centuries, yet while always capitalism, it has taken a series of distinct forms over time and space. Such a particular form, once established, lasts for an extended period of time. A particular form of capitalism is defined by particular economic and political institutions, associated dominant ideas (the particular form of bourgeois ideology), and a particular form of the main class relations of capitalism, most importantly the capital–labor relation. Each form of capitalism is still capitalism: a system of generalized commodity production and the wage–labor relationship through which capital appropriates surplus value from labor.

The forms of capitalism have been given a variety of labels in the Marxist literature: stages, social structures of accumulation, or modes of regulation. A common depiction of the main forms is a sequence that starts with competitive capitalism, followed by monopoly or finance capitalism after around 1900, then state monopoly or regulated capitalism after World War II, and most recently neoliberal capitalism (or globalized or financialized capitalism in some accounts) since around 1980.

This level of analysis is different from the level of state policy. A state policy is narrow and in principle subject to change at any time. By contrast, a form of capitalism is a coherent entity with mutually reinforcing elements, which make it relatively stable for a significant period of time. A form of capitalism will give rise to certain kinds of state policies, but such policies are constrained by the existing form of capitalism and hence have a stability and coherence that is not captured by the level of analysis that focuses just on state policies.

The prevailing form of capitalism is central to analyzing capitalist economic crisis because it is a major determinant of which crisis tendency inherent in capitalism will emerge and cause a crisis, as well as determining whether the emergent crisis will be a long-term one. Individual state policies are likely to be involved in the origin of every crisis, as are contingent events. Hence, the third and fourth levels of analysis are also relevant to the analysis of every crisis, along with the analysis of capitalism-in-general and the form of capitalism.

2.2 THE CURRENT CRISIS

The initial outbreak of a severe economic crisis in 2008 in the US had two sides. One was a financial crisis, whose dramatic character grabbed most of the attention. The other was a slower-moving real sector crisis, often called the Great Recession, although at times that aspect of the crisis produced gripping headlines as monthly job losses of 700 000 to 800 000 were reported from November 2008 through March 2009 (Kotz 2015: Chapter 5, Figure 5.10). This structural crisis has causal factors at all four levels: capitalism-in-general, the prevailing form of capitalism, state policies and contingent events. This author provides an analysis of the causes of the crisis in Kotz (2009) and in more detail in Kotz (2015: Chapters 4–5). However, neither of those works explicitly locates the crisis causes with respect to the four levels of analysis of capitalism.

Kotz (2009) and Kotz (2015) make the following argument. The period from 1979 to 2007 in the US showed three important economic developments: (1) increasing inequality, in the form of a large and growing gap between profits and wages, and rising inequality among households; (2) a series of large asset bubbles, with one in each decade; and (3) a shift in the practices of financial institutions toward speculative and highly risky activities. The rising inequality was noted as early as the 1980s (Kotz 1986) but achieved widespread recognition only in the 2000s. The Occupy movement forced it into the public discourse in 2011, and the stir caused by Piketty (2014) brought a focus on rising inequality into the mainstream. The series of large asset bubbles began with one in Southwestern commercial real estate in the 1980s, followed by the big stock market run-up in the 1990s, and culminating in the giant nationwide housing bubble of the 2000s.

Financial institutions in the US prior to 1980 represented a quiet, convention-bound sector of the economy. Commercial banks made business loans, profiting from the spread between lending and borrowing rates. Savings banks did the same for conventional home and commercial mortgages. Insurance companies insured life and property, with reserves held against expected payouts. Investment banks were a bit more flamboyant, floating securities and promoting mergers, but typically doing so by risking the partners' own capital and with funds not insured by the government. After 1980 the financial sector changed, gradually over time, and, as is well known, by the 2000s it had become a high-flying, risk-seeking sector gaining huge profits. The profits of financial institutions in the US more than doubled from 20 percent of all corporate profits in 1979 to an astonishing 40 percent in 2001–03 (Kotz 2015: Chapter 2, Figure 2.8). As even non-financial corporations began gaining significant profit from financial investments, the view arose that capitalism had been fundamentally transformed by 'financialization'.

Kotz (2009, 2015) argues that the above three developments, interacting with one another, gave rise to three trends that were unsustainable over the long run. First, both household and financial sector debt relative to GDP rose from 1979 to 2007, with the former ratio doubling while the latter rose almost sixfold by the eve of the crisis (Kotz 2015: Chapter 5, Figure 5.1).

The rapid growth in household debt resulted from household borrowing to support consumer spending. By 2007 both sectors had so much debt that any drop in cash flow would be disastrous. Second, so-called 'toxic' financial assets spread throughout the financial system. These included subprime and other unconventional mortgage-backed securities, collateralized debt obligations and credit default swaps. They were toxic in that, far from reducing risk as their promoters claimed, these assets had values that could be sustained only if the housing bubble inflated forever.

The third long-term trend, of growing excess productive capacity, has not been widely noticed. Over time the share of industrial capacity in use trended downward. Figure 2.1 shows the capacity utilization rate in industry for selected business cycle peak years. For the last three peak years since 1980, each saw a lower rate of capacity utilization than the preceding one. By contrast, capacity utilization was higher and trended upward between the last two peak years through 1973 prior to the onset of an earlier long-run economic crisis.[4]

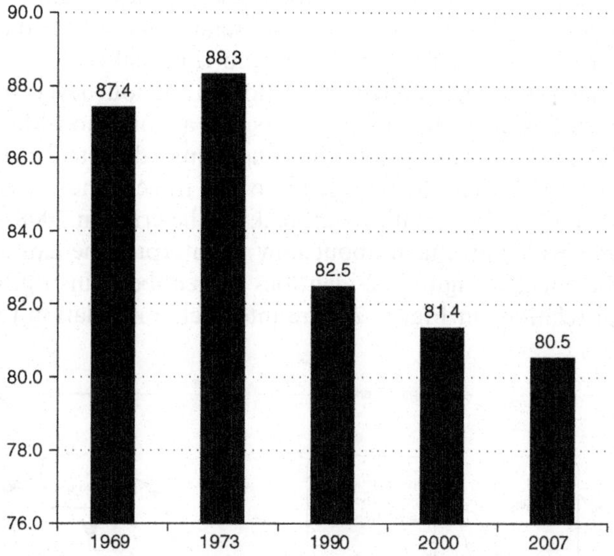

Note: The industrial capacity utilization rate, which is the broadest capacity utilization rate series, covers manufacturing, mining, and utilities.

Source: Board of Governors of the Federal Reserve System (2014).

Figure 2.1 Industrial capacity utilization for selected business cycle peak years

The spark that ignited the crisis, in both real and financial sectors, was the deflation of the housing bubble. In 2006 housing prices stopped rising and in 2007 they began to fall. As a result, households could no longer borrow to support consumer spending and instead had to begin paying off loans, leading to a drop in consumer spending. The falling consumer spending, together with the effect of the housing bubble deflation on profit expectations, led to falling business investment. These together turned expansion into contraction in the first quarter of 2008. Finally, the housing bubble deflation caused the market value of all those toxic securities to plummet, rendering most of the highly indebted big financial institutions insolvent and setting off a financial panic. The common belief that the financial crisis caused the Great Recession by cutting off funds for the real sector finds no support in the data, which show huge increases in cash in the hands both of financial institutions and non-financial corporations from the start of the crisis. However, the financial panic worsened profit expectations further, accelerating the decline in business investment and contributing to the severity of the recession.

Figure 2.2 shows this analysis of the causes of the current crisis. Three developments led to three unsustainable trends which, once the big asset bubble deflated, led to the real sector and financial sector crises. How can this analysis be interpreted in relation to the four levels of analysis of capitalism? Many Marxist analysts, as well as some non-Marxist ones, agree with some, or even all, of the causal links depicted in Figure 2.2 that go from the three developments to the three trends in the period 1979–2007 and to the resulting outbreak of the crisis in 2008. However, there is not wide agreement about how to interpret the cause of those three trends, which Figure 2.2 identifies as neoliberal institutions. How the causal relations in Figure 2.2 are interpreted in relation to the four

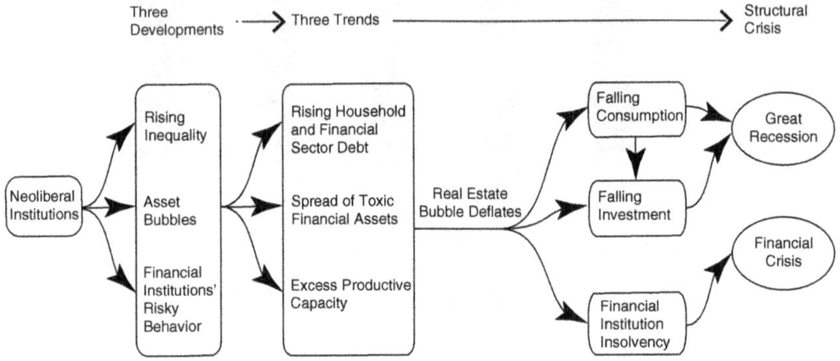

Figure 2.2 Causes of the economic crisis

levels of analysis of capitalism matters for our understanding of this crisis.

2.3 THE FORM OF CAPITALISM AND THE CURRENT CRISIS

To make any definitive determination about the role of capitalist crisis tendencies in this crisis, it is necessary to move from an abstract analysis of capital in general to take account of the particular form of capitalism that prevailed after 1980. While the fundamental Marxist crisis tendencies are the starting point for analysis of a particular crisis, the prevailing form of capitalism is a key determinant of which crisis tendency or tendencies will be the operative one(s).

Marxist analysts have proposed three different ways to characterize the stage or form of capitalism that emerged around 1980: globalization, financialization and neoliberalism. Kotz (2015: Chapter 2) offers a comparison of those three interpretations and argues that neoliberalism is the best of the three for understanding contemporary capitalism.[5] Here I will show how the concept of neoliberalism, or more accurately neoliberal capitalism, can form the basis for explaining the roots of the current crisis as well as the character of the capital accumulation process in the decades before the crisis broke out. Important policy decisions that played a role in the crisis can be understood as flowing from the logic of the neoliberal form of capitalism.

Some analysts interpret the term 'neoliberalism' as referring to a set of ideas (Foster 2007). Here neoliberalism is viewed as something broader, namely the form of capitalism that emerged after 1980. That form of capitalism is embodied in institutions, ideas and the form of the main class relations of capitalism, particularly the capital–labor relation.

The institutions of neoliberal capitalism are located in the state relation to the economy, the labor market, the corporate sector and the international arena. In the international arena neoliberalism is marked by free movement of goods and capital across national boundaries and a high degree of global integration of the production process. Institutions governing the state relation to the economy include deregulation of the financial sector and other previously regulated sectors, privatization of public enterprises and public services, renunciation of Keynesian aggregate demand management aimed at a low unemployment rate, cutbacks in social programs, and reduced taxes for business and the rich.[6] Other institutions include marginalization of collective bargaining, unrestrained competition among large corporations, the penetration of market principles inside corporations, and the hiring of chief executive officers (CEOs) from the outside rather than promotion from within.

The dominant ideas of neoliberal capitalism are a highly individualistic conception of society, the idealization of market relations, and a view of the state as an enemy of individual liberty, private property and economic efficiency. The main class relation of neoliberal capitalism is a capital–labor class relation based on a high degree of domination of capital over labor, with capital able to set wages and working conditions with little effective resistance from labor. The extreme domination of capital over labor is the central feature of this form of capitalism, a relation that is enforced by the institutions and dominant ideas of neoliberal capitalism.

The institutions and ideas cited above are not just a list; they make up a coherent social structure with mutually reinforcing parts that has some stability and durability. While not every aspect of US capitalism was entirely consistent with this structure, major initiatives in the realm of government policy or other realms that would run contrary to the neoliberal structure were relatively easily repelled, at least until the system went into crisis in 2008.

Why use the term 'neoliberal' for this structure? In every part of the world other than the US, a liberal position means one favoring relatively free markets with limited intervention in or regulation of markets. The term 'neoliberal' capitalism means a new instance of a liberal form of capitalism. Its use is justified by the fact that after 1980 market relations and market forces have expanded to play the predominant role in regulating economic activity, while non-market institutions, such as states, trade unions and corporate bureaucracies, have played a reduced role. The economic and political institutions of neoliberal capitalism all promote an increasing role for market relations and market forces while restricting the role of non-market institutions. At the same time, those institutions and ideas also reinforce the power of capital over labor, which is not only a central feature of this form of capitalism but also explains why big capital promoted neoliberal transformation starting in the mid-1970s (Kotz 2015: Chapter 3).

The neoliberal form of capitalism has suppressed some crisis tendencies while fostering others. Neoliberal capitalism undermines workers' bargaining power, strengthening capital's ability to raise the rate of exploitation over time. This tends to give rise to an upward trend in the rate of profit, although other factors could outweigh that effect. Basu and Vasudevan (2013) analyzed the movement of the rate of profit in the US using a variety of measures, and they found that almost every measure showed a long-term increase in the profit rate after the early 1980s rather than a decrease. Basu and Vasudevan also found that the long-term trend in the profit share was upward over this period, as one would expect given labor's rapidly declining bargaining power. Thus, neither the tendency of the rate of profit to fall, nor the reserve army or profit squeeze crisis tendency, would be a strong candidate for explaining the crisis.

Since neoliberal capitalism gave rise to increasing inequality and a stagnating real wage for non-supervisory workers after 1980 in the US, it would seem to set the stage for a crisis of underconsumption. However, consumer spending trended upward, not downward, over the period 1979–2007, relative both to GDP and to disposable income (US Bureau of Economic Analysis 2015: Tables 1.1.5 and 2.1), despite the rising inequality and a stagnating real wage. Below I will argue that this suppression of the underconsumption crisis tendency resulted from the way the accumulation process proceeded under neoliberal capitalism, and that the crisis tendency fostered by neoliberal capitalism has been overaccumulation of fixed capital.

The concept of neoliberal capitalism can explain the emergence of the three developments cited above that led eventually to the current crisis. The institutions and ideas of neoliberal capitalism fostered rising inequality, the shift in financial practices and the series of large asset bubbles. Those three developments determined the form of capital accumulation in the neoliberal era, holding some of the fundamental crisis tendencies of capitalism at bay for several decades while limiting other crisis tendencies to the production of short-run crises only, and promoting a series of long economic expansions interrupted by relatively mild recessions that surprised many Marxist analysts. However, the contradictions embodied in those three developments led eventually to a structural crisis, in 2008.

Most of the institutions of neoliberal capitalism have directly promoted rising inequality, with a particularly important role for the open world economy, renunciation of aggregate demand management (resulting in a higher average unemployment rate), deregulation of basic industries, privatization, cuts in social programs, tax cuts for business and the rich, marginalization of collective bargaining, casualization of jobs, and a market for corporate CEOs (which led to the skyrocketing of CEO pay). More generally, relatively free markets inherently tend to promote rising inequality, as the strong, the quick and the unscrupulous grab a rising share of the value produced.[7] The institutions that can potentially reduce inequality in capitalism are non-market institutions such as states that can reduce inequality through social welfare programs, progressive taxes, regulation of business that limits competition, regulation of global competition, and the provision of free or subsidized public goods. Trade unions can reduce inequality by both increasing labor's share of income and reducing wage inequality among workers. Even corporate bureaucracies can reduce inequality through job ladders that prescribe pay rates independent of market forces, sometimes based on trade union pressure, but also to achieve policy aims of the top officers (reduced turnover of workers, limiting the labor cost of managerial employees).[8]

The shift from traditional financial practices to pursuit of speculative and risky activities stemmed from several features of neoliberal capitalism. Many observers point to financial deregulation, thought of as an individual policy, as the cause of this shift in the financial sector. It is undeniable that the policy choice to deregulate finance was a key reason for the shift in financial institution practices, a shift that had been blocked under the previous policy regime of financial regulation that originated in the 1930s. However, an inference from this that a state policy explains the rise of a speculative and risk-seeking financial sector misses the full story. Financial deregulation was not the only factor underlying this shift in the financial sector. Other factors associated with neoliberal capitalism include the following: an intensification of competition in the economy, in the financial sector as well as the real sector; the expanding practice of hiring corporate CEOs from the outside; the shift from a long-term to a short-term time horizon for corporate decision-makers; and the rise to dominance of free-market theories of finance. Furthermore, financial deregulation was not a lone government policy, but a part of the mutually reinforcing set of institutions and ideas that compose the neoliberal form of capitalism.

Some regard asset bubbles as inherent in capitalism, in which everything is for sale. However, there were no big asset bubbles in the US during 1948–80. Something changed after 1980 that encouraged the development of asset bubbles in the US. The operation of the neoliberal form of capitalism can explain the series of large asset bubbles, as a consequence of the growing inequality and the transformed financial sector that in turn resulted from neoliberal capitalism. Rising inequality meant a growing flow of revenue into corporate profit and the incomes of rich households, which exceeded the available productive investment opportunities. Some of that flow found its way into an asset, which tends to start the asset price rising. The speculative, risk-seeking financial institutions of neoliberal capitalism enthusiastically supported speculation in assets, which enabled incipient asset bubbles to grow over time.[9]

Thus, the neoliberal form of capitalism gave rise to increasing inequality, big asset bubbles and a risk-seeking financial sector that together led eventually to the crisis in 2008. However, those three developments also explain the 'successes' of neoliberal capitalism. Some Marxists initially doubted that neoliberal capitalism could bring a period of sustained capital accumulation since stagnating wages, along with the limited growth of state spending, would prevent the growing demand required to sustain accumulation. Yet the US economy starting in the early 1980s produced three long economic expansions, in 1982–90, 1991–2000, and 2001–07. Inflation remained mild even at the end of cyclical expansions when the unemployment rate fell to a relatively low level.

The explanation for the long expansions is found in the same three developments. The imbalance between profit and wages meant a rising rate of profit which stimulated accumulation. The tendency for a shortage of demand to emerge was forestalled by debt-fueled consumer spending made possible by the other two developments: asset bubbles and risk-seeking financial institutions. The stock market bubble of the 1990s enabled upper-income households to borrow against their inflating stock portfolios, causing an unusual lurch upward in consumer spending growth in the last three years of the 1990s that prolonged that expansion to become the longest one on record (Kotz 2003). In the 2000s an even bigger bubble in housing provided an appreciating asset against which a large swath of the population could borrow to support rising consumer spending despite stagnating real wages (Kotz 2009). The risk-seeking financial institutions found new ways to lend money even to low-income homeowners, which supported the growing debt-fueled consumer spending. The stable prices are explained by the intensely competitive markets of neoliberal capitalism which made it difficult for firms to raise prices while the low degree of worker bargaining power averted cost-push inflation.

The mode of accumulation in neoliberal capitalism tells us which fundamental crisis tendency was operative in 2008. The debt-fueled consumer spending averted a crisis of underconsumption, but it did so by elevating consumer spending far above the trajectory that was sustainable based on ordinary household income. Firms invested in fixed capital to serve, and profit from, the rising sales due to debt-fueled consumer spending. This produced productive capacity that was required yet would become surplus once the asset bubble deflated and consumer spending returned to a normal relation to disposable income. That is, the crisis tendency of over-accumulation of fixed capital, one of the crisis tendencies of capitalism-in-general, was fostered by the neoliberal form of capitalism and was the operative crisis tendency in 2008.[10] By June 2009, after debt-fueled consumer spending had evaporated, the industrial capacity utilization rate fell to 66.9 percent, by far the lowest rate in the post-war period.[11]

Individual policy decisions played a role in the process that led to the crisis. In 1998 the head of a regulatory agency, the Commodity Futures Trading Commission, called for regulation of financial derivatives. This led to a political battle that was won by Treasury Secretary Lawrence Summers, who was able to first postpone the proposed regulation and then inserted a ban on any regulation of derivatives into the last financial deregulation act of that era, the Commodity Futures Modernization Act of 2000. This was followed by the very rapid spread of toxic financial derivatives in the US and global financial system, which played a central role in the financial panic of 2008. In 2004 the Securities and Exchange Commission decided to grant an exemption for the five biggest investment banks to the Commission's rule regulating the maximum permissible level of debt leverage, on the grounds that giant investment banks were sophisticated enough to handle additional leverage. Over the following years the leverage ratio of four of the five rose to 30:1. After 2007 all five teetered on the edge of bankruptcy, contributing to the financial crisis (Kotz 2015: 129).[12] While these two policy decisions contributed to the severity of the financial crisis of 2008, they were not isolated events but occurred in the context of the dominance of neoliberalism which strongly favored such policy decisions.

Contingent events also played a role in 2008. The failure of the big investment bank Lehman Brothers contributed to the financial panic in September 2008. If Lehman had been more cautious in the preceding years, it might not have failed. If the Fed had bailed Lehman out, the effect would have been lessened. However, neither alternative history would have forestalled the structural crisis.

2.4 CONCLUDING COMMENTS

The particular prevailing form of capitalism played an important role in the origin of the current crisis. An analysis that ignores the form of capitalism is left only with tendencies emerging from capitalism-in-general on the one hand and individual state policies and contingent events on the other. Since an analysis at the level of capitalism-in-general cannot determine which crisis tendency is operative in a given time and place, the analyst is stuck with either a highly abstract account that cannot be persuasive or an account that gives policies and/or contingent events a bigger role than they deserve.[13] The particular form of capitalism is a systematic entity, one that emerges from the contradictions of capitalist development. By including the form of capitalism in crisis analysis, we can show how a crisis emerges from the concrete form of capitalism rather than just policies and contingent events.

An advantage of the framework presented here for analyzing the current crisis is that it sheds light on the possible future directions of restructuring, which is helpful for developing political strategy for the socialist movement. Kotz (2015: Chapters 6 and 7) uses this framework to develop an analysis of the possible future directions of economic change.

In brief, both theory and history suggest that one of three alternative directions of restructuring is likely to emerge in coming years: a right-wing nationalist and statist form of capitalism, a social-democratic form of capitalism, or a transition to socialism. The analysis can provide the forces that favor a transition to socialism with arguments in favor of that direction of change.

Critics of the view that the current crisis is a structural crisis of neoliberal capitalism often argue that this approach 'lets capitalism off the hook' for the crisis by 'diverting attention' from capitalism to neoliberalism. It must be admitted that the analysis presented here does suggest that a shift away from the neoliberal form of capitalism, toward a social democratic form, has the potential, if it could be achieved, to resolve the crisis. Policy advocates associated with the labor movement and some left-Keynesians in the US have been calling for a return to a social democratic form of capitalism as the solution to the problems that brought the current crisis. However, Marxists arguing that this is a crisis of capitalism itself, not of neoliberal capitalism, will not quiet such reformist demands.

To counter the possibility that a focus on neoliberalism might lead someone to think that a social democratic form of capitalism is the best direction of change, Marxists can point out the roots of neoliberal capitalism in the evolution of capitalism. Capitalism always takes some institutional form, and each such form accentuates one or more crisis tendencies which will eventually cause a structural crisis of that form of capitalism. The post-World War II 'regulated capitalism' empowered the working class and gave play to crisis tendencies associated with a declining profit rate: the profit squeeze crisis tendency and the tendency of the rate of profit to fall. At the same time, that form of capitalism suppressed the underconsumption and overaccumulation of fixed capital crisis tendencies. As for any form of capitalism, post-World War II regulated capitalism eventually gave rise to a structural crisis, in the 1970s, which led to neoliberal restructuring. No form of capitalism is permanently stable since the contradictions of capitalism cannot all be held at bay indefinitely.

Marxists can make several criticisms of the reformist resolution of the current crisis. A social democratic form of capitalism, despite being better for working people than neoliberal capitalism, still leaves many social and economic problems of capitalism unresolved, including inequality, dangerous working conditions, harmful products, and unemployment of some while others are overworked. Marxists can point out that another long period of social democratic capitalism, even if it were politically feasible, would spell disaster for humanity. Unlike in the 1940s, today the natural environment cannot absorb another several decades of the rapid capital accumulation and economic output growth that social democratic capitalism would bring. The result would be an acceleration of global warming that would spell disaster for civilization.

Of the three possible directions of economic change in this period, only a transition to socialism can avoid environmental disaster. Socialism does not have the economic growth drive of capitalism and could be structured to meet human wants and needs through a sustainable relationship to the natural environment. Only socialism can overcome the exploitation and oppression inherent in capitalism. Only socialism can provide the whole population with material comfort and security, guaranteed employment for all, and an evolution of the labor process toward forms that develop human capabilities rather than repressing them.

NOTES

1. Keynes rejected the stability claim for a capitalist economy and argued that capitalism can undergo a prolonged crisis with no self-correcting mechanism to resolve it. However, the cause remained unchanged from the neoclassical view in the form of a contingent event (herd-like worsening of expectations about the future rate of return) or a mistaken policy (aiming for a balanced budget at the wrong time).
2. Marxist theory argues that the crisis itself creates conditions that tend to eventually resolve the crisis and lead to the resumption of accumulation. However, it is argued below that in a long-run crisis that tendency is blocked.
3. Some Marxists view the reserve army or profit squeeze crisis tendency as one that can bring only a short-term, self-correcting crisis. However, some Marxist analysts have presented a case that a version of the profit squeeze crisis tendency led to the long-run crisis of the 1970s (Bowles et al. 1990).
4. The Federal Reserve's series for industrial capacity utilization is available only starting with 1967. The narrower series for manufacturing alone, which includes the 1960 cyclical peak year, shows the same pattern as in Figure 2.1.
5. Some analysts argue that financialization is a better overall conception of post-1980 capitalism (Lapavitsas 2013), and others view globalization as the best way of framing post-1980 capitalism (Bowles et al. 2005).
6. When the crisis broke out in the fall of 2008, the resulting panic led some of these institutions to shift temporarily. For example, the US and the other major capitalist states introduced large fiscal stimulus programs. However, by 2010 the panic subsided and neoliberalism returned in the guise of austerity policy.
7. Typically the cases of accumulation of great wealth through overseeing productive activity involve seizure of some kind of monopoly position in a market, such as the fortunes of John D. Rockefeller and Bill Gates. However, that is not contrary to a framework of unregulated markets, which should not be confused with the neoclassical concept of a perfectly competitive market. Fortunes gained in financial activity involve different dynamics, typically including various forms of misrepresentation, inside information and outright fraud that flourish in a system of unregulated markets. Also, the state, which does not disappear in neoliberal capitalism, remains a lucrative source of private appropriation in that form of capitalism.
8. In some cases non-market institutions can have the opposite effect of increasing inequality, such as professional associations that elevate the pay of already highly paid professions or craft unions that obtain very high wages. However, on balance, unregulated markets have a universal inequality-increasing impact that far outmatches the

instances of inequality that arise in capitalism from the operation of some non-market institutions.

9. Big asset bubbles can arise in other socio-economic forms besides neoliberal capitalism. A huge real estate bubble has arisen in the cities of China recently although China's economy is heavily state-regulated.
10. See Kotz (2013).
11. In addition to the excess productive capacity that was revealed only after debt-fueled consumer spending evaporated, as was noted earlier Figure 2.1 showed that the capacity utilization rate in industry was lower in each successive business cycle peak in the neoliberal era through 2007 despite the debt-fueled consumer spending at the last two cyclical peaks. This suggests a tendency of overaccumulation of fixed capital even apart from the effect of asset bubbles on consumer spending. A possible explanation is the effect of large asset bubbles, which tend to create a sense of euphoria among investors, on expectations of future profits from investment in fixed capital.
12. Of the five biggest investment banks, one went bankrupt, two had to be acquired by larger institutions, and two were bailed out by the government.
13. An analysis of crisis tendencies in capitalism-in-general can be combined with a study of the empirical data to seek to find out which crisis tendency operates in a given period. Weisskopf (1979) followed that approach. While that approach can yield useful information, it cannot explain why one particular crisis tendency was the operative one at a particular time and place.

REFERENCES

Basu, D. and R. Vasudevan (2013), 'Technology, Distribution and the Rate of Profit in the US Economy: Understanding the Current Crisis', *Cambridge Journal of Economics*, 37, 57–89.

Board of Governors of the Federal Reserve System (2014), 'G.17 – Industrial Production and Capacity Utilization', available at http://www.federalreserve.gov/datadownload/Choose.aspx?rel=G17 (accessed 29 July 2014).

Bowles, S., R. Edwards and F. Roosevelt (2005), *Understanding Capitalism: Competition, Command, and Change*, 3rd edn, New York, USA and Oxford, UK: Oxford University Press.

Bowles, S., D.M. Gordon and T.E. Weisskopf (1990), *After the Wasteland: A Democratic Economics for the Year 2000*, Armonk, NY, USA and London, UK: M.E. Sharpe.

Foster, J.B. (2007), 'The Financialization of Capitalism', *Monthly Review*, 58(11), 1–12.

Kotz, D.M. (1986), 'How Many Billionaires Are Enough?', *New York Times*, 19 October, F3.

Kotz, D.M. (2003), 'Neoliberalism and the US Economic Expansion of the 1990s', *Monthly Review*, 54(11), 15–33.

Kotz, D.M. (2009), 'The Financial and Economic Crisis of 2008: A Systemic Crisis of Neoliberal Capitalism', *Review of Radical Political Economics*, 41(3), 305–317.

Kotz, D.M. (2013), 'The Current Economic Crisis in the United States: a Crisis of Over-Investment', *Review of Radical Political Economics*, 45(3), 284–294.

Kotz, D.M. (2015), *The Rise and Fall of Neoliberal Capitalism*, Cambridge, MA: Harvard University Press.

Lapavitsas, C. (2013), *Profiting without Producing: How Finance Exploits Us All*, London, UK and New York, USA: Verso.
Piketty, T. (2014), *Capital in the Twenty-First Century*, Cambridge, MA: Belknap Press of Harvard University Press.
US Bureau of Economic Analysis (2015), 'US Economic Accounts', last revised 23 December 2014, available at http://www.bea.gov.
Weisskopf, T.E. (1979), 'Marxian Crisis Theory and the Rate of Profit in the Postwar US Economy', *Cambridge Journal of Economics*, 3(4), 341–378.

PART II

Crisis and Profitability

3. Crisis theory and the falling rate of profit

David Harvey

In the midst of crises, Marxists frequently appeal to the theory of the tendency of the rate of profit to fall as an underlying explanation (e.g. Carchedi 2011; Kliman 2012; Shaikh 2010; Moseley 1990). In a recent presentation, for example, Michael Roberts (2014) attributes the current long depression to this tendency. The tendency or law operates as follows:

1. Competition forces capitalist producers to invest in labor-saving technologies in order to preserve market share.
2. The value of the means of production consumed (*c*, the constant capital) tends to outstrip the value of labor power (*v*, the variable capital) employed.
3. The ratio of constant to variable capital employed (the productivity or value composition of capital, *c*/*v*) rises. If the rate of exploitation (*s*/*v*, the ratio of surplus value produced to variable capital employed) is unchanged, then the rate of profit, (*s*/*c* + *v*) will fall.
4. There are, however, counteracting tendencies. The rate of exploitation of labor power can rise. Constant capital can become cheaper with increased productivity in the sectors supplying machinery, raw materials and intermediate products. But these counteracting tendencies are insufficient, it is held, to offset the downward trend in the profit rate in the long run. 'Thus,' Roberts concludes, 'profitability tends to fall and capitalism tends towards crises, a movement interrupted only by short periods of growth'.

This law paints a feasible theoretical scenario for the course of capital's profitability over time. Roberts bolsters his case by attaching an array of graphs and statistical data on falling profit rates as proof of the validity of the law. Whether the data actually support his argument depends on: (1) the reliability and appropriateness of the data in relation to the theory; and (2) whether there are mechanisms other than the one Roberts describes that can result in falling profits. So what might be wrong with his argument?

Marx approached his theoretical task by way of a critique of classical political economy. In the *Grundrisse* it was primarily Ricardo's version of the law of falling profits that Marx set out to critique and displace. Ricardo attributed falling profits to Malthus's thesis of the falling marginal productivity of land. This would mean rising food prices that would have to be matched by wage increases. Rising food prices would empower the landlord class and lead to rising rents particularly on the most fertile land. The profits of production capital would thus be squeezed between rising wages and rising rents. This would ultimately spell the end of industrial capitalism.

Marx was obviously attracted to this idea but he was loath to attribute social change to natural causes (such as natural scarcity or Malthusian limits). So he sought a reason for falling profits deriving from the internal contradictions of capital. This is what his version of the theory does. It is the ever-rising productivity of capital, forged out of the perpetual competitive search for relative surplus value, that leads the profit rate to fall. In the *Grundrisse*, Marx (1973: 750–754) even went so far as to suggest that this would prove to be the ultimate 'grave-digger' of capitalism. Marx derived the law under certain assumptions. He confined his theorizing throughout much of *Capital*, as I have shown elsewhere, to what he called the sphere of law-like generality. He excluded any consideration of universal conditions (the vagaries of the relation to nature), particularities (distributional arrangements, class and other struggles over surplus value appropriation and the state of competition) and singularities (such as the whims of consumer fashion and the effects of state policies) from his reasonings. He examined how capital functioned in what he considered a 'pure' state (Harvey 2012). The fact that Marx excluded so much in his magnum opus should not be taken to mean that he thought the relation to nature, the particularities of distributional and market arrangements, and the singularities of human choice were irrelevant or in any way minor features of any social system. His more historical and political writings suggest the exact opposite. But the theoretical landscape he chose to explore in *Capital*, and which encloses his theory of the falling rate of profit, is far more restricted.

Marx spelled out even more specific assumptions in constructing his 'general law of capital accumulation' in Volume 1 of *Capital*. Firstly, capitalists have no problem selling their goods at their value in the market or recirculating the surplus value they gain back into production. All commodities trade at their value (with the exception of labor power, the value of which rises or falls depending upon the vigor of accumulation); there is no problem in finding a market and no lack of effective demand. Secondly, the way in which the surplus value is 'split up into various parts . . . such as profit, interest, gains made through trade, ground rent, etc' (Marx 1976: 709–710) is excluded from consideration. Thirdly, Marx states: 'in order to examine the object of our investigation in its integrity, free from all disturbing subsidiary circumstances, we must treat the whole world of trade as one nation, and assume that capitalist production is established everywhere and has taken possession of every branch of industry' (Marx 1976: 727).

All these assumptions carry over to Marx's derivation of the falling rate of profit in Volume 3. In both volumes Marx constructs highly simplified models of the dynamics of capital accumulation derived from the theory of absolute and relative surplus value operating in a closed system characterized by perfect competition and no difficulties of realization or distribution of the surplus value. While the two models reveal important features of capital's dynamics, they cannot be accorded the status of anything close to the absolute truth of those dynamics when capital is viewed as a whole. Both models are only as good as their common assumptions allow. The contradictory unity of production and realization is repressed, as are the contradictions between production and distribution, between monopoly and competition and much else besides. This severely restricts the applicability of the laws derived.

I am not criticizing Marx for dealing in such abstractions. He was a brilliant pioneer in teaching us how to come to grips with the complexities of capital accumulation by formulating abstractions and engaging in what we would now call modeling of economic systems. While Marx scrupulously lays out his assumptions in Volume 1 he does not do so in the case of the falling rate of profit theory. This is understandable given the preparatory nature of the materials that have come down to us. Some proponents of the law of falling profits have, however, given a different and in my view unfortunate reading to Marx's exclusions. If Marx could ignore questions of distribution (in particular the role of finance, credit and interest-bearing capital) in his statement of the law of falling profits then this implies, they suggest, that financialization had nothing to do with the crash of 2007–08. This assertion looks ridiculous in the face of the actual course of events. It also lets the bankers and financiers off the hook with respect to their role in creating the crisis.

The draconian nature of Marx's assumptions should make us cautious about pressing his theoretical conclusions too far. The production of an increasingly impoverished industrial reserve army in Volume 1 and the tendency of the profit rate to fall in Volume 3 are contingent propositions. Both tendencies are driven exclusively by the dynamics of technological change. A reading of his original notebooks suggests that Marx increasingly viewed crises not as a sign of the impending dissolution of capitalism but as phases of capitalist reconstruction and renewal. Thus, he writes:

'Crises are never more than momentary, violent solutions for the existing contradictions, violent eruptions that re-establish the disturbed balance for the time being' (Marx 1981: 357). Crises that flowed from rising labor productivity did not disappear from his thinking, but they could and should be supplemented or related to other contradictions, such as the periodic 'plethora of capital' and the chronic tendency towards overaccumulation (Marx 1981: Chapter 15; Harvey 1982: 176–203).

Michael Heinrich (2009, 2013), one of the German scholars responsible for editing the original manuscripts, has caused a storm of controversy by suggesting that Marx was far less enthusiastic about the law of falling profits than Engels's edited version allows (see also Thomas and Reuten 2014). The protests on the part of adherents to the law have been, to put it mildly, vigorous. Since I do not read German I will leave it to the scholars to sort this out. But I find Heinrich's account broadly consistent with my own long-standing skepticism about the general relevance of the law. We know that Marx's language vacillated between calling his finding a law, a law of a tendency or even on occasion just a tendency. Marx made no mention of any tendency of the rate of profit to fall in his political writings such as *The Civil War in France*. Even in Volume 3 of *Capital*, where he did consider the two crises of 1848 and 1857, these crises were depicted as 'commercial and financial crises' and were analyzed in the chapters on banking, credit and finance. Only passing reference is made to the falling rate of profit in these analyses (Marx 1981: Chapters 30–34). We also know that Marx never went back to the falling rate of profit theory – in spite of its evident incompleteness and supposed importance – after 1868 (Moseley 2014). While we cannot say why this was so, it does seem strange that Marx would chose to ignore in the last dozen years of his research what he had earlier dubbed in the *Grundrisse* 'the most important law of political economy' (though even there it is not entirely clear whether Marx is talking about Ricardo's political economy or his own).

'At the end of the 1870s,' Heinrich (2013) observes, 'Marx was confronted with a new type of crisis: a stagnation lasting for years, which is distinguished sharply from the rapid, conjunctural up and down movement which he had hitherto known.' The idea of crises as 'momentary' disruptions must have no longer seemed adequate:

> In this context, Marx's attention is drawn to the now internationally important role of the national banks, which have a considerable influence upon the course of the crisis. The observations reported by Marx make clear that a systematic treatment of crisis theory is not possible on the immediate basis of the law of the tendential fall in the rate of profit (as suggested by Engels's edition of the third volume of *Capital*), but rather only after a presentation of interest-bearing capital and credit (Heinrich 2013).

This would explain why the crises of 1848 and 1857 are called 'commercial and financial crises' and examined in the chapters on banking and finance. If, however, 'the national banks play such an important role,' says Heinrich, 'then it is very doubtful whether the credit system can be categorically presented while excluding an analysis of the state. The same holds for the world market.' Marx evidently found it necessary to abandon the formal assumptions within which he had earlier confined his derivation of the law of falling profits in order, presumably, to make it relevant to the dynamics of accumulation actually occurring. He also left the level of generality behind and incorporated the particularities of distribution (the credit system in particular) and the state of market competition into his theorizing (Harvey 2012).

Heinrich (2013; cf. also Thomas and Reuten 2014) concludes that 'a systematic treatment of crisis theory cannot . . . follow immediately from the "law of the tendency of the rate of profit to fall," but only after the categories of interest-bearing capital and credit have been developed'.

How seriously we should take Marx's apparent vacillation and ambivalence depends not only upon what we make of his draconian assumptions but also on the strength and generality of the counteracting tendencies he identified. Proponents of the law typically downplay the counteracting tendencies. Marx lists six of them in *Capital* but 'two of these (foreign trade and an increase of stock capital) fail to conform to his initial assumptions (a closed economy and a concept of surplus value that precludes the facts of distribution)' (Harvey 1982: Chapter 6; Marx 1981: Chapter 14). But under real crisis conditions we cannot afford, as his commentaries on the crises of 1848 and 1857 show in Volume 3, to exclude questions of finance and stock capital since they play such an important part in the form of appearance if not the underlying causes of crises. Nor can we afford, on the evidence offered in the chapters on money and finance, to ignore the vacillating influences of foreign trade imbalances ('bullion drains', as they were then referred to). Marx emphasizes, of course, the two counteracting influences given by Roberts, but adds 'depression of wages below the value of labor power; and an increase in the industrial reserve army' which protects certain sectors from the ravages of technological progress by lessening the incentive to replace labor power by machines; technologies invented in Britain were not deployed there, he points out in Volume 1 of *Capital*, because of surpluses of labor power but were used in the United States where labor power was scarce (see Marx 1976: 516–517).

In the *Grundrisse*, Marx lists a variety of other factors that can stabilize the rate of profit. If the profit rate is to be resuscitated then one way a crisis can do so is to produce a massive devaluation of the existing constant capital (the fixed capital in particular). But Marx also mentions the constant devaluation of a part of the existing capital (by which I presume he means premature obsolescence and devaluations particularly of fixed capital equipment as a result of technical change), the transformation of a great part of capital into fixed capital which does not serve as agency of direct production (investment in public works and urbanization, for example, all of which could circulate in return for interest only without any regard for profit of enterprise) and unproductive waste (such as military expenditures, which Marx considered equivalent to making commodities to be ditched in the ocean). He also importantly notes that the fall in the rate of profit can be 'delayed by creation of new branches of production in which more direct labor in relation to capital is needed, or where the productive power of labor is not yet developed'. And finally, monopolization is treated as an antidote to the falling rate of profit presumably because of the reduced competitive pressure to innovate (Marx 1973: 750–751).

This is, I long ago argued, 'a somewhat motley array of factors' to be taken into account (Harvey 1982: 178). Some of them (such as monopolization and the opening up of new production lines) could be of overwhelming significance. Others, such as investment in fixed capital on the land and urbanization more generally, as I have also tried to show elsewhere, are playing a critical role (as was most obviously the case in 2007–2008 and its aftermath) in crisis formation and crisis resolution.

The state-monopoly capitalism theorists of the French Communist Party towards the end of the 1960s (Boccara 1974) considered the circulation of collective fixed capital in return for interest as one way to offset the falling rate of profit (collective constant capital could circulate at a discount, as it were). The history in the United States of getting out of crises by 'building houses and filling them with things' is well known (and was crucial in the 1960s) and is now being replicated in China, where a quarter of the recent growth in gross domestic product (GDP) has been attributed to housing construction alone. Conversely, property market crashes are a familiar trigger for more general crises, with 2007–2008 the most obvious recent example, but 1928 in the United States of America (USA) being a critical and overlooked historical example (Harvey 2013b: Chapter 2).

It is not hard to add a few more countervailing influences. Engels, for example, recognized that speed-up and accelerating turnover times in both production and circulation (subjects examined in Volume 2) could affect the profit rate, and inserted (I think quite correctly) a chapter on that topic into Volume 3 of *Capital* but did not take up the impact on the falling rate of profit (Marx 1981: Chapter 4). This feature has been generally ignored by the proponents of the law. Marx vaguely indicated other possibilities. If productivity in a given industry doubles then the unit prices of the commodities produced can be cut in half and the total output can be doubled (provided there is a need, want or desire for the commodity backed by sufficient effective demand). The effect would be to keep employment (and surplus value production) in industry constant even as labor productivity doubled. With rising effective demand backed by unfulfilled needs, wants and desires, employment and surplus value production could even increase. This is what in effect happened with the history of Henry Ford's assembly-line production of the Model T, and we have witnessed a similar phenomenon in recent years with computers and cellphones. In all these cases, a consumer world was created in which a luxury quickly became a necessity, and where rising (credit-based?) effective demand expanded the market for the good. Rising productivity and rising employment and surplus value production can comfortably go hand in hand in certain circumstances. It is hard not to conclude that at the end of the day profits could just as easily rise or fall. Here Engels's intervention was crucial because it was he who added the fateful words in Volume 3 of *Capital*: 'In practice, however, the rate of profit will fall in the long run, as we have already seen' (Marx 1981: 337).

In the subsequent chapter in Volume 3 on 'The Development of the Law's Internal Contradictions', matters get much more interesting. The misleading title of the chapter was imposed by Engels. It implies that the law or tendency remains intact but has inner contradictions when the chapter is really about what happens when the assumptions made in deriving the law are dropped. The result is a far vaster portrait of the processes of crisis formation with multiple cross-cutting contradictions. The language changes such that crises are here firmly represented as violent explosions that serve to restore equilibrium, not moments that betoken the end of capitalism. Problems of realization in the market, the production of the world market, relations with non-capitalist social formations, degrees of centralization and decentralization of capital, monetary disturbances and speculative excesses located within the credit system, devaluations and the problematics of fixed capital circulation, are all introduced along with concepts such as the overaccumulation of capital, the role of the so-called 'plethora' of capital and the chronic inability to meet the needs of whole populations in a 'humane way'. Even a fresh bout of primitive accumulation in the form of 'decapitalization' of existing capitals makes an appearance. These all become part of the story of crisis formation. Marx here poses multiple questions, where Engels's editing suggests he had clear and unequivocal answers. 'The problem is,' says Geert Reuten (2009: 229), one of those deeply familiar with the manuscripts, 'that Engels, in his editorial work, polished away most of Marx's worries and so made it appear as if *Das Kapital*, Volume III was a near-to-final text instead of just a research manuscript'. It is out of this maelstrom of intersecting forces and multiple contradictions that I have constructed over the years my own sense of how crises unfold under capitalism and how the crisis tendencies never disappear but get moved around (Harvey 2010).

So what were some of the other contradictions and mechanisms that might lead to a falling rate of profit? In Volume 3 of *Capital*, for example, Marx (1981: 615) suggests that 'the ultimate reason for all real crises always remains the poverty and restricted consumption of the masses, in the face of the drive of capitalist production to develop the productive forces as if only the absolute consumption capacity of society set a limit to them'. In Volume 2 we also read:

> Contradiction in the capitalist mode of production. The workers are important for the market as buyers of commodities. But as sellers of their commodity – labor power – capitalist society has the tendency to restrict them to their minimum price. Further contradiction: the periods in which capitalist production exerts all its forces regularly show themselves in periods of over-production; because the limit to the application of the productive powers is not simply the production of value, but also its realization. However, the sale of commodities, the realization of commodity capital, and thus of surplus value as well, is restricted not by the consumer needs of society in general, but by the consumer needs of a society in which the great majority are always poor and must always remain poor. (Marx 1978: 391)

This turns up in the crucial Chapter 15 of Volume 3 as a restriction on the capacity for realization due to 'antagonistic conditions of distribution, which reduce the consumption of the vast majority of society to minimum level' (Marx 1981: 352).

The above commentaries are rarely treated in the literature with the same seriousness as Marx's elaboration of the theory of the falling rate of profit. This may be because Marx confuses matters by exploring opposing possibilities. After remarking that it is 'a pure tautology to say that crises are provoked by a lack of effective demand or effective consumption' because capitalism 'does not recognize any other form of consumer other than those who can pay', he then adds that 'crises are always prepared by a period in which wages generally rise, and the working class actually does receive a greater share in the part of the annual product destined for consumption' (Marx 1981: 352). Crises can therefore occur in periods of rising working class wages and/or rising expectations as well as in periods of wage repression and inadequate demand. Marx had shown in his general law of capital accumulation how wage increases accompanying phases of vigorous accumulation would cut into profits and so diminish accumulation (Glyn and Sutcliffe 1972). Crises can come, one can conclude, from quite different directions. If wages go too high then there is a crisis of accumulation as the profit share contracts; while if wages are too low then lack of effective demand will pose a problem. Crises consequently depend on conjunctural and even highly localized conditions. The teleology of falling profits gives way to fluctuating contingencies.

Marx's theory of the falling rate of profit should itself be treated, I conclude, as a contingent rather than a definitive proposition. It says, in effect, that if there is a fall in the rate of profit, here is one of many ways in which it could come about. Whether or not this particular mechanism is the one at work depends, however, upon careful analysis of actually existing dynamics. My own guess is that crises produced by this mechanism are relatively rare.

This in no way contradicts Marx's broader point concerning the destabilizing and often disruptive effects of technological change in the history of capitalism. These effects have frequently been implicated in crisis formation but for quite disparate reasons. In the case of fixed capital formation and use, for example, accelerating technological changes have sparked waves of devaluation of the existing fixed capital including the massive amounts invested in the built environment and in physical infrastructures. We should take seriously Marx's observation that 'the cycle of interconnected turnovers embracing a number of years, in which capital is held fast by its fixed constituent part, furnishes a material basis for the periodic crises' (Marx 1978: 264). This observation parallels some of the arguments put forward regarding the role of devaluation of existing fixed capital as a counteracting influence over the profit rate. I find it interesting, however, that Marx's explanation of this material basis for periodic crises has drawn very little commentary compared to that given over to the falling rate of profit.

The waves of technological change that have had the effect of creating a disposable reserve army of unemployed workers can likewise feed back into the circulation of capital as diminishing effective demand. The sharp crash that initiated the crisis of 2007–08 looks very different from the long-drawn-out saga of deindustrialization and devaluation that swept across traditional industrial production districts throughout the world after 1980 or so. The factories in the Ruhr, the American Midwest, industrial Britain and even in Mumbai were closed down, in part as a result of revolutions in the technologies of transport and communications that made a new globalization possible. While some may reasonably claim that these were all localized and not general crises engulfing places like Detroit, Essen, Sheffield, Mumbai and the industrial cities of northern China, it turns out that there never has been a truly global crisis where everyone everywhere was simultaneously engulfed, even within what we broadly refer to as 'the capitalist world' (that is, not including that part of the world outside of capital's trading networks). There were in fact plenty of places scarcely affected by the events of 2007–2008 (much of Latin America, for example) and the long-drawn-out, slow-burning and painful deindustrialization of the traditional centers of manufacturing during the period 1980 to 2000 was felt all across the capitalist world. So maybe we should distinguish between the short sharp crashes such as those of 1929, 1973, 2007–2008 and the long-drawn-out adjustments that Marx encountered after 1873 and which totally reshaped the face of capitalism during the 1980s.

So has there been a general tendency for the rate of profit to fall over time, as many Marxist economists maintain? And how does that falling rate, if it exists, explain a crisis which on the surface at least was a commercial and financial crisis that began in the housing markets of California, Arizona, Nevada, Florida and Georgia (with outliers in Spain, Ireland, Hungary and various other countries) before going worldwide through contagions in a global financial system that infected all manner of sectors differentially with different intensities in different places and times?

Before submitting pacifically to the weight of the empirical evidence that has been amassed by Roberts and many other proponents of the falling rate of profit theory, some serious questions have to be asked. Since I am not inclined or qualified to attempt any sophisticated counter-analyses of data sets, I shall confine my remarks to some very general observations on the difficulties of assembling relevant and meaningful data.

Data that show a falling rate of profit do not necessarily confirm the existence of the specific mechanism to which Marx appealed. This is, for me, the most important objection to much of the literature on the subject. Profit rates can fall for any number of reasons. As we have seen, lack of adequate aggregate effective demand in the market could produce falling profits, as could rising wages impelled by heightened class struggle. When technological change is introduced then the net effect is to produce greater inequalities. In the absence of any opposition or countervailing force the rich get richer and the poor get poorer. This is how Marx's general law of capital accumulation works. On the other hand, an organized working class backed by powerful state institutions could force wage rates so high as to generate a crisis of falling profits. This happened during 1965–1975 in North America and Europe as wages rose, profits fell and productivity stagnated thanks to recalcitrant working-class power.

Resource scarcities and constraints (particularly with respect to food, energy and raw materials) can lead to falling profits by the mechanism that Ricardo described. There is no need to appeal to Malthusian nature-imposed limits to make this argument. Scarcity can be orchestrated through speculative activity and restraints on effective demand. Scarcities of oil and food are clearly manipulated to extract higher rents. Increasing monopoly power and, perhaps even more important for our times, the rising powers of rent extraction can lead to falling profits on industrial capital. Marx conceded that falling rents could augment profits, so why not also accept that rising rents would have the opposite effect? Rent on money capital itself (interest) is rationed by conditions of demand and supply, competition and the factional class power of the financiers. The rentiers, far from suffering the euthanasia that Keynes wishfully predicted, are currently carving out niches to procure greater and greater shares of the surplus at the expense of industrial capitalists, which means falling returns for the direct producers.

There are all sorts of reasons why profit rates might fall and no amount of graphs depicting falling profit rates give us any reason to accept any one particular mechanism rather than another. The only way forward here would be to measure the direct impacts of changing labor productivity on profit rates. In measuring labor productivity, Marx distinguished between the organic and the value compositions of capital: the former being defined by the ratio of constant to variable capital within an enterprise or even within a whole sector or 'department', while the latter measures productivity for capital as a whole. Most theorists treat the two terms as synonymous when they are not. Both cases are highly sensitive to turnover times (of fixed capital in particular) and to degree of vertical integration in production (Harvey 1982: 125–133). The form of industrial organization is a crucial issue to its measure. Imagine an iron ore mine on top of which is built a steel plant that feeds the production of cars directly. The constant capital would be that used in the iron mine plus the energy inputs and fixed capital in the other phases of such an integrated production system. Most of the total value would be attributed to that added by labor. Now split the process up into separate firms producing iron ore, steel and then cars. The constant capital on average would increase while the labor share would decrease markedly. While the example I use may seem a bit extreme, consider how the increase in subcontracting these last 40 years might have affected value compositions within firms and across sectors.

While it is possible to make sense of the average organic composition of capital within an enterprise or even in industries or 'departments' (as specified in Volume 2 of *Capital*), the value composition for capital as a whole appears at best as tautological and at worst as a totally incoherent concept. This is so because the only measure of productivity relevant to capital is surplus value production, and this is what changes in productivity are supposed to explain (Marx 1976: 644). There are all sorts of other problems: is constant capital the value of capital employed (including fixed capital of long life) or the value of the capital used up (the fraction of fixed capital value worn out) in a production period (of what length)? Are capitalists interested in the rate or mass of surplus value?

The second major problem arises because Marx specified his theory in value terms, while the data used to prove or illustrate it are expressed in money terms. Money is not equivalent to value, but an indispensable representation of value. The relation between value and its representation as money is deeply contradictory: the generality of immaterial social values were traditionally represented by the particular materialities of gold and silver as commodities; this is how the immateriality of a social relation acquired its material representational form. The problem is that the particular conditions of gold production stand in for the generality of all human labor, and that the sociality of value is thereby opened up to appropriation by private persons. Money then acquires a social power which can be used as an instrument of domination and class rule. When the metallic base to the world's monetary system was abandoned in the 1970s, however, money took on a life all of its own such that it could diverge substantially from that which it is supposed to represent. The disciplinary power once exercised by gold and silver is replaced by the disciplinary powers of the central banks. The fetish focus of the monetary authorities on inflation control after 1980 or so is a stark indicator of this shift. On the other hand, when the Federal Reserve adds trillions to the money supply through quantitative easing, this has no necessary relation to value creation. Most of it seems to have ended up in the stock market to boost the asset values that are so important to the rich and powerful.

There is, Marx notes, nothing to prevent not only a quantitative but a qualitative divergence between market prices and values such that honor, conscience, raw land, carbon emissions futures and God knows what can be traded as if they are commodities, when they clearly are not (Harvey 2014: contradiction 2). Investing in corruption (or its legalized version called lobbying) is big (and lucrative) business in our times. Some of the most profitable businesses are illegal, and the various mafias around the world are major centers of capital accumulation. Successful lobbying can raise profits substantially in certain sectors without investing anything in production. It is far more profitable for the power industry to invest in lobbying than to install pollution reduction technologies in coal-burning power plants.

The profitability of housing construction is heavily dependent on speculative movements in housing prices and rent extractions (both land and interest) via the credit system. The value profit rate, as Marx defined it, has little or no relation to the profitability of Nike shoes whose monetary value has been augmented by a successful branding campaign (do advertisers produce value?; Arvidsson and Pieterson 2013). A stock market price likewise depends as much upon reputation as it does on productive activity and capacity. The gap between value creation and what money does grows wider and wider. This contradiction between value and its representation is usually ignored by those who use monetary measures as definitive proof of a theory specified in value terms. It underpins Marx's theory of fictitious capital.

This does not mean that the profit data are worthless. Quite the contrary. We live in the world of money and operate in the shadowy presence of the value it represents. The money profit rate is real; after all, businesses close down if they do not make enough of it. These are the monetary signals that affect our lives, our behaviors and frequently guide our actions. Policy-makers look at monetary aggregates and devise strategies to guide the economy – also a very real fiction – this way or that depending upon whose class interest is being served or gored. Convincing evidence that the rate of monetary profit is falling is a significant social fact which affects us all and to which we typically react.

But there are some tricky questions that have to be negotiated. There is a gap between where profit (value) is produced and where it may be realized. Value produced in the factories of China may be realized by Walmart in the United States, and part of what Walmart realizes in Oklahoma may be taken by the rentiers or the financiers in New York City (Marx 1978: Chapters 1–4; Harvey 2013a). The recorded rate of profit in manufacturing may be falling because the extractions of the merchants, the financiers and the landlords may be rising. The marginal profit rate of Apple (in the USA) is reported to be 27 percent, whereas Foxconn (in China) which produces Apple computers reports 3 percent. The power relation between merchant and producer capital prevents the equalization of the profit rate. Conversely, as Marx points out, profit rates in industry may rise with reductions in rents and taxes. The direct producers may concede higher wages and receive lower profits, but the workers may then have their gains extracted back by predatory landlords, merchants, telephone and credit card companies, and the like. Capital is a flow, as are the revenues generated out of value production, and the patterns of such flows are intricate. Data collected at one point in the system may or may not accurately represent the movements in their totality.

All sorts of other considerations can affect reported profits. Much of the world's trade occurs within corporations that fix internal transfer cost pricing arrangements across currency borders so as to either disguise their profits or record them in that jurisdiction with the lowest tax rate. It sometimes seems that the only reason corporations report any actual profits at all is to jack up their stock price. The monetary profit data tell us something, but exactly what is not always easy to assess.

There are good reasons to be skeptical, therefore, of some of the data sets available. Reports in the business press these days suggest that businesses in the United States are operating at a high rate of profit, while the data series that Roberts and others produce point to the opposite conclusion. A report from the Federal Reserve shows a startling growth in the mass if not the rate of profit. 'From 2000 to the present, quarterly corporate after-tax profits have risen from $529 billion to $1.5 trillion. On an annual basis, growth was from $2.1 trillion to $6 trillion in annual after-tax profits' (Edsall 2014). The business press also reports that the rate of reinvestment is at an all-time low. There is little interest in expansion (hence low growth and sustained wage repression), which some attribute to lack of effective demand. This is due in part to lack of reinvestment, but the three big centers of lagging effective demand in the US are the housing market and state and federal government expenditures. We seem to be at a very odd conjuncture in the United States in which the rate of profit is high but the rate of return on new capital investment is low.

Most of the data sets on profit rates are compiled from within the nation-state framework of data reporting and in all but a very few instances make no pretence of representing the global situation (but see Maito, n.d.). What the profit rate is in China, Indonesia, India, Bolivia and Mali (to say nothing of contemporary Syria and Iraq), and how all of this might be aggregated into some global data on the rate of return on capital, is simply unknown and probably unknowable. A data set compiled for the USA is useful in its own right, of course, but it cannot be taken as evidence of what is happening to global capital even assuming all the other objections already raised are laid aside.

There is, however, one data set which has potential relevance as an indicator of what might be going on in the realm of value production, and which is relatively easy to procure. If the general theory of the tendency for profit rates to fall is correct, then the spread of labor-saving technological changes (forced by the competitive pursuit of relative surplus value) should mean a tendency for the number of waged workers employed by capital to decrease. We know that employment in agriculture has dramatically decreased with industrialization and that the proportion of the global labor force in manufacturing has remained fairly constant (this has been true even in China) in spite of expanding production because of automation. This tends to support the falling rate of profit thesis.

But when we look at the overall labor participation rate on a global scale, we see a massive increase in the global labor force. An International Labour Organization (ILO) report from 2007 concluded, for example, that 'in 2005, there were an estimated 3.05 billion individuals in the global labor force, a figure that represents an increase of more than 1.1 billion – more than 35 per cent – since 1980' (Kapsos 2007). Much of the growth in these years was driven by population growth and the accession of ex-communist states to the world market. Over a much longer time horizon the movement of women into the labor force has been hugely significant, along with the destruction of peasant ways of subsistence living. Without dwelling on the regional details and differences (important though these are) this clearly does not suggest any decrease in the global labor force available for value creation and surplus value extraction. The extra 1.1 billion workers suggests a dramatic increase in the prospects for rising rather than falling surplus value extractions and possibly rising rather than falling profit rates. It speaks to a situation in which absolute surplus value is just as easy to appropriate as relative surplus value.

The only argument against this conclusion is that the increase in the active waged workforce was absorbed in non-productive labor, or that it was not employed by capital at all (for example, as personal security guards for the ultra-rich). Much of the influx is certainly attributable to the growth of the so-called service economy rather than to increasing employment in agriculture, mining and manufacturing. But the distinction between unproductive and productive labor is a difficult one. Like many of Marx's categories it becomes murkier and murkier the more he distanced himself from Adam Smith's views, and the more he embraced the idea that value production involved the 'collective' rather than the individual laborer, and the more he sought to integrate science, technology and knowledge production into the concept of value-producing activities (Vercellone 2007). Even sticking with his more restrictive definitions, there are plenty of situations where what we normally call services are clearly productive of value.

For example, Marx (1978: 225–229) insisted that transportation is value and potentially surplus value producing. The booming logistics sector is therefore rife with value and surplus value production. And while General Motors has been displaced by McDonalds as one of the largest employers of labor in the US, why would we say that making a car is productive of value while making a hamburger is not? Restaurants are value and surplus value producing (even waiters can be viewed as part of the 'collective laborer' in value production). All we then have to do is to suggest that the subcontracted designers, branding and advertising firms, scientists and technical personnel, even consultants and accountants, are all part of the collective laborer and we are well on the way of taking on board a very significant portion of the 1.1 billion extra workers in the field of value production. Misperceptions arise because what are conventionally defined as services often turn out to be productive activities. If Marx is correct in arguing that the definition of productive labor is anyone who creates a surplus value that can be appropriated by capital, then for-profit educational or security services (for example, teachers and security guards) are productive workers. 'A schoolmaster,' says Marx (1976, 644), 'is a productive worker when, in addition to belaboring the heads of his pupils, he works himself into the ground to enrich the owner of the school. That the latter has laid out his capital in a teaching factory, instead of a sausage factory, makes no difference to the relation.'

In much of the advanced capitalist world most of the large factories have been long gone and so it would seem that value and surplus value producing labor has disappeared. But when I stand at the corner of 86th and Second Avenue in Manhattan I see innumerable delivery, bus and cab drivers, the workers from Verizon and Con Edison digging up the streets to fix the cables, down the street the water mains are being fixed while other workers are constructing the new subway, workers are putting up scaffolding on one side of the street while taking it down on the other, the coffee shop is making coffees, and in the local 24-hour diner workers are scrambling eggs and serving soups. These are the kinds of jobs (along with all manner of teaching factories) that have increased markedly in recent times, and they are all value and surplus value producing. If only half of those employed in the production and reproduction of urban life are employed in the production of this sort of value and surplus value, then this easily compensates for the losses due to the industrialization of agriculture and the automation of manufacturing.

This rapidly expanding value-producing workforce has very little collective bargaining power (compared to the factory labor of yore) to curb exploitation. The conditions for rising rather than falling profitability are therefore very much in place. Certainly the mass of surplus value has been increasing even if the rate of profit may have been falling. It is unlikely, however, that the huge expansion in labor force participation that has occurred over the last 40 years will ever be repeated. There are still substantial reserves of labor untapped in Africa, and some in the Middle East and South and Southeast Asia. But the absorption of women into the labor force and the entry of China and the ex-Soviet empire into global labor market competition cannot be repeated, and any falling-off in rates of population growth (already negative in much of Southern Europe and Japan) might change conditions for profitability sometime in the future. Right now, however, those who attribute the difficulties of contemporary capitalism to the tendency of the profit rate to fall are, judging by the evidence of increasing labor participation, seriously mistaken. The conditions suggest a vast increase and not a constriction in surplus value production and extraction.

It may seem that I am unduly picking on the falling rate of profit theorists and singling them out for criticism. I do so, however, because of all the divergent theories of crisis that have emerged from the Marxist tradition, this one holds an iconic position within the Marxist imaginary and it is typically presented in such a way as to exclude consideration of the other possibilities that Marx laid out.

There is, I believe, no single causal theory of crisis formation in Marx's works. Marx (1972: 120) himself made this clear. 'The contradictions existing in bourgeois production,' he wrote, 'are reconciled by a process of adjustment, which, at the same time, however, manifests itself as crises, violent fusion of disconnected factors operating independently of one another yet correlated'. Much of his research focused on the kinds of disconnected but correlated factors that come together in particular crises. This undermines the teleology of the falling rate of profit and replaces it with contingent forces that move one way or another depending on the interplay of multiple but correlated contradictions. Capitalism, in short, moves its crisis tendencies around, geographically, sectorally and from one nodal point to another (as money, commodity or production, for example) within the overall circulation process of capital (Harvey 2010). The multiple contradictions and crisis tendencies internal to capitalism are perpetually re-created even as they appear in different guises (Harvey 2014). The relation between what is systemic and what is conjunctural begins to fuse even as it sharpens. I believe this was the determination that Marx was coming to as his studies progressed. And even if it was not, capital's complicated history would suggest that this is how we should think of it in the here and now. While Marx was, I think, correct never to let go of the principle that of the many barriers that capital accumulation had to confront, the greatest was capital itself, and that capital, like many other organic systems, was destined at some point to mutate or die, he needed an increasingly nuanced theory of how and why this might be so. As good historical-geographical materialists, we should surely be pursuing the same goal.

REFERENCES

Arvidsson, A. and N. Pietersen (2013), *The Ethical Economy: Rebuilding Value after the Crisis*, New York: Columbia University Press.

Boccara, P. (1974), *Etudes sur le Capitalisme Monopoliste d'Etat, sa Crise et son Issue*, Paris: Seuil.

Carchedi, G. (2011), *Behind the Crisis: Marx's Dialectics of Value and Knowledge*, Leiden: Brill.

Edsall, T. (2014), 'America Out of Whack', *New York Times*, Opinion Section, 23 September.

Glyn, A. and R. Sutcliffe (1972), *British Capitalism, Workers and the Profit Squeeze*, Harmondsworth: Penguin.

Harvey, D. (1982), *The Limits to Capital*, Oxford: Basil Blackwell.

Harvey, D. (2010), *The Enigma of Capital*, London: Profile Press.

Harvey, D. (2012), 'History versus Theory: A Commentary on Marx's Method in Capital', *Historical Materialism*, 20(2), 3–38.

Harvey, D. (2013a), *A Companion to Marx's Capital, Volume 2*, London: Verso.

Harvey, D. (2013b), *Rebel Cities: From the Right to the City to the Urban Revolution*, London: Verso.
Harvey, D. (2014), *Seventeen Contradictions and the End of Capitalism*, London: Profile Press.
Heinrich, M. (2009), 'Reconstruction or Deconstruction? Methodological Controversies about Value and Capital, and New Insights from the Critical Edition', in R. Bellofiore and R. Fineschi (eds), *Re-Reading Marx: New Perspectives after the Critical Edition*, London: Palgrave Macmillan.
Heinrich, M. (2013), 'Crisis Theory, the Law of the Tendency of the Profit Rate to Fall, and Marx's Studies in the 1870s', *Monthly Review*, 64(11), available at http://monthlyreview.org/2013/04/01/crisis-theory-the-law-of-the-tendency-of-the-profit-rate-to-fall-and-marxs-studies-in-the-1870s/.
Kapsos, S. (2007), 'World and Regional Trends in Labour Force Participation: Methodologies and Key Results', *Economic and Labour Market Papers*, Geneva: International Labour Organization.
Kliman, A. (2012), *The Failure of Capitalist Production: Underlying Causes of the Great Recession* London: Pluto Books.
Maito, E.E. (n.d.), 'The Historical Transience of Capital: The Downward Trend in the Rate of Profit since XIX Century', unpublished paper, University of Buenos Aires, Argentina.
Marx, K. (1972), *Theories of Surplus Value*, Volume 3, London: Lawrence & Wishart.
Marx, K. (1973), *Grundrisse*, Harmondsworth: Penguin.
Marx, K. (1976), *Capital Volume 1*, Harmondsworth: Penguin.
Marx, K. (1978), *Capital Volume 2*, Harmondsworth: Penguin.
Marx, K. (1981), *Capital Volume 3*, Harmondsworth: Penguin.
Moseley, F. (1990), *The Falling Rate of Profit in the Postwar United States Economy*, New York: St Martin's Press.
Moseley, F. (2014), 'The Development of Marx's Theory of the Falling Rate of Profit in the Four Drafts of Capital', paper delivered to the MEGA symposium at the Institute for Economic and Historical Research, Amsterdam, 10–12 October.
Reuten, G. (2009), 'Marx's General Rate of Profit Transformation', in R. Bellofiore and R. Fineschi (eds), *Re-Reading Marx: New Perspectives after the Critical Edition*, London: Palgrave Macmillan.
Roberts, M. (2014), 'The Nature of Current Long Depression', presentation at Marxism 2014, London, 11 July.
Shaikh, A. (2010), 'The First Great Depression of the 21st century', in L. Panitch, G. Albo and V. Chibber (eds), *Socialist Register* 2011: *The Crisis This Time*, London: Merlin Press.
Thomas, P. and G. Reuten (2014), 'Crisis and the Rate of Profit in Marx's Laboratory', in R. Bellofiore, G. Starosta and P. Thomas (eds), *In Marx's Laboratory: Critical Interpretations of the Grundrisse*, London: Haymarket.
Vercellone, C. (2007), 'From Formal Subsumption to General Intellect: Elements for a Marxist Reading of the Thesis of Cognitive Capitalism', *Historical Materialism*, 15, 13–36.

4. Monocausality and crisis theory: a reply to David Harvey

Michael Roberts

This chapter aims to refute the arguments of David Harvey that Marx's law of the tendency of the rate of profit to fall (TRPF) is not relevant to any Marxist theory of crises under capitalism. The chapter will argue that, contrary to recent revisionist scholarship, Marx did not abandon his law of profitability or ignore it as a theory of crises in his later years. It will attempt to defend the view that Marx's law is logically consistent with his law of value; that the law is relevant to a coherent theory of crises; and, moreover, that the law provides the underlying explanation and ultimate cause of crises in the capitalist mode of production.

The law provides a clear causality for crises that is backed up by a growing amount of empirical evidence compiled by many scholars. The nature of the law as a tendency along with counter-tendencies can explain the cyclical development of capitalist production better than any alternative theories of crises presented by Marxists in the past and Harvey now.

The matter at debate is simple: is Marx's TRPF the main or ultimate cause of recurrent and regular crises in capitalist production that lead to sharp and sustained drops in output, employment and incomes in modern economies? In Chapter 3 in this volume, Harvey basically concludes that the TRPF is not the only or even the principal cause of crises. Thus it cannot be the basis of a Marxist theory of crisis. I contend the opposite.

Harvey opens by saying that 'Marxists frequently appeal to the theory of the tendency of the rate of profit to fall as an underlying explanation' of crises. Well, some like me do. But actually most Marxists and Marxist economists, even now, do not do so. The view that Marx's TRPF is relevant to cyclical booms and slumps under capitalism has never been a majority view. The early Marxists after Marx – Kautsky, Lenin, Bukharin, Luxemburg, Hilferding and the Stalinist economist Varga – rejected the TRPF as the driver behind a Marxist theory of crises.[1] Indeed, it was only in the 1920s and 1930s that Grossman (1992) and Mattick (1974) put forward the TRPF as a theory of crisis.

In the post-war period (at least from the 1970s), more Marxist economists adopted the TRPF as the basis of crisis theory (Cogoy 1987; Yaffe 1972; Carchedi 1992). But it was still a minority view (see Sweezy 1946; Baran and Sweezy 1962) and remains so now. The most prominent Marxist economists now, including of course Harvey himself, do not accept it (Aglietta, Dumenil, Husson, Uno, Itoh, Wolf, and so on). Moreover, most of the revolutionary Marxist groups around the world, particularly in Europe and the United States (US), reject Marx's TRPF as relevant to crises.[2]

Indeed, back in March 2011, Costas Lapavitsas, Marxist professor at the School of Oriental and African Studies (SOAS), University of London, at a meeting where he spoke along with Gerard Dumenil (who also rejects the TRPF as the main or sole cause of crises) claimed that this 'monocausal' view of the TRPF was an invention of a recent 'Anglo-Saxon school' of Marxist economists and never had been in the 'classical tradition' (Roberts 2011a). Whether Grossman, Mattick or, for that matter, Cogoy or Carchedi, can be considered 'Anglo-Saxon' is doubtful. But I certainly am Anglo-Saxon.

Given the weight of rejection of Marx's TRPF as the basis for a theory of crises, it is encouraging that the work done recently by such as Anwar Shaikh, Fred Moseley, Guglielmo Carchedi, Andrew Kliman, Alan Freeman, Mick Brooks, Peter Jones, Esteban Maito, Sergio Camara Izquierdo, Tapia Granados, Juan Mateo and myself has gained some traction (Roberts 2013a, 2011b). As a result, Harvey is able to conclude that a Marxist theory of crises based on the TRPF now 'holds an iconic position within the Marxist imaginary' and thus needs to be demolished by Harvey – a compliment indeed.

4.1 MONOCAUSALITY

The majority of Marxists still consider that crises under capitalism can have different causes at different times. Indeed, as Harvey says towards the end of his chapter, 'There is, I believe, no single causal theory of crisis formation in Marx's works'.[3] Dumenil and Levy (2011) reckon that each major crisis as they defined them (1890s, 1930s, 1970s and the Great Recession) had a different 'conjunctural' (to use Harvey's term) cause (Roberts 2011a). Similarly in their recent award-winning book, Panitch and Gindin (2013) claim that each crisis has a different origin.

My immediate response to this eclectic or 'conjunctural' view is that of Carchedi (2010a: note 3), namely:

> some Marxist authors reject what they see as 'mono-causal' explanations, especially that of the tendential fall in the rate of profit. Instead, they argue, there is no single explanation valid for all crises, except that they are all a 'property' of capitalism and that crises manifest in different forms in different periods and contexts. However, if this elusive and mysterious 'property' becomes manifest as different causes of different crises, while itself remaining unknowable, if we do not know where all these different causes come from, then we have no crisis theory . . . if crises are recurrent and if they have all different causes, these different causes can explain the different crises, but not their recurrence. If they are recurrent, they must have a common cause that manifests itself recurrently as different causes of different crises. There is no way around the 'monocausality' of crises.

Monocausality must be tempered with a modification: namely, a Marxist theory of crises must look beneath the appearance of events, beneath the proximate causes to the essential or ultimate cause. We need to identify the underlying or ultimate cause of crises in the same way that Newton identified the underlying cause of motion of earthly bodies in the law of gravity and in force and counter-force. But we must also recognize that the 'trigger' for each crisis can be different: it could start from a collapsing stock market (1929) or a bursting housing boom (2007), or a sharp jump in commodity prices (oil in 1974). This is where each 'conjunctural' event can be different (Roberts 2014a).

Capital starts with the 'general', or should we say with the 'abstract', and proceeds step by step to the concrete (Rodolsky 1977; Grossmann 2015). This is vital to understand because the biggest sin committed by the method of mainstream bourgeois economics is to look only at the appearance of things and not see the essence. But, of course, you cannot stay with the essence and must proceed to flesh out any critique of an economy so that the appearances can be explained.

Marx's TRPF refers to profit as surplus value in the whole economy, prior to the division of that value into 'profit of enterprise', rent and interest, which are dealt with towards the end of *Capital* Volume 3. Yes, as Harvey says, Marx's *Capital*, even Volume 3, is at the abstract level of 'capital-in-general' (capital's extraction of surplus value from labour) for the most part. That is for a very good reason, as Marx wants to bring out the key laws of motion of capitalism, including the most important, the TRPF, that drives accumulation and contains its own downfall. Marx ignores the issues of credit, interest-bearing capital and the state until he deals with 'many capitals', that is, competition and division of the surplus value among capitalists.

Harvey says 'Marx derived the law under certain assumptions', which later on he refers to as 'draconian', thus implying that they are so strict as to be irrelevant to reality or the appearance of things. But models or laws are always only as good as their assumptions allow. The point is that Marx's assumptions for the TRPF are very realistic. They boil down to just two: that value is only created by labour power; and that capital must accumulate more value, but can only do so, as a rule, by increasing the organic composition of capital.

The organic composition of capital is the ratio between value of the means of production (or stock of assets) and the value of labour power (wages). Over time, this ratio rises. That does not mean that wages fall necessarily. Wages can rise, but the value of the means of production will rise more. Labour creates value and the organic composition of capital will rise over time as capitalism expands and covers the globe. Two assumptions, that is all – and realistic, in my opinion.

By the way, 'perfect competition' is not an assumption of Marx's TRPF, as Harvey claims. Or that value must be 'realized' during accumulation, again as Harvey claims. Also, the TRPF is not affected if commodities trade at their production prices or market prices rather than at values and does not depend on a fall in 'effective demand'. This is the strength of the theory: the rate of profit would fall even in the case of all commodities being sold. And Marx's law is not 'restricted' by ignoring monopolization or a failure to realise value created. On the contrary, these latter processes are the result of the operation of the law.

Harvey contends that Marx's TRPF is 'contingent'. This could mean that it must be tested in reality. In that sense, every law is contingent. You start with some realistic assumptions, that are contingent, but then the law leads logically to a result that can be tested in reality and may also lead to predictions about what will happen; for example, if the rate of profit or the mass of profits falls on a sustained basis, we can expect a crisis in capitalist production to follow. But I suspect that what Harvey means by contingent that is there no logic that leads from Marx's TRPF to crises; because the law itself is 'indeterminate'. This latter charge is indeed the line that comes from Michael Heinrich and before him, Paul Sweezy (1946) and the modern-day *Monthly Review* 'school'. Carchedi and I have answered this charge of indeterminacy in the TRPF (Roberts 2013b) already and so have others (Miller 1995; George 2013).

4.2 MARX ABANDONED THE LAW?

We are told by the eminent Marxist scholars of the *Marx-Engels-Gesamtausgabe* (*MEGA*) (published by Karl Dietz Verlag Berlin), like Michael Heinrich (2013), that Marx probably abandoned the TRPF as relevant to crises in his later years and it was Friedrich Engels in his editing of *Capital* after Marx's death who reinserted the law and distorted it into a theory of crisis. Indeed, we are told by Harvey that Engels put a 'gloss' and misleading title on Marx's Chapter 15. Harvey accepts this interpretation (and that is all it is): 'I find Heinrich's account broadly consistent with my own long-standing skepticism about the general relevance of the law'. Well, that may be comforting to Harvey, but it does not bear up with the facts, or with the views of other *MEGA* scholars.[4]

Poor old Freddy Engels has really come in for it by our modern Marxist *MEGA* scholars who apparently know better what Marx meant than his close comrade-in-arms and contributor.[5] Despite what Heinrich says, there is no evidence anywhere that Marx (1973) dropped or rejected his TRPF, considered by him as 'the most important law of political economy'. In my view, he never went back to his theory because he had dealt with it – instead he then spent some time trying to work out how to apply it in an explanation of the cyclical nature of capitalist crises.[6] Fred Moseley has recently published a paper on Engels's editing of Volume 3 from Marx's notebooks and concludes that Engels got as close as he could to Marx's meaning.[7]

4.3 TENDENCIES AND COUNTER-TENDENCIES

Harvey tells us that 'we know that Marx's language vacillated between calling his finding a law, a law of a tendency or even on occasion just a tendency'. Well, let us ask the question. Is the TRPF a law or a tendency? In fact, all 'laws' in Marx's analysis are tendencies, that is to say they operate as a force pulling in a certain direction. For instance, 'Such a general rate of surplus-value – viewed as a tendency, like all other economic laws – has been assumed by us for the sake of theoretical simplification' (Marx 1967: 275).

Harvey says near the very beginning of his chapter that I '[attribute] the current long depression to this tendency' (the TRPF). That is not correct because a tendency implies counter-tendencies and thus the tendency alone cannot entirely be the cause of crises. Marx's TRPF is the tendency, the 'law as such'. But with tendencies, dialectically, come counter-tendencies. The difference between the two is important. The tendency is the law that will eventually override counter-tendencies. But counter-tendencies can delay, reverse or slow the tendency, for some time.[8] The TRPF says the rate of profit will fall over time; but it does not do so all the time because of counter-tendencies. Indeed, the counter-tendencies operate in such a way as to give a cyclical character to the operation of the TRPF.

Harvey tells us that 'proponents of the law typically downplay the countervailing tendencies'. Really? I am sure Harvey has read Henryk Grossmann (1992), that arch 'monomaniacal' supporter of the TRPF as a theory of capitalist breakdown and recurrent crises. In his book, Grossmann takes 68 pages to explain the 'law as such', the tendency. He takes 71 pages to outline all the counter-tendencies. In my book, *The Great Recession*, the whole point of my proposition that the TRPF operates as a cyclical as well as a secular process is based on the role of the counter-tendencies (Roberts 2009). It is the same with that other 'monocausal' author, Carchedi (2010b).

Indeed, there are lots of counter-tendencies. Harvey calls them a 'motley array'. But he notes that I usually identify the two key ones: a rising rate of surplus value and the cheapening of constant capital. That is precisely because they are at the level of abstraction of the 'law as such', namely 'capital-in-general'. The other counteracting factors, such as taxation, foreign earnings, state credit, monopolization and so on, are at the level of 'many capitals'. The counteracting tendency of the globalization of capital, as it searches for new sources of value creation in the urbanization of cheap rural labour of the so-called emerging economies (something which Harvey correctly makes a big play of) (Smith 2010), is really a product of the dominance of the tendency over the key counter-tendencies, leading to downward pressure on profitability in those national economies that have nearly exhausted such sources of value.

Harvey also makes a point of an accelerating turnover of capital as another counteracting tendency. Accelerated turnover will certainly boost the rate of profit for an individual capitalist but only at the expense of other 'slower' capitalists. An average rate of turnover comes into play at the aggregate. And that can be speeded up by better communications and transport and inventory efficiency, but that will only raise the rate of profit if constant capital is not increased at the same time.[9]

Harvey says that the supporters of the TRPF like me suggest that 'financialization had nothing to do with the crash of 2007–08. This assertion looks ridiculous in the face of the actual course of events. It also lets the bankers and financiers off the hook with respect to their role in creating the crisis.' But this charge of omission certainly does not apply to me. Anybody who has read my book (Roberts 2009) knows that I devoted large amounts of space to the US housing boom and bust, the banking crisis, the role of derivatives, and so on. Indeed, my current blog has at least 25 posts on the relation between profitability, credit (debt), banking and the crisis. And in 2012, the year after Harvey gave his intriguing Isaac Deutscher memorial speech at the Historical Materialism conference in London,[10] I presented a long paper entitled 'Debt Matters' (Roberts 2012a). This monomaniac is not so mono (even if maniacal).

4.4 CYCLES AND BREAKDOWN

Harvey says that Marx 'increasingly viewed crises not as a sign of the impending dissolution of capitalism but as phases of capitalist reconstruction and renewal'. If Harvey means that Marx did not have a theory that capitalism would collapse and only one of cyclical crises, then I do not think that is correct. He had both: the cyclical and the secular. Yes, crises, by the destruction of value (and use value) create the conditions for 'renewal' by restoring profitability, previously driven down by the TRPF. But there is no permanent escape, just as there is no permanent crisis. The law will exert its power again and profitability will head down again, eventually, provoking a new crisis (slump). So, as Marx put it, 'Once the cycle begins, it is regularly repeated. Effects, in their turn, become causes, and the varying accidents of the whole process, which always reproduces its own conditions, take on the form of periodicity' (Marx 1987, Part VII, Ch. 25, 633).

This cyclical process of crises is not to restore some equilibrium. Crises do not restore some neoclassical notion of equilibrium but instead jolt the accumulation process back from collapse only to push it forward dynamically again; equilibrium is by chance only.

Moreover, as the delaying or reversal power of the counteracting tendencies wanes, capital finds it more and more difficult to appropriate value and surplus value. And capital is no longer able to develop the productive forces to their full potential. So Marx's TRPF not only provides a causal explanation of crises; it also shows the transitory nature of the capitalist mode of production.

4.5 THE EVIDENCE

Moving on from methodology and the law, Harvey refers to my 'array of graphs and statistical data' to 'bolster' my case, but seems to dismiss their value or relevance. Well, there are two points here. First, are the data correct: has there been a falling rate of profit in the major capitalist economies over the life of modern capitalism, or even since World War II (WWII)? Second, if there is good evidence that there has been a secular fall (interspersed by periods of rising profitability), is this explained by Marx's law? Or are there other (more valid) reasons for profitability to fall? These are questions that Harvey poses early on.

Well, the evidence for a secular fall in the rate of profit of capital is overwhelming both for the most important capitalist economy of the nineteenth century, Britain, and for the most important capitalist economy of the twentieth century, the US.[11] And we have had new work by Marxist scholars who have attempted to measure the rate of profit for many national capitals across the globe since 1870, and since the end of WWII. They show a secular fall (Maito 2014; Roberts 2012b).

The next question is, even if we accept that capitalism does exhibit a tendency for the rate of profit on capital to fall that is borne out in reality, maybe this is caused by other factors than Marx's law. As Harvey puts it: 'Profit rates can fall for any number of reasons'. He cites a fall in demand (the post-Keynesian explanation), a rise in wages (the profit squeeze explanation), 'resource scarcities', monopoly power (rent extraction from industrial capital). Yes, a 'motley array' again.

But is not the point of scientific research to try to identify the main cause from an array of possibilities? If we can show that, when the rate of profit falls, it is caused by a rising organic composition of capital that is not counteracted sufficiently by a rising rate of surplus value, then we have good evidence that Marx's law is the cause. And indeed, that is what the work of several Marxist economists have been able to show, particularly in relation to the movement of profitability in the US, but not only there (Roberts 2013a).

Indeed, that is what I have shown in my 'array of graphs': an inverse relationship between the rate of profit and the organic composition of capital (Roberts 2011b). The fit is almost perfect. When the rate of profit is rising, the organic composition of capital is falling, and vice versa. In other words, this is strong evidence that movements in the rate of profit are caused by inverse movements in the organic composition of capital. And I am not the only researcher to show this.

The 'motley array' of other causes either reinforces or counteracts this movement. They are contingent in the sense that they are liable to happen or not, according to circumstances. And when they happen, they give a specific shape to the crisis.

4.6 RISING ORGANIC COMPOSITION AND PRODUCTIVITY

Harvey says that '[t]he only way forward here would be to measure the direct impacts of changing labor productivity on profit rates'. But that is what the TRPF can do. The law says that a rising organic composition of capital is accompanied by rising labour productivity; it is the flipside of capital accumulation. But the great contradiction is that rising labour productivity is eventually combined with falling profitability. That is because, even if capital appropriates all that new value created by increased productivity of labour and workers get no wages and so 'live on air', profitability will eventually fall because of the rising organic composition of capital. The impact of rising productivity of labour on profit depends on the rate of exploitation of that labour. In and of itself, higher productivity does not influence profitability because productivity measures use values.

After all, what gives the first push to these revolutions in productivity, like, for instance, the decision by Henry Ford to move to assembly line techniques? It is surely the increased expenditure on capital goods relative to living labour, thus the increase in the organic composition of capital. So increased productivity lowers the value of labour power and also cheapens constant capital. That should raise profitability. But increased productivity is only possible through a rising organic composition of capital and that lowers profitability. The latter tendency eventually predominates.

Harvey wants to differentiate between the value composition of capital (VCC) and the organic composition (OCC). He asserts that 'the value composition for capital as a whole appears at best as tautological and at worst as a totally incoherent concept'. This, Harvey argues, is because 'the only measure of productivity relevant to capital is surplus value production, and this is what changes in productivity are supposed to explain'. But Harvey is mistakenly identifying productivity with profitability. If the rate of profit is only a measure of productivity, changes in productivity cannot explain changes in the rate of profit and that would be tautological. But what explains changes in the rate of profit are variations in the organic composition of capital, and so there is no tautology.

And the supposed 'incoherence' is partly incurred by Harvey's misunderstanding of the two concepts. He refers to 'the organic and the value compositions of capital: the former being defined by the ratio of constant to variable capital within an enterprise or even within a whole sector or "department", while the latter measures productivity for capital as a whole'. That is not correct. Fine and Saad-Filho (2004: 110) do a better job at Marx's meaning: 'The OCC measures the results of accumulation by exclusive reference to the sphere of production . . . while the VCC reflects this process in the sphere of exchange.' They go on to say, '[T]he rise of the OCC associated with the specifically capitalist methods of production is the source of the "law as such", whilst the formation of the VCC is associated with the counteracting tendencies.'

Exactly: changes in productivity are accompanied by a rising organic composition of capital (even if moderated by the cheapening effect of rising productivity), while surplus value 'production' is indicated by the rate of surplus value or exploitation.

There we have it again, Marx's two assumptions for the law: only labour power creates value (and surplus value), and capital can only expand and accumulate through a rising organic composition of capital. Are these assumptions borne out in reality? Does the organic composition of capital rise (and the value composition)? Does the rate of profit fall over time as the organic composition of capital rises and vice versa? The evidence is that they do.

Harvey uses as an example of the 'incoherence' of Marx's concept, the level of vertical integration within an economy. If more economic activity is subcontracted out, does that mean that the OCC has changed? He is right to point out that this makes measurement of the actual OCC more difficult. But if the same number of workers are using exactly the same capital equipment to perform exactly the same tasks, whether they are all part of the same firm or if their activities have been subcontracted, then that is surely irrelevant to the economy as a whole. And I and others use aggregate figures for business investment in the economy as a whole, so the problem of the level of vertical integration that Harvey points to is not as important as it would be in the case of an individual firm.

Harvey reckons that money distorts the data anyway, particularly in the modern era of inflation, so that the 'gap between value creation and what money does grows wider and wider'. And we data collectors ignore this anomaly. On the contrary, many of us have spent much time isolating the effect of monetary inflation so that we can discern the underlying changes in as close to value terms as possible (see Kliman 2011; Carchedi 2011).[12]

Harvey clearly does not accept that I and others have found data and evidence that support the conclusion that Marx's TRPF is the best explanation of falling profitability. Yet he is kind enough to say that this 'does not mean that the profit data are worthless. Quite the contrary', as the money rate of profit is real enough. Harvey goes on: 'Convincing evidence that the rate of profit specified in money terms is falling is a significant social fact which affects us all and to which we typically react.' This would seem to invalidate all his previous objections to the empirical work of TRPF supporters.

4.7 OTHER POSSIBILITIES

But Harvey goes further than being sceptical about the data. He doubts that there has been falling profitability, however you measure it, and he also reckons that there are better explanations of recurrent crises of capitalism than falling profitability.

On the first point, Harvey cites rising profits in various parts of the modern economy: in housing, stock market investing, branded products and so on. He states that 'in the business press these days' it is suggested that US businesses are operating 'at a high rate of profit' and cites the 'startling growth in the mass, if not the rate of profit'. Ah well, that is where proper research and data analysis are necessary, rather than relying on the 'business press' for 'anecdotal evidence'.

First, Marx's law is about falling profitability of capital, not falling mass of profits, although the former can lead to the latter in a very decisive way. Harvey makes a slip when he refers to Marx's law as an explanation of 'falling profits'.[13] To extol from newspapers that business profits are up is not good enough, because profitability can be falling at the same time. Indeed, that is usually the case: the mass of profits in an economy is always rising, except just before a slump when businesses (starting with the weakest ones) find that renewed production delivers not just a lower rate of profit but lower absolute profits.

Second, I and others spend a lot of time and effort trying to ascertain what is happening to the rate and mass of profit. As Marx himself argued, there is a point in the accumulation process when the rate of profit on the stock of investment falls to a level where new investment actually leads to a fall in the mass of profit and new value.[14] This 'absolute overaccumulation' of capital is the trigger moment for the collapse of investment and then bankruptcies, unemployment and falling incomes; in other words, a slump.[15]

A study by Tapia Granados (2012) has shown that this causal sequence holds for the US economy since 1945 and Carchedi and I (Carchedi and Roberts 2013) have shown that it holds for the Great Recession too.[16] And so has Mick Brooks (2012).[17] Once again, there are a 'motley array' of graphs and data from me and others to support this explanation of crises.

But Harvey prefers other reasons for capitalist crises than Marx's law. There is the effect of credit, financialization and financial markets; the devaluation of fixed constant capital in the form of obsolescence; and, above all, the limits on consumer demand imposed by the holding down of real wages relative to capitalist investment and profits.

4.8 THE OLD CHESTNUT

Harvey brings up that old chestnut of the 'poverty and restricted consumption of the masses' as the 'ultimate reason for all real crises'. The quote actually comes from a section of *Capital* Volume 3 on money capital and real capital that Marx called 'the confusion'. And no wonder. It mainly consists of undigested quotes on debates on monetary policy relating to the Bank Act of 1844. This part of *Capital* Volume 3 has few clear conclusions and seems to be in the form of preliminary notes by Marx to himself for further study. By comparison, the chapters in Volume 3, Part 3 on the rate of profit are closely argued and extremely taut and coherent.

The quote on the 'poverty and restricted consumption of the masses' sticks out like a sore thumb. Scholars of the *MEGA* note that it was originally a bracketed note that Engels incorporated into the text. 'The ultimate reason' is '*der letzte Grund*' in the *MEGA*. So 'reason' is an incorrect translation in the old chestnut. It has nothing in common with the notions of 'cause' as suggested by those who use the quote as an explanation for the onset of capitalist crisis.[18]

The quotation from Volume 3 can only support the view that Marx had an underconsumptionist view of crises if it is taken out of context. It appears in Marx's discussion of the relation between commercial credit and real crises. Marx (1967: 483) argues that, in periods of crises, markets are glutted and yet credit is contracted. It is thus clear that Marx refers here to realization crises, to the impossibility of selling all commodities at an unchanged price.

Marx's argument is that competition 'develops the productive forces', that is, raises productivity 'as though only the absolute consuming power of society constituted their limit'. But the development of the productive forces goes hand in hand with the ejection of labour, and when crises explode this ejection reduces the masses' consumption. The capitalists' productive and unproductive consumption is also reduced. Underconsumption is a consequence and not the cause of crises.

What causes underconsumption? The answer is obvious: lower wages. But why do wages fall? Wages fall either because employment falls with the same wage rate or because the wage rate falls with the same employment. In other words, wages fall either because less value is produced or because more value is appropriated by capital. A generalized decrease in employment implies that the downward cycle, and possibly the crisis, has already begun. If wages fall because profits increase, then this cannot be the cause of crises because the rate of profit rises.[19]

So Marx did not '[confuse] matters' (Harvey) when he specifically rejected an underconsumptionist explanation of crises in saying that 'it was a pure tautology to say that crises are provoked by a lack of demand or more effective consumption'. Underconsumption assumes what it wants to explain. A lack of demand is the description of a realization crisis, or slump, not an explanation of its cause. To accept otherwise is to accept the inadequate Keynesian 'explanation' (not that Keynes's followers really bother to have one).

4.9 NO THEORY AT ALL

If we do not accept that Marx's TRPF is the basis of his theory of crises, then we must accept that Marx did not have any theory of crisis at all. Indeed, this is what our *MEGA* scholars Heinrich and Kratke (2015) want us to conclude, perhaps so we can fall back on various theories from bourgeois economics based on credit booms (Austrian school), financial speculation (Minsky), lack of demand (Keynes), low wages and inequality (Stiglitz and the post-Keynesians) (Roberts 2010, 2014b). They all have one thing in common: that if their particular theory is right, then capitalism can be corrected through financial regulation (Wolf 2014), higher wages (post-Keynesians), or progressive taxation (Piketty 2014) without replacing the capitalist mode of production itself. That is because these theories argue that there is no fundamental contradiction in the capitalist mode of production that causes recurrent and cyclical crises (as Marx claimed); there are only problems with circulation.

Indeed, that is what Harvey concludes. He wants us to consider alternative theories based on the secondary circuit of capital – that is, outside that part of the circuit to do with the production of value and surplus value – and instead look at that part concerned with the distribution of that value among 'many capitals' involving, in particular, speculative overproduction. Again, Harvey wants us to look at the crises caused by a redistribution of the value created by 'dispossession', a form of 'primitive accumulation' where wealth is accumulated by force or seizure and not by the exploitation of wage labour in production as in fully developed modern capitalism.

Harvey (Chapter 3 in this volume) asks:

> How does that falling rate, if it exists, explain a crisis which on the surface at least was a commercial and financial crisis that began in the housing markets of California, Arizona, Nevada, Florida and Georgia (with outliers in Spain, Ireland, Hungary and various other countries) before going worldwide through contagions in a global financial system that infected all manner of sectors differentially with different intensities in different places and times?

But the bursting of the house price bubble and the credit crunch (begun in 2007) came after a fall in the rate and mass of profit in 2006. That is attested to by official figures from the US BEA. Capitalism went through a 'roadrunner moment', when the system charged ahead – over a cliff.

Furthermore, this was a world economic crisis, affecting countries that undoubtedly had a house price bubble and credit out of control but also others that did not. If we accept that the credit crunch was triggered by the bursting of the house price bubble in a few states of the US, why did it spread all over the world so quickly?[20] For all the major economies, the rate of profit was falling before the onset of recession. Financial manias, panics and crashes cannot yield an explanation of the recurring boom–slump cycle of capitalism. The credit crunch was a trigger for world recession, not the fundamental cause.

4.10 EXCLUDING THE UNLIKELY

Harvey says that those who advocate Marx's TRPF as the underlying or ultimate cause of recurrent and regular crises or slumps in production typically present the law 'in such a way as to exclude consideration of the other possibilities that Marx laid out'. Well yes, at the level of an underlying law, other possibilities have been excluded, if you like by a process of elimination, because they do not explain crises and cannot predict any new ones.

Harvey says at the end of his chapter that 'Marx was, I think, correct to never let go of the principle that of the many barriers that capital accumulation had to confront, the greatest was capital itself'. But, apparently, 'he needed an increasingly nuanced theory of how and why this might be so'. I contend that Marx was more 'monomaniacal' in preserving this 'principle' and did not 'increasingly nuance' it away. We should follow Marx here.

In sum, Marx's TRPF remains integral to any Marxist theory of crises under capitalism. There is no evidence to suggest that Marx abandoned it as illogical or irrelevant. The law of the tendency and the counter-tendencies offers a causal explanation of the cyclical nature of capitalist accumulation, with an increasing body of empirical evidence to back it up. Nothing offered as an alternative by Harvey or others is as compelling.

NOTES

1. Henryk Grossmann (2014) provides an excellent account of theories of crisis adopted by the Marxists after Marx up to the 1930s. See also Howard and King (1989).
2. Latin American groups seem more committed to TRPF.
3. I have been accused of monomania. Mike Treen (2014), national director of the New Zealand Unite Union, recently commented when discussing Marxist crisis theory: 'But the almost monomaniacal attachment to the TROPF [TRPF] to explain crises leads them astray. Michael Roberts even tries to explain the 10-year cycle under capitalism as a result of the fall in the rate of profit. It is of course true that every crisis is associated with a fall in the rate of profit, but that temporary decline is a result of the crisis not the cause.'
4. Kratke (2015). While Kratke also denies that Marx's TRPF was his theory of crisis, Kratke disagrees with Heinrich that Engels distorted Marx's chapters on the TPRF in Capital Volume 3.
5. Jerrold Seigel (1993) had a look at the manuscripts. Yes, Engels made significant

editorial changes to Marx's writing on the law as in *Capital* Volume 3. He divided it into three chapters, 13–15; Chapter 13 was the law; 14 was counteracting influences and 15 described the internal contradictions. But in doing so, Engels shifted some of the text into Chapter 13 on the 'law as such', when in fact in Marx's manuscript they came after the counteracting factors in Chapter 14. In this way, Engels actually makes it appear that Marx balances the counter-tendencies in equal measure with the law as such, when the original order of the text re-emphasizes the law after talking about counter-influences. So, as Seigel (1993: 339) puts it: 'Engels made Marx's confidence in the actual operation of the profit law seem weaker than Marx's manuscript indicates it to be'.

6. The key point for Marx (1987) was that 'the cycle of related turnovers, extending over a number of years, within which the capital is confined by its fixed component, is one of the material foundations for the periodic cycle [crisis] . . . But a crisis is always the starting point of a large volume of new investment. It is also, therefore, if we consider the society as a whole, more or less a new material basis for the next turnover cycle'.
7. Fred Moseley (2015) recently introduced a new translation into English of Marx's four drafts for Volume 3 of *Capital*, where Marx's law of profitability is developed and shows how Engels edited those drafts for *Capital*. Moseley shows that the much-maligned Engels did a solid job of interpreting Marx's drafts and there was no real distortion. 'One can, therefore, surmise that Engels' interventions were made on the basis that he wished to make Marx's statements appear sharper and thus more useful for contemporary political and societal debate, for instance, in the third chapter, on the tendency of the rate of profit to fall' (Moseley 2004).
8. As Marx (1967: 239) put it clearly: 'the same influences that produce a tendency in the general rate of profit to fall also call forth counter-effects, which hamper, retard and partly paralyse this fall. The latter do not do away with the law, but impair its effect. Otherwise, it would not be the fall of the general rate of profit, but rather its relative slowness, that would be incomprehensible. Thus the law acts a tendency. And it is only under certain circumstances and only after long period that its effects become strikingly pronounced'. I do not think that could be clearer.
9. For more on the role of the turnover of capital, we must await an unpublished paper by Carchedi and Roberts (n.d.).
10. For an account of that speech by Harvey, see Roberts (2011c).
11. See Roberts (2011b), which compiles all the empirical research on the rate of profit, *à la* Marx, showing a fair degree of agreement on the movement of the rate of profit and also explaining how falling profitability affects investment and causes crises.
12. In a chapter for a joint book that Carchedi and I are working on, Carchedi (forthcoming) shows that quantitatively the rates of profit (in value and in money terms) differ, but that they track each other fairly closely.
13. Harvey also makes another slip when outlining how the TRPF operates at the beginning of his chapter when he says that 'competition forces capitalist producers to invest in labor-saving technologies in order to preserve market share'. No, it is in order to increase profitability, not market share.
14. Marx (1967: 255): 'because capital would be unable to exploit labour . . . to the degree which would at least increase the mass of profit along with the growing mass of employed capital'.
15. See my evidence for this causal process in Roberts (2014a).
16. And in an unpublished paper, Carchedi (forthcoming) finds that crises occur in years of negative percentage growth of value and surplus value.
17. Brooks (2012): 'The US Bureau of Economic Analysis (BEA) shows that in the 3rd quarter of 2006 the mass of pre-tax profits peaked at $1,865 bn. By the 4th quarter of 2008 it bottomed out at $861bn. This represents a fall of more than one half. The collapse in profits that the BEA records from 2006 would have caused a recession in any case, with or without a banking crisis. A halving in the mass of profits is catastrophic for capitalism and explains on its own the severity of the Great Recession.'

18. What is the meaning of '*grund*' within this context? The famous paragraph consists of two sentences. The first one goes from 'The ultimate reason' to 'of the masses', and the second one from 'as opposed to' to 'their limit'. A better translation of the famous paragraph would be: 'Ultimately, the ground/base upon which all real crises develop remains the poverty' and so on. To make their point, underconsumption supporters disregard the second sentence, but this is the starting point of the argument.
19. The Keynesian reply is that lower wages decrease sales and thus affect negatively profits and the rate of profit. However, Carchedi (2012) has shown that the rate is unchanged if all commodities remain unsold, and rises if some commodities are purchased by capital.
20. Roberts (2009) for an analysis of the global role of securitized debt and derivatives. But note that many banks collapsed in Europe because of the lack of credit and not because they purchased too many derivatives and mortgage-backed collateralized debt obligations (CDOs) from US banks.

REFERENCES

Baran, P. and P. Sweezy (1962), *Monopoly Capital: An Essay on the American Economic and Social Order*, New York: Monthly Review Press.
Brooks, M. (2012), *Capitalist Crisis, Theory and Practice*, Warsaw: Expedia.
Carchedi, G. (1992), *Frontiers of Political Economy*, London: Verso.
Carchedi, G. (2010a), 'Zombie Capitalism and the Origin of Crises', *International Socialism*, 125(5 January), accessed 5 June 2015 at http://www.isj.org.uk/index.php4?id=614&issue=125.
Carchedi, G. (2010b), 'Behind and Beyond the Crisis', *International Socialism*, 132(11 October), available at http://gesd.free.fr/carchedi11.pdf.
Carchedi, G. (2011), *Behind the Crisis – Marx's Dialectics of Value and Knowledge*, Leiden: Brill.
Carchedi, G. (2012), 'Could Keynesian Policies End the Slump? An Introduction to the Marxist Multiplier', *International Socialist Review*, 136(October), available at http://gesd.free.fr/carch12.pdf.
Carchedi, G. (forthcoming), 'Crises and Marx's Law', in G. Carchedi and M. Roberts (eds), *The World in Crisis*, Portland, OR: Zero Books.
Carchedi, G. and M. Roberts (2013), 'The Long Roots of the Present Crisis', *World Review of Political Economy*, Spring, available at http://gesd.free.fr/robcarch13.pdf.
Carchedi, G. and M. Roberts (n.d.), 'Measuring the Turnover of Capital and Variable Capital', unpublished paper.
Cogoy, M. (1987), 'The Falling Rate of Profit and the Theory of Accumulation', translated from M. Cogoy (1974), 'Baisse du taux de profit et theorie de l'accumulation', *Les Temps Modernes*, 31(330), 1231–1255.
Dumenil, G. and D. Levy (2011), 'The Crisis of the Early 21st Century: A Critical Review of Various Interpretations', accessed 5 June 2015 at http://www.jourdan.ens.fr/levy/dle2011h.pdf.
Fine, B. and A. Saad-Filho (2004), *Marx's Capital*, London: Pluto Press.
George, E. (2013), 'But Still It Falls: On the Rate of Profit', 4 July, available at http://gesd.free.fr/stillitf.pdf.
Grossmann, H. (1992), *The Law of Accumulation and Breakdown of the Capitalist System, being also a Theory of Crises*, London: Pluto Press.
Grossmann, H. (2014), *50 Years of Struggle over Marxism 1883–1932*, transl. by Rick Kuhn, London: Marxist Left Review.

Grossmann, H. (2015), *Marx, Classical Political Economy and the Problem of Dynamics*, transl. by Rick Kuhn, Victoria, Australia: Marxist Left Review.
Heinrich, M. (2013), 'Crisis Theory, the Law of the Tendency of the Rate of Profit to Fall and Marx's Studies in the 1870s', *Monthly Review*, 64(11), accessed 5 June 2015 at http://digamo.free.fr/heinrich13.pdf.
Howard, M.C. and J.E. King (1989), *A History of Marxian Economics Volume 1*, New York: Macmillan Press.
Kliman, A. (2011), *The Failure of Capitalist Production*, London, Pluto Press.
Kratke, M. (2015), 'Marx's Theory or Theories of Crisis', paper presented to Capitalism Workshop, King's College London, May.
Maito, E. (2014), 'The Historical Transience of Capital: The Downward Trend in the Rate of Profit since the 19th Century', accessed 5 June 2015 at http://gesd.free.fr/maito14.pdf.
Marx, K. (1967), *Capital Volume 1*, New York: International Publishers.
Marx, K. (1973), *Grundrisse*, London, Penguin.
Marx, K. (1987), *Capital Volume 2*, New York: International Publishers.
Mattick, P. (1974), *Economic Crisis and Crisis Theory*, Paris: Editions Champ Libre.
Miller, J. (1995), 'Must the Profit Rate Fall – a Defense of Marx against Paul Sweezy', accessed 5 June 2015 at http://gesd.free.fr/miller95.pdf.
Moseley, F. (2004), 'Marx, Engels, and the Text of Book 3 of *Capital*', *International Journal of Political Economy*, 32(1), 3–13.
Moseley, F. (ed.) (2015), *Marx's Economic Manuscript of 1864–65*, transl. by Ben Fowkes, London: Brill.
Panitch, G. and S. Gindin (2013), *The Making of Global Capitalism: The Political Economy of the American Empire*, London: Verso.
Piketty, T. (2014), *Capital in the 21st Century*, New York: Belnap Press.
Roberts, M. (2009), *The Great Recession, Profit Cycles and Crises: A Marxist View*, London: Lulu Press.
Roberts, M. (2010), 'The Causes of the Great Recession', paper presented to the Association of Heterodox Economists Conference, July, available at http://hetecon.net/.
Roberts, M. (2011a), 'The Crisis of Neoliberalism and Gerard Dumenil', accessed 5 June 2015 at http://thenextrecession.wordpress.com/2011/03/03/the-crisis-of-neoliberalism-and-gerard-dumenil/.
Roberts, M. (2011b), 'Measuring the Rate of Profit, Profit Cycles and the Next Recession', paper to the 13th annual conference of the AHE, July, accessed 5 June 2015 at http://gesd.free.fr/mrobprof.pdf.
Roberts, M. (2011c), 'David Harvey, the Marxist Method and the Enigma of Surplus', accessed on 5 June 2015 at https://thenextrecession.wordpress.com/2011/11/13/david-harvey-marxs-method-and-the-enigma-of-surplus/.
Roberts, M. (2012a), 'Debt Matters', paper to Historical Materialism Conference, London, November, accessed on 5 June 2015 at https://thenextrecession.files.wordpress.com/2012/11/debt-matters.pdf.
Roberts, M. (2012b), 'A World Rate of Profit', paper presented to the AHE/IPPE joint conference in Paris, accessed on 5 June 2015 at http://gesd.free.fr/mrwrate.pdf.
Roberts, M. (2013a), 'The US Rate of Profit: Extending the Debate', 19 December, accessed on 5 June 2015 at http://gesd.free.fr/mr1213.pdf.
Roberts, M. (2013b), 'Michael Roberts and Guglielmo Carchedi on Heinrich', accessed 5 June 2015 at http://gesd.free.fr/mrhtprof.pdf.

Roberts, M. (2014a), 'Tendencies, Triggers and Tulips', presentation to the Third Economics Seminar of the International Institute of Research and Education (IIRE), 14 February, Amsterdam, accessed 5 June 2015 at http://thenextrecession.files.wordpress.com/2014/02/presentation-to-the-third-seminar-of-the-fi-on-the-economic-crisis.pdf.

Roberts, M. (2014b), 'Is Inequality the Cause of Capitalist Crises?', accessed 5 June 2015 at https://thenextrecession.wordpress.com/2014/03/11/is-inequality-the-cause-of-capitalist-crises/.

Rodolsky, R. (1977), *The Making of Marx's Capital*, London: Pluto Press.

Seigel, J. (1993), *Marx's Fate: the shape of a life*, University Park, PA: Pennsylvania State University Press.

Smith, J. (2010), 'Imperialism and the Globalisation of Production', PhD thesis, University of Sheffield, July, accessed 5 June 2015 at https://thenextrecession.files.wordpress.com/2012/12/imperialism-the-globalisation-of-production.pdf.

Sweezy, P. (1946), *The Theory of Capitalist Development*, London: D. Dobson.

Tapia Granados, J. (2012), 'Does Investment Call the Tune?', May, accessed 5 June 2015 at http://sitemaker.umich.edu/tapia_granados/files/does_investment_call_the_tune_may_2012__forthcoming_rpe_.pdf.

Treen, M. (2014), Speech at the annual conference of the socialist organisation Fightback, Wellington, 31 May – 1 June, and a seminar hosted by Socialist Aotearoa in Auckland, 12 October, available at *Links International Journal of Socialist Renewal*, http://links.org.au/node/4156.

Wolf, M. (2014), *The Shifts and the Shocks: What We've Learned – and Have Still to Learn – From the Financial Crisis*, New York: Penguin.

Yaffe, D. (1972), 'The Marxian Theory of Crisis and the State', *Bulletin of the Conference of Socialist Economists*, Winter, 5–58, available at https://www.marxists.org/subject/economy/authors/yaffed/1972/mtccs/index.htm.

5. Booms, depressions and the rate of profit: a pluralist, inductive guide

Alan Freeman

This chapter is a guide to theories of the profit rate, its effect on economic performance, and its role in economic recessions and booms. The chapter aims to get the reader, with a minimum of mathematics, to a point where she can continue studying the topic alone. It is a work of historical recovery, not an all-inclusive exposition; more detail can be found in standard sources (Howard and King 1989; Walsh and Gram 1980) or the recent debates listed in the References.

There is a context. As the economic woes of the advanced capitalist countries increase, with ever more serious consequences for their geopolitical order, people want to know why. The finger of suspicion points to a culprit which economists identified two centuries ago, and have since studiously ignored or, indeed, exonerated. This guide is thus not a simple learning exercise, like a new language; it is a history of a contested subject. The contest is at the heart of a fundamental political discussion: is capitalism responsible for its own difficulties?

This chapter is partisan; it argues that in the battle to explain what is going wrong, the profit rate is the only contestant left standing. However it is not dismissive. It aims to provide readers with sufficient information to make independent judgements. Two principles are therefore applied: systematic pluralism (ISIPE 2014; Denis 2009), to ensure that alternative explanations are properly identified and fairly stated; and inductive consistency, to judge which best explains those facts.

5.1 THE CRISIS OF ECONOMICS AND THE CASE FOR THEORETICAL INTEGRITY

The 2007 financial crash provoked a crisis of public confidence in economics (Freeman 2009); nine years later we may justifiably speak of a crisis of economic theory. With no end in sight to what the International Monetary Fund (IMF) (Blanchard 2015) oxymoronically terms 'stagnant growth', as popular majorities emerge for policies that orthodoxy finds indefensible, the question is not just who is still listening to the economists, but whether they have anything useful to say.

This is clearest from their treatment of their own most disturbing discovery: that long-run declines in the profit rate, occupying much of capitalist history, are caused by capitalism itself. Economists have ignored this fact with an evasiveness which would convince any rational Martian that their job is to perpetuate ignorance. The rate of profit should by rights occupy the same place in any serious understanding of capitalist dynamics as the study of materials in bridge-building, gravity in physics or enzymes in biology: It is a non-ignorable factor, which no complete theory can dispense with.

Yet economics does dispense with it. The question is: why? At stake is theoretical integrity. The history of the subject, I will show, comprises a kind of long-wave alternation between facts unexplained by theory, and theories unsupported by facts. During long booms (1893–1914, 1942–1968), when everything seems to be going well, it is dominated by its 'esoteric' function (Freeman 2015): justification of the existing order. During long depressions (1870–93, 1929–42, now) brute facts intrude and 'new' theories break through to account for them.

This contest is the theoretical expression of a real, material battle between classes whose interests are bound up with the explanations which economists offer for their condition. If we wish to become collective agents of our destiny, we need to engage in theoretical struggle: a comprehensive striving to understand the world we live in, based on principles of rational enquiry. Such an emancipatory social science, breaking from 'pure' economics (Desai, Chapter 8 in this volume), would study the historical relation between the action of conscious humans and that which the commodity conceals from them, whilst empowering those same conscious humans to acquire reliable knowledge though the systematic study of the facts. This chapter is a contribution to that endeavour.

5.2 INVESTMENT, GROWTH AND PROFIT IN THE LONG DEPRESSION

Table 5.1 summarizes some basic facts of the current long depression. The most notable point is the simple size of gross investment, a major component of demand comparable with, or greater than, government spending. The second point is the clear correlation between investment and growth, accounting almost entirely for post-crash differences between the major economies. This relation is confirmed in countless studies; most notably the IMF's own gloomy diagnosis (Blanchard 2015).

Table 5.1 Investment and growth in major economies

Country	Investment[a] (%)	Post-crash growth rate[b] (%)	Memo: government spending[a] (%)
China	48	9.0	29
India	31	6.5	27
Korea	29	3.2	21
United States	19	0.9	37
Germany	17	0.7	45
France	22	0.3	57
United Kingdom	14	0.2	44
Japan	21	0.1	40

Notes:
a. Post-crash average share of GDP, current local currency.
b. Average GDP growth, constant local currency, 2008–13.

Source: IMF WEO Database 2014.

Among the variables affecting investment, the profit rate is impossible to ignore. As Kliman (2012: 91) notes:

> variations in the rate of profit account for 83 percent of the variations in the rate of accumulation of the following year . . . if there were actually no relationship between the rates of profit and accumulation, there would be less than one chance in 900 trillion that the observed relationship between them would be as strong as the one we observe.

These facts are not a proof of causal relation. However, we should suspect any theory which cannot account for them. The reality is even stranger: with honourable exceptions, most theories contain explanations of this relation which they choose to ignore. This, in and of itself, is a fact that requires explanation.

To set out the problem systematically, I will first express the basic identities arithmetically. These are uncontroversial; differences revolve around how the magnitudes involved should be interpreted and, in consequence, how the causal relations between them may be explained.

Suppose a private owner invests a sum k which yields a profit s over a given period of time. The return on capital, or rate of profit r over this period is:

$$r = \frac{s}{k} \tag{5.1}$$

From this we can deduce the average rate of return on two or more capitals. With two investments k_1, k_2 yielding profits s_1, s_2, this is:

$$r = \frac{s_1 + s_2}{k_1 + k_2} \tag{5.2}$$

Likewise the average profit rate for any set of capitals k_i yielding returns s_i (i = 1. . .n) is the sum of these returns divided by the sum of the capitals:

$$r = \frac{\sum_{n}^{1} s_i}{\sum_{n}^{1} k_i} \tag{5.3}$$

Writing for brevity:

$$K = \sum_{n}^{1} k_i; \tag{5.4a}$$

$$S = \sum_{n}^{1} s_i \tag{5.4b}$$

we get:

$$r = \frac{S}{K} \tag{5.5}$$

where capital letters signify aggregates. If K is now total privately invested capital and S the total return on it, (5.5) gives the rate of profit in the whole economy.

Part of the surplus – say, some quantity A – is invested: this is what accumulation consists of. The measure of A however depends on the theory concerned; if a writer argues that K falls through devaluation by D, whilst some portion B of S is not invested, then that theory defines A to be:

$$A = S - D - B \tag{5.6}$$

Just like (5.1)–(5.5), every theory conforms to this identity. If, therefore, over any period of time T the total accumulated surplus is A_T, then K will grow to $K + A_T$ and the new rate of profit will be:

$$r_T = \frac{S_T}{K + A_T} \tag{5.7}$$

All differences about the rate of profit reduce to differences about *S* and *A*; r_T can be greater than *r* only if the increase in *S* offsets the fact that *K* grows by *A* as long as accumulation continues, or if *A* becomes negative – disaccumulation. Much obscurity vanishes if we study theories in these simple, basic terms.

5.3 FACTS AND THEIR CAUSES: THE PROFIT RATE IN THE HISTORY OF THEORY

Political economy's founders were unequivocal about the profit rate. Smith ([1776] 1904: Vol. 1, Chapter 9) and Ricardo ([1817] 1990: 71–73) paid great attention to a downward trend in the rate of return on capital[1] which practical businessmen regarded as an established fact. Mill thus notes that:

> The tendency of profits to fall as society advances, which has been brought to notice in the preceding chapter, was early recognized by writers on industry and commerce; but the laws which govern profits not being then understood, the phenomenon was ascribed to a wrong cause. (Mill [1848] 2008: 573)

As Mill indicates, Marx's contemporaries sought to explain what everyone knew to be true.[2] When Marx writes: '[G]iven the great importance that this law has for capitalist production, one might well say that it forms the mystery around whose solution the whole of political economy since Adam Smith revolves' (Marx [1894] 1991: 319), the 'mystery' is that capitalism itself is responsible for the observed fall, as the following makes clear:

> The *true* barrier to capitalist production is *capital itself*. . . What disturbs Ricardo is the way that the rate of profit, which is the stimulus of capitalist production and both the condition for and the driving force of in accumulation, is endangered by the development of production itself. (Marx [1894] 1991: 358, 368)

Twentieth-century discussions, focussed on breakdown (Rosdolsky 1977: 392; Grossman 1992; see also Kuhn 2007) have tended to portray Marx's law of the tendency of the rate of profit to fall (LTRPF) as a proof that it cannot possibly recover (Carchedi and Roberts 2013). An opposite camp, basing itself on Okishio ([1961] 1993) has tried to prove that it cannot possibly fall.

All attempts to prove that reality is impossible are, in the last instance, unenlightening. The resulting intellectually bizarre polarization is rooted in a mutual denial that the philosopher need pay any attention to mere facts, as long as he can demolish the opposition's theories. Empirically, the rate falls for most of the time; at certain points, empirically, it recovers. The question is why, and when, the transitions occur.

What did the economists think the falling rate of profit (FRP) would lead to? Smith and Ricardo concerned themselves with long-term trends: they wanted to know if capitalism could survive. Marx ([1867] 1990: 762–872) is equally concerned with historical tendencies. However, he is unambiguous that there are also short-term or cyclic consequences:

> In view of the fact that the rate at which capital is valorized, i.e. the rate of profit, is the spur to capitalist production . . . a fall in this rate slows down the formation of new, independent capitals and thus appears as a threat to the development of the capitalist production process; it promotes overproduction, speculation and crises, and leads to the existence of excess capital alongside a surplus population. (Marx [1894] 1991: 349–350)
>
> The periodical depreciation of existing capital, which is a means, immanent to the capitalist mode of production, for delaying the fall in the profit rate and accelerating the accumulation of capital value by the formation of new capital, disturbs the given conditions in which the circulation and reproduction process of capital takes place, and is therefore accompanied by sudden stoppages and crises in the production process. (Marx [1894] 1991: 358)

The conclusions are that capitalism produces crises; that these crises repeat and cannot be averted; and that the problems thus arising accumulate, to produce long-term historical threats to the existence of capitalism. These hypotheses are empirically verifiable and widely acknowledged as true.

The debate centres on whether, and to what extent, the LTRPF is their 'cause'. It would benefit from attention to the concept of 'cause', covered by an extensive and informative literature. The simplest confusion is to look for some kind of mechanism, making the FRP an 'immediate' cause in Aristotle's sense, as for example a burst pipe 'causes' a flood, or heart failure 'causes' death.

For Marx, in contrast, the LTRPF 'causes' crisis by exacerbating all other contradictions, just as old age exacerbates all the conditions that threaten life, or rising water pressure produces a spate of burst pipes. Actually, Marx recognizes dozens of immediate 'causes' of crisis:

> [A]ll these necessary premises [for capitalism to reproduce] demand one another, but they are brought about by a very complicated process, including three processes of circulation which occur independently of one another but intermingle. This process is so complicated that it offers ever so many occasions for running abnormally. (Marx 1969: 301–302)

This is brought out in his sustained demolitions of Say's law in *Theories of Surplus Value* (Marx 1969: 470–546). Say, he argues, fails to separate purchase from sale, assuming that anything that is produced will automatically find a buyer. That is, Say assumes that reproduction will succeed, before it has done so. This is a characteristic methodological error. The 'mechanism' of crisis is problematic only if one presupposes that capitalism has to work: '[C]risis is precisely the phase of disturbance and interruption of the process of reproduction. And this disturbance cannot be explained by the fact that this does not occur in those times when there is no crisis' (Marx 1969: 503).

Does Marx then offer a theory of crisis based on the LTRPF? Yes; but he does not reduce a theory to a mechanism. A law – which he defines in keeping with most philosophy[3] – underlies these 'mechanisms'. The 'occasions for running abnormally' all multiply in the presence of low profit rates, and diminish in the presence of high ones. The confusion surrounding this simple idea arises, primarily, from the alien notion that causes are exclusive, as if crisis were a 'whodunit' mystery. The protagonists write (Howard and King 1989) as if by proving that underconsumption is one cause of crisis, they have somehow proven that the FRP cannot be – or vice versa. Causal laws are never exclusive; just because 'age' does not appear on a death certificate, we cannot conclude that people will live forever.

Equal confusion arises from the idea that there are no relations between causes, which underlies the spurious problem of 'multicausality' (Harvey 2015; Kliman 2015). Every death involves multiple organ failure, but this does not mean that people cannot die of old age; it explains why old people's organs fail. The question Marx correctly poses is: why do the many mechanisms of crisis multiply in certain circumstances, and not in others? A phrase apocryphally attributed to golfer Jerry Barber runs: 'The more I practice, the luckier I get'. Marx's concern is: what makes capitalism get unlucky?

To take one example: he notes that a shortage of means of payment is a phase in every cycle. Credit shortage is a 'mechanism'. But if we make this an alternative theory of crisis, how can we explain why, on the one hand, cheap credit fuelled the 1945–68 expansion, while on the other, the years of quantitative easing since 2009 have failed to restore even the growth levels of the 1980s, never mind the golden years?

These confusions all lead up to the modern discussion on whether some new phenomenon, such as financialization, neoliberalism or inequality, 'took over' from the FRP in the 1980s. Such causes can only be designated 'new' if we either insist on causal exclusion, or employ multicausality to issue a ban on general causes. The point is: what caused financialization or neoliberalism? Did the contradictions which erupted in the 'Second Slump' of 1974 (Mandel 1978) simply slink away? Or did these, and the twin crises of the 1980s, create an abscess which burst in 2008?

This directs us to the missing half of the discussion: how, and when, can we say a crisis is over? The question is rarely included in discussions on the

LTRPF, yet it sets crisis theory on its feet. Once we recognize that capitalism does not automatically reproduce itself, we grasp that the failure has to be understood as the absence of success. Twentieth-century economists, we shall see, confronted the question 'What causes depressions?' via their debate on how to end them; that is, 'What causes booms?'

5.4 DON'T BLIND ME WITH FACTS: EQUILIBRIUM AND THE DOGMA OF MARKET PERFECTION

Certain facts are so obvious as to be undeniable. Economists may differ on how to explain the Great Depression of 1929–42, but none now claim that it did not happen. Yet the prevailing consensus of the time – neoclassical theory – furnished incontrovertible proofs that it could not happen. Such a discordance between fact and theory cannot be explained by supposing that economics behaves like a normal science. We must recognize that its function, in part or whole depending on the historical period, is not to explain the existing social order but to justify it.

Economic theory removed crisis from its agenda in a retrogression (Freeman 2010) which declared capitalism to be incapable of it. Having reconstructed the social sciences on Weberian lines at the end of the nineteenth century (Desai, Chapter 8 in this volume), it embarked on fabricating proofs of capitalist perfection. This fulfilled two esoteric functions: it dethroned labour and removed all capitalism's contradictions.

The result was the method of general equilibrium, or comparative statics (Freeman 2015), which replaced the temporal method (Freeman and Carchedi 1996; Kliman 2007) which Marx inherited from Sismondi. General equilibrium systems begin by presupposing that the market works perfectly, and deduce their theories from this supposition. Unsurprisingly, internally generated crisis becomes theoretically impossible.

In this religious phase, the prime imperative is to show that all deviations from the theoretical ideal arise from causes external to capitalism. This is a classic neoplatonic formulation: the ideal is the real, of which the sinful society around us is an imperfect manifestation. Market imperfection in economics takes over the function of Satan in Christianity. As John Weeks (pers. comm.) has aptly put it, a horse becomes an imperfect unicorn.

Having no exoteric pretensions, these theories openly admit that their numbers cannot add up to what is observed. The scholar has to grasp that to these authors this failure is of no consequence: the numbers would add up, were it not for the imperfections. Their real concern, as with mediaeval scholars discussing proofs of God's existence, is: what are the properties of a completely ideal system?

Two versions emerge, mirrors of each other. Marginalist general equilibrium, formulated by Walras (1977) in the 1930s and perfected by Arrow and Debreu in the 1950s (Walsh and Gram 1980), replaces the notion of surplus with the idea of payment for capital services. However, actual output is not equal to the sum of payments for factors and so the actual empirical data does not obey equations (5.4) and (5.5), except in the stationary state – which never exists. The result is not so much a theory as a confession: the theorist admits in advance that the numbers cannot work, and calls the outcome an 'imperfect market'.

The Marxist variant is physicalism, otherwise known as simultaneism. It begins with von Bortkiewicz's ([1905] 1952) famous 'correction' to Marx, in which value and price of production becomes the solution to a set of simultaneous equations. Bortkiewicz is quite open: he recognizes Marx as a 'successivist' – his term for 'temporalist' – and offers a new theory of value which he designates a 'correction' of Marx, in line with his Walrasian convictions:

> Alfred Marshall said once of Ricardo: 'He does not state clearly, and in some cases he perhaps did not fully and clearly perceive how, in the problem of normal value, the various elements govern one another mutually, not successively, in a long chain of causation'. This description applies even more to Marx . . . [who] held firmly to the view that the elements concerned must be regarded as a kind of causal chain, in which each link is determined, in its composition and its magnitude, only by the preceding links . . . Modern economics is beginning to free itself gradually from the successivist prejudice, the chief merit being due to the mathematical school led by Léon Walras. (Bortkiewicz [1905] 1952: 23–24)

A complication arises when Sweezy ([1942] 1970), in a controversial reading of Sraffa (1962), declares Bortkiewicz's system the received version of Marx, fertilizing a vast literature 'proving' that Marx was inconsistent. This literature has fallen into disrepute; it rests on the disproven attribution to Marx of an equilibrium viewpoint.

The confusion is best dispelled by recognizing simultaneist Marxist systems for what they really are: distinct theories of value. They share, with marginalist general equilibrium, a series of presuppositions without which they yield no solution; in the 70 years since Sweezy first called them 'simplifying assumptions', these have never been relaxed. There is a single, uniform rate of profit, all capital turns over completely at exactly the same time, markets clear completely in every period, and prices and values at the end of each period are required to equal those at the start of the same period. The term 'physicalism' arises because, as Steedman (1977) famously pointed out, value in this system is redundant. All magnitudes depend only on the 'physical quantities' consumed and produced.

Famously, as established by Okishio's ([1961] 1993) rigorous theorem, such systems cannot yield a falling rate of profit. The reason is that when values fall, the losses arising from moral depreciation of capital goods purchased at the old prices are simply wiped out; the capitalists are excused from paying for them. This would be a neat trick if any real capitalist could behave thus; as is the supposition that the sellers receive more money for their goods than the buyers pay them. But again, this does not matter to the authors concerned because in an imaginary state of perfect reproduction, the numbers would work. Thus Roemer (1981: 380):

> Responses to this claim, of Okishio and others, have been of three types. These are, first, what Fine and Harris (1976) call fundamentalist positions on RPF. Second, there are empirical discussions of whether or not the organic composition of capital is indeed rising. While this sort of investigation may be useful, it does not bear upon the *theoretical* issue of whether or not the rate of profit falls due to technical change . . . empirical investigations, then, are certainly necessary, but they cannot provide refutation of a theory.

The formal claim that facts cannot refute a theory simply loses sight of what theory is for, namely, to explain the said facts. But how can we tell whether any given theory achieves this end? To this we now turn.

5.5 DATA PLURALISM AND THE INDUCTIVE METHOD

Once economists embark on such basic debates as 'Has the profit rate recovered?' or 'Is the recession over?' they encounter a fundamental issue: data are constructed. In order to test these propositions we have to measure and define the profit rate and the other quantities involved. This is why the major theoretical revolutions in economics are all accompanied by revolutions in measurement.

Curiously, economists tend to treat data as incontrovertible, even though, as Shaikh (1999) notes, every single variable in the profit rate involves a theoretical construction. The national accounts themselves originate in Keynes's redefinition of such key variables as savings and investment; they embody a theory (Assa 2014). Economists' debates about theoretical explanations are therefore inseparable from their differences on how to interpret the data.

The case of finance is instructive. The national income accounts (NIA) deduct an 'imputed' (fictitious) magnitude called financial intermediation services indirectly measured (FISIM) from all industrial sectors and add it to the output of the financial sector. Interest payments are hence attributed to a productive activity. This is an ideological assumption, which Mohun (2000) and Moseley (1992) attempt to correct for; whether or not we accept their solutions, we cannot but agree that if finance is inconsistently accounted for, the NIA's ideological bias will be imported uncritically.

Freeman (2012) corrects a further inconsistency in conventional measures, which include financial profits in *S* but exclude from *K* the financial assets which yield these profits. Once this correction is made, the 'recovery' in the profit rate observed by other authors (Kotz 2009; Basu and Vasudevan 2013) disappears. Both United Kingdom (UK) and United States (US) profit rates continue uninterrupted on the downward trend which started in 1946. NIA measures of fixed assets themselves are also problematic. Kliman (2010) shows that if the Bureau of Economic Affairs (BEA) historic cost measures of assets and profits are used, the rate of profit unambiguously declines from 1980 to 2000, the disputed period. Other differences arise if, following Shaikh (1999, 2010), we correct for capacity utilization.

When data yield different answers to such basic questions as whether the profit rate is rising or falling, a rigorous enquiry has to accept that factual claims depend on how the data are constructed. We can draw no final conclusions from the widest conceivable range of measures, if that range excludes results which refute those conclusions, any more than a court can reach a just decision by refusing to hear the defence's star witness.

Does this drive us into relativism? To the contrary, inductive consistency imposes a stringent further constraint: a theory must explain *all* the data it yields. The standard measures of the profit rate lead to two implausible conclusions: that in the financial sector it is in excess of 80 per cent; and that in the UK it has risen continuously from 1974 onwards, while the UK's economic performance was unambiguously awful. No theory which deploys such measures can be accepted, unless it accounts for these uncomfortable predictions as well as the phenomena they were constructed to explain.

Data pluralism is not a licence to produce numbers that do not add up, or predictions which conflict with a theory's own data: it is a duty to scrutinize data using inductive principles routinely applied elsewhere. With this in mind, let us now study how, faced with the incontrovertible facts of the Great Depression of 1929, economic theory reacted. Three of its reactions are pertinent. First, it embarked on a theoretical discussion of the conditions for exit from the crisis leading to the emergence of Keynesianism. Second, it evolved substantially new methods of measuring the facts, giving rise to the national accounts. Third, and most fundamental, it put politics back into political economy, as the role of the state came to centre stage. At stake was a three-way discussion: can capitalism restore itself, can it be saved at all, and if so, what actions might save it?

5.6 KEYNES, KONDRATIEFF, SCHUMPETER AND THE REDISCOVERY OF REALITY

The second Great Depression confronted economic theory with a new problem,[4] confirmed by a comprehensive data set on the profit rate assembled by Maito (2013). On the one hand, long declines in the profit rate (20–40 years) appear in every mature capitalist economy. On the other, except in the UK, these reverse sharply at definite points, wiping out prior losses in the short space of 5–10 years. It is also striking that no single, uniform profit rate applies to all national economies; the rate of profit does not equalize on a world scale.

The primary theoretical puzzle is that the business cycle itself does not restore the profit rate. This is an outstanding historical fact; the new data strikingly confirm it. Accounting for it remains the central theoretical problem facing modern political economy. If the negative growth which accompanies downturns were sufficient to wipe out the value of accumulated capital, there would be no long-term trends to observe in capitalism. Yet this is not, empirically, the case. The modern debate around whether the US profit rate was 'restored' in the 1980s does not absolve us from explaining why it fell from 1948 until the alleged upturn, nor why even this claimed upturn in no way restores it to boom-time levels.

As indicated, the problem cannot be solved without studying it from the correct perspective. Before we can understand why the profit rate fell from 1948 we must grasp what raised it to its 1948 levels and set off the post-war expansion. We can then understand depressions properly, as the absence of the factors that produce these long, expansive booms: this is, actually, the only historically known form a 'recovery' takes. A gloomy fact is that the first such recovery coincided with imperialism, and the second with fascism and World War II. What is the role of such external, political causes in restoration?

We can approach this problem by starting from Marx's explanation of the law, namely, the accumulation of capital values in the denominator of equation (5.5). Cyclical downturns do potentially reverse this, though the question is: by how much? If accumulation goes into reverse, capital stocks will run down. This requires A in equation (5.7) to be sufficiently negative. Unlike other 'countervailing tendencies' I know no theoretical objection to the hypothesis that disaccumulation can restore the profit rate during the short cycle. Yet, empirically, it does not. Instead the profit rate recovers infrequently, under definite but rare historical circumstances. What are these circumstances?

Economic theory divided, in the 1930s, on exactly this issue. Schumpeter (1939; see also Freeman 2014a) locates recovery in endogenous circumstances. He holds that long depressions themselves create the conditions, completing the long-postponed liquidation of accumulated capital values in a frenzy of creative destruction.[5] Schumpeter's is thus the purest and most coherent form of the widely held, even dominant, notion of self-restoration (Freeman 2014b) which lies behind both neoliberalism and endogenous long wave theory (Menshikov 1989).

The second great camp argues that a boom requires conscious intervention by non-market – that is to say, political and institutional – forces. Though Keynes's account is best-known, its clearest expression comes from Trotsky's (Day 1981: 50) definitive 1924 criticism of Kondratieff's theory of long waves:

> One can reject in advance the attempts by Professor Kontrad'ev to assign to the epochs that he calls long cycles the same 'strict rhythm' that is observed in short cycles. This attempt is a clearly mistaken generalisation based on a formal analogy. The periodicity of short cycles is conditioned by the internal dynamic of capitalist forces, which manifests itself whenever and wherever there is a market. As for these long (50-year) intervals that Professor Kontrad'ev hastily proposes also to call cycles, their character and duration is determined not by the internal play of capitalist forces, but by the external conditions in which capitalist development occurs. The absorption by capitalism of new countries and continents, the discovery of new natural resources, and, in addition, significant factors of a 'superstructural' order, such as wars and revolutions, determine the character and alteration of expansive, stagnating, or declining epochs in capitalist development.

Wars and revolutions may seem distant from the issue of the profit rate; however Trotsky's explanation makes sense if we interpret it to mean that political events are required to destroy capital values, because purely economic mechanisms do not suffice. This coincides with Keynes's own theory of the profit rate, which appears in his concept of the marginal efficiency of capital (MEC), his key explanator for investment behaviour. He distinguishes this from marginal productivity:

> The ordinary theory of distribution, where it is assumed that capital is getting *now* its marginal productivity (in some sense or other), is only valid in a stationary state. The aggregate current return to capital has no direct relationship to its marginal efficiency . . . the extent of investment in any direction will depend on a comparison between the rate of return over cost and the rate of interest (Keynes 1971: 139–140)

The opportunities for productive investment are capitalized over their expected lifetime and discounted by the expected rate of interest; only those are undertaken whose discounted return is above zero. Thus it is the difference – Marx's surplus profit – between the return on productive investment, and that on financial hoarding or accumulation, which determines the level of investment.

For Keynes, moreover, the rate of profit is restricted for precisely the reason proposed by Marx: $K_T + A$ in equation (5.7) outstrips S_T:

> The demand for capital is strictly limited in the sense that it would not be difficult to increase the stock of capital up to a point where its marginal efficiency had fallen to a very low figure. This would not mean that the use of capital instruments would cost almost nothing, but only that . . . the aggregate return from durable goods in the course of their life would, as in the case of short-lived goods, just cover their labour-cost of production plus an allowance for risk and the costs of skill and supervision. (Keynes 1971: 375)

It is sometimes argued that Keynes's analysis is unconnected with Marx's, because Keynes speaks of the expected, and Marx the actual rate of return, and Keynes speaks of value while Marx speaks of price. Neither objection holds water.

Marx makes no claim that the profit rate directly enters the consciousness of the capitalists. He repeatedly asserts (e.g., Marx [1894] 1991: 142, 300, 780–782) that what matters to the individual capitalist is surplus profit, the difference between his own profit and that of other capitalists. He makes it clear that fictitious capital itself seeks and obtains a return on what is paid for it, which determines its price (Marx [1894] 1991: 597).

Since for Marx, the temporalist, rates of profit do not equalize but form a distribution, it must follow that the lower the average of this distribution, the more individual capitalists will find it profitable to place their money with a financier than to throw it back into production. Keynes is not merely similar to Marx; on this he is virtually identical.

Equally, both writers recognize that false expectations are punished. Inflated asset prices are brought back to earth in the crashes that normally accompany downturns. Expectations, moreover, are formed on the basis of real data, no matter how fantastical the computation, it being assumed that capitalists possess no supernatural powers. At stake is thus only the manner in which a falling average rate imposes itself on expectations. This is an interesting question which could fund many dissertations, but it is not a difference of principle.

What about the difference between price and value? Once we recognize the temporal character of Marx's concept of value, this difference too vanishes. We begin from the work of Kalecki who explicitly theorized the rate of profit in Keynesian terms (Toporowski 1999), arguing in effect that the impositions of identity (5.7) could be overcome by an indefinite increase in output. Clearly, if the magnitudes of (5.7) are values, this cannot happen because output cannot rise faster than the natural growth rate of the labour force – the core of Marx's argument. To see this, we should recognize that the surplus S_T is bounded above by output Y_T, so the profit rate cannot rise above a maximum R_T where:

$$R_T = \frac{Y_T}{K_T + A_T} \quad (5.8)$$

Only if A becomes vanishingly small over time – that is, accumulation tends towards zero – can the maximum rate be prevented from falling. Since r is always smaller than R, it follows that a rising surplus cannot offset the rising composition of capital.[6]

However, if Y can be inflated arbitrarily, this constraint no longer holds. Thus, another way of looking at the differences between Marx's theory and those of his critics is that, their measure of output being unrelated to the magnitude of labour time, they recognize no constraint on output.

Inductive consistency requires us to stand this debate on its feet. Actually, the profit rate falls. Since, actually, the value rate imposes itself on behaviour, the question is: how does this happen? The issue is how to adapt the theory to explain reality, not the other way around.

Marx's and Keynes's analysis converge on an answer to this question. If the average level of investment is determined by differences between rates of return, rather than any absolute level, then a general inflationary trend in prices relative to values will not alter anything, since all rates of return will rise equally, by an amount equal to the proportionate rate of growth of prices in comparison with values.[7]

The value rate of profit is, in effect, a canonical form, independent of its monetary measure. All results of value theory that are expressible in terms of relative profit differences also apply to the price forms. Where specifically monetary effects arise, such as asset price inflation, we can obtain an absolute measure of these effects by reducing prices to values using the monetary equivalent of labour time (MELT). Value analysis thus is a practical, not merely theoretical, instrument of analysis. The final step is to draw out the political consequences of this economic result.

5.7 STRUCTURES OF DISACCUMULATION: SELF-RESTORATION AND THE MODERN DEBATE

We now have an explanation for long depressions which begins to make sense: they are the twin outcome of the forces that produce decline, and the absence of forces that lead to restoration. Seen in this light, the true subject of the debate is: what might lead to restoration? This points us to a much-neglected feature of Marx's theory of the profit rate: it is an instrument of class analysis.

In Volume 3 of *Capital* (Marx [1894] 1991) the profit rate does not only, or even primarily, explain crisis; it explains capitalist classes. Each such class receives shares of total profit determined by a specific kind of property. This lies behind Marx's emphatic rejection of Smith's notion of the profit rate as the 'price of capital'. In the classical 'trinity formula' (Marx [1894] 1991: 953), land, labour and capital are independent sources of value, or 'factors'. In contrast, Marx presents all revenues – the wage itself, industrial profit, commercial profit, interest and rent – as redistributed parts of a single surplus produced by one factor: labour.

In consequence, everything that affects the revenue of a class will cause it to grow or shrink relative to others. If interest rises relative to profit, it will support either more financiers or a larger army of flunkeys for existing financiers. The class of financiers, as a social and political power, will grow. Conversely, a public or class action which affects a type of property income – deregulation, rent controls or tax breaks, for example – will strengthen one class of owners at the expense of others.

These clearly interrelate. Marx speaks in several places of an inverse relation between the growth of industry and the influence of banking capital. Yet by 1914 almost all commentators noted an exorbitant growth of finance capital which had begun during the Great Depression; Hobson and Lenin's famous theory of imperialism took specific account of it (Desai 2012: 49).

The critical question is whether this interrelation acts to exacerbate, or to ameliorate, the original causes of the crisis. Is it a beneficial or parasitic development? To be even temporarily stable, a 'regime of accumulation', to use a regulationist phrase, requires a beneficial relation. The growth of the industrial capitalist class in expansionist booms – the two industrial revolutions, the belle époque and the post-war Golden Age – was directly related to relative surplus value, continuous improvements in productivity and accelerated investment.

The relation between the morbid growth of financial capital and its political manifestation – neoliberalism, extractionism, rising inequality, aggressive and militaristic expansionism – are the outcome of an opposite, unstable process. To understand this we can begin from the law of crisis upon which Marx certainly does insist: in a crisis, capital condenses into the form of money hoards, and withdraws from production. But money, in modern capitalism, is not kept under mattresses. It is neither passive nor idle, but a very aggressive source of incomes – huge ones. Marketable financial instruments are simply the modern form of money capital. The unbridled growth of the class that owns and manages it is not an expression of capitalism's great vitality, but a manifestation of a parasitism arising from capitalism's failure to sustain those sources of revenue which arise from investment in new forms of production.

The source of financial income being unproductive, it does nothing to raise the level of production. Productive investment increases, as in China, precisely and only where external measures are taken to support industry and restrain finance capital;[8] conversely, it collapses, as in much of Europe, where the twin illusions that industry requires no support and finance needs no regulation are given full sway.

The debate is thus whether financialization or neoliberalism are alternative causes of crisis to the FRP (Duménil and Lévy 2011; Kotz 2009; Lapavitsas 2009) or whether they themselves are explained by the FRP. They are. Financial assets are precisely the form that money hoards take in modern times. It makes perfect sense to suppose that the low profit rates of the 1970s and 1980s made these assets into an attractive alternative to productive investment. As Freeman (2012) shows, this explanation is completely consistent with the data. It makes equal sense to recognize the rise of neoliberalism not as a 'solution' to crisis but as the political expression of the material interests of those rentier classes who became the owners and managers of this idle capital, making it a morbid consequence of the LTRPF, not an 'alternative mechanism' of crisis.

It is a classic error of causal reasoning to reject the FRP as a cause of crisis on the grounds that its place has been taken by institutional factors of which it is in turn a cause. The real issue is whether its interrelation with these institutional consequences is stable or unstable. If the former, we should expect to see some kind of oscillatory interaction around an attractor. But what we actually see since the mid-1980s is a degenerative process in which economic and institutional obstacles to a 'boom' reinforce each other.

If we interpret, as an unstable degenerative process, the interaction between rising non-productive incomes which occurs towards the end of an expansive boom, and the changing class relations that the latter induces, we get an alternative account to those benign Schumpeterian theories which, whilst recognizing that capitalism has plainly not mended itself, suppose without factual grounds that it has been mended by stable political mechanisms of accumulation which it produced out of itself.

Which account is true? The issue is clouded by the prior discussion around data. Those authors who elevate institutional factors to the status of prime cause also argue that recovery has already occurred, as they must do since if there has been no recovery, there is no 'new' crisis of which institutional factors may be a cause; rather, writers in the opposed strand (Desai 2012; Freeman 2012; Kliman 2012; Shaikh 2010) tend to argue, institutional factors are a new expression of the same underlying problem.

The standard of comparison is critical. All claims of a post-1984 recovery adopt, as their standard, the prior years of recession, which were the previous worst experience capitalism went through, after the war. But after any downturn, any rise appears like an improvement. A 'dead-cat' bounce 'looks like' a recovery only because things were already so bad. What is required is a comparator independent of arbitrary periodization. History provides such a comparator: previous long booms. How does the post-1985 period compare with prior long expansions, notably the post-war boom?

Trough-to-trough US growth over 2001–09 was 1.4 per cent, the lowest in post-war history; though at the time hailed as a great bull run.[9] Again averaging trough to trough, average growth from 1939 to 1970 was 4.6 per cent; from 1970 until 2009 it was 2.8 per cent. These are not spurious averages. For 15 of the 30 years from 1939 to 1970, growth was above 4.6 per cent; growth exceeded this figure in only six of the 39 years from 1970 to 2009. All other economic indicators – long-term unemployment, the rate of investment, capacity utilization and the balance of trade – confirm the sharp contrast between post- and pre-1970s performance.

On a world scale, in no year between 1960 and 1970 did gross domestic product (GDP) grow by less than 4 per cent; in no year since 1991 has it grown by more than 4 per cent. Even in the rocky 1970s, world growth fell below 4 per cent in only two years: 1974 when it dropped to 1.1 per cent, and 1975 when it reached 1.0 per cent. At the time, such growth rates were regarded as catastrophic. Yet, world growth in 2001 was only 0.4 percentage points above the worst of these two years.

Such a 'recovery' is best described as Carthaginian. With recoveries like these, who needs recessions? In an ironical inversion, those writers most exercised to show that the rate of profit no longer matters are the most dependent on the claim that it has risen; it is almost the only statistic that supports their case.

Yet their proof of its rise depends, critically, on the theoretical constructs which are most called into question by the events of the past decade. This chapter, if critical, is written to suggest a way out of this dilemma and promote a return to a genuinely inductive and therefore genuinely pluralist attempt to grasp the reality in which we now live.

NOTES

1. This downward trend is termed the falling rate of profit (FRP).
2. See Heinrich (2013) and the response by Kliman et al. (2013) on this point.
3. A law is 'a theoretical principle deduced from particular facts, applicable to a defined group or class of phenomena, and expressible by the statement that a particular phenomenon always occurs if certain conditions be present' (*Oxford English Dictionary*).

4. A boom followed the Great Depression of 1870, generally referred to as the 'belle époque' and described by C. Freeman (2002) as the age of steel, electricity and imperialism.
5. Theories that have dispensed with the category of value systematically underestimate the disruption needed to reverse the decline in the profit rate because they confuse disaccumulation – which runs down underlying values – with crashes, which merely restore asset prices to these values.
6. Heinrich (2013) represents the issue as if Marx's LTRPF only holds in the extreme case that S is actually equal to Y. He fails to see that since S is bounded by Y, it can only offset accumulation if the latter tends to zero.
7. See the Appendix for a proof of this result. The non-mathematical reader may skip this proof.
8. As is still the case in India, at the time of writing, to a degree unrecognized by most commentators.
9. Data from Freeman (2012).

REFERENCES

Assa, J. (2014), 'Gross Domestic Power: Geopolitical Economy and the History of National Accounting', in R. Desai (ed.), *Theoretical Engagements in Political Economy: Research in Political Economy*, Bingley: Emerald Books.

Basu, D. and R. Vasudevan (2013), 'Technology, Distribution and the Rate of Profit in the US Economy: Understanding the Current Crisis', *Cambridge Journal of Economics*, 37, 57–89.

Blanchard, O. (2015), 'The IMF's Top Economist On Weak Global Growth', *Wall Street Times*, 19 January, available at http://blogs.wsj.com/economics/2015/01/19/the-imfs-top-economist-on-weak-global-growth-tumbling-oil-prices-and-market-turmoil/.

Bortkiewicz, L. von ([1905] 1952), 'Value and Price in the Marxian System (Part I)', *International Economic Papers*, 2, 5–60.

Carchedi, G. and M. Roberts (2013), 'A Critique of Heinrich's "Crisis Theory, the Law of the Tendency of the Rate of Profit to Fall, and Marx's Studies in the 1870s", *Monthly Review*, 1 December.

Day, R. (1981), *The Crisis and the Crash*, London: Verso.

Denis, A. (2009), 'Pluralism in Economics Education', *International Review of Economics Education*, 8(2), 6–22.

Desai, R. (2012), *Geopolitical Economy: After Globalization, Empire, and US Hegemony*, London: Pluto Books.

Duménil, G. and D. Lévy (2011), *The Crisis of Neoliberalism*, Cambridge, MA: Harvard University Press.

Fine, B. and L. Harris (1976), 'Controversial Issues in Economic Theory', *Socialist Register*, 13, available at http://socialistregister.com/index.php/srv/article/view/5398/2297#.VsI7MdDxzU4.

Freeman, A. (2009), 'The Economists of Tomorrow: The Case for a Pluralist Subject Benchmark Statement for Economics', *International Review of Economics Education*, 8(2), 23–40.

Freeman, A. (2010), 'Marxism without Marx', *Capital and Class*, 34(1), 84–97.

Freeman, A. (2012), 'The Profit Rate in the Presence of Financial Markets', *Journal of Australian Political Economy*, 70, 167–192.

Freeman, A. (2014a), 'What Causes Booms?', in A. Bagchi and A. Chatterjee

(eds), *Marxism: With and Beyond Marx*, New Delhi, India and Abingdon, UK: Routledge.
Freeman, A. (2014b), 'Schumpeter's Theory of Self-Restoration: A Casualty of Samuelson's Whig Historiography of Science', *Cambridge Journal of Economics*, 38(3), 663–679.
Freeman, A. (2015), 'Heavens Above: What Equilibrium Means for Economics, with an Appendix on Temporality, Equilibrium, Endogeneity and Exogeneity, in Physics and Economics', available at www.geopoliticaleconomy.academia.ca/AlanFreeman.
Freeman, A. and G. Carchedi (eds) (1996), *Marx and Non-Equilibrium Economics*, Cheltenham, UK and Northampton, MA, USA: Edward Elgar.
Freeman, C. (2002), 'The Third Kondratieff Wave: Age of Steel, Electrification and Imperialism', draft of Chapter 7 of C. Freeman and F. Louça (eds), *As Time Goes By*, Oxford Scholarship Online.
Grossman, H. (1992), *The Law of Accumulation and Breakdown of the Capitalist System*, London: Pluto Press.
Harvey, D. (2015), 'Crisis Theory and the Falling Rate of Profit', available at https://thenextrecession.files.wordpress.com/2014/12/harvey-on-ltrpf.pdf.
Heinrich, M. (2013), 'Crisis Theory, the Law of the Tendency of the Profit Rate to Fall, and Marx's Studies in the 1870s', *Monthly Review*, 64, 11, available at monthlyreview.org/2013/04/01/crisis-theory-the-law-of-the-tendency-of-the-profit-rate-to-fall-and-marxs-studies-in-the-1870s.
Howard, M. and J. King (1989), *A History of Marxian Economics*, Princeton, NJ: Princeton University Press.
ISIPE (2014), *An International Call for Pluralism in Economics*, accessed 8 October 2014 at http://www.isipe.net/open-letter/.
Keynes, J. (1971), *The General Theory of Employment, Interest and Money*, London: Macmillan.
Kliman, A. (2007), *Reclaiming Marx's Capital: A Refutation of the Myth of Inconsistency*, Lanham, MD: Lexington.
Kliman, A. (2010), 'The Persistent Fall in Profitability Underlying the Present Crisis', Marxist–Humanist Initiative, available at http://www.marxisthumanistinitiative.org/literature/the-persistent-fall-in-profitability-underlying-the-current-crisis-new-temporalist-evidence.
Kliman, A. (2012), *The Failure of Capitalist Production*, London: Pluto.
Kliman, A. (2014), 'The Whiggish Foundations of Marxian and Sraffian Economics', *Cambridge Journal of Economics*, 38(3), 643–661.
Kliman, A. (2015), 'Harvey versus Marx on Capitalism's Crises Part 1: Getting Marx Wrong', available at http://www.newleftproject.org/index.php/site/article_comments/harvey_versus_marx_on_capitalisms_crises_part_1_getting_marx_wrong.
Kliman, A., A. Freeman, N. Potts, A. Gusev and B. Cooney (2013), 'The Unmaking of Marx's Capital: Heinrich's Attempt to Eliminate Marx's Crisis Theory', available at SSRN: http://ssrn.com/abstract=2294134.
Kotz, D. (2009), 'The Financial and Economic Crisis of 2008: A Systemic Crisis of Neoliberal Capitalism', *Review of Radical Political Economy*, 41(3), 305–317.
Kuhn, R. (2007), *Henryk Grossman and the Recovery of Marxism*, Chicago, IL: University of Illinois Press.
Lapavitsas, C. (2009), 'Financialised Capitalism: Crisis and Financial Expropriation', *Historical Materialism*, 17(2), 14–148.

Maito, E. (2013), 'The Historical Transience of Capital: The Downward Trend in the Rate of Profit since XIX Century', available at https://mpra.ub.uni-muenchen.de/59285/3/MPRA_paper_59285.pdf.

Mandel, E. (1978), *The Second Slump: Marxist Analysis of Recession in the Seventies*, London: Verso.

Marx, K. ([1867] 1990), *Capital*, Vol. 1, London: Penguin.

Marx, K. ([1894] 1991), *Capital*, Vol. 3, London: Penguin Classics.

Marx, K. (1969), *Theories of Surplus Value*, Book II, Moscow: Progress Publishers.

Menshikov, S. (1989), 'The Long Wave as an Endogenous Mechanism', International Colloquium on the Long Wages of the Economic Conjuncture, 12–14 January, Brussels.

Mill, J. ([1848] 2008), *Principles of Political Economy and Chapters on Socialism*, Oxford World's Classics, Oxford, UK and New York, USA: Oxford University Press.

Mohun S. (2000), 'Productive and Unproductive Labor in the US Economy: Does the Distinction Matter? A Reply to Houston and Laibman', paper presented to the mini-conference of the International Working Group on Value Theory (IWGVT), Washington, DC.

Moseley F. (1992), *The Falling Rate of Profit in the Postwar United States Economy*, New York: St Martin's Press.

Okishio, N. ([1961] 1993), 'Technical Change and Rate of Profit', in M. Krüger and P. Flaschel (eds), *Nobuo Okishio – Essays on Political Economy: Collected Papers*, Frankfurt am Main: Peter Lang.

Ricardo, D. ([1817] 1990), *Principles of Economy and Taxation*, in *Works and Correspondence of David Ricardo*, Vol. 1, Cambridge: Cambridge University Press.

Roemer, J.E. (1981), *Analytical Foundations of Marxian Economic Theory*, Cambridge: Cambridge University Press.

Rosdolsky, R. (1977), *The Making of Marx's Capital*, London: Pluto Press.

Schumpeter, J. (1939), *Business Cycles*, Vol. I, New York, USA and London, UK: McGraw-Hill.

Shaikh, A. (1999), 'Explaining the Global Economic Crisis', *Historical Materialism*, 5(1), 101–134.

Shaikh, A. (2010), 'The First Great Depression of the 21st Century', *Socialist Register*, 47, available at http://socialistregister.com/index.php/srv/article/view/14330#.VsI2w9DxzU4.

Smith, A. ([1776] 1904), *An Enquiry into the Nature and Causes of the Wealth of Nations*, ed. Edwin Canaan, 4 vols, London: Methuen, accessed 28 April 2014 at http://www.econlib.org/library/Smith/smWN.html.

Sraffa, P. (1962), *The Production of Commodities by Means of Commodities*, Cambridge: Cambridge University Press.

Steedman, I. (1977), *Marx after Sraffa*, London: New Left Books.

Sweezy, P. ([1942] 1970), *The Theory of Capitalist Development: Principles of Marxian Political Economy*, New York: Modern Reader Paperbacks.

Toporowski, J. (1999), 'Kalecki and the Declining Rate of Profits', *Review of Political Economy*, 11(3), 355–371.

Walras, L. (1977), *Elements of Political Economy*, transl. W. Jaffé, Fairfield: Augustus Kenney.

Walsh, V. and H. Gram (1980), *Classical and Neoclassical Theories of General Equilibrium*, Oxford: Oxford University Press.

APPENDIX: DIFFERENCES BETWEEN RATES OF RETURN ARE UNAFFECTED BY A GENERAL INFLATION OF PRICES

First note that if all capital is invested, then S is simply the growth of capital over any given period. We can this rewrite equation (5.5) as:

$$r = \frac{K'}{K} \tag{5.9}$$

If e is the MELT, then using $\$K$ to represent K in money terms and $\$r$ for the money rate of profit on any investment, we get:

$$\$K = eK \tag{5.10}$$

whence:

$$\$r = \frac{(eK)'}{eK} = \frac{e'K + K'e}{eK} = \frac{e'}{e} + \frac{K'}{K} = r + \frac{e'}{e}$$

This is easily generalized to the case where part of the surplus is consumed.

PART III

The Crisis in Economic and Social Reproduction

6. A global approach to the global financial crisis

John Weeks

6.1 ANALYTICAL FRAMEWORK

6.1.1 Defining 'Crisis'

Capitalist societies have historically unique relations of production. Some are older than capitalism, money and commodities, and take on new and qualitatively different significance in capitalist society. Price, profit, money, credit, competition and fixed means of production all acquire specifically capitalist form in the circulation and reproduction of capital. These social forms interact to generate the most concrete manifestation of the historical uniqueness of capitalism, crises.

A crisis is a disjuncture that prevents complete reproduction of the circuit of capital.[1] A slowing of the rate of accumulation is not a crisis. The rationale for this definition is that measured rates of accumulation vary over time and across countries, which I show in a subsequent section. As well as sharing common characteristics, each capitalist country has historically and culturally specific relations and institutions of production. One should not expect each to possess precisely the same potential for pace of accumulation.

National institutions change slowly, implying less variation over time in the potential for accumulation. National economic systems respond to transitory forces ('shocks') that do not derive directly from the contemporaneous accumulation process. An example is the dramatic increase in the prices of petroleum at the beginning and end of the 1970s. Many Marxists have pointed to the 1970s as a 'crisis' of accumulation resulting from the internal tensions or contradictions in capital, implicitly or explicitly dismissing explanations based on the petroleum price increase (Harvey 2010; Kotz 2013).

One need not delve deeply into United States (US) economic performance in the 1970s to have scepticism about the hypothesis of a 1970s crisis. While US economic growth in the 1970s fell more than 1 percentage point below that in the 1960s, 3.3 compared to 4.4 per cent per annum, it was higher or the same than in the 1980s (3.1 per cent), the 1990s (3.3 per cent) and during 2000–2007 (2.7 per cent; see annex tables in Office of the President, various years). If a crisis of accumulation occurred in the US in the 1970s, it was very different from the Great Depression of the 1930s and the global financial collapse of 2008.

During the worse performing post-World War II (WWII) period, 1974–82, average growth was 2 per cent and the nine years include three of rapid expansion (1974–76, with rates of 5.4, 4.6 and 5.6 per cent). The less esoteric explanation presents itself as credible, that oil price increases in 1973–74 generated a short decline, and the subsequent recovery was cut off by another round of increases in 1978.

The definition I use of crisis presupposes capitalist society and capitalist social relations.[2] The division of social life into the economic and the non-economic reflects the twofold nature of commodities. Labour performed for exchange becomes subject to regulation by monetary costs. In this way, human labour that produces commodities is formally separated from labour performed for other reasons.

At least since the time of Ricardo,[3] economic crisis referred to interruptions in the circuit of capital manifested as overproduction, in which use values pile up idle, unused and unusable due to relations of ownership. Overproduction necessarily means overproduction of value, when some commodities cannot be sold. Realization is the necessary condition for their consumption as use values. Overproduction of value is the overproduction of capital. When products do not circulate as commodities and are produced directly for consumption, overproduction is impossible.[4]

A theory of capitalist reproduction must account for economic crises.[5] Marx's mature writings were devoted to explaining economic crises, and his theory of crisis is inseparable from his theory of accumulation. In the process of accumulation, all of the tensions and contradictions of capitalist production and circulation are intensified, and economic crisis is the predictable outcome of the accumulation process (Marx 1971: Chapter XV).

The analysis of causation encounters three major questions: (1) whether all moments of overproduction are crises; (2) whether crises have a common cause; and (3) whether all crises are systemic. The next section addresses these questions.

6.1.2 Systemic and Non-systemic Crises

Like other great thinkers, on occasion Marx contradicts himself, or 'seems to', if one is loath to attribute this human failing to him. One would expect apparent and real differences during an intellectual and activist career of more than four decades. Few people hold the same views in middle age that they did in their twenties. The ones that they do still hold are not very interesting as a result of that slavish consistency.

Therefore, I quote from Marx with some caution. I do not use this quotation as authority to justify the argument I shall develop. I use it as a guide to dispel the ambiguities associated with the concept and reality of economic crises. In the second volume (Part II) of *Theories of Surplus Value*, Marx specifies what creates the possibility of economic crises. He writes:

> The general *possibility* of crisis is given in the process of metamorphosis of capital itself, and in two ways: in so far as money functions as *means of circulation*, [the possibility of crisis lies in] the separation *of purchase and sale*; and in so far as money functions as *means* of payment, it has two different aspects, it acts as *measure* of *value* and as *realization of value*. These two aspects [may] become separated. If *in the interval* between them the value has changed, if the commodity at the moment of its sale is not *worth* what it was *worth* at the moment when money was acting as a measure of value and therefore as a measure of reciprocal obligation, then the obligation cannot be met from the *proceeds of-the sale of the commodity*.
>
> . . .[I]t is quite clear, that between the starting-point, the prerequisite capital, and the time of its return at the end of one of the periods, great catastrophes must occur and elements of crises must have gathered and developed. (Marx 1968: 513–514, 495)

In this discussion of crises the words 'profit' and 'surplus value' do not appear. Their absence makes the passage suggestive of my analysis of systemic crises as resulting from the inability of capital to realize the full value of fixed means of production. The crisis causality can be summarized as follows. Fixed means of production are put in place and have a useful life time of many circuits of capital (production cycles). Their replacement fund is accumulated in each production period, as the material productivity of the fixed means of production declines, technical change reduces their value productivity.

Marx applied the term 'moral depreciation' to this process by which the development of new and better machines undermines the profitability of the old. The companies using the old machinery seek to match the prices of the companies using the new. Since the latter almost always are fewer than the former, the market value of the majority of fixed capital in the industry declines. Most competitors discover that they cannot completely recapture the value of their machinery through the sale of their output. As Marx comments in several places in *Capital* and *Theories of Surplus Value*, the dynamism of capitalism undermines the accumulation process.

Productivity growth, not stagnation, is the source of the tensions in capitalism.

Inability to realize the value of fixed means of production implies a fall in profitability for all but the companies using the latest techniques. The fall in profitability is not the result of an increase in what some call 'the organic composition of capital'. It does not result from an increase in constant capital in the famous formula for the rate of profit, π = (surplus value)/(variable plus constant capital).

Technical change tends to make it impossible for many producers to realize the value of their fixed means of production. Since capitalists finance their fixed investments by borrowing, the failure to realize the value of those fixed investments has the potential to manifest itself as a financial crisis. This interpretation is consistent with the characterization of the way in which economic crises manifest themselves: 'In a system of production, where the entire continuity of the reproduction process rests upon credit, a crisis must obviously occur – a tremendous rush for means of payment – when credit suddenly ceases and only cash payments have validity' (Marx 1971: 490).

Crises occur because production and sale are not simultaneous. While the separation refers to two moments in time, it takes no insight to infer that this could result in incomplete sales or shortages, a trivial issue discussed endlessly by mainstream economists as an aspect of the 'coordination problem' of market economies. I refer, as Marx did, to the change in commodity value between different moments in the circuit of capital. In Marx's analysis the 'separation' does not refer to a problem of realizing commodity value. On the contrary, it presumes commodities are realized, but at values that do not match their value when they emerged from production.

The crisis manifests itself in a financial collapse. The crisis derives from the fundamental tension ('contradiction') in capitalist society, the twofold (dual) nature of commodities. As Marx makes clear in the first chapters of *Capital* Volume I, the tension within the commodity form is the origin of all crises. We have the fundamental tension, production and sale do not coincide; and a specific form that it takes, that the replacement of the value of fixed means of production does not coincide with their material replacement. To put that another way, in the absence of technical change the value of fixed capital deteriorates slowly over time, and its material form must be replaced at a specific moment. The combination of technical change and competition renders this tension between value and use value the source of crises.

In what follows I reserve the word 'crisis' for episodes when this value–use-value tension results in severe economic contraction. These qualify as economic disruptions caused by systemic tensions that could not be resolved within the existing institutions and regulations of the accumulation process, both public and private. The tension is resolved through the general destruction of fixed capital value and associated debt.

Especially in the US, severe financial disruptions have occurred without resulting in a systemic crisis. An obvious case is the US stock market crash of 1987, so-called Black Monday when the Dow Jones Index fell by more than 20 per cent. Though temporarily wiping out billions in asset prices, the crash had no notable effect on production or employment. Almost all other post-WWII financial collapses had little impact on the major economies of the world, including the infamous Asian financial crisis of 1997 (see Weeks 2014b: Chapter 3). The collapse of fictitious capital value is the necessary manifestation of a capitalist crisis, but not all financial collapses signal a capitalist crisis.

6.1.3 Crises National and Global: Analytical Framework

To what extent does an economic crisis in a national economy result in a global crisis? Few writers in recent years have directly addressed this question. The most obviously erroneous reason for overlooking this issue has been the frequent practice of implicitly or explicitly treating the US economy as synonymous with 'world capitalism'. I show empirically that this carried some superficial verisimilitude up to the early 1970s and the first oil price boom, but subsequently had no credibility. After the mid-1980s even the assertion that the US economy served as the driver of the world economy becomes difficult to verify empirically.

A variation on 'the US economy equals the global economy' is the argument that capitalism is an integrated social formation, implying that national boundaries are irrelevant. While this concept of the capitalist mode of production generates important insights at a high level of abstraction, it provides little guide to concrete circumstances. In the analysis of crises it represents an empirical hypothesis that requires rigorous specification and testing before it can be endorsed.

The empirical claim that a crisis is 'global' might be justified by one or more of several theoretical arguments. First, it might be argued that capitalism contains flaws that can manifest themselves simultaneously in all countries. The clearest example of this line of argument is the overproduction mechanism of Luxemburg (Luxemburg 1913: Chapter 25; Kemp 1967: Chapter IV).[6] Luxemburg argued that inherent in capital accumulation is a tendency for the overproduction of fixed capital, implying that output expands in excess of total domestic consumption. As a result, capitalists seek markets in non-capitalist regions to sell the excess production.

This mechanism clearly implies that crises tend to be international, because the same problem arises in every capitalist country. It suffers from theoretical problems, as well as the obvious empirical difficulty that in the twenty-first century non-capitalist regions have declined to insignificance as measured by their economic weight in global markets.

The typical 'falling rate of profit' mechanism fails to get out of the starting gate as a candidate for generating cross-country crises, much less global ones without a complementary mechanism of global demand failure. I shall disregard the Okishio critique[7] and pursue the argument that the process of accumulation leads to a 'rising organic composition of capital'. Should this be the case, the analysis requires some critical value for the 'organic composition' that provokes a crisis. This is a necessary element because the alleged rise is monotonic with respect to accumulation; that is, it starts when accumulation begins. To argue that all or most national capitals would hit this critical value at approximately the same moment hardly carries credibility. If this theoretically suspect argument has relevance for global crises, it must be augmented by some cross-country transfer mechanism.

Whatever might cause a fall in either the rate or the 'mass' of surplus value (to use Marx's term), it does not follow that a fall is the cause of a crisis. Lower surplus value and lower profit are likely to result in a slower rate of accumulation, and this is not a crisis. On the contrary, fluctuations in profit rates and levels commonly occur in capitalist societies. They are neither unusual nor harbingers of disaster.

Any falling rate of profit argument in support of global crises must have a clear explanation for the decline. Empirical evidence of falls in profit rates, even a cyclical pattern of declines, provides little guide to understanding crises be they national or global. Whether the decline is causal or derivative from demand failure must be specified theoretically and tested empirically.

A plausible argument would be that a crisis in a major capitalist country, whatever the cause, could generate spread effects via either aggregate demand failures due to falls in world trade, or instability in financial asset prices. As I show below, this line of argument appears more plausible during 1950–1985 than before or subsequently. My empirical assessment implies that 'capitalist crisis' should be considered a concept relevant to the national, not global level. If the crisis-affected country is large, crisis affects can spread across countries through demand effects.

6.1.4 Crises National and Global: Empirical Assessment

The challenge is to move from the crisis-generating tensions in the abstract to crises in the concrete. The Global Financial Crisis that began in

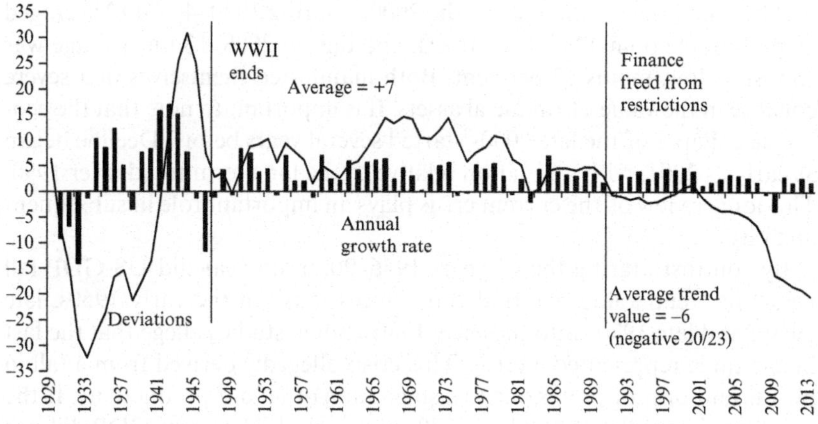

Note: Trend is 3.5% per annum (@ .00).

Source: Office of the President (various years).

Figure 6.1 USA: GDP, constant price, annual growth rate and percentage point deviations from period trend, 1929–2013

2007–2008 certainly qualifies for Marx's assessment that when a 'reproduction process rests upon credit', then 'a crisis must obviously occur'. To proceed I consider whether such a crisis can be conjunctural, or must by its nature be systemic.

Inspection of empirical evidence demonstrates that all disruptions in the accumulation process are not 'crises' in the sense of being systemic or severe. Figure 6.1 demonstrates this for the US. For the 85 years of consistent gross domestic product (GDP) statistics, 1929–2013, I calculate each year as the percentage point deviation from the year's trend value and the year-on-year growth rate. For the entire period the trend is 3.5 per cent per annum, which is statistically significant at far below 1 per cent probability.

Extreme declines occur at end periods of these 85 years of statistics. For this reason it might be objected that the resulting trend-adjusted pattern distorts long- and medium-term patterns. This objection reflects a misunderstanding of trend adjustment, since the same objection could be raised wherever extreme values occur in the time series. The relevant issue is not measurement but interpretation. As we see, the growth rates and the trend deviations convey the same message.

Inspection of movements in US gross national product suggests that over the nine decades only two episodes qualify as 'crises' by the definition explained above, the Great Depression of the 1930s and the contraction that began in the second half of the 2000s. During 1930–40 GDP averaged 20 percentage points below its trend, and during 2008–13 the average was almost as low, minus 17 per cent. Both manifested themselves in a severe collapse in the value of financial assets. It is important to note that the economic collapse of the late 2000s started several years before. Decline began as early as 2001, with stagnation relative to the long term trend after 1990. This longer view of the current crisis plays an important role in subsequent analysis.

By contrast, during the 45 years 1946–90, in no year did US GDP fall below its trend value. We find three 'recessions', in the early 1950s, late 1950s, and late 1970s into the early 1980s. Some studies allege that the last of the three represented a crisis. This crisis allegedly derived from a fall in profits and/or profit rates due to a stagnation of labour productivity. If the word 'crisis' applies to the late 1970s and early 1980s when GDP did not fall below its trend value, we require another term for 1930–40 and 2008–13 ('catastrophes', perhaps). Whatever words we use, it is obvious that the US economy during 1930–40 and 2008–13 suffered outcomes qualitatively different from all other years (Weeks 2010a: Chapters 10 and 11).

The exercise in Figure 6.1 is repeated in Figure 6.2 for the United Kingdom (UK), the only other high-income country for which the calculations are relevant. All other major capitalist countries during these nine decades – France, Germany, Italy and Japan – suffered catastrophic damage in

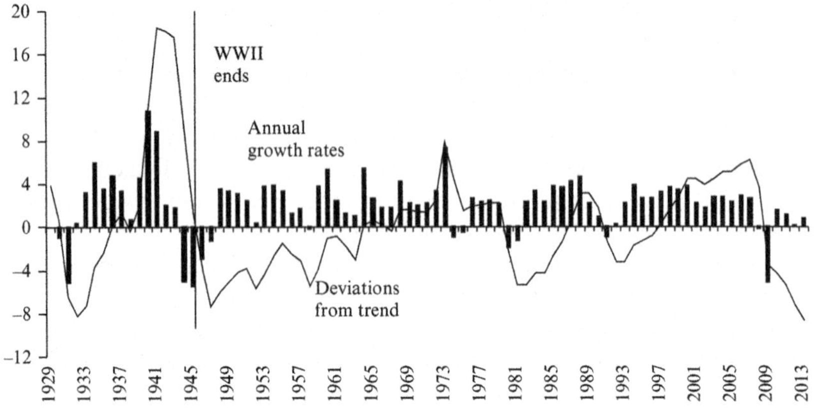

Note: Trend is 2.6% per annum (@ .00).

Source: www.bankofengland.co.uk/publications/. . ./threecenturiesofdata.xls.

Figure 6.2 UK: GDP, constant price, annual growth rate and percentage point deviations from period trend, 1929–2013

World War II and underwent profound social and political changes. A glance at the two figures reveals substantial differences in the movement of national production over time. While four decades, 1950–90, involved continuous expansion for the US economy, the UK economy passed through two substantial and extended recessions or disruptions in accumulation, immediately after the war (1945–60) and during the first half of the 1980s. In addition, during 1990–2007, when the US economy grew at well below its trend value, the British economy expanded considerably faster than its long-term tendency.

Subsequent figures show that of all major economies, the interaction between those of the US and the UK is by far the closest for deviations from trend over the long run. A scatter diagram of the deviations from trend for the two economies demonstrates that while the link is statistically significant, it is quite weak (correlation coefficient of 0.07).[8] Inspection of the long-term statistics for these two economies suggests that in most years the movements in national output respond to domestic factors.

Comparing more countries requires shortening the time period. Figure 6.3, which uses statistics from the 'Penn World Tables',[9] adds France, Italy and Japan to the analysis and covers six decades, 1950–2013, with trend rates reported in the legend.[10] Germany is not included because unification in 1990 resulted in a disjuncture in all economic time series statistics. Two observations stand out. First, both the UK and the US economies stick relatively

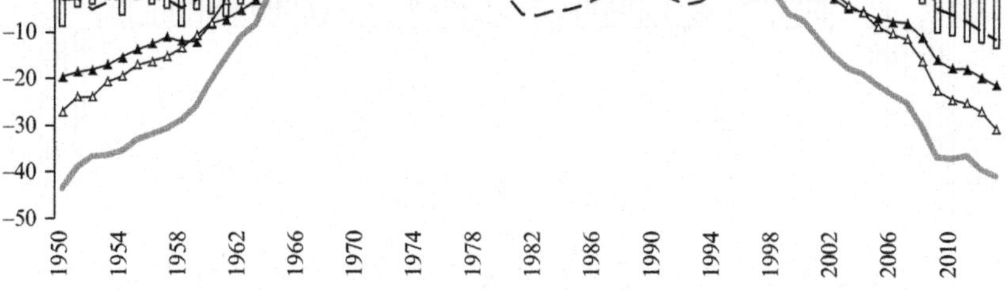

Source: www.oecd.org/statistics and Penn World Tables, https://pwt.sas.upenn.edu/php_site/pwt_index.php.

Figure 6.3 USA and four high-income countries, constant price GDP, percentage point deviations from period trend, 1950–2013

close to their trend values, while the economies of the other three countries have pronounced convexity with respect to the horizontal (time) axis.

Second, the common growth pattern for France and Italy in the figure reflects two extremes: very rapid recovery from the devastation of WWII in the first two decades, and relative or absolute decline after 2000. Output fell well below its trend value for these two countries in the early 2000s, while UK and US output remained above trend. For France and Italy the drop below the trend coincided with adoption of the euro (Weeks 2014a). The patterns in Figure 6.3 demonstrate the differences in accumulation among the major capitalist countries. These patterns specifically emphasize the importance of war and major policies, as well as level of development. One explanation of the inverted 'U' pattern of French, Italian and Japanese growth is the relative underdevelopment of these countries before WWII compared to the US and UK.

For Japan the contrast between post-war recovery and subsequent stagnation is greatest. As is well documented, the Japanese economy stagnated during the 1990s and 2000s, a deflationary process that began well before what we now call the Global Financial Crisis (Ito and Mishkin 2004). As in France and Italy, the disruption in accumulation for Japanese capital preceded the onset of the financial crisis.

Reducing the coverage by another decade allows for inspection of additional countries using World Bank statistics. Figure 6.4 compares the US and two groups, upper- and lower-middle-income countries, for 1960–2013

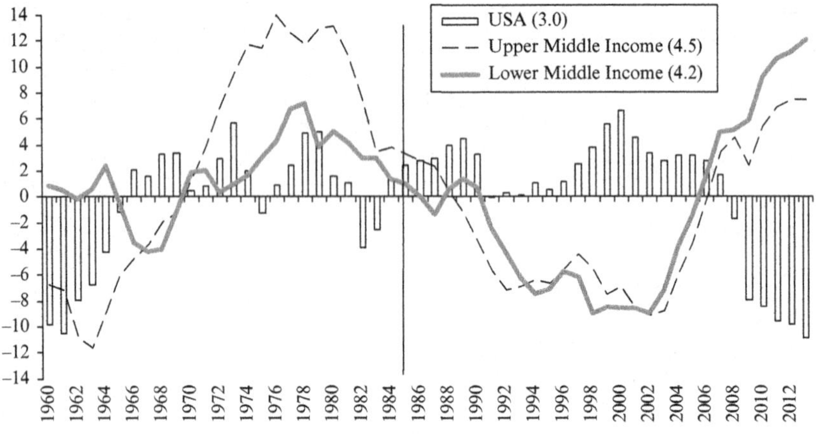

Source: World Bank (2013).

Figure 6.4 USA and middle-income countries, constant price GDP, percentage point deviations from period trend, 1960–2013 (trend rates appear in the legend).[11] Inspection of the figure suggests that the growth pattern of these countries was similar to that of the US until the mid-1980s (noted by the vertical line). Subsequently the two middle-income groups appear almost the mirror image of the US pattern. As for the major capitalist countries, domestic factors seem to have more impact on national accumulation patterns than international influences. It is clear that in recent decades the influence of the US economy on global growth patterns declined.

6.1.5 Cross-Country Patterns During 1994–2014

The end of the Soviet Union and the unification of Germany fundamentally transformed Europe and the global economy. This section inspects some consequences of these changes. What is perhaps the most important change for the global economy, the rise of China as a major capitalist power, is discussed briefly in the next section.

Figure 6.5 compresses the time period into 20 years, 1994–2014, using quarterly data, in order to inspect both financial collapse of 2007–09 and the route to it for six developed capitalist countries: the US, France, Germany, Italy, Japan and the UK. Quarter-on-quarter deviations from trend GDP appear in the legend to the figure (the annual equivalent trends are approximately four times the quarterly value).

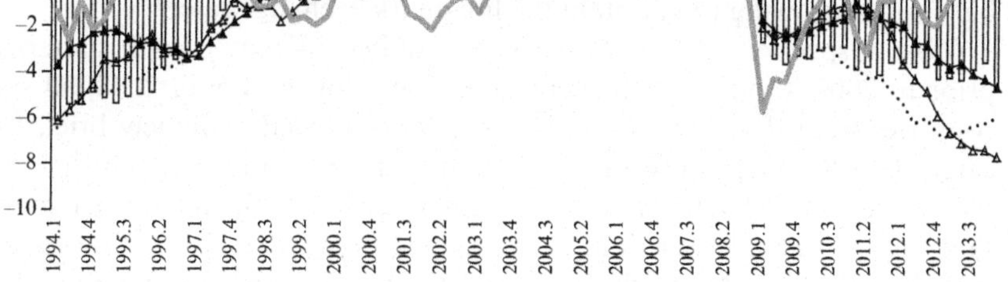

Source: www.oecd.org/statistics.

Figure 6.5 USA and four high-income countries, constant price GDP, percentage point deviations from period trend, 1994–2014

The growth patterns are quite similar with the exception of Japan. The Japanese pattern reflects the long period of stagnation and deflation, only weakly influenced by external economic events. Due to this secular stagnation the crisis that racked the other mature capitalist countries affected Japanese accumulation less. The economies of all six countries suffered absolute declines beginning at approximately the same moment, the first quarter of 2008. However, of the countries in the figure the economy of only one, the UK, collapsed as a direct result of financial 'contagion' from the US. The common pattern for the three continental European countries should be placed in the context of the eurozone rather than as a direct extension of the US crisis.

Until 2007 the contraction or stagnation of the major economies of the eurozone resulted from causes only loosely related to influences emanating from the US. During the 1990s the German economy suffered from the growth-depressing policies of the Deutsche Bundesbank which maintained high interest rates in the erroneous belief that the reunification in 1990 would provoke inflation.[12] As a result, the German economy stagnated during the 1990s. It did not return to growth until the Social Democratic government of Gerhard Schröder adopted beggar-thy-neighbour export policies at the end of the decade. Ideologically opposed to stimulating growth through a fiscal expansion, the Schröder government induced trade union leaders to agree to an indefinite freeze on real wages and a dual labour market allowing for a low-paid segment of the workforce. To this was added an export subsidy by changing payroll taxes to value added taxes from which exports were exempt. These measures generated massive German trade surpluses by the mid-2000s, and would result in the euro crisis (Weeks 2014a).

For France and Italy the 1990s brought low growth, though not as low as Germany's, in the successful but ultimately disastrous attempt to 'track' the German mark, which was a condition to join the eurozone at the end of the decade. Italy's relatively large debt resulted not from fiscal deficits, but from borrowing to maintain the lire–mark exchange rate.[13]

Close inspection of Figure 6.5 shows quite different growth patterns prior to 2007, though when financial collapse hit the US in 2008, all six countries went down together. This similarity proved extremely brief. In early 2009 the German economy began to recover and was the first to rise above its trend value, followed by Japan which unlike the former soon sank into a second recession, as would Germany after 2011. The fiscal stimulus of 2009 arrested the decline of the US economy, though provoking no sustained recovery. Relative to their trend growth rates, France and Italy displayed no hint of recovery by early 2014. The absence of recovery for these two countries resulted directly from the fiscal austerity policies of the governments, slavishly adhering to the ideology of the European

Commission and the Bundesbank. The recovery claimed by the right-wing Coalition government in the UK was weak and sluggish, the slowest on record (ONS 2013).

The decidedly dismal performance of the US and the European economies stands in striking contrast to the recovery and growth among the major middle-income countries, China, the Republic of Korea (South Korea) and Indonesia.[14] The Asian financial crisis caused the severe dips for the latter two during 1997–1998. Exchange rate speculation combined with dysfunctional 'support' from the International Monetary Fund turned into disasters what would otherwise have been mild recessions (Weeks 2010b).

Of the three, the correlation between US and Korean growth rates is quite high and positive, but for China and Indonesia it is negative with respect to the US, and strongly positive with respect to each other. These calculations suggest that the long-term military and trade links between the US and Korea have maintained a strong interactive economic relationship. However, the correlation between Indonesian and Chinese growth may reflect the development of a new sphere of influence.

When we turn to Latin America, changing global economic power becomes even more obvious. Of the three largest Latin American countries only Mexico appears to remain tightly linked to the US economy, with almost a one-to-one correspondence in deviations from their trends. In contrast, for Brazil and Argentina the links to the US growth are negative, and strongly positive to China. The statistics are consistent with non-quantitative judgements about the rise of Chinese influence in Latin America (Kotschwar 2014).

All six middle-income capitalist countries suffered growth declines along with the US economy in 2008, but in two cases, China and Indonesia, these were very small and brief. By far the worst affected were Korea and Mexico, long-standing members of the US sphere of economic and political influence.

In the previous section I suggested that economic crises are rare and essentially national not global. National crises manifest themselves globally when the crisis country represents a large share of global output, and financial markets serve as the major transmission mechanism. Severe disruption in the US economy provoked the two great capitalist crises of the last 90 years, in the first case as US capital was emerging as globally dominant, and in the second case when that dominance was on the wane.

6.1.6 Decline of the US Economy

As stated previously, two changes determined the nature of the global economy of the first half of the twenty-first century: the dissolution of the

Soviet Union and the capitalist transformation of China. These changes resulted in a capitalist global social system. So-called globalization has been the rapid process of capitalist integration, unchecked by any rival social formation. Initially US capital took the lead in establishing the deeply reactionary nature of the post-Soviet capitalist epoch. Over the last decade its lead has been challenged and reduced by two rising capitalist powers: foremost China, and to a lesser but substantial extent Germany.

If one accepts the general Marxian principle that production not circulation determines economic power, then the two primary determinants of global economic power are commodity exports and direct investment. The two are closely related, in that a national export surplus determines the growth of foreign investment in productive capital. From an extremely low base below US$100 billion, mainland China exports rose to more than US$2.5 trillion by 2013, passing Germany in 2010 and the US in 2011. When one adds exports of Hong Kong, many of which derive from the mainland, total China exports rise far above the other two, more than US$3 trillion (UNCTAD 2013: Annex Table 1).

For Germany and China, the massive level of exports implied in the 2000s the largest trade balances in the world, while the US claimed the smallest, far into deficit. The continuous trade surpluses resulted in the Chinese government holding the largest amount of foreign exchange of any country in the world, US$4 trillion in mid-2014; Germany was far behind in eleventh place with US$208 billion, and the US held US$143 billion (in eighteenth place).[15] The growing foreign exchange reserves of China and Hong Kong have financed a surge in foreign investment, from below US$50 billion in 1990 to more than US$200 billion in 2013. This total is far below the US figure of about US$350 billion, but easily the second-largest amount for any country (World Bank 2014).

The relative reduction in the global power of US capital began as early as the 1960s when the post-war recovery in Europe and Japan gathered pace. The dissolution of the Soviet Union appeared to reverse this decline, but this was more appearance than substance. The rise of China and its imminent claim to being the leading capitalist country rendered US global economic dominance a thing of the past. A crisis of US capital is a necessary but no longer sufficient condition for a crisis of capital to manifest itself globally.

6.2 CRISIS AND FINANCE

I have argued that crises result from the inability to recapture the value of fixed capital through the circuit of capital. A necessary implication of this argument is that proposed alternative explanations either confuse cause with appearance (overproduction and underconsumption), or misidentify a transitory disruption with a systemic crisis. My argument is consistent with the identification of long-term trends in capitalist social formations that weaken the resilience of capital to adjust to and recover from crises.

For example, stagnant productivity in sectors producing surplus value can make the circuit of capital more prone to generate a systemic crisis. But the failure of productivity to rise, due to production-level class struggle or the increase in unproductive supervisory labour, does not itself generate a crisis or require one to resolve it.

It follows from my argument linking realization of fixed capital to finance that perhaps the most important trend in advanced capitalist societies has been the rise of financial capital. Lenin made this argument 100 years ago, though the justification was empirical rather than an analytical discussion of the circuit of capital (Lenin 1963, 226ff). Prescient as it was, Lenin's book did not anticipate perhaps the most fundamental aspect of the rise of finance: the conversion of industrial corporations into financial institutions (Toporowski 2010, 27ff). This process has been most intensive in the US, less so in Europe, and has hardly happened at all in China, which helps to explain the rise of German and Chinese capital relative to US capital.

Within my analytical framework for understanding crises, the financialization of previously non-financial corporations is by far the most important intra-capital development of the last several decades. If a process of financialization has had a transformative effect on contemporary capitalism, this is its most important element.

The financialization phenomenon results from the attempt to extract surplus value from the circuit of capital without producing surplus value. Marx, like his contemporaries, argued that surplus value arises in production. He went on to explain that surplus value divided into the 'Trinity': profit of enterprise, interest and rent (Marx 1971: Parts IV and V). In the twenty-first century we must expand the meaning of the word 'interest' to include profits appropriated through financial transactions, especially financial speculation.

The Great Depression, which was primarily a US financial collapse, resulted from the unregulated rise of financial capital. In 1933 the famous Glass–Steagall Act, formally the Banking Act of 1933, severely restricted financial activities for all private institutions (see Weeks 2014b: 39–41).[16] The relentless process of dismantling the protective provisions of the Act from the late 1970s through the 1990s liberated finance to assert its dominance of US capital.

The so-called Global Financial Crisis was the result of the unchecked ascendancy of finance in the US economy. At the end of World War II manufacturing generated value added over ten times greater than value added attributed to financial activities. At the end of the 1960s the ratio fluctuated between six and seven.[17] Financial deregulation initiated under President Jimmy Carter brought the ratio down to about four in 1980. Since 2000 it dropped below two in every year but one, in 2008. The simple correlation between percentage changes in manufacturing and financial value added over the 65 years is not significantly different from minus one.

The absolute rise of financial revenue and the corresponding decline in manufacturing value added encapsulates the decline of the global power of US capital. After decades of dominating global capital, the power of US capital to control international markets is more than on the wane. It is in retreat, and not a willing retreat.

6.3 CONCLUSION

The analytical and empirical parts of this chapter point to several conclusions. First and most importantly, the advanced capitalist countries – the US, the United Kingdom, those in Western Europe and Japan – are highly integrated through financial markets. While the US has the largest economy in this group, it has not determined the economic performance of the others for several decades. Put another way, these economies are integrated through trade and capital flows, but domestic conditions, random events and policies determine their medium-term growth performances. For none of them does a major crisis result in a crisis of global capitalism.

Second, over the last 100 years capitalist countries have suffered many disruptions, most of which did not result in global disruptions. Those that did, worked their destruction through financial markets, and these became increasingly frequent after 1980. Third, at the national level the US suffered from two disruptions that qualify for the term 'crisis': 1929–1940 and 2008 to through the present. The first did not generate crisis-level disruption in the other major capitalist countries, though all to some degree suffered lower rates of accumulation. The second crisis has struck all of the major capitalist countries of Europe, though not those in Latin America or Asia.

NOTES

1. I refer to the full circuit including both production and finance capital:

$$M^{*} \rightarrow M \rightarrow [CC + VC] \ldots P \ldots C' \rightarrow M'$$

[M^* to M] is financial capital lending to industrial capital to initiate production. [$CC + VC$] is money paid for the elements of productive capital, means of production and labour power. P is the moment of production yielding commodity capital [C], and M' is the realization of commodity capital as money capital.

2. In his famous and frequently misunderstood discussion of commodity fetishism, Marx writes in a footnote:
'It is one of the chief failings of classical economy that it has never succeeded, by means of its analysis of commodities, and, in particular, of their value, in discovering that form under which value becomes exchange value. Even Adam Smith and Ricardo, the best representatives of the school, treat the form of value as a thing of no importance, as having no connection with the inherent nature of commodities. The reason for this is not solely because their attention is entirely absorbed in the analysis of the magnitude of value. It lies deeper. The value form of the product of labour is not only the most abstract, but is also the most universal form, taken by the product in bourgeois production and stamps that production as a particular species of social production, and thereby gives it its special historical character. If then we treat this mode of production as one eternally fixed by Nature for every state of society, we necessarily overlook that which is the *differentia specifica* of the value form, and consequently of the commodity form, and of its further developments, money form, capital form, &c.' (Marx 1970: Chapter 1, footnote 33).
3. For a discussion of why Adam Smith did not deal with the problem of general overproduction, see Marx (1968: II, 484ff).
4. As surprising as it may be, few non-Marxist economists consider capitalism to be fundamentally different from previous societies in which exchange was common. A rare exception is the Keynesian Liejonhufvud: '[T]he dynamic properties of an economic system depend upon what I will call its "transaction structure". That labor services are sold for money and that households obtain their consumption goods in exchange for money is one aspect of the transaction structure in Keynes' system. In an economy of self-employed artisans [the problem of] unemployment cannot appear' (Leijonhufvud 1968: 90).
5. Shaikh (1978) provides a brief survey of crisis theories, Marxist and non-Marxist.
6. A useful source is Bellofiore (2009) and the review essay by Jaffe (1972).
7. See Okishio (1961), where he demonstrates that if capitalists apply a profit maximization rule, they will always reject techniques that lower the profit rate. It should be noted that the Okishio 'theorem' refers to the level of the production unit, not capital as a whole.
8. The figure and associated calculations appear in the conference version of this chapter, and it is available from the author.
9. These statistics were compiled in an ongoing University of Pennsylvania research project, found at https://pwt.sas.upenn.edu/php_site/pwt_index.php.
10. Figures for each country appear in the conference version of this chapter.
11. The World Bank defines middle-income countries as those with per capita incomes from about US$1000 to US$12000. The lower and upper limits change over time due to inflation and changes in the base year. See http://go.worldbank.org/BDZHSEY4J0.
12. The perennial Bundesbank obsession with inflation derived superficially from the decision of the conservative government of Helmut Kohl to set the conversion of the East German mark at one-to-one with the West German mark.
13. Throughout 1990–2006 the Italian government maintained primary surpluses every calendar year, which no other major European Union (EU) country did, certainly not Germany with a primary deficit every year, 2001–2005 (Weeks 2014a).
14. These are shown in a figure in the conference version of this chapter. I omitted India because its quarterly growth statistics began considerably later than 1994.
15. International Monetary Fund balance of payments statistics are accessed at http://elibrary-data.imf.org/FindDataReports.aspx?d=33061&e=170784.

16. The sovereign debt crisis of the 1980s demonstrated the effectiveness of the Banking Act of 1933 in virtually prohibiting risky behaviour by US banks. Legally forbidden to speculate on stocks, bonds and real property, US banks found in the Act a loophole that allowed them to lend to foreign governments (see Weeks 1989: Chapter 3).
17. This can be calculated from the sectoral value added tables in various issues of the *Economic Report of the President*. See Weeks (2010a: Chapter 11).

REFERENCES

Bellofiore, R. (2009), (ed.), *Rosa Luxemburg and the Critique of Political Economy*, Oxford: Routledge.

Harvey, D. (2010), 'The Enigma of Capital and the Crisis this Time', paper prepared for the American Sociological Association Meetings, Atlanta.

Ito, T. and F.S. Mishkin (2004), 'Two Decades of Japanese Monetary Policy and the Deflation Problem', NBER Working Paper 10878, Cambridge, MA, available at http://www.nber.org/papers/w10878.

Jaffe, D. (1972), 'Imperialism and the Accumulation of Capital', *Bulletin of the Conference of Socialist Economists*, 2(2), 70–77, available at https://www.marxists.org/subject/economy/authors/yaffed/1972/impaccrev/impacckreview.htm.

Kemp, T. (1967), *Theories of Imperialism*, London: Dennis Dobson.

Kotschwar, B. (2014), 'China's Economic Influence in Latin America', *Asian Economic Policy Review*, 9(2), 202–222.

Kotz, D. (2013), 'Social Structure of Accumulation, the Rate of Profit, and Economic Crises', PERI Working Paper No. 329, Political Economy Research Institute, Amherst, MA.

Leijonhufvud, A. (1968), *Keynesian Economics and the Economics of Keynes*, Oxford: Oxford University Press.

Lenin, V.I. (1963), 'Imperialism: The Highest Stage of Capitalism', in V.I. Lenin, *Selected Works, Volume I*, Moscow: Progress Publishers.

Luxemburg, R. (1913), *The Accumulation of Capital*, available at http://www.marxists.org/archive/luxemburg/1913/accumulation-capital/.

Marx, K. (1968), *Theories of Surplus Value, Part II*, Moscow: Progress Publishers.

Marx, K. (1970), *Capital, A Critique of Political Economy, Volume I: A Critical Analysis of Capitalist Production as a Whole*, Moscow: Progress Publishers.

Marx, K. (1971), *Capital, A Critique of Political Economy, Volume III: The Process of Capitalist Production as a Whole*, Moscow: Progress Publishers.

Office for National Statistics (ONS) (2013), *Economic Review, July 2013*, London: Office for National Statistics.

Office of the President (annual, various years), *Economic Report of the President*, Washington, DC: Government Publishing Office.

Okishio, N. (1961), 'Technical Changes and the Rate of Profit', *Kobe University Economic Review*, 7, 85–99.

Shaikh, Anwar (1978), 'An Introduction to the History of Crisis Theories', in Union for Radical Political Economics (ed.), *US Capitalism in Crisis*, New York: URPE.

Toporowski, J. (2010), *Why the World Economy Needs a Financial Crash*, London: Anthem.

United Nations Conference on Trade and Development (UNCTAD) (2013),

World Investment Report 2013 – Global Value Chains: Investment and Trade for Development, Geneva: UNCTAD.
Weeks, J. (ed.) (1989), *Debt Disaster? Banks, Government and Multilaterals Confront the Crisis*, New York: New York University Press.
Weeks, J. (2010a), *Capital, Exploitation and Economic Crisis*, Oxford: Routledge.
Weeks, J. (2010b), 'Miracles and Crisis: Boom, Collapse and Recovery in East and Southeast Asia', in Richard Westra (ed.), *Confronting Global Neoliberalism: Third World Resistance and Development Strategies*, Atlanta, GA: Clarity Press.
Weeks, J. (2014a), 'Euro Crises and Euro Scams: Trade not Debt and Deficits Tell the Tale', *Review of Political Economy*, 26(2), 171–189.
Weeks, J. (2014b), *Economics of the 1%: How Mainstream Economics Serves the Rich, Obscures Reality and Distorts Policy*, London: Anthem Press.
World Bank (2013), *World Development Indicators, 2013*, Washington, DC: World Bank.
World Bank (2014), *World Development Indicators, 2014*, Washington, DC: World Bank.

7. The incubator of the great meltdown of 2008: the structure and practices of US neoliberalism as attacks on labor

Al Campbell and Erdogan Bakir

There are now a significant number of good articles and books describing the Great Recession and the related subsequent lethargic recovery. The number of these articles is constantly increasing as the weak recovery continues, written by both liberal critics[1] of neoliberalism, and radical critics[2] of both neoliberalism and capitalism. The intent of this chapter therefore is not to discuss the recent United States (US) crisis and anemic recovery themselves. Rather, the intent of this chapter is to address two underdiscussed prequel questions: why US capitalists abandoned the previous form of capitalism that had served them so well in the first two decades after World War II (WWII), and (related to that, we will see) why they adopted the specific practices and structure of neoliberal capitalism that existed in the US in 2007.

A second intent of this chapter is to go beyond only analyzing the origins of today's deeply troubled economy, to contribute to building a human-centered alternative. The possibility of the majority in the US beginning a process of building a fundamentally different economy has become a reality today exactly because the dissatisfaction with the existing economy is markedly higher now than at any time since WWII. While not dead, the 'American Dream', that since the country's birth has been so central to its stability and its very self-identity, is now for the first time in its history believed in by only a minority of the population. Polls now regularly show that about 50 percent of the population thinks it is no longer 'possible for just about anyone in America to work hard and get rich', and only about 25 believe that it is possible.[3] Even more devastating to the American Dream, the percentages are similar for the statement: 'today's children [will] be better off than their parents' (Rasmussen Reports 2012). Coming out of this fundamental change is a growing popular questioning of the US economic system itself. While still a minority, a growing number of people have begun to think of the capitalist system as problematic, and some of these to even consider a socialist alternative as preferable.[4] The depth of the social penetration of these attitudes is unprecedented.

Operating from the conviction that such an alternative must be the product of the members of society themselves, this chapter carries out its analysis of the origins of the Great Recession in terms of economic issues that are today most disconcerting to the non-privileged majority of US society. Specifically, it is concerned with replacing the currently dominant popular desire to fix the existing problems within the frame of capitalism with a desire to fix the problems by transcending capitalism. To do that it is necessary that the popularly perceived problems must come to be understood as existing because of the practices adopted by capitalism in accordance with its goals, and not as policy errors that capitalism will readily abandon if their costs to society as a whole are only presented clearly enough to capitalism's centers of power. The specific content of this chapter is selected to carry out the chapter's central intent of analyzing the causes of the Great Recession, in terms that will promote the efforts for a fundamental economic-social transformation.

The analysis in this chapter of why US capitalism chose the particular practices and structure for the neoliberalism which it had developed by the eve of the post-2007 crisis will be presented in two sections. Section 7.1 will address the first prequel question indicated above: why capitalism came to feel compelled to abandon the post-war-compromise[5] structure that had served it so well for two decades. It establishes that beginning in the late 1960s capitalism's central concerns became its falling rates of profit and accumulation, and that explains why it abandoned its existing model. The new model of capitalism in time was to become known as neoliberalism, and its heart was a consciously intensified attack on the working class. Section 7.2 then goes on to address the second prequel question posed above: why capitalism chose the particular practices it did to address its general concerns with its profits and accumulation. From among its many changes, four aspects of US capitalism's neoliberal restructuring that are central to both its resulting functioning and to the current popular discontent with the economy are: (1) the direct attack (that is, at the point of production) on wage gains and labor costs; (2) the effects of the changed immediate objective of corporate governance;[6] (3) the essential indirect (that is, not at the point of production) attack on labor by making government, the broader state and even general social attitudes (still) friendlier to capital and the very wealthy; and (4) various aspects of financialization. The presentation will make clear that the changes were not simply some automatic result of the functioning of capitalist markets, but rather were the result of a broad political-economic project that was consciously executed by capital.

On the one hand, it is a fundamental liberal misunderstanding of neoliberalism to consider the dramatic financialization of capitalism as the essence of neoliberalism instead of its intensified attack on labor. But on the other hand, the importance of financialization must not be underestimated. In particular, the interaction of financialization with the real sector was essential to the particular way in which neoliberalism carried out its attack on labor. 'Excessive' financialization therefore is treated here not in accord with the liberal position that it is harmful to capitalism, nor as something 'accidental', nor as something driven strictly by its own interests separate from those of capital as a whole, though it does have such self-interests in addition to its central common interest with the rest of capital. Rather, financialization is treated in this chapter as one important aspect of the actual neoliberalism that developed, and as something which made important contributions to neoliberalism's central goal of intensifying capital's attack on labor.

7.1 WHY US CAPITALISM FELT COMPELLED TO ABANDON THE POST-WAR COMPROMISE

There are two reasons why capital felt compelled to abandon its post-war-compromise structure: the fall in the rate of profit, and the fall in the share of national income and wealth of the very rich. The rate of profit and changes in its level are understood here, as in the standard broad Marxist tradition, as centrally important indicators of the general health of capitalism. Profits are both the source of value for the self-expansion of capital and the 'goad of capitalist production' (Marx [1894] 1988: 240). Changes in the very rich's share of the national income need to be considered separately because, while they can be merely the result of changes in the profit rate, they can also occur for other reasons. Two such other reasons that are important in the current popular discontent with the economic system are pro-wealthy changes in taxation,[7] and mushrooming chief executive officer (CEO) and upper financial sector salaries and bonuses. These outsized salaries and bonuses are important to keep in mind as examples where the drive by the very rich to increase their income can actually lower a firm's rate of profit.

While most Marxist discussions of the causes of the Great Recession focus only on the rate of profit, it is important to include the drive by the very rich to restore their share of the national income as a secondary cause.

Without it, one cannot fully explain all the specific features that were the trigger for the current crisis. For example, the greatly increased inequality, a much-discussed characteristic of neoliberalism which played such an important role in the onset of the current crisis, was partially driven by the recuperating rate of profit over the first half of the neoliberal period, but only partially. As will be discussed below, the increase in inequality began in the late 1960s and early 1970s, at a time when the rate of profit was still falling. Two possible errors need to be avoided regarding the cause of neoliberalism's increased inequality. First, it is incorrect to treat the success of capital in partially restoring its rate of profit as the sole cause. Second, it would also be incorrect to treat the other cause – the drive by the very rich to increase their share of the national income – as an equally important cause.

7.1.1 The Fall in the Rate of Profit and Capital's Declared Response

Profits were so high in 1966 that the (pro-business, of course) Chairman of the Council of Economic Advisers, Gardner Ackley, asked publically if profits any higher would be harmful to business (Brooks 1971: 298). The following year profit rates began their decade-and-a-half steep decline. The large majority of the empirical work over the last four decades on the post-WWII rate of profit in the US presents results very similar to our results presented in Figure 7.1.[8] For a sample of this rich body of work, see Weisskopf (1978, 1979), Duménil et al. (1987), Michl (1988), Cipolla (1992), Devine (1994), Brenner (1998, 2002), Wolff (2001, 2003), Duménil and Lévy (2002a, 2002b, 2011), Harvey (2005), Glyn (2006), Bakir (2006), Bakir and Campbell (2006, 2009, 2010), Kotz (2007), Basu and Vasudevan (2013) and Cámara Izquierdo (2014).

Figure 7.1 shows that from 1947 to 1973 the aggregate rate of profit for the US private sector was always between 14 percent and 18 percent. Starting from the top of that range in 1966, it then suffered a decade-and-a-half fall to 10.5 percent by 1982. Operating from the premise that capital is driven to self-expand or accumulate through the pursuit of maximum profits implies that capitalists would consider such a steep and extended decline in the rate of profit to be a major problem which needed to be addressed. As background to the changes in the operation of capitalism which this chapter will discuss, this 42 percent decline over 16 years is taken as the major cause for capital's conscious decision to launch its neoliberal restructuring.

While an understanding of the nature and dynamics of capitalism make it clear that capital will react to a sustained significant decline in its rate of profit by increasing its aggression against labor, in this case it also openly

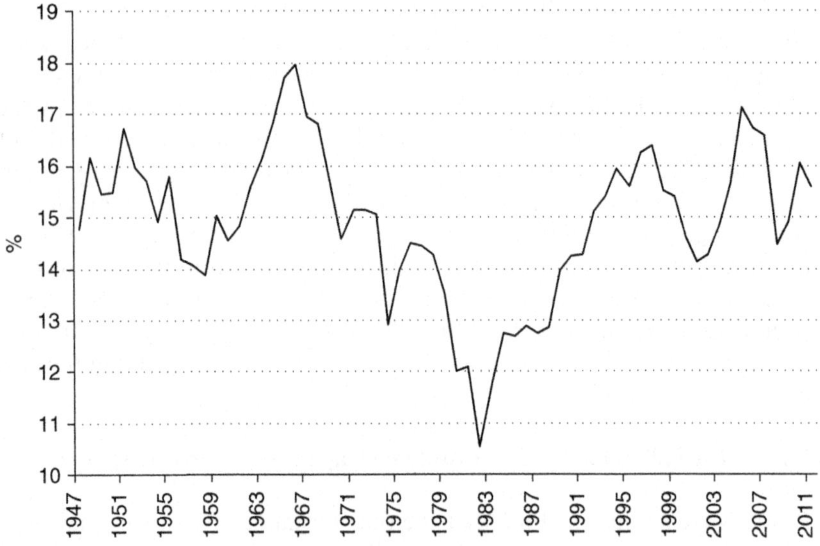

Source: Authors' calculations based on national income and product accounts tables, gross domestic product (GDP) by industry accounts tables and fixed assets accounts tables from Bureau of Economic Analysis. For details of calculation, see Bakir and Campbell (2013), or at greater length in the technical appendices in Bakir (2006).

Figure 7.1 Profit rate in the private sector

declared its intention to do so. The Construction Users Anti-Inflation Roundtable was formed in 1969, headed by the CEO of US Steel, and published material proposing ways to reduce the wage gains of unionized construction workers. The Labor Law Study Committee from the same time, composed mostly of the executives of large corporations responsible for labor relations, likewise published material directed to reforming labor law to hold down wage gains. In 1971 business openly called for and lobbied for the government to restrict wage gains as much as politically possible in the 'wage-price controls' introduced then.[9] But the most important and most often referred-to document from that time that openly declared the need for capital to escalate its fight against labor was the Powell Memo[10] from August 1971, 'Attack on the American Free Enterprise System' (Powell 1971). This multidimensional call to battle and blueprint for the 1970s 'corporate mobilization'[11] went beyond openly calling on business to coordinate itself to both directly hold down wages and lobby the government for changes in labor law to that end. It was a clear call for the coordination of capitals to enable them to become more aggressive in shaping all US laws and controlling US politics, including going beyond simply pressuring legislators to instead use capital's vast resources to assure the election of business-friendly legislators and the defeat of labor-friendly ones. Below we will look at some of the results of capital's actions that were quickly to follow these open declarations: here the point is merely to indicate clearly that capital was very open (as it had to be as part of mobilizing itself for the battle) about the need first to sharply reduce workers' wage gains, and then beyond that to more directly capture and fully control the government to use it in pursuit of all of capital's interests in its escalated aggression against labor.

The concern in this section is to indicate the reasons capitalism felt compelled by the 1970s to restructure itself as neoliberalism. Two striking aspects of Figure 7.1 should be briefly noted here even though they concern its subsequent evolution that will be discussed below. First, the early neoliberal restructuring was successful from 1982 to 1997 in achieving a major, albeit not complete, restoration of the rate of profit. But second, despite the existence of mature neoliberalism, the profit rate then suffered a four-year significant decline followed by four years that did little more than recover from that fall. After 15 years of impressive growth in the profit rate following the early consolidation of neoliberalism, mature neoliberalism was unable to deliver further gains over the decade leading up to the Great Recession.

7.1.2 The Fall in the Share of National Income of the Very Rich

As argued above, a second motivation for the neoliberal project, secondary in importance to the desire to restore the rate of profit but partially independent of it, and necessary to include to fully understand the specific US neoliberalism that developed, was the desire of the very rich to restore their share of the national income. Their income share had fallen as a result of the restructuring of the economy during the New Deal, WWII and the first three decades of the post-war period, and then began to recover as first isolated neoliberal policies and then full-fledged neoliberalism were implemented from the 1970s onward. The work by Piketty and Saez (2003) has today become the best-known and most frequently referenced support for this position, though there was a small handful of work documenting this behavior before them.[12] From a bubble-induced peak of 19.6 percent in 1928, first the Great Depression and WWII and then (more important and more sustained) the social policies that began under Roosevelt and continued through the 1960s brought the share of total income of the top 1 percent down to 10.5 percent by 1944 and 7.7 percent by 1973. The early effects of neoliberalism then caused it to begin a slow rise to 8.2 percent in 1980 and 9.0 percent in 1985. Following that, consolidated neoliberalism caused its mercurial return in just two decades to a pre-Great Depression level of 18.3 percent in 2007. Most authors see this inequality as one important aspect of the structure of capitalism that caused the Great Recession and subsequent anemic recovery, generally as operating through its effects on aggregate demand as discussed below.[13]

7.2 THE STRUCTURE AND PRACTICES OF US NEOLIBERALISM IN 2007 AS ATTACKS ON LABOR

Given the fall in the rate of profit and the income share of the super-rich documented in the last section, those negatively affected launched a multifaceted project to reverse these trends. The result over time was a restructured capitalism. The most important changes from the structure and practices of the post-war-compromise capitalism to neoliberalism arose from the direct efforts by capital to restore its rate of profit and its related broader project of increasing its political power, and secondarily from the efforts of the super-rich to restore their share of the national income.

In this section we consider the four aspects of neoliberalism indicated in the introduction that are central to those changes, that at the same time are key to the continually growing popular discontent with the functioning of the US economic system.

7.2.1 The Direct Attack (at the Point of Production) on Wage Gains and Labor Costs

The most direct increased aggression against labor occurred in the form of a sharply increased resistance to any increases in labor compensation. While real wages had grown 2.3 percent annually from 1947 to 1967 and a still healthy 1.9 percent from 1967 to 1973,[14] the above-indicated offense by capital turned it negative by 1974. It then stayed slightly negative for most of the next two decades until a short period of healthy growth started in the mid-1990s, after which it returned to extremely weak growth (Mishel et al. 2012: 184). The ubiquitous 'growing together, growing apart' graph[15] shows this frozen wage growth sharply by comparing it to productivity growth, that is supposed to be the source of wage growth. From 1947 to 1973 in the post-war-compromise economy, wages and compensation grew almost identically to labor productivity. This changed completely under neoliberalism, where wage growth (just discussed above) turned negative after 1973 and the growth of wages and benefits together turned negative after 1979, despite productivity growth continuing the same general upward trend as before. The benefits of productivity growth were partially shared in the post-war compromise, but retained almost entirely for capital under neoliberalism. Weak wage growth, both in absolute terms compared to the post-war-compromise period and in relative terms compared to the growth of labor productivity, is a central component of the popular discontent with the US economic performance.

In addition to conceding smaller wage gains, four other key components of capital's 'reduction of labor costs' at the point of production were the increased use of (lower-paid) temporary workers, reduced total wages through two-tier wage systems, actual 'givebacks' (reduction of previously agreed-upon wages or benefits, or 'speed-up' of existing working conditions) and the reduction of the national union density through 'union avoidance' at new plants or actual union busting (Harrison and Bluestone 1988: 39).

7.2.2 The Effects of the Changed Immediate Objective of Corporate Governance

There certainly is a significant, though relatively small, literature on the neoliberal corporate governance paradigm of 'shareholder value'.[16] We believe, however, that most radical analyses have tended to pay insufficient attention to, if not entirely overlook, this extremely important dimension of the neoliberal transformation in the US in favor of (very important) discussions of macroeconomic variables. While the ultimate goal of obtaining maximum profits and accumulating capital remains the same under all organizational forms of capitalism, the change in the ancillary goals of corporations between post-war-compromise capitalism and neoliberalism has been one important part of capital's increased aggression. In the first place the negative effects on labor have concerned their compensation and conditions of work, but additionally they have affected them as consumers and members of society.

Under post-war-compromise capitalism the key to maximizing profits was generally considered to be growth, often (not always) involving the belief that the best way to achieve this was to develop better or new products, or more efficient production processes. From this the standard business ideology of the period, as detailed in the 1956 eminent classical study of that ideology *The American Business Creed*, was that corporate managers 'have four broad responsibilities: to consumers, to employees, to stockholders, and to the general public . . . Stockholders have no special priority' (Sutton et al. 1956: 64–65). By the 1980s it was no longer possible for top management of any major US corporation to publically declare a view of stakeholder capitalism as the chairman of Standard Oil of New Jersey Frank Abrams had in 1951: 'the job of management is to maintain an equitable and working balance among . . . . stockholders, employees, customers and the public at large' (Smith 2012: 37). Notwithstanding that the earlier view was of course neither universally adopted by business nor fully implemented by those who did profess it, it is essential to understand the importance of the change to a corporate consciousness of 'shareholders *über alles*' in promoting a number of practices that were elements of neoliberalism's overall increased aggression against labor.

Making the increase in a firm's stock price the central measure of a firm's performance, and in many cases tying top management's compensation directly to it, had both direct and indirect negative effects on labor. Since such measures as reducing wage or benefits gains or sometimes even achieving their reduction, cutting the workforce or breaking or blocking unions, almost always caused an immediate increase in the stock price, the new governance paradigm increased such attacks on workers even as they sometimes also caused medium-term harm to profits.[17] Many of the indirect negative effects on workers operated through neoliberalism's depression of the rates of growth and capital accumulation.[18] One example is neoliberalism's much commented-on short-termism: the replacement of the previous longer-term corporate planning time horizon needed to pursue growth by the short-term time horizon involved in performance evaluation according to stock prices. A second example of neoliberalism's indirect harm to workers through the depression of growth is its practice of boosting a stock price by increasing dividend payouts and stock buybacks and then borrowing to invest because of the reduced retained earnings. This increases finance's role in the reproduction and expansion of capital, resulting in a greater share of capital being tied up in finance and hence less in productive capital, again lowering the rate of accumulation (Bakir and Campbell 2010).

The shareholder-value argument that shareholder interests not only have priority over the interests of workers *qua* workers, but also that shareholder interests have priority over the interests of workers in their roles as consumers (product quality, product safety, and so on) or as members of the community where the enterprise operates (pollution, traffic congestion, and so on) is an important further aspect of neoliberalism's increased aggression against workers. All these direct and indirect aspects of the shareholder-value paradigm of corporate governance are elements of neoliberalism's increasingly aggressive attack on labor.

7.2.3 The Essential Indirect (not at the Point of Production) Attack on Labor by Making Government, the Broader State and General Social Attitudes (Still) Friendlier to Capital and the Very Wealthy

It is a serious error when studying capitalism to think of capital's attack on the working class as occurring only, or even primarily, at the point of production. To the contrary, it is essential to always keep in mind the central role of the government and the broader state in all economic considerations. In section 7.1 we indicated that when capital decided in the late 1960s and early 1970s to qualitatively increase its aggression against labor, it quickly moved from its initial focus on the point of production to pressuring government to change laws (especially labor laws, taxes, and anti-trust and banking regulation) to strengthen it in the struggle, and from there to assuring the election of 'business-friendly' legislatures.

A plethora of organizations were either newly created or revitalized and reinvented as direct voices of business in the corporate mobilization.[19] Two of the most important of these organizations were the Business Roundtable and the US Chamber of Commerce. In June 1973 the informal March Group of CEOs of large corporations merged with the Construction Users Anti-Inflation Roundtable and the Labor Law Study Committee discussed above and took the name Business Roundtable. This rapidly expanded by 1997 to consist of 180 CEOs from the country's largest companies, and effectively became the political voice of big business. Spending $136 million lobbying in 2012, the US Chamber of Commerce with more than 300 000 member businesses has been the largest business lobbying organization since 2000 in the US,[20] and additionally spends massively in supporting conservative candidates in elections. It provides the most important 'grass roots' support for business, from a network it has built which can provide tens or even hundreds of thousands of emails, telephone calls or letters to Congress in support of pro-capital legislation (Edsall 1984: 121–128; Vogel 1989: 198–199).

For the still broader component of the class battle that involves the structures and practices of the state beyond the government, and beyond that society's general attitudes toward capital (which capital always refers to as 'business'), capital created or revitalized a plethora of 'think-tanks'. Sometimes the nearly universally poor quality[21] (with a few exceptions) of the research and the reports of these think-tanks causes progressive commentators discussing the 50-year shift to the right in US politics to treat them as almost irrelevant. In fact, they played the important dual role they were designed for. On the one hand they turned out conservative research reports to put in the hands of congressmen fighting legislative battles, who until then had frequently been at a disadvantage as most scientific academic reports supported the positions of the progressives. On the other hand, a second goal of these think-tanks was to make public opinion still friendlier to capital ('business') in order to create a very broad balance of forces that would allow them to push forward their legislative agenda of transformation. From the start of the business rebellion, the think-tanks developed outreach divisions whose job it was to disseminate the political messages of their 'research reports' to the public, by all channels possible, but in particular at first focusing largely on newspapers, and later on television and radio talk shows. A few of the more prominent and important of the many such conservative think-tanks are the Hoover Institution, American Enterprise Institute, Heritage Foundation (founded 1973), American Council for Capital Formation (founded 1973), Center for the Study of American Business (founded 1975; renamed as the Weidenbaum Center, 2001), Cato Institute (founded 1977), and a conservative think-tank that does careful economic analysis and therefore progressives often forget that it is part of the conservative think-tank complex, the National Bureau of Economic Research (Edsall 1984: 117–120).

It is broadly accepted among economic and political historians that capital accomplished a major step in its declared plan of creating a more business-friendly government with the election in 1976. Though the party composition of the Congress changed little, it was radically more pro-business than the preceding two Congresses, which had still been typical of the post-war-compromise period. With the election of President Carter, who was mostly perceived as a progressive, labor thought it would win some major battles it had long been fighting. Its three biggest concerns were labor law reforms, common situs picketing, and indexing the minimum wage to inflation and average wages. Unexpectedly to almost everyone, all three were stopped. The labor reform bill was passed by a healthy majority in Congress, but filibustered and killed in the Senate. The common situs bill had been passed by the last Congress but vetoed by Gerald Ford, and given the similar party composition of the new Congress and Carter's declared support, passage was assumed to be a sure thing. Its defeat showed the shift in the nature of this Congress, and more specifically the specific aggressive role (including monetary support) that the above-mentioned business associations played in both electing new pro-business legislators and winning over (buying) fence-sitting existing ones (Stein 2010: 183–190; Hacker and Pierson 2010: 128–131; Vogel 1989: 210–211). The change was permanent, and every subsequent Congress has been business-friendly as planned by capital. With the election of Reagan in 1980 (or arguably the political change in Carter in 1978), capital completed its planned creation of a business-friendly government with the capture of the executive branch.

7.2.4 Financialization

Financialization is arguably the most universally commented-on aspect of neoliberalism. Very broadly, 'financialization' can be defined as the expanded influence of finance on real production. Being more concrete, we can list the following seven highly interrelated central aspects of financialization: (1) expansion of the financial sector; (2) numerous fundamental changes in the operation of the financial sector; (3) an expanded role for financial operations in the non-financial sector (with this finance possibly coming from the non-financial sector itself); (4) an increased economic and political power of the financial sector; (5) a change in corporate governance to pay more attention to financial goals; (6) increased debt throughout the economy; and (7) asset inflation (including bubbles).

Liberal treatments of financialization usually focus on it as a struggle between financial interests and productive interests (which it partially is), and from that conclude that it is bad (at least in its excessive neoliberal form) for capital as a whole.[22] Neither the direct conflict of interests between finance and labor (personal debt, as one example), nor the indirect conflict between them through finance's necessary role in the increased aggression of productive capital against labor (the shareholder-value paradigm of corporate governance, as one example), are considered.

A number of radical works, in addition to presenting excellent descriptions of the decades-long process of financialization, have implicitly addressed the conflict of enhanced financialization with labor by documenting the relative and absolute deterioration of labor's condition over the course of financialization. There has been very little written, however, on the specific ways in which financialization has played a necessary enabling role for the real-side drive to lower the value of labor-power, neoliberalism's *raison d'être*. Within the space limitations of this chapter we will here qualitatively describe this role of the last three of the seven aspects of financialization listed at the beginning of this subsection. These three aspects of financialization are also important parts of today's popular dissatisfaction with the US economy.

The first aspect of financialization that we will discuss is the change in corporate governance. Its operation was already sketched in section 7.2.2 above. Our purpose in mentioning it again here is only to underline its two-sided relation to neoliberalism's financialization of capitalism. Considering the relation in one direction, this new paradigm in which finance plays such a central role is one of the changes in capitalism that constitute its neoliberal financialization. Considering the relation in the other direction, without neoliberalism's broad financialization of capitalism, theoretical as well as practical, the shareholder-value paradigm would never have been developed and adopted by business. Particularly, we want to underline it as one example of the integral relation of financialization to many of the real-side attacks on labor: without financialization, many of the most important specific ways in which US neoliberalism increased its aggression against labor could not have occurred. Even most radical presentations of neoliberal financialization generally fail to include the shift to the shareholder-value paradigm of corporate governance as one of its important components.

The second aspect of financialization that we will discuss is the much commented-on explosion of debt. The hypertrophy of household debt served the increased attack on the value of labor-power in four different ways. First, what workers pay in debt service is fundamentally a reduction in their wages (in the extreme case, 'debt slavery'). Second, debt-supported consumption helped to maintain a necessary level of effective demand in the face of the slowed growth of wage-supported consumption. The third way is less commented on by economists because of its political or sociological nature. The explosion of household debt reduced the immediate fall in the growth of labor's purchasing power to within limits which labor would accept (even if unhappily) without the type of major fight-back that would end capital's project. Fourth, the expansion of household debt combined with the expansion of financial sector debt (to be discussed next) to fuel the asset inflation (first stocks, then especially housing), the third aspect of financialization that we will briefly comment on below.

The first consideration on financial sector debt is that the sector's net lending (net debt in credit market instruments as a percentage of GDP) grew twice as fast from 1980 to 2008 as it did from 1952 to 1980 (Duménil and Lévy 2011: 105). In the first instance, this enabled the increased household debt just discussed. Beyond that, the financial sector's sources for funds to lend shifted even more dramatically to credit market borrowing. Gross debt of the financial sector in credit market instruments was 3 percent of GDP in 1952 and still only 20 percent in 1980, but 119 percent in 2008 (Duménil and Lévy 2011: 104). Much of that came from issuing asset-backed securities, which in turn drove inflation of the underlying assets. Expanded financial net debt (lending) was an essential aspect of the entire neoliberal financialization of capitalism, and expanded gross borrowing via issuing asset-backed securities made an important contribution to asset inflation and bubbles, that will be discussed next.

The third aspect of financialization that we will consider here is asset inflation and bubbles. Again, our concern here is not to describe the now well-known dynamics of bubbles,[23] but rather to sketch how this financial aspect was an integral part of neoliberalism's central project of attacking the working class. It provides essential support to neoliberalism's central project in three different ways. The first two are the same as the second and third effects discussed above for increased household debt: the inflation of housing values cushioned the fall in income for that part of the working class that owned their home. As with debt, this helped neoliberalism to address both its problem of maintaining sufficient aggregate demand and its problem of sufficiently pacifying the working class to prevent a fight-back against the increased aggression. Asset bubbles, associated with high debt levels, reinforce several of these ways in which high debt levels serve the neoliberal system. The third way in which asset inflation and bubbles serve the goals of neoliberalism concerns neoliberalism's secondary goal of shifting the distributions of income and wealth in favor of the super-rich.[24]

7.3 CONCLUSION

In the mid-1960s US capitalism began to experience a decade-and-a-half crisis in the process at the heart of its existence, the accumulation of capital, indicated by a prolonged decline in its rate of profit. To reverse this fall, and secondarily to reverse the preceding three decades of increased income and wealth equality, the capitalists launched a process of restructuring of capitalism from its previous post-war form to what has become known as neoliberalism.

At the heart of the neoliberal project is a markedly more aggressive relation of capital to labor than existed in the previous post-war form of capitalism, aimed at driving down the value of labor-power to increase profits. This increased aggression occurs through many different channels. Among the most important channels are capital's increased direct resistance to wage gains, a change in the corporate governance model, and more aggressively using the government against the working class. The latter issue of the increasingly active use of the government against labor includes weakening labor's ability to fight both for direct wage gains and for its more general interests.

Financialization is universally viewed to be a centrally important aspect of neoliberalism. One of the theses of this chapter is that it must additionally be understood to be an important fourth channel for capital's aggression against labor. In addition, financialization must also be understood to have been able at times to provide short-term relief to the system from problems the neoliberal system generates for itself from the lowered wages, in particular inadequate effective demand and popular discontent with the stagnant wages.

For one-and-a-half decades beginning in 1983, US neoliberalism succeeded in increasing the aggregate rate of profit, though it never was able to fully recover to where it was before the long fall that began in 1967. But subsequent to that, the empirical record shows nearly no net gain for the next decade leading up to the onset of the Great Recession, indicating that neoliberalism's continued intense aggression against the working class had lost its ability to deliver a continually improving rate of profit. Instead, the contradictions built into neoliberalism's basic structure on which its (capitalist) success had rested then came to the fore. By the middle of the first decade of the 2000s it was clear to many radical and some liberal economists[25] that the constantly expanding debt and the associated bubbles that were essential components of neoliberalism's short-term resolution of the systemic contradiction from its stagnant wages could not continue, and that at least 'a correction' if not a crisis was coming. But almost no one, even among the voices who perceived the intrinsic fragility of the system years ahead of others, could see that the result would be as severe as what in fact occurred.

The result of the crisis that emerged from the structure of neoliberalism in 2007 is that today US working people are more discontented with their economic system than ever before in the history of the country. Half have lost faith in the 'American Dream', and an additional quarter are not sure. Issues particularly disconcerting to them include their stagnant wages, the increased inequality, their deteriorating working conditions, the growing perception that their deteriorating situation is the source for the continued healthy improvement of the situation of the rich, their growing debt problems and the increased economic instability.

NOTES

1. Valuable works by high-profile liberal authors include Krugman (2009, 2012), Stiglitz (2010) and Reich (2011).
2. See for example Baker (2008), Foster and Magdoff (2009), Albo et al. (2010), Rasmus (2010, 2012), Duménil and Lévy (2011), Vasudevan (2013) and Kotz (2015).
3. For a particularly reputable poll that regularly reports on this now fairly commonly commented-on belief, see the Rasmussen Reports, for example Rasmussen Reports (2013).
4. In a Rasmussen Reports (2009) poll, while a majority 53 percent of adults found capitalism better than socialism, a full 20 percent believed socialism is better than capitalism and 27 percent said they were not sure, a large shift from traditional US public opinion on capitalism. Even more indicative of how far these changes have gone, adults under 30 were evenly divided as to which system was better. These of course must not be interpreted as something more than they are. These are responses to polls, not people engaging in class struggle to change the social system. Beyond that, as always, one has to be very careful with the interpretation of responses to simple poll questions. As an example, the vision of 'socialism' by most US respondents favorably disposed to it would be social democracy, perhaps as it existed in Scandinavia several decades ago, certainly not the post-capitalist system that Marx and Engels meant by the term.

Nevertheless, the magnitude and importance of these changes in consciousness is clearly enormous.

5. A key aspect of the structure of US capitalism coming out of WWII was a compromise between capital and labor in that a number of fundamental issues would not be contested at that time, such as workers' complete exclusion from management decisions, the existence of unions, significant sharing of productivity gains, and so on. There was never a class 'truce' (Rosenberg 2003: 65; Campbell 2005:188).
6. Because we hold that the central project of neoliberalism has been to drive down the value of labor-power, we here discuss the important contribution to this from the effects of the changed governance paradigm. Since the changed governance paradigm itself involves substituting financial targets for real targets, we will also refer to this in the discussion on financialization.
7. It is widely understood by both radicals and liberals that 'recent changes in the tax system have [only] exacerbated the problem' of inequality, even when they are large such as the Bush tax cuts, and that the fundamental 'inequality developments are all based on market outcomes' (Mishel et al. 2009: 3). Detailed supporting evidence for the secondary (but still important) significance of taxes is presented in the work just cited.
8. Note that this general pattern of this graph, and in particular the fall of the rate of profit from the mid-1960s to the early 1980s and subsequent partial recovery, hold up if considered broadly for the whole private (corporate non-financial plus corporate financial plus non-corporate) sector as we do here, more narrowly for the corporate sector, or still more narrowly for the non-financial corporate sector.
9. Phase I of the 'wage-price controls' initiated 15 August froze wages. Phase II initiated 15 November ended the freezes and instituted a system in which all wage increases had to be approved by a Pay Board consisting of five members each from business, labor and 'the public'. By June 1973 when a 'price freeze' was reinstituted in response to the rekindled inflation under Phase III deregulation, wage growth was considered to have been so reduced that it was not necessary to have any accompanying wage freeze. Real wage growth was in fact completely halted by 1973, though real wage and benefit growth was not stopped until 1979, as will be discussed further below (Rosenberg 2003: 185).
10. This was much more than simply one person's opinion. It was written at the behest of capital's most 'grass roots' organization, the US Chamber of Commerce, and distributed through its broad channels.
11. This well-documented sharp change in behavior by business toward government has many names in the literature, among them: business mobilization, corporate mobilization, business rebellion, revolt of the bosses and politicization of the business community. Its goal was to 'refine its ability to act as a class, [to submerge] competitive instincts in favor of joint, cooperative action' (Edsall 1984: 128). Four works that detail this changed behavior are Edsall (1984), Harrison and Bluestone (1988), Stein (2010) and Smith (2012: Chs 1–2).
12. For example, while the book was more focused on the related but different issue of wealth inequality, Wolff (1996: 28) also presented the family income of the top 5 percent from 1920 to 1990.
13. See for example Krugman (2009, 2012), Stiglitz (2010, 2012) and Duménil and Lévy (2011).
14. Note that while as indicated above capital reacted to its falling profits first by attacking labor for 'excessive wage gains', the wage gains in the period the attacks began were actually lower than in the preceding two decades. What had changed was that productivity growth had dramatically slowed, but successfully driving down wage growth could nevertheless of course improve capital's profits.
15. For a plethora of graphs of different data that all show this robust effect, type 'images for productivity and wages' into Google.
16. See Jacoby (2005) for a good short popular introduction to the issue; Lazonick and O'Sullivan (2000) for a lengthier article; Lazonick and O'Sullivan (2002) and Aglietta

and Rebérioux (2005) for critical books; and Useem (1993) for a standard attempted defense.
17. This can occur through such well-known channels as increased worker antagonism to the company and the associated decrease in productivity, more rapid worker turnover with the associated loss of experience and increased training costs, and so on.
18. It is not true that improved growth and capital accumulation will automatically benefit workers through some sort of 'trickledown'. That depends on the basis for the growth. The current better growth in the US than Europe is an example of few benefits of the growth in the US going to its workers, who typically are worse off than Western European workers. But the converse is generally true: if growth and accumulation decline, capital generally can pass a large part of the economic deterioration onto the workers.
19. Besides the two organizations discussed, these included the Business Council, Committee for Economic Development, Conference Board, National Association of Manufacturers, National Federation of Independent Businesses and National Small Business Association, plus several thousand trade associations.
20. Spending two to three times as much as the second-place business lobbying spender, which varied from year to year, since 2002.
21. Typically these 'research institutions' will not release the data or methodology they claim to have used in their analysis – a prerequisite for any scientifically serious work – so that others can duplicate and either confirm or challenge the derivation of the results.
22. Liberals of course suppress considerations of class and so refer to this as 'the interests of the economy'.
23. Among the recent liberal and radical works that strongly emphasize the centrality of the housing bubble to US neoliberalism's structure in 2007 and describe the dynamics of the formation of such bubbles, see for example Baker (2008), Hudson (2012), Krugman (2009) and Vasudevan (2013).
24. For stock market bubbles this benefit goes very disproportionally to the super-rich. The benefits from the housing bubble went further down the wealth scale to also significantly benefit the rich and even significant sectors of the broadly defined middle class.
25. See Baker (1997) and Krugman (1999) as examples of the few who were discussing this by the end of the 1990s.

REFERENCES

Aglietta, M. and A. Rebérioux (2005), *Corporate Governance Adrift*, Cheltenham, UK and Northampton, MA, USA: Edward Elgar.

Albo, G., S. Gindin and L. Panitch (2010), *In and Out of Crisis. The Global Financial Meltdown and Left Alternatives*, Oakland, CA: PM Press.

Baker, D. (1997), *Saving Social Security with Stock: The Promises Don't Add Up*, New York: Twentieth Century Fund and Economic Policy Institute.

Baker, D. (2008), *Plunder and Blunder: The Rise and Fall of the Bubble Economy*, Sausalito, CA: Polipoint Press.

Bakir, E. (2006), 'The Post WWII Nonfinancial Corporate Rate of Profit in the US: Cycles, Trends and the Effects of Financialization', PhD Dissertation, University of Utah.

Bakir, E. and A. Campbell (2006), 'The Effect of Neoliberalism on the Fall in the Rate of Profit in Business Cycles', *Review of Radical Political Economics*, 38(3), 365–373.

Bakir, E. and A. Campbell (2009), 'The Bush Business Cycle Profit Rate: Support

in a Theoretical Debate and Implications for the Future', *Review of Radical Political Economics*, 41(3), 335–342.
Bakir, E. and A. Campbell (2010), 'Neoliberalism, the Rate of Profit and the Rate of Accumulation', *Science and Society*, 74(3), 323–342.
Bakir, E. and A. Campbell (2013), 'The Financial Rate of Profit: What Is It, and How Has It Behaved in the United States?', *Review of Radical Political Economics*, 45(3), 295–304.
Basu, D. and R. Vasudevan (2013), 'Technology, Distribution and the Rate of Profit in the US Economy: Understanding the Current Crisis', *Cambridge Journal of Economics*, 37(1), 57–89.
Brenner, R. (1998), 'The Economics of Global Turbulence', *New Left Review*, 229, 1–264.
Brenner, R. (2002), *The Boom and the Bubble. The US in the World Economy*, London: Verso.
Brooks, T. (1971), *Toil and Trouble: A History of American Labor*, New York: Dell.
Cámara Izquierdo, S. (2014), 'The Role of Long and Short-Term Dynamics of the US Rate of Profit in the Current Crisis', *International Journal of Management Concepts and Philosophy*, 8(1), 1–22.
Campbell, A. (2005), 'The Birth of Neoliberalism in the United States', in A. Saad-Filho and D. Johnston (eds), *Neoliberalism: A Critical Reader*, London: Pluto Press.
Cipolla, F. (1992), 'Profit Rate and Public Deficit in the USA', *Review of Radical Political Economics*, 24(2), 76–82.
Devine, J. (1994), 'The Causes of the 1929–33 Great Collapse: A Marxist Interpretation', *Research on Political Economy*, 14, 119–194.
Duménil, G., M. Glick and J. Rangel (1987), 'Theories of the Great Depression: Why did Profitability Matter?', *Review of Radical Political Economics*, 19(2), 16–42.
Duménil, G. and D. Lévy (2002a), 'The Field of Capital Mobility and the Gravitation of Profit Rates (USA 1948–2000)', *Review of Radical Political Economics*, 34(4), 417–436.
Duménil, G. and D. Lévy (2002b), 'The Profit Rate: Where and How Much Did It Fall? Did It Recover? (USA 1948–2000)', *Review of Radical Political Economics*, 34(4), 437–461.
Duménil, G. and D. Lévy (2011), *The Crisis of Neoliberalism*, Cambridge, MA: Harvard University Press.
Edsall, T. (1984), *The New Politics of Inequality*, New York: W.W. Norton & Company.
Foster, J.B. and F. Magdoff (2009), *The Great Financial Crisis*, New York: Monthly Review Press.
Glyn, A. (2006), *Capitalism Unleashed*, Oxford: Oxford University Press.
Hacker, J. and P. Pierson (2010), *Winner-Take-All Politics: How Washington Made the Rich Richer – and Turned Its Back on the Middle Class*, New York: Simon & Schuster.
Harrison, B. and B. Bluestone (1988), *The Great U-Turn. The Corporate Restructuring and the Polarizing of America*, New York: Basic Books.
Harvey, D. (2005), *A Brief History of Neoliberalism*, Oxford: Oxford University Press.
Hudson, M. (2012), *The Bubble and Beyond. Fictitious Capital, Debt Deflation and Global Crisis*, Dresden: ISLET-Verlag.

Jacoby, S. (2005), 'Corporate Governance and Society', *Challenge*, 48(4), 69–87.
Kotz, D. (2007), 'Contradictions of Economic Growth in the Neoliberal Era: Accumulation and Crisis in the Contemporary US Economy', available at http://people.umass.edu/dmkotz/Contradictions_07_05.pdf.
Kotz, D. (2015), *The Rise and Fall of Free-Market Capitalism*, Cambridge, MA: Harvard University Press.
Krugman, P. (1999), *The Return of Depression Economics*, New York: W.W. Norton & Co.
Krugman, P. (2009), *The Return of Depression Economics and the Crisis of 2008*, New York: W.W. Norton & Co.
Krugman, P. (2012), *End this Depression Now!*, New York: W.W. Norton & Co.
Lazonick, W. and M. O'Sullivan (2000), 'Maximizing Shareholder Value: A New Ideology for Corporate Governance', *Economy and Society*, 29(1), 13–35.
Lazonick, W. and M. O'Sullivan (2002), *Corporate Governance and Sustainable Prosperity*, New York: Palgrave.
Marx, K. ([1894] 1988), *Capital. A Critique of Political Economy. Volume III. The Process of Capitalist Production as a Whole*, reprinted (1988) in *Karl Marx Frederick Engels Collected Works*, Vol. 37, New York: International Publishers.
Michl, T. (1988), 'The Two-Stage Decline in US Nonfinancial Corporate Profitability, 1948–1986', *Review of Radical Political Economics*, 20(4), 1–22.
Mishel, L., J. Bernstein and H. Shierholz (2009), *The State of Working America, 2008/2009*, Ithaca, NY: ILR Press.
Mishel, L., J. Bivins, E. Gould and H. Shierholz (2012), *The State of Working America*, 12th edn, Ithaca: ILR Press.
Piketty, T. and E. Saez (2003), 'Inequality in the United States, 1913–1998', *Quarterly Journal of Economics*, 118(1), 1–39.
Powell, L. (1971), 'Attack on the American Free Enterprise System', accessed September 2014 at http://law.wlu.edu/powellarchives/page.asp?pageid=1251.
Rasmus, J. (2010), *Epic Recession. Prelude to Global Depression*, London: Pluto Press.
Rasmus, J. (2012), *Obama's Economy. Recovery for the Few*, London: Pluto Press.
Rasmussen Reports (2009), 'Just 53% Say Capitalism Better Than Socialism', 9 April, accessed 1 May 2013, at www.rasmussenreports.com/public_content/politics/general_politics/april_2009/just_53_say_capitalism_better_than_socialism.
Rasmussen Reports (2012), 'New Low: Just 14% Think Today's Children Will Be Better Off Than Their Parents', 29 July, accessed 1 May 2013 at http://www.rasmussenreports.com/public_content/business/jobs_employment/july_2012/new_low_just_14_think_today_s_children_will_be_better_off_than_their_parents.
Rasmussen Reports (2013), '54% Think It's Not Possible to Work Hard and Get Rich in America', 8 April, accessed 1 May 2013 at http://www.rasmussenreports.com/public_content/business/jobs_employment/march_2013/54_think_it_s_not_possible_to_work_hard_and_get_rich_in_america.
Reich, R. (2011), *Aftershock. The Next Economy and America's Future*, New York: Vintage Books.
Rosenberg, S. (2003), *American Economic Development since 1945*, New York: Palgrave Macmillan.
Smith, H. (2012), *Who Stole the American Dream?*, New York: Random House.
Stein, J. (2010), *Pivotal Decade: How the United States Traded Factories for Finance in the 1970s*, New Haven, CT: Yale University Press.

Stiglitz, J. (2010), *Freefall: America, Free Markets, and the Sinking of the World Economy*, New York: W.W. Norton & Co.
Stiglitz, J. (2012), *The Price of Inequality*, New York: W.W. Norton & Co.
Sutton, F., S. Harris, C. Kaysen and J. Tobin (1956 [1962]), *The American Business Creed*, New York: Schocken Books.
Useem, M. (1993), *Executive Defense: Shareholder Power and Corporate Reorganization*, Cambridge, MA: Harvard University Press.
Vasudevan, R. (2013), *Things Fall Apart*, Los Angeles, CA: Sage.
Vogel, D. (1989), *Fluctuating Fortunes*, New York: Basic Books.
Weisskopf, T. (1978), 'Marxist Perspectives on Cyclical Crises', in URPE (ed.), *US Capitalism in Crisis*, New York: Union for Radical Political Economics.
Weisskopf, T. (1979), 'Marxian Crisis Theory and the Rate of Profit in the Postwar US Economy', *Cambridge Journal of Economics*, 3(4), 341–378.
Wolff, E. (1996), *Top Heavy*, New York: New Press.
Wolff, E. (2001), 'The Recent Rise of Profits in the United States', *Review of Radical Political Economics*, 33(3), 315–324.
Wolff, E. (2003), 'What's Behind the Rise in Profitability in the US in the 1980s and 1990s?', *Cambridge Journal of Economics*, 27(4), 479–499.

8. The value of history and the history of value

Radhika Desai

This chapter argues that Marxist economics cannot explain the present crisis because, as a discipline, it is not geared to. It is an oxymoron, attempting fit Marxism to the antithetical methodological frame of marginalist neoclassical economics. Though Marxist economists are critical of neoclassical economics and have radical political commitments, their most important scholarly contributions have been made despite their discipline. And the genetic defects of Marxist economics have their effect. Most recently, they have ensured that some of the most prominent Marxist economists deem the second major crisis of capitalism in the twentieth century as merely one of financialization (Lapavitsas 2009; for a critique see Desai and Freeman 2011) or neoliberalism (Duménil and Lévy 2011; who had earlier, in Duménil and Lévy 2004, argued that neoliberalism has resolved the 1970s crisis of capitalism). Their predecessors had done little better in the 1930s (Howard and King 1992).

It is high time the formative problems of Marxist economics were brought to light so that Marxists, including many Marxist economists themselves who may only be dimly aware of them, may return to their real intellectual heritage – Marxist political (and geopolitical) economy – and deploy its intellectual power to understand and respond to the crisis. The heart of the problem lies (Desai 2013, 2010a) in the abandonment of classical political economy's historical approach (not to be confused with that inconsequential cul-de-sac in intellectual history, the German Historical School of economics). In classical political economy up to and including Marx and Engels's critique of it, the actions of historically constituted agents – classes, parties, states – drove history forward. They acted in unchosen circumstances to understand and deal with them. Whether or not they were successful, their actions changed the terrain. Marx and Engels's understanding was historical in two critical ways: in seeing that value production distinguished capitalism from previous forms of social production; and that its exploitative, contradictory, crisis-prone and, above all, esoteric dynamics constituted the testing terrain on which historical actors were compelled to pursue their goals – whether of aiding and stabilizing or hindering these dynamics.

Neoclassical economics emerged in the late nineteenth century marginalist revolution and displaced classical political economy precisely because Marx and Engels's intervention had made it useless as an instrument for bourgeois legitimation. Neoclassical economics essentialized and eternalized capitalism just like the 'vulgar economics' whose commodity fetishism Marx criticized as 'proclaiming for everlasting truths, the banal and complacent notions held by the bourgeois agents of production about their own world, which is to them the best possible one' (Marx [1867] 1977: 175n). The new discipline, around which the rest of the modern and equally ahistorical social sciences developed, became established in universities just when intellectuals began to engage with and even gravitate to Marxism in greater numbers. With their neoclassical economics training, they found the historical method of Marx alien and their attempts to fit it to the methods they were trained in never worked. The result was that Marxist economists jettisoned history for social science, and value for the ahistorical conceptions of subjective utility and price.

Though Marxist economists proclaim their loyalty to the labor theory of value, their neoclassical methodological commitments constitute a powerful undertow pulling them toward a view of capitalism as a 'purely economic' system of equilibrium price (not contradictory value) relations, unchanging and eternal, without inherent contradictions and thus not in need of state and political actions, domestic or international, to resolve them. Such a view is also necessarily cosmopolitan: national states and their plurality are incidental to it (for a critique of attempts to pin this interpretation on Marx see Desai 2012, 2014). Marxist economics originated in the early twentieth-century works of the Russian legal Marxist, Tugan Baranowski, and was rejuvenated by Joseph Schumpeter confounding Marxist ideas of crises with those of business cycles during the Great Depression (Freeman 2014, 2015). Marxists outside economics simply accepted the verdict of Marxist economists on the nature of capitalism: 'economics' was not their 'discipline'.

This rejection of the value of history and the displacement of the history of value by the neoclassical economics of price has been the elephant in the Marxist salon. Most Marxists are unaware of it because they remain in one of the numerous passageways that connect Marxism with the various social science disciplines. Marxist economists, to whom it is most embarrassing, have persuaded the rest either to look away or refrain from asking questions. This chapter ventures to contribute to the vital effort to break that silence.

In what follows, I first briefly outline a critique of Marxist economics and follow it up with a discussion of the variety of forms of capitalist crises. These discussions clear the ground for a historical view of value production, of capitalism and its crises. A full account of it being impossible here, I outline the political and geopolitical economy of two key elements of the crisis: the issues of consumption demand and international capital flows.

8.1 FROM THE HISTORY OF VALUE TO ECONOMICS OF PRICE

When Marx identified the source of surplus value by distinguishing labor and labor-power and operationalized the law of value by showing how competition pushed values down to their 'socially necessary' level, he laid bare the mechanisms of exploitation and crises, exposing capitalism's injustice and anarchy. Classical political economy could no longer legitimize capitalism and, as if on cue, circa 1870, the marginalist revolution delivered neoclassical economics. Its 'objective function' as Mandel observed, 'was, no doubt, purely apologetic – to justify the capitalist order as more or less inevitable; to justify wages, prices and profits as the result of exchanges carried out on an equal footing' (Mandel [1962] 1968: 717); (note that Mandel was that rare post-war Marxist whose link to revolutionary politics set him apart from Marxist economics, though he used the term to describe his work).

Bukharin 's critique was similar: neoclassical economics, he averred, was the best an enervated bourgeoisie transformed into a rentier class could muster in response to the Marxist challenge. It was an 'economic theory of the leisure class', a class removed from production, given to an anomic individualism and psychologism, and fearful of revolution. Hence marginalism's focus on consumption, its subjectivism and its ahistoricism, respectively (Bukharin [1914] 1972: 29–30). Partisans of the new discipline, like Pareto, also proclaimed neoclassical economics 'the best reply to Marx's theory of value' (Meek 1973: 243).

After Bukharin, major accounts of marginalism's origins first emerged in the 1950s and 1960s, when economics increased its importance in public discourse and policy through its (bastard) Keynesian revolution and needed a respectable genealogy. More emerged in the 1970s, when Marxist economics consolidated itself in its own founding discourse. It included criticisms of neoclassical economics which reveal as much about the discipline's Marxism as about its economics. It proclaimed Bukharin's account too schematic. While greater sophistication is always welcome, the devil lay in the Ricardian detail of this discourse.

8.1.1 Ricardo versus Ricardo

Of marginalism's three founders, Jevons and Walras clearly saw themselves as reaching back to and developing Ricardo's ideas via John Stuart Mill (Meek 1973: 244). However, Menger and his Austrian followers saw themselves as attacking Ricardo's labor theory of value. The new Marxist economists concurred (Meek 1973: 244; Dobb 1973: 166–170), and even spoke of a single 'Ricardo–Marx approach to the problems of value and of distribution' in which 'relative prices are independent of the pattern of consumption and demand' (Dobb 1973: 257).

In the post-war period, Marxist economists were dominated by neo-Ricardians or Sraffians at pains to refute the (bastard) Keynesian idea that capitalism's difficulties could be solved through fiscal and monetary tinkering. They distinguished themselves from their Keynesian counterparts by claiming to focus on production, as opposed to the rest of neoclassical economics which belonged to a 'Smithian' strand focusing on exchange. While problems with this claim abound, three are immediately pressing.

Firstly, while Ricardo undoubtedly shared classical political economy's general inclination to believe that value arose from labor, like his predecessors he was unable either to explain surplus value or to operationalize value theory. That was Marx's contribution. No one familiar with Marx's critique of Ricardo's understanding of value (Marx 1969: 164–216) can assimilate the two.

Secondly, Marx's labor theory of value served Marxist economics as little more than an incantation. Operationally, Marx's theory is rejected because it allegedly suffers from a 'transformation problem', unable to consistently transform values into prices. Nothing could be more ironic: Marx rooted his understanding of value production in his critique of Say's Law (and of Ricardo's adherence to it) and his insistence that money played an independent role in the economy. For Marx ([1894] 1981: 264–269), values and prices did not exist as two separate systems and there was never any question of 'transformation' or 'translation', but one of understanding their dynamic relationship. The temporal single-system interpretation (Kliman 2007; Freeman in Freeman and Carchedi 1996) which points this out has generally been met with silence. It is as though, when faced with the choice between Marx's value and neoclassical prices, Marxist economists cannot break their umbilical tie to the latter, despite their political commitment to Marxism; the spirit may be willing but the flesh is weak.

Finally, without a theory of value, Marxist economists see the dynamics of capitalism as Ricardian ones of cost prices versus prices determined by demand and supply. And here two other, usually hidden, Ricardian ideas – the two 'Ricardian fictions' (Desai 2013) – are smuggled in: his acceptance of Say's law (Keynes [1936] 1967: 32) and his own notion of 'comparative advantage'.

They are the two indispensable components of an ideological legitimation of capitalism and, not surprisingly, the chief targets of the greatest analysts of capitalism: Marx and Keynes. Say's law denied the possibility of gluts, and crises more generally, because it failed to understand that money transformed exchange into something qualitatively different from barter. Comparative advantage then served as its international counterpart: its claims about mutually beneficial free trade papered over international tensions that resulted when capitalist countries sought to externalize the consequences of capitalism's contradictions, for example by exporting excess production to colonial or otherwise unprotected markets and undermining prospects for industrial development there (I discuss Marx's critique of both in Desai 2013, 2014).

Now economists, Marxist and others, could deny that there were crises in capitalism, particularly any arising from the paucity of demand, and insist that imperialism, unfortunate as it was, was not 'necessary to capitalism' (Zarembka 2002). These fictions provide the foundation for neoclassical economics' assumption of an eternal, purely economic, crisis-free and cosmopolitan capitalism.

Ricardo with his twin fictions was the true inspiration for neoclassical economics in all respects but his (in any case never operationalized) idea of the source of value in labor, and Tugan Baranowski pioneered the foundation of a Marxist economics on its basis. Reinforced by Sraffa, the Ricardianism of contemporary Marxist economics is so entrenched that today the paucity of consumption demand is not even discussed, only dismissed as 'underconsumptionism', an allegedly madcap idea allegedly dismissed by Marx himself (for a detailed textual and historical critique see Desai 2010b). While the rejection of the more hotly debated tendency of the rate of profit to fall (TRPF) is usually traced to Okishio, it too originated in Tugan Baranowski (Desai 2010b). Marxist economists who debate the TRPF are divided between those who reject it because they believe the profit rates tend to rise with cost-saving innovation and those who try to demonstrate the TRPF empirically through this or that measure of the rate of profit. However, even in the latter group, the law is divorced from Marx's historical account of value.

8.1.2 History in Value and Value in History

The emergence of neoclassical economics and the resulting separation of economics and sociology (Clarke 1991: 243ff) gave rise to the wider social scientific division of labor which is lamented today and to which inter- and multidisciplinarity are the solutions. However, these developments struck a far greater blow against understanding social reality historically.

They were aimed at the heart of Marx's advance: his operationalization of the law of value. Its replacement, the neoclassical conception of prices and utility (not to be confused with Marx's historical conception of use value), drained history from our understanding of capitalist society in four important ways. Firstly, in Marx's view, the production of (abstract) value distinguished capitalist production from all previously known forms of social production. Value is the measure of labor embodied in its alienated products which the mechanisms of competition, by forcing the incorporation of technology in the production process, push down to a 'socially necessary' level, thus improving human productivity. Secondly, therefore, value production constitutes the motor that drives capitalism to develop the forces of production. Thirdly, in that it unifies the two main types of contradictions – the inter-class contradiction of exploitation and the intra-class contradiction of competition – value production, rather than proceeding smoothly, lurches from crisis to crisis and is subject to increasing legitimacy deficits thanks to its anarchy and injustice. Finally, these very contradictions require that political agents – pre-eminently the state – intervene and modify the parameters in which value production takes place, whether they succeed or fail. Once value as the historical distinctiveness of capitalism and its contradictory as well as progressive motor is eliminated, we have ahistorical capitalism: stable, eternal and unchanging. We lose the central plot that makes its tumultuous history intelligible.

Now capitalism could be seen as 'purely economic', an eternal and cosmopolitan system. The ever-present role of states and other actors in managing capitalism's contradictions through domestic and international actions, actions which gave political (and geopolitical) economy its historical – that is to say, its agential and dynamic – character, was written out of the script. The intellectual impoverishment accompanying neoclassical economics would have remained confined to bourgeois theory had Marxists not themselves wheeled its Trojan horse into the Marxist citadel.

8.1.3 The Schumpeterian Gloss

The distinctive virtue of historical approaches is the understanding of change but, having dispensed with it, Marxist economists proved not much better than neoclassical ones in the face of the Great Depression. While the latter were challenged by Keynes, Schumpeter sought to rescue the neoclassical understanding in ways that have proved particularly congenial to Marxist economists.

Against Marx's view that, like all class societies hitherto, capitalism too would cease to be able to develop the forces of production, Schumpeter's entrepreneurial and innovative capitalism is a Promethean system which ceaselessly develops the productive forces. Schumpeter's phrase, 'creative destruction', is quoted *ad nauseum* by Marxists. Schumpeter also conflated crises with business cycles, which he considered regular purges that cleansed the system of excess capital. Given the gravity and depth of the Great Depression, he threw in 'long waves' for good measure: should the crisis be really big, and the purge not capable of restarting accumulation, a 'long wave' of expansion would rescue it (Freeman 2014). Marx's portrayal of a capitalism in which the development of the productive forces is not guaranteed, which is inherently prone to crisis and can break down, vanished. Now Schumpeterian Marxists could lampoon any Marxists who retained notions of contradiction for predicting ten of the last two crises.

Having failed to explain the Great Depression (Howard and King 1992: 19), Marxist economics is once again on the intellectual back foot amidst the current crisis. It is left to non-Marxist, even bourgeois, economists to make elementary but important historical observations such as that the lesser severity of the Great Recession in comparison to the Great Depression is due to 'automatic stabilizers' built into the system out of the lessons learned, however distortedly, from the Great Depression which have put a floor below demand.

8.1.4 Returning to Political and Geopolitical Economy

In a properly historical political and geopolitical economy, the present crisis would constitute a chapter in the rocky history of value production in whose course social agents, pre-eminently the state, have modified its parameters through domestic and international actions. Given Marxist economists' tendency to write states out of the script of capitalism, the extent and nature of states' economic roles have been registered chiefly in non-Marxist work: economic histories of nationally specific capitalisms, accounts of national 'regimes of accumulation' as the Regulationists would have it, and 'comparative capitalisms' and 'developmental states' as other large and interesting swathes of literature would put it (see Anderson 1992 for an overview of the principal European cases, and Woo-Cumings 1999 on the developing world).

The geopolitical economy (which can be traced to Marx and Engels themselves; see Desai 2013, 2014) of the present crisis, would also place it in the changing international configuration of value production. The powerful Marxist tradition of theorizing capitalist international relations in relation to value production and its contradictions was inaugurated by the classical theories of imperialism; they were also the first theories of international relations, as I have argued (Desai 2013). However, Marxist economists' view of a pure and cosmopolitan capitalism diverted post-war Marxist theorizing of international relations towards a Marxisant version of hegemony stability theory, as the world systems writers did in the 1970s (Wallerstein 1974, 1976; Arrighi 1994 are the principal works) and towards seeking to gainsay globalization theories by holding Marx up as the original globalization theorist (as in Rosenberg 2000; criticized in Desai 2010b). In these cosmopolitan theories conceiving world capitalism as a single seamless whole, either no state matters or only one does. The co-evolution of capitalism and the international system of nation-states through a dialectic of uneven and combined development (Desai 2013) has no place here and nor does competition, let alone the sharp political and geopolitical contestation that has historically characterized relations between capitalist states, and between them and others. Some Marxists have worked against this trend (Mandel 1970, 1972; Van der Pijl 2006a, 2006b) and Robert Brenner's historiography (if not his theory; Desai 2013, 2015) of 'the economics of global turbulence' features inter-capitalist competition centrally.

In geopolitical economy nation-states are material products of capitalism as much as classes are. Just as capitalist society is divided into classes, so the capitalist world is divided into struggling and competing, imperial and contender states. To the class struggle within nations corresponds that between them in the form of uneven and combined development: imperial capitalist countries seek to reinforce a given configuration of unevenness in capitalist development; and contenders, both capitalist and 'communist', undertake combined – that is, state-directed, hot-housed economic development – to undermine it.

8.2 CAPITALISM AND ITS CRISES

Geopolitical economy returns to the idea of inherent crisis tendencies in capitalism, taking seriously the full variety of crisis mechanisms embedded in the dynamics of value production and manifested in capitalism's history so far. Marx certainly referred to many although, given his famously incomplete analysis, not systematically. Mandel and Sweezy, very different Marxist scholars, also noted the plurality of crisis mechanisms. Mandel (1981: 38–53) criticized those who privileged one crisis mechanism, and believed that several could be seen at play in different phases of the development of a particular crisis. Paul Sweezy (1970: 145–146), for his part, divided Marxist accounts of crisis into those associated with falling rates of profit and those associated with realization.

However, these lists remained far from systematic and excluded finance and the state. In 2010, I tabulated crises along two axes: their source, the realm of capitalist society they emerge from – production, realization, credit and geopolitics; and their form, whether intra-class (related to inter-capitalist competition) or inter-class (related to class struggle). When a few years later David Kotz kindly shared with me a list of crisis mechanisms carefully gleaned from decades of engagement with Marx's oeuvre (personal communication, 2013), I added another source of crisis, that of money, separate from credit. On further reflection, and in the interests of completeness, I then added a sixth source of crisis: the (domestic) political, to match the geopolitical. The result was Table 8.1.

The sources and forms should be relatively uncontroversial. Accumulation and realization are intrinsic to the circuit of capital since surplus value must be extracted in production and realized through the sale of goods embodying it. There can be no capital without money, and money is inseparable from credit. Finally, capital accumulation is impossible without the state securing its political and legal framework, facilitating its rise and securing its continued growth. Finally, the unevenness of capitalist development calls forth the response of combined development and constitutes the dialectic of uneven and combined development (Desai 2013), ensuring the plurality of nation-states and competition and conflict between them. The two forms of crisis emerge from exploitation and competition which are united in the operation of the law of value as its vertical and horizontal, inter-class and intra-class, axes. Both are contradictory and prone to crises.

There are five main things to note about the Marxist economics treatment of the intra-class crisis of accumulation, the TRPF, the tendency of increasing organic composition of capital to reduce the profit rate in the long run unless counteracted, temporarily, by one or more counteracting factors (Marx [1894] 1981: 339–348). Firstly, Okishio and Tugan-Baranowski rejected this thesis because, they asserted, no capitalist would invest unless doing so increased his profits. They failed to consider that the capitalist 'may be *forced* to introduce new machinery in order to keep his market share or even to save his firm from bankruptcy', and that '[n]o capitalist knows in advance what the result of this decision to buy new machinery will be' (Mandel [1894] 1981: 35–36, see also Marx 1894/1981: 373–4). Secondly, until Henryk Grossman's work in the 1930s, while Marxists generally accepted the TRPF they did not link it to crises (Howard and King 1989: 316). Thirdly, they may have had a point. Mandel spoke of 'the *memento mori* [the TRPF] implies for capitalism in a secular perspective' (Mandel [1894] 1981: 51); Alan Freeman elaborates the rationale for this view (Chapter 5 in this volume) and Keynes anticipated private investment winding down in a surfeit of capital. The TRPF

Table 8.1 Crises by source and form

Source Form	Production	Realization	Money	Finance	Political	Geopolitical
Intra-class	Tendency of the rate of profit to fall (TRPF)	Disproportion	Deflation	Credit crunch/ speculative bubbles	Fiscal crisis	Uneven vs capitalist combined development
Inter-class	Profit squeeze	Overproduction/ underconsumption	Inflation	Mortgage crisis	Legitimation crisis	Uneven vs popular or socialist combined development

is probably best seen as a secular downward trend, punctuated but not reversed by up-ticks, which makes accumulation ever more difficult with time. Fourthly, therefore, Mandel argued against explaining overproduction crises by the TRPF:

> because it confuses the impossibility of valorizing *additionally* accumulated capital with the impossibility of valorising all *previously invested* capital; because it identifies fluctuations in the *investment decisions* of capitalist firms with the fluctuations of current surplus-value production. (Mandel 1981: 39)

Neo-Ricardians did so nevertheless, because their exclusive focus on production left out problems of realization and the role of expectations.

Finally, and most importantly, therefore, for all the heat generated by debates over how exactly to measure the profit rate, it sheds little light on the relationship between falling profits, profit rates and the rate of investment (the slowdown of which would constitute a crisis). While differences in rates of profit may explain the shift of capital from less to more profitable sectors, can it explain rises or falls in aggregate investment? In any capitalist country with a reasonably developed financial system, low average profits should hardly be a barrier to investment, and may even be a spur, if promising new technology appears. And high profits in a situation of low demand and profit expectations only leads capitalists to hoard their money in the form of financial 'investment', which simply increases the capital seeking a share of existing returns, reducing the rate of profit further (Freeman 2013), as in the 2000s.

Profits are squeezed when rising wages reduce the rate of exploitation and profits. While critics have attempted to dismiss this source of crisis theoretically by showing that it is possible to raise the rate of exploitation even when profits are falling (e.g. Shaikh 1978: 239), and empirically by noting that other factors, particularly international price pressures, explained most of the decline in profitability between 1965 and 1973 (Brenner 1998: 101–102), they do not demonstrate that upward pressure on wages cannot decrease profit rates. And certainly wage pressures did threaten profits in the economic crisis of the 1970s as productivity growth slowed at least in some countries (Glyn and Sutcliffe 1972; Glyn 2006).

Crises of 'disproportionality' between sectors or departments of production include shortfalls in investment demand, while those of overproduction or underconsumption refer to those of consumption demand. While the two make up aggregate demand, investment demand for production goods relies on demand for final products. As Marx pointed out, the production of constant capital is 'ultimately limited' by consumption demand, 'for production of constant capital never takes place for its own sake, but simply because more of it is needed in those spheres of production whose products do go into individual consumption' (Marx [1867] 1977: 420). The idea of capitalism as a never-ending production of producers' goods which would make the paucity of consumption demand irrelevant is largely a fantasy of many Marxist economists; it is logically faulty and historically irrelevant (Desai 2010b).

Deflation is rooted in overcompetition depressing prices and reducing the inducement to invest. While inflation can have diverse causes, one critical one is cost-push inflation due to high bargaining strength of labor or primary commodity producers. Credit crunches occur when one set of capitalists, bankers, become unwilling to lend to others – bankers or productive investors – as experienced in 2008; and asset bubbles arise from overcompetition between financial capitals chasing thinning margins and making them ever thinner by throwing ever more leveraged money into speculation, as happened in the recent housing and credit bubbles. Mortgage crises occur with high default rates of credit extended for consumption. The recent subprime crisis in the United States (US) was an important but not the only instance: mortgage crises had preceded the Crash of 1929 (Dollars and Sense 2009).

Fiscal crises are typically results of capitals competing to offload common costs onto one another while appropriating the benefits of public spending for themselves, and can handicap the state in performing its role in ensuring accumulation. Inter-class political crises of capitalism I propose to conceive in Polanyian form: they involve struggles to advance decommodifcation of land, labor and money (say by introducing elements of public utility banking) intolerable to capital and its resistance.

Geopolitical crises of the intra-capitalist sort could arise out of competition between nationally organized blocs of capital, including those undertaking capitalist combined development such as culminated in World War I, though they can also arise from competition for markets of the sort Brenner blames for the onset and persistence of the 'long downturn' (Brenner 1998). Geopolitical crises of an 'inter-class' form typically can be traced to refusals of the periphery to contribute to the stability of core capitalism – such as oil price increases of the 1970s or contemporary surges in commodity prices (Patnaik 2009) – and undertake non-capitalist forms of combined development.

Are any of these crisis mechanisms more fundamental than the others? Not only are they all, as we have seen, connected and not only are there usually several at work at once in any historical instance of capitalist crisis, but which one ends up being fatal to any capitalism is impossible to tell in advance.

8.3 THE CRISIS OF WESTERN CAPITALISM

In the historical approach of geopolitical economy, the 2008 crisis appears as a new phase in the series of attempts to reverse Western capitalism's long growth slowdown since the 1970s on Western capitalists' terms, attempts whose aims and achievements cannot be understood within national parameters. There are reasons to believe that the crisis is a particularly grave one. It may not seem that way given the relative quiescence of working classes, except in parts of the European periphery, but these attempts have cumulatively mired Western capitalism in stagnation. What little growth it can now muster must rely on inflating destructive and volatile asset bubbles, as its left- and right-wing commentators admit (Krugman 2012; Summers 2013). Breaking out of this cycle may well require putting the capitalist character of Western economies into question. That Western capitalism has run out of neoliberal road is particularly clear internationally. The more state-managed Brazil, Russia, India, China (BRIC) and other emerging economies are growing and, for the first time in the history of capitalism, putting an end to Western supremacy. While it is impossible to reconstruct this full story here, what follow below are outlines of a historical perspective on two key aspects: consumption demand and international financial flows.

8.3.1 Consumption Demand

As the regulationists classically emphasized, the historically unprecedented economic dynamism of post-war capitalism rested on a historically unprecedented expansion of working class demand thanks to rising working class wages and the socialization of a large part of working class consumption through the public provision of education, pensions, and insurance against illness and temporary unemployment. They worked to prevent '*a cumulative shortfall in effective demand* when the conditions of surplus-value production deteriorate' (Aglietta [1975] 1978: 181–182). Ernest Mandel added that, with rising real wages, working class consumption shifted to the products of the monopoly sector (Mandel 1972: 536). Brenner, for his part, while stressing that the real post-war growth story lay not in the US but in the recovering economies of Western Europe, also noted that, system-wide, it was reliant on expanded consumption demand (Brenner 1998: 91). How important the expansion of Western working class consumption demand was in laying the foundation of the 'golden age' is best thrown into relief by comparing it with what preceded and succeeded it.

Industrial maturity and imperialism

The late nineteenth-century second industrial revolution, the previous major phase of capitalist expansion, expanded the production of producers' goods massively through high levels of investment. It culminated in 'industrial maturity' in the advanced industrial world and thereafter growth manifested a new pattern, focused on consumer goods production. It needed to be sustained by an expansion of consumption demand and public investment (Nasser forthcoming, 2013 on the US case).

Of course, even capitalism's needs are not automatically met and the Great Depression was the result of expanding Fordist production of consumer goods unmatched by rises in public spending and wages sufficient for its successful realization. It was sharpest in the US, in which highly productive Fordist production methods originated and were most highly developed and which lacked the colonial markets that other capitalist countries had to compensate for the restricted size of the home market. Historically, the US had enjoyed a number of functional equivalents for colonies: the historically higher wages of its working classes; its centuries-long process of 'internal colonization' until around 1890; the pursuit of markets overseas, including in its Latin American 'informal empire' that followed, with merchandise exports rising from 2.5 percent of gross domestic product (GDP) in 1870 to 3.6 percent in 1913, faster than any industrialized country except Japan (Maddison 2006: 361–362); wars that became boom periods for US capitalism (Desai 2013; Freeman, Chapter 5 in this volume) with two world wars pulling it out of recession; and finally, when export growth dipped to 2.2 percent per annum in the inter-war period and consumer goods began to lead growth, the development of consumer credit in the US in the 'roaring twenties' which ended in a mortgage and credit crisis in the lead-up to the 1929 stock market crash (Livingston 2009: 39).

The rises in wages and the social wage are usually traced to the strength of working class organization enhanced by mobilization for war. However, external and colonial markets were also drying up. As long as they existed, working class consumption remained less important to capitalist expansion. With decolonization and development efforts involving protection of home markets, the old suppliers to these markets had to find others. The social liberal, J.A. Hobson, had foreseen the possibility of replacing colonial markets by expanding working class consumption:

> If the consuming public in this country raises its standard of consumption to keep pace with every rise of productive powers, there could be no excess of goods or capital clamorous to use Imperialism in order to find markets: foreign trade would indeed exist, but there would be no difficulty in exchanging a small surplus of our manufactures for the food and raw material we annually

> absorbed, and all the savings we made could find employment, if we choose, in home industries. (Hobson [1902] 1965: 81)

The post-war 'golden age' realized this possibility. The importance of the 'agricultural countries', effectively the non-settler colonies, to Britain as markets, already almost 60 percent of exports at the height of its industrial supremacy in the mid-nineteenth century, grew as that supremacy declined after 1870, going up to about three-quarters in 1913 (Hobsbawm 1968: Diagram 28). That they were replaced by working class mass consumption upon decolonization is indicated by the one-time increase in the share of wages and salaries in national income: it had remained less than 50 percent to 1914 and rose to above 70 percent in the post-war period (Deane and Cole 1962: 247). Available US figures indicate that the share of wages in net domestic income rose from 55 percent in 1929 to a peak of 67 percent in 1970 and another slightly higher peak in 1980 before falling (Bureau of Economic Analysis website).

Wages could rise without eating into profits, and thus be tolerated by capitalists, as long as productivity rose. By the late 1960s, however, productivity increases slowed. While the Regulationists attributed this to the inherent limits of the Fordist labor process, the doyen of US productivity scholars, Robert Gordon, saw it as a more general exhaustion of cost-reducing innovation (Gordon 2012). It would now be difficult to prevent rising wages, pushed upward by an organized and militant working class, from eating into profits (Glyn 2006:7). The rise of commodity prices, preeminently oil, was the international counterpart of this inter-class crisis mechanism. Meanwhile, 'overcapacity and overproduction' sharpened inter-capitalist competition as Western Europe and Japan recovered and all capitalists chafed at the limits placed on demand as wages stagnated (Brenner 1998).

The neoliberal wager

A strong organized working class, increasingly assertive developing countries, their demand for a new international economic order (Hudson [1977] 2003; Murphy 1984), rising protectionism, failure of Bretton Woods and defeat of the leading capitalist nation by a poor country: these constituted the sharply contested terrain on which the 'new right' attained its hard-won victory. It would now seek to resolve the crisis on Western capitalist terms. The alternative is worth recalling: the Brandt commission had suggested expanding demand in the developing world to provide the West with a new demand stimulus (Desai 2013: 163).

While the new right's victory undoubtedly inflicted great pain on working people and the developing world, whether it constituted a viable resolution to the capitalist crisis is another question altogether; for neoliberalism was simply the vapid idea that capitalism would grow, left to itself. Clearly, Western capitalists were scraping the bottom of the intellectual barrel: the ideology had survived only in sectarian milieus (Desai 1994) and had never guided policy. It ensured that there would be no stable strategy to revive growth. Perhaps none could be had on capitalist terms.

The neoliberal era was, unsurprisingly, no era of free markets and competition (Crouch 2011). Instead, Western capitalist classes used the state to deregulate their own activity, promote the interests of the biggest corporations, attack working class power and obtain risk-free profits – through privatizations, the infamous public–private partnerships, non-competitive contracts on one-of-a-kind infrastructure construction and, of course, state debt. Such measures may have increased profitability for some corporations, but they did not resolve the underlying demand problem, instead they exacerbated it, expanding demand, at best, only among the better-off, aided by military and credit Keynesianism. This was too little to resolve the problem of overcapacity and overproduction.

The result was a growth pattern with three characteristics: Firstly, it was significantly lower on average than that of the 'golden age'. Secondly, given the stagnation in demand, it had a distinctive geopolitical economy: growth became a zero-sum game between the major centers of capitalist accumulation, 'flowing' to the area with low exchange rates in a sort of 'hydraulic mechanism', as Brenner (1998) put it. For Brenner, this was because, in the face of overproduction and overcapacity, firms and states prevented or refused a 'slaughter of capital values'. However, this also raises a question Brenner does not ask: barring the 25 percent contraction Mrs Thatcher imposed on British manufacturing in the early 1980s, in the context of perhaps the most bitter class struggle of the Western world of the 1970s, when was the last time an advanced industrial country permitted such a 'slaughter of capital values' provided it was within its power to prevent it? The scale of destruction of capital in the US during the Great Depression must be attributed to the limited development of regulatory structures of the US state, and since then such recourse is unimaginable given the geopolitical economy of capitalist competition (Desai 2013). Just as firms are loath to lose capacity, something that can only benefit their competitors, so are nationally organized blocs of capital. Thirdly, while neoliberal measures probably helped capital in a number of ways, they only exacerbated the underlying problem of limited markets. Now, most capitalist countries became reliant on the inflation of asset bubbles and their wealth effects to provide what demand stimuli they could to power growth. This brings us to financialization, which also had a distinctive geopolitical economy.

8.3.2 Dollar-Denominated Financializations

Though it was being discussed in the decade before 1995 (Lipietz 1985; Hutton 1995) as financial activity increased with the slowdown in growth and accumulation, discussion of financialization really took off in the late 1990s and 2000s as the wilder party, in which financial investment and international capital flows twice grew to several multiples of their previous peaks with the US stock market and housing bubbles, got going. What that party was about requires understanding more than generic 'financialization': it requires a geopolitical economy of the end of Western supremacy and of US attempts at world dominance. Trying to make sense of the 2008 crisis without an appreciation of these aspects is like trying to understand the Russian Revolution without an understanding of the Great War.

Used in the singular, 'financialization' is too generic and therefore misleading. Distinct national financial systems mean that financial bubbles and crises remain primarily national and contagion travels along distinct paths rather than overspilling uniformly onto the rest of the world. So, nationally and historically discrete 'financializations' is a more apt description. While they do tend to appear as productive investment declines, the drivers and patterns of each are constituted by the shape and institutional structure of the national economy. And how these are related to the succession of discrete dollar-denominated international financializations upon which the dollar's international role has come to depend since the 1971 breakdown of Bretton Woods is an equally important question. These financializations, rooted in the Anglo-American financial system, were necessary, and necessarily short-lived, requirements of maintaining the dollar's world role by creating a financial demand for US dollars to counteract the downward pressure on the dollar thanks to the Triffin dilemma.

In the twentieth century, the US had attempted to emulate the United Kingdom's (UK) nineteenth-century world dominance with little heed to how the dialectic of uneven and combined development had not only bought the UK's dominance to an end circa 1870, when contender powers challenged British industrial and imperial supremacy, but also made such dominance unrepeatable. Productive power had now spread too widely and economies were becoming more national, rather than remaining imperial. Even in the diluted form of making the dollar the world's currency and New York the world's financial center (rather than attempting to emulate the UK's formal empire), the US's goal of world dominance could not be realized: what appears as a continuous post-war reign of the dollar is in fact a series of efforts, each more volatile and short-lived, to maintain its world role. Not only did Bretton Woods never work, but since its 'end', the inevitable downward pressures on a national currency attempting to be an international one in twentieth-century conditions – in which capital exports on the requisite scale were not possible and current account deficits were the only way to provide international liquidity which was, however, subject to the Triffin dilemma – needed to be counteracted by a series of financializations.

Each dollar-denominated financialization temporarily prevented the dollar from declining faster by increasing the demand for dollars, but reversed that decline only three times: the Volcker Shock-induced rise in the dollar's value; the considerably less spectacular rise associated with the stock market bubble of the late 1990s; and the more recent post-crisis rise in the dollar's value fueled first by a stock market bubble in the US which rested on low interest rates and later, even more powerfully, by the Federal Reserve's promises of rises in interest rates. As their hollowness was becoming clear by early 2016, the dollar was back on a downward trajectory.

There were other financializations, of course, including the vast increase in national and international bank loans in the 1970s which culminated in the Third World debt crisis; the centrifugal flow of funds into the big emerging markets in the mid-1990s that led to the East Asian financial crisis; the US stock market bubble of the 1990s; and the gigantic subprime house price and credit bubbles of the 2000s which burst in 2008.

While the connection between these dollar-denominated financializations to individual national ones needs to be studied, some key relationships are clear. The 2008 financial crisis was neither 'global' nor 'imperial' or 'hegemonic': it did not affect all countries in a comparable fashion, nor was it transmitted from the US along skeins of domination and dependence to the rest of the world, and magnified there. Originating in the US, it inflicted most pain on Europe, whose financial institutions were significantly invested in the subprime assets of the US housing bubble of the 2000s (Borio and Disyatat 2011). These financial strains sharpened formative problems of the euro and led to independent financial and economic crises in the eurozone two years later.

There are indications that the dollar's volatile career as world money is finally ending. Concern about the effects of its financialized volatility is voiced increasingly widely. Despite historically lax monetary policy and its inflation of new dollar-denominated bubbles since 2008 – in emerging-market currencies, commodities and in the US stock market – international capital flows remain 60 percent short of their pre-crisis levels (McKinsey Global Institute 2013). Bi- and multilateral measures by many systemically important countries are reducing the dollar's role in transactions with third countries. The Chinese-led Asian Infrastructure Investment Bank (AIIB) is the latest and strongest: it offers stable long-term finance for production and development to capital-starved countries, against the surfeit of depreciating short-term unproductive and dangerously volatile capital which is all the much-touted sophistication of the US financial system has to offer. Even the UK, whose financial sector has been such an important support for the dollar's volatile career since the 1970s, sees the future of its own financial sector in joining the AIIB.

8.3.3 2008 and Beyond

The economic crisis that accompanied the financial crisis is even more instructive. It too afflicted mainly the US and Western Europe, while Japan continued on the singular low-growth track it had shunted onto since the 1990s (Mikuni and Murphy 2003). On the other hand, after the short sharp fall in world trade in late 2008, the emerging economies continued to post the higher growth rates and, despite recent slowdowns, they remain considerably higher than those in the advanced industrial economies.

It is noteworthy that the developing world had originally begun to gain on the developed world in the 1970s before the trend was interrupted by the Volcker Shock, the Third World debt crisis and the two 'lost decades of development' that ensued. In neoliberal decades, growth resumed primarily in countries that were able to refuse its stipulations, and to the extent that they did. The end of Western dominance that this development spells is historic.

To recap: Western capitalism arrived at industrial maturity in the early twentieth century and could enjoy the 'golden age' of growth thanks only to the state-organized expansion of working class consumption made more urgent by the loss of colonies. It could only last as long as productivity increases permitted wages to rise without eating into profits. As soon as that limit was reached, further expansion of working class consumption proved intolerable to capitalism. The ferocious attempts to restore growth by every means other than expanding working class and Third World demand could only deliver short bursts of bubble-driven growth inevitably punctuated by financial crises.

Given its strident opposition to state intervention, neoliberalism after 2008 required that attempts to revive growth on capitalist terms – that is, by leaving the reins of the economy and, above all, the investment prerogative, in the hands of Western capitalists – had to rely on manipulating monetary policy alone. Ostensibly geared to get growth going by providing capital cheaply, unconventional monetary policy is actually designed to facilitate continued financial speculation in whatever asset classes – emerging-economy assets, commodities, stocks – that remain available for asset price inflation. There is an elaborate pretense that growth is just around the next unconventional monetary policy corner, and that monetary policy is geared to levels of unemployment. However, this only dissimulates the reality that only massive fiscal stimulus, only fiscal stimulus of a size and scale guaranteed not only to take the reins of the economy out of the hands of capitalists but also to make it blindingly clear that they have been so taken, can revive growth in the Western world. Such a revival can only empower working people further because only the fulfilment of their needs can be the goal of such a stimulus (Freeman 2009). US capitalism at least has arrived at the historical point where it is pertinent to ask, as Marx and Engels did in 1848, whether the ruling class is fit any more to rule.

Marxists can only explain this outcome, and the series of crises that neoliberal capitalism caused in attempting to resolve the long downturn on Western capitalist terms, by putting the world capitalist system as a whole in the sort of historical perspective suggested above, and illustrated in relation to consumption demand and international capital flows. This historical perspective must be one on the effective unit, the world economy, which in turn must be seen as driven not by markets or some purely economic logic, nor by hegemony, but by the dialectic of uneven and combined development. It is this dialectic, between a West intent on perpetuating its dominance and emerging economies increasingly challenging it and widening already existing rifts within the West, that can really account for capitalist crises in general and the recent one in particular. In such a geopolitical economy of world capitalism, class struggles that determine national and international trajectories of capitalism, and are the route humanity must take beyond it, are also central.

REFERENCES

Aglietta, M. ([1975] 1978), *A Theory of Capitalist Regulation: The US Experience*, London: Verso.
Anderson, P. (1992), 'The Light of Europe', *English Questions*, London: Verso.
Arrighi, G. (1994), *The Long Twentieth Century: Money, Power, and the Origins of Our Times*, London: Verso.
Borio, C. and P. Disyatat (2011), 'Global Imbalances and the Financial Crisis: Link or No Link?', Bank for International Settlements, Working Paper No. 346, May.
Brenner, R. (1998), 'The Economics of Global Turbulence', *New Left Review*, I/229(May–June), 1–265.
Bukharin, N. ([1914] 1972), *The Economic Theory of the Leisure Class*, New York: Monthly Review Press.
Clarke, S. (1991), *Marx, Marginalism and Modern Sociology: From Adam Smith to Max Weber*, 2nd edn, Basingstoke: Macmillan Academic and Professional.
Crouch, C. (2011), *The Strange Non-Death of Neoliberalism*, Oxford: Polity.
Deane, P. and W.A. Cole (1962), *British Economic Growth, 1688–1959*, Cambridge: Cambridge University Press.

Desai, R. (1994), 'Second-Hand Dealers in Ideas: Think-Tanks and Thatcherite Hegemony', *New Left Review*, 203, 27–64.
Desai, R. (2010a), 'Consumption Demand in Marx and in the Current Crisis', *Research in Political Economy*, 26, 101–141.
Desai, R. (2010b), 'The Absent Geopolitics of Pure Capitalism', *World Review of Political Economy*, 1(3), 463–484.
Desai, R. (2012), 'Marx, List and the Materiality of Nations', *Rethinking Marxism*, 24(1), 47–67.
Desai, R. (2013), *Geopolitical Economy: After US Hegemony, Globalization and Empire*, London: Pluto Press.
Desai, R. (2014), 'Geopolitical Economy, Or How Marx Understood the World Order', in A.K. Bagchi and A. Chatterjee (eds), *Marxism with and beyond Marx*, New Delhi: Routledge.
Desai, R. (2015), 'Look Back in Hope? Reassessing Regulation Theory', in Kees Van der Pijl (ed.), *The International Political Economy of Production*, Handbooks of Research on International Political Economy series, Cheltenham, UK and Northampton, MA, USA: Edward Elgar Publishing.
Desai, Radhika and Alan Freeman (2011), 'Value and Crisis Theory in the Great Recession', *World Review of Political Economy*, 2(1), 35–47.
Dobb, Maurice (1973), *Theories of Value and Distribution since Adam Smith: Ideology and Economic Theory*, Cambridge: Cambridge University Press.
Dollars & Sense (2009), 'The Great Real Estate Bubble of the 1920s', *Dollars & Sense* blog, available at http://dollarsandsense.org/blog/2009/02/the-great-real-estate-bubble-of-the-1920s.html.
Duménil, Gérard and Dominique Lévy (2004), *Capital Resurgent: Roots of the Neoliberal Revolution*, Cambridge, MA: Harvard University Press.
Duménil, Gérard and Dominique Lévy (2011), *The Crisis of Neoliberalism*, Cambridge, MA: Harvard University Press.
Freeman, A. (2009), 'Investing in Civilization', in Wayne Anthony and Julie Guard (eds), *Bailouts and Bankruptcies*, Winnipeg: Fernwood Press.
Freeman, A. (2013), 'The Profit Rate in the Presence of Financial Markets: A Necessary Correction', *Journal of Australian Political Economy*, 70 (summer 2012/13), 167–192.
Freeman, A. (2014), 'Schumpeter's Theory of Self-Restoration: A Casualty of Samuelson's Whig Historiography of Science', *Cambridge Journal of Economics*, 38, 663–679.
Freeman, A. (2015), 'Introduction to Chris Freeman's "Schumpeter's 'Business Cycles' Revisited"', *European Journal of Economic and Social Systems*, 27(1–2), 37–46.
Freeman, A. and G. Carchedi (eds) (1996), *Marx and Non-Equilibrium Economics*, Cheltenham, UK and Northampton, MA, USA: Edward Elgar Publishing.
Glyn, A. (2006), *Capitalism Unleashed*, Oxford: Oxford University Press.
Glyn, A. and B. Sutcliffe (1972), *British Capitalism, Workers and the Profit Squeeze*, Harmondsworth: Penguin.
Gordon, R. (2012), 'Is US Economic Growth Over? Faltering Innovation Confronts Six Headwinds', Policy Insight No. 63, September, Washington, DC: Center for Economic Policy Research.
Hobsbawm, E. (1968), *Industry and Empire*, Harmondsworth: Penguin.
Hobson, J.A. ([1902] 1965), *Imperialism: A Study*, Ann Arbor, MI: University of Michigan Press.

Howard, M.C. and J.E. King (1989), *A History of Marxian Economics*, Volume I, Basingstoke: Macmillan.
Howard, M.C. and J.E. King (1992), *A History of Marxian Economics*, Volume II, Basingstoke: Macmillan.
Hudson, M. ([1977] 2003), *Global Fracture*, London: Pluto Press.
Hutton, W. (1995), *The State We're In*, London: Jonathan Cape.
Keynes, J.M. ([1936] 1967), *General Theory of Employment, Interest and Money*, London: Macmillan.
Kliman, A. (2007), *Reclaiming Marx's Capital: A Refutation of the Myth of Inconsistency*, Lanham, MD: Lexington Books.
Krugman, P. (2012), *New York Times*, blog, 16 November, accessed 18 March 2014 at http://krugman.blogs.nytimes.com/2013/11/16/secular-stagnation-coal mines-bubbles-and-larry-summers/?_php=true&_type=blogs&_r=0.
Lapavitsas, C. (2009), 'Financialised Capitalism: Crisis and Financial Expropriation', *Historical Materialism*, 17(2), 114–148.
Lipietz, A. (1985), *The Enchanted World: Inflation, Credit and the World Crisis*, London: Verso.
Livingston, J. (2009), 'Their Great Depression and Ours', *Challenge*, 52(3), 34–51.
Maddison, Angus (2006), *The World Economy*, 2 vols, Paris: OECD Publishing.
Mandel, E. ([1962] 1968), *Marxist Economic Theory*, London: New Left Books.
Mandel, E. (1970), *Europe versus America? Contradictions of Imperialism*, London: New Left Books.
Mandel, E. (1972), *Late Capitalism*, London: New Left Books.
Mandel, E. (1981), 'Introduction', Karl Marx, *Capital*, Vol. III, London: Penguin.
Marx, K. ([1867] 1977), *Capital*, Vol. I, London: Penguin.
Marx, K. ([1894] 1981), *Capital*, Vol. III, London: Penguin.
Marx, K. (1969), *Theories of Surplus Value*, Vol. I., London: Lawrence & Wishart.
McKinsey Global Institute (2013), 'Financial Globalization: Retreat or Reset?', available at http://www.mckinsey.com/insights/global_capital_markets/financial_globalization.
Meek, R. (1973), *Studies in the Labour Theory of Value*, 2nd edn, London: Lawrence & Wishart.
Mikuni, A. and R.T. Murphy (2003), *Japan's Policy Trap*, Washington, DC: Brookings Institution.
Murphy, C. (1984), *The Emergence of the NIEO Ideology*, Boulder, CO: Westview.
Nasser, A. (2013), 'Against Investment-Driven Growth: The Economics of Over-Ripe Capitalism', *CounterPunch*, 3–5 May.
Nasser, A. (forthcoming), *United States of Emergency: American Capitalism and its Crises*, London: Pluto Press.
Patnaik, P. (2009), *The Value of Money*, New York: Columbia University Press.
Rosenberg, J. (2000), *The Follies of Globalisation Theory: Polemical Essays*, London: Verso.
Shaikh, A (1978), 'An Introduction to the History of Crisis Theories', US Capitalism in Crisis, New York: URPE.
Summers, L. (2013), Speech at the IMF's Fourteenth Annual Research Conference in Honor of Stanley Fischer, 8 November, accessed 18 March 2014 at http://larrysummers.com/imf-fourteenth-annual-research-conference-in-honor-of-stanley-fischer/.
Sweezy, P.M. (1970), *The Theory of Capitalist Development: Principles of Marxian Political Theory*, New York: Monthly Review Press.

Van der Pijl, K. (2006a), *Global Rivalries from the Cold War to Iraq*, London: Pluto Press.
Van der Pijl, K. (2006b), 'A Lockean Europe', *New Left Review*, 31(January–February), 9–37.
Wallerstein, I. (1974), *The Modern World-System: Studies in Social Discontinuity*, New York: Academic Press.
Wallerstein, I. (1976), *The Modern World-System: Capitalist Agriculture and the Origins of the European World-Economy in the Sixteenth Century*, New York: Academic Press.
Woo-Cumings, M. (ed.) (1999), *The Developmental State*, Ithaca, NY: Cornell University Press.
Zarembka, P. (2002), 'Rosa Luxemburg's *Accumulation of Capital*: Critics Try to Bury the Message', *Research in Political Economy*, 21, 3–45.

9. The systemic failings in framing neoliberal social policy

Ben Fine[1]

The main purpose of this chapter is to argue that the welfare regime approach (WRA) to social policy is, as I put it, well past its use-by date. There is obviously some distance between this aim and interrogating whether the current economic crisis is systemic or not in some broader sense. However, part and parcel of the current crisis is how scholarship, ideology and policy respond to it. In casting aside the WRA, I will argue that its warranted demise, although almost certainly it will continue its dominance over social policy scholarship, is part and parcel and a reflection of the systemic nature of the crisis. Why this should be so in general terms is laid out in the remainder of this introduction. Subsequently, I offer a critical overview of the WRA, highlighting its undue and inappropriate reliance on ill-fitting ideal types; its inappropriate extension in application in time and place beyond both developed countries and the post-war boom and its most immediate aftermath (for both of which it is arguably also more or less analytically inappropriate); its increasingly casual approach to theory and convergence towards mainstream thinking; and its failures in capacity to address policy alternatives. These devastating weaknesses of the WRA derive primarily from its failure to incorporate a full understanding of neoliberalism in general and of the financialization at its heart in particular. Born out of the post-war boom and the early clash of its conditions with neoliberalism, the WRA has failed to move on even though it has consolidated its position as the leading way in which to understand social policy. As a result, as taken up in the concluding remarks, just as paralysis in the discipline of economics can be taken as an index of the systemic nature of the current crisis (being exposed as both inadequate and unable to change), so the same is exposed as applied to WRA and social policy.

But what of the crisis itself? The most obvious way in which to view the current global crisis is in terms of its being a crisis of neoliberalism. Not only has the economy dramatically failed, but it has done so on the basis of those markets most closely associated with the neoliberal project, those of finance. The failure has also witnessed extraordinarily extensive state intervention to support financial markets, quite apart from rescuing particular financial institutions themselves. Such a perspective, however, raises more questions than it answers. What exactly is the nature of neoliberalism? What is its relationship to finance? Does the current crisis represent a crisis within or of neoliberalism? And what is the relationship between the ideologies and policy practices of neoliberalism?

To address these questions appropriately is far from easy, not least because positions must be adopted, implicitly, unwittingly or otherwise, on a number of deeper issues, including what constitutes one period of capitalism as opposed to another and what signals transition from one period to another. For the purposes of this chapter, I confine myself to a minimally asserted posture on these, related and some other issues.[2]

First, what distinguishes one period of capitalism from another primarily concerns the way in which capital is accumulated and restructured. For example, in the post-war boom, this occurred through a combination of extensive state intervention, internationalization of production and their interaction.

Second, such economic restructuring is closely associated with social restructuring (and economic and social reproduction). Again, taking the post-war boom as illustration, this is marked by the rise of the welfare state in diverse form and content within and across countries.

Third, in these respects, neoliberalism does signify a separate stage of development, one that is marked by the heavy and increasing role of finance in both economic and social restructuring. This is reflected most obviously in the phenomenal rise of financial markets themselves and also their influence on how economic restructuring takes place, together with the increasing role of finance in social reproduction, not least with privatization of public services, and so on.

Fourth, this signifies that financialization is at the heart of neoliberalism, and is what has sustained it over three decades (as opposed to temporary and contingent interventions on behalf of finance). Neoliberalism promotes financialization, and financialization impacts directly and indirectly on economic and social restructuring and reproduction. Significantly, precisely because of this, financialization has been understood in many different, often complementary rather than competing, ways, since the empirical forms that it takes, and the influences that it exerts, are so extensive.

Fifth, the growth and influence of finance (and financialization) are extremely uneven geographically and sectorally. In addition, not least because neoliberalism is not reducible to financialization, that unevenness is intensified in terms of how finance is incorporated into economic and social restructuring. It follows that far from being homogenizing, and heterogeneity being evidence against its existence, neoliberalism by its nature is highly variegated.

Sixth, this implies that, whilst neoliberalism is to be associated with the promotion of private capital in general and of finance in particular (usually put ideologically in terms of favouring the market over the state), there is considerable dissonance between neoliberal ideologies and neoliberal policies in practice, with the latter contingent upon considerable state intervention (and necessarily so), as sharply revealed by, but not originating with, the crisis.

Seventh, two broad and roughly delineated phases of neoliberalism can be discerned. The first ran from the mid-1970s for two decades and, essentially, as 'shock therapy', promoted private capital by 'rolling back', or rather transforming, the state with limited regard for consequential dysfunctions. Such, in developmental terms, is the era of the Washington Consensus. The second phase, continuing through the current crisis, does seek to place more emphasis on 'rolling out' the state, if in more market-friendly forms, to address the dysfunctions that have accrued out of the first phase, and the struggles over them, whilst continuing to sustain financialization itself. Such is the nature of the post-Washington Consensus and Third Wayism as the scholarly and ideological forms of neoliberalism in its second phase.

Now, each of these perspectives could itself command a chapter of its own, to elaborate and justify. And the course of the crisis makes demands of its own in terms of squaring off the imperatives of financialization against its past and continuing dysfunctions in economic and social restructuring. What stands out in this, itself an index of systemic crisis, is the abysmal failure of mainstream policy and intellectual responses. The poverty of the dismal science has been well documented, with some degree of ineffectual *mea culpa* from within the discipline, with the International Monetary Fund (IMF) for example effectively admitting that it had not realized that finance could be macro, there is fiscal as well as monetary policy, and the latter need not be reduced to interest rate manipulation. But the same applies equally to 'micro', with no firewall between it and macro for other issues as well as for finance. Market imperfection economists are, for example, lining up to celebrate and support the minimalist return of industrial policy, by which they mean selective intervention to support private capital as opposed to systemic policies for economic and social development (e.g. Fine and Van Waeyenberge 2013).

Characteristic of such responses are two aspects. First is the more or less conscious commitment to return to some diluted form of the post-war boom, with corresponding intellectual and policy concessions to neoliberalism. Second is the failure to get to grips with the systemic transformations that have taken place since the end of the post-war boom, seeking Keynesian policies or the like even within the firmly established neoliberal period. This means in particular having failed to take account of financialization on the potential for, and impact of, their alternative policies should they, indeed, manage to become adopted.

To some degree, this reflects a misrepresentation of the causes of the post-war boom in terms of Keynesianism, possibly stretched to include welfarism. By contrast, in focusing upon economic and social restructuring through internationalization of production and state intervention, and a much more subordinated role for finance (that is, relative absence of hegemony of financialization), it is possible to see why mainstream proposals both misjudge the past and project it to the present and future as an alternative to neoliberalism. The prospects for industrial as much as macroeconomic policy rest upon a necessary if far from sufficient condition of wresting hegemony in policy-making from the deadweight of finance and the momentum of financialization, neither of which has been addressed by the momentary, knee-jerk clamour to re-regulate finance that has subsided with little trace in its wake.

This all provides background to the focus of this chapter: how (scholarly) discussion of social policy reflects the systemic nature of the crisis. No one can doubt the strains placed on social policy by neoliberalism and the crisis. Levels of unemployment, poverty, inequality and access to housing, health, education, pensions, and so on have all been hit hard, intensifying the contradictions across leaving things to the market, supporting the market to target relief, or even residualizing the hard to serve outside of the market. Initially, the response to the crisis was some expansion of social protection but this has subsequently been clawed back with a vengeance as austerity has reigned supreme (Ortiz and Cummins 2013a; see also Ortiz and Cummins 2013b; ILO 2014). But the process is highly uneven, especially for pensions, for example, where the forward march of privatization has been halted or even reversed (Saritas 2013).

To a large extent, if not on the same scale, account of such developments has been common fare for the social policy literature. Death of the welfare state, let alone episodes of austerity, have been announced and denied alongside predictions of convergence and divergence, and appeals to path dependence to explain apparent inertia in provision (or subordination to neoliberalism if otherwise). Scandinavia serves as the exemplar of the welfare state, both to be emulated and as under threat. As such perspectives have enjoyed a life almost as long as neoliberalism itself, they have been repeatedly applied without sufficient regard to the transformations in capitalism from which they derive. Although much is made of the globalization-neoliberalism dualism, financialization (as opposed to financing and access to resources) has been notably absent from social policy discourse (with housing and pensions as understandable exceptions).

This is especially true of the WRA, that stands, and has increasingly stood, head and shoulders above other approaches in the social policy literature for more than 20 years, with little or no sign of abatement of its prominence. This is despite the increasing distance in its frame of analysis from the key characteristics of neoliberalism and, as a consequence, indicative of the systemic nature of the crisis in the realm of scholarship.

9.1 FROM WELFARE REGIMENTING . . .?

The most striking aspect of the recent social policy literature is the continuing presence, dominance even, of the WRA. In their 'audit' of welfare modelling, Powell and Barrientos (2011: 69) open with: 'The "welfare modelling business" . . . initially a one person firm (Esping-Andersen 1990) has become in recent years a multinational corporation' (see also Scruggs and Allan 2006: 69; Kam 2012: 108). Given this, it is unsurprising that there are considerable attractions, merits even, within the WRA. First, and most prominent, it does seek to identify, and possibly as a first step, begin to explain, diversity across different national systems of welfare provision. Second, it does so by looking at templates for the specification of provision, the different welfare regimes themselves (see below). Third, it does allow for intra- and inter-country empirical analysis of provision: what are the differences by one or more elements of provision across countries, and what are the differences within countries across different elements of provision in cases where the regimes within a country differ according to what is provided. Fourth, the WRA also readily accommodates a variety of theories, causal variables and methodologies although these are often middle-range, casual or not closely specified. Consequently, we have gained much from the WRA, which has been bountiful in organizing our understanding and knowledge of welfare provision. And, by the same token and hardly surprisingly, it has underpinned colossal programmes of research and publications over the past two decades and more.

However, despite its many positive features in these respects, there is a huge tension across the contributions collectively taken together, as well as from particular contributions that take the WRA as a critical point of departure without necessarily breaking with it. The need to break with the WRA is the conclusion drawn here. To put it polemically, whatever purposes the WRA has served in the past, it has long since passed its use-by date. Or, in understanding the continuing evolution of welfare provision, it is only with a huge sense of relief that we should unburden ourselves by discarding the baggage of tyranny that goes with the WRA. I am not the first to be drawn to this drastic solution. For Bambra (2005: 53–54):

> Five substantive critiques of this [WRA] typology have emerged: the range of countries and number of regime types; the methodology used; the usefulness of the regime concept; the analytical dominance of income maintenance schemes over welfare services; and the omission of gender in the analysis . . . Some assert that a distinctive fourth type of welfare state regime is emerging in the countries of the Latin rim of the European Union (Spain, Portugal, Greece and to a lesser extent Italy) and [some] argue that the UK, Australia and New Zealand constitute another 'radical' fourth type of welfare state regime . . . Esping-Andersen's methodology has been widely critiqued . . . and the use of cluster analysis has also suggested that there could be four or five 'worlds of welfare' . . . the validity of the regimes concept itself [has been questioned], asserting that instead of internal policy homogeneity or cohesion, welfare states and welfare regimes exhibit significant variation across different areas of provision. Esping-Andersen's decision to organize the principle of classification around the study of cash benefit programs, ignoring the fact that welfare states are also about the actual delivery of services, has also been a source of contention . . . Feminist commentators . . . have offered the most extensive critique, arguing that Esping-Andersen's 'three worlds of welfare' typology is deeply flawed because it marginalizes women.

Letting go, however, is not purely a negative exercise, given the positive aspects attached to the WRA. As a result, its critical rejection allows for the constituent parts and ethos of alternatives to be identified. I deal with a number of such issues in turn.

First, it is apparent that the more the WRA is applied, the more it is found to be inadequate. But corresponding criticism, and this is crucial, has not led in practice to the rejection of the WRA, but its extension, in part explaining its increasingly heavy and continuing presence as it absorbs criticism. Thus, the most favoured sort of contribution to the literature is through empirical case study, ranging across the grand looking at, or for, regimes as a whole for greater or smaller numbers of countries, to focusing upon particular programmes within particular countries. As is well known, Esping-Andersen initially proposed three ideal types of welfare regimes: the Scandinavian social democratic, the Bismarckian corporatist-statist and the Anglo-Saxon liberal. These, though, have long been supplemented by a proliferating set of extras to accommodate empirical diversity. There has been the Southern European or Mediterranean welfare model,[3] with emphasis on familial provision, to which there has been added a Middle Eastern regime (or even as many as five of them; Jawad and Yakut-Cakar 2010) as well as Latin American and East Asian ideal types. Varieties of cluster analyses give rise to varieties of outcomes, with five regimes for Bambra (2007) looking at defamilization, five also for Kuitto (2011) investigating varieties of cash transfers, and four ways of supporting the working-aged for Pfeifer (2012) across 14 European countries. Equally, it is now acknowledged that there is not a one-to-one relationship between countries and regimes, with an attempted resolution through appeal to hybrids. Thus, for Aybars and Tsarouhas (2010: 761), 'The picture painted above is mixed and points to the "hybrid" character of the Turkish welfare regime, illustrating important features of both the Middle Eastern and Southern European welfare models, but remaining an outlier to both in certain respects.'[4] And, as Mätzke and Ostner (2010: 390) observe, '"hybridization" increases once family policies are studied comparatively . . . and even more so when change is taken into account – rendering comparisons across Esping-Andersen's "worlds" problematic'.[5]

Much the same applies to the transition economies of Eastern Europe, whose existence, of course, post-dates the WRA, with Greve (2009: 103) seeing:

> the welfare states in Eastern Europe moving very much towards a more liberalistic approach, but at the same time maintaining in principle a universal approach in relation to health care. The mix between public and private is perhaps thus not dependent on the welfare state type or society we are looking at, but instead more dependent on the welfare sector we look into.

Similar conclusions arise for country- and/or sector-specific regime studies with ideal types proving elusive, as with Willemse and de Beer (2012: 105), for whom, across 19 developed Western countries:

> by applying the central concepts of welfare state analysis of decommodification and stratification, as proposed by Esping-Andersen, to the field of higher education . . . We conclude that including higher education in comparative welfare states analysis might result in a less clear-cut categorization of welfare regimes than when the analysis is restricted to social protection and labor market policies.

And, for Berggren et al. (2010: 409–410), in the context of care management in a study of provision for the elderly and psychiatric disabled in Sweden, 'A move from "ideal types construction" to "real types descriptions" in positioning and understanding welfare state differences and similarities would be fruitful'. Also this study allows for variation within national provision according to how it is decentralized to the local, as is confirmed by Künzel (2012: 4) for whom, for minimum income policies across France and Germany: 'At the local level, however, we have discovered very different outcomes of active inclusion reforms, ranging from market-oriented, integrated and participatory variants of active inclusion to the persistence of standardized benefits.' More broadly, Wendt (2009) finds that there is no reason for health regimes to match with welfare regimes, especially as more countries are taken into account as well as in addressing the specificities of health itself (see also Kam 2012: 108).

In short, as summarized by Powell and Barrientos:

> Regimes are broader than individual programmes such as pensions, and broader than the welfare state . . . A number of authors have attempted to apply Esping-Andersen's typology to specific programmes, or groups of programmes . . . Their findings are mixed. Some find the welfare regime typology works, while others find it does not . . . Britain – supposedly the residualist welfare state – had the largest social rented sector; French economic policy was the most orthodoxly neo-liberal; and corporatist Germany had gone furthest in privatizing social housing . . . focus on 'social assistance regimes' or 'poverty regimes' . . . find only a limited relationship to wider welfare regimes . . . welfare regimes tend to be based on transfers rather than services, but the relationship between them is far from clear. Moreover, there are important differences between the patterns of health and social care . . . welfare states are composed of different approaches to different social risk, and the approach to each social risk is often 'hybrid'. (Powell and Barrientos 2011: 75; see also Kasza 2006: 153)

Proliferating hybrids of proliferating regimes increasingly suggests a chaotic classificatory scheme.[6]

9.2 THROUGH SCOPE OF APPLICATION . . .

This is especially so when the WRA is extended to developing countries, as with Sharkh and Gough (2010: 28) for which three critical issues are explicitly raised: the WRA's scope of application, its theory, and its policy implications. Consider each in turn. Initially, especially in light of its subsequent coverage, the scope of application of the WRA was both ambitious (categorizing different welfare states as a whole) and, paradoxically, relatively limited in two significant aspects. For the latter, on the one hand, it was confined to (a sample of) developed countries. On the other hand, although a product of the neoliberal era by timing (early 1990s), its origins are heavily marked by the lingering influences of the conditions of the post-war boom and its association with Keynesian welfarism, however this might be interpreted. As a result, there is at least an implicit presumption that the welfare states or regimes concerned are at a mature stage, rather than being in the process of being established, and in the context of advanced capitalist economies in which Keynesianism, and so on, still appears to be a viable intellectual and policy option. Inevitably, this places considerable logical and historical limitations on the scope of applicability of the WRA irrespective of its merits otherwise for understanding the conditions that have spawned it and which have long been in the process of being dissolved. The WRA is confined, initially and however consciously, to those advanced societies that have benefited from the post-war boom even if subsequently already deeply into the period of neoliberalism. And scholarly ethos at the time the WRA emerges does remain in major part focused on explaining relatively minor differences in performance across otherwise similarly (potentially) expanding economies; especially for growth, with Germany and Japan to the fore for example, if also for welfare provision where Scandinavia is the exemplar.

Most obviously, in such societies average incomes are high, formal employment and working conditions are normal, and unemployment is variable but contained. There will be a modern industrial sector, possibly in relative decline in terms of weight of economic activity, and long-established and well-functioning (government) bureaucracies and institutions. The family of welfare regimes in such narrowly delimited circumstances will only be challenged to discern and categorize differences of a minor degree, compared to if they were spread wider over both historical (long before and longer after the post-war boom) and logical (different stages of development) canvases.

In addition, as already indicated in passing, the WRA was primarily focused upon income transfers as opposed to welfare services (something equally more prominent in the sorts of societies under consideration at a particular stage in their development). Now, in retrospect, with the hindsight both of a further two decades of neoliberalism and the extensive application of the WRA to a range of other societies, it is scarcely surprising that it should flounder on the relatively slender foundations upon which it was constructed. Just why should the specific approach to select welfare states around the period of the post-war boom be of general applicability to other times, places and programmes?

Indeed, the expansive scope of the WRA is indicative of a (narrow) Eurocentric conceptual imperialism (see Izuhara 2013; Walker and Wong 2013; Wong 2013; Chang and Ku 2013), in which other countries are illegitimately seen through its prism with modifications to suit where the fit is poor, blurred or even more or less non-existent. And the ultimate option remains to add another ideal type. This is itself indicative of the poverty of theory attached to the WRA which should, at least in principle, delimit its historical and logical scope of application (rather than bordering on the universal in its substance); is the theory suitable for other societies than those that gave it birth and for welfare programmes at other points in world history and national stages of development?

9.3 AND THEORETICAL MALAISE . . .

Such considerations are a reflection of a deeper theoretical malaise across the welfare regime approach. As put by Arts and Gelissen (2002: 155) more than a decade ago, 'A better formulation of the theory on which it is based deserves priority'. This is amply confirmed by the more recent review of Powell and Barrientos (2011: 81):

> The main conclusion of the article is that the 'welfare modelling business' requires investment in its more neglected elements. There has been a great deal of attention on the empirical validity of Esping-Andersen's *Three Worlds*. However, apart from the feminist critique and de-familization, the conceptual and theoretical aspects which the typology was expected to facilitate remain under-developed. It is a little ironic that a work aiming to lay bare the 'theoretical substance of welfare states' (Esping-Andersen 1990: 19) has led to a largely atheoretical debate.

To some extent, then, this theoretical deficiency is a reflection of the neglect of Esping-Andersen's original intentions concerning theoretical scrutiny of the role of resources and power as the structural underpinnings for factors such as decommodification and stratification, and how these give rise to more or less complex outcomes across ideal types of welfare regimes. Such reflect the previously delineated intellectual origins of the WRA in the conditions of the post-war boom, and the potentially progressive roles played by an industrial working class and its organizations, politics and ethos. Subsequently, even for the latter, specification of a proliferation of regime types has taken precedence over explaining and understanding their nature, with more or less casual appeal to a range of other considerations and categorizations such as hybrids, gender, decommodification and defamilization.

There are a number of issues involved here. One is whether whatever theory is present is appropriate to its object of study: specifying and understanding the provision of welfare, presumably across some form of geographically, historically and logically delimited application (associated with capitalist development). Here, there will be a need to finesse the general (capitalism), the historical (over what period and how characterized) and the specific (provision of what, to whom, through what mechanisms, and so on). The initial power-resources hypothesis deployed by Esping-Andersen is arguably inadequate for purpose along a number of dimensions, not least because it is universal in method (all societies deploy power and resources), fails to address explicitly the nature and period of capitalism under consideration (although, as already argued, it is itself very much a product of the Keynesian period, or just beyond into its decline), and equally fails to (have the potential to) fill the gap between the more abstract theoretical considerations and the chain of causation linking these to outcomes (see the third point in section 9.4 below).

Another issue is that the theory underpinning the WRA has not remained static. Indeed, as observed, it has stagnated or even decayed in deference to, or even because of the strain imposed by, empirical case studies involving regime classification and extension. Reference to power and resources as explanatory factors are increasingly, even absolutely, notable for their absence. This decline might reflect an unconscious response to the rise of neoliberalism and a corresponding shift in balance, composition and organization of forces across and within capital and labour. Thus, the theory underpinning the WRA may well be a victim of its own limitations, the weight of empirical studies in its image, and the demise of the Keynesian period that inspired it.

With this decline and shift in WRA theory, it would, of course, be unduly harsh to blame such developments in the literature in this regard on Esping-Andersen himself. He can hardly be held responsible for his followers. But nor would this be entirely a case of blaming the entirely innocent victim. As argued as early as Fine (2002), Esping-Andersen himself seems to have abandoned the power-resources theory for flirtation with, if not embrace of, mainstream concepts such as collective risk management and market failures. Significantly, Esping-Andersen (1999: 36) heads a section, 'The Foundations of Welfare Regimes: Risk Management', with opening sentence, 'social policy means public management of social risks'. Compare this with his classic text Esping-Andersen (1990: 11) for which: 'The central question, not only for Marxism but for the entire contemporary debate on the welfare state, is whether, and under what conditions, the class divisions and social inequalities produced under capitalism can be undone by parliamentary democracy.'

In his subsequent work, *The Incomplete Revolution* (Esping Andersen 2009: 174), he informs us that, 'Some years ago I solemnly promised to myself that I would from then on dedicate my research and writing to anything but the welfare state'. Here, as previously, he has commendably taken the criticism of neglect of gender considerations to heart, redefining welfare provision in terms of household life chances from cradle to grave, especially emphasizing early years of life and, 'to conclude [literally the end of the book], if the welfare state can help accelerate the revolution of women's roles, we will probably also harvest major equality and efficiency gains across the board'. Otherwise the volume is marked by: (1) continuing identification of ideal types (associated with gender roles and their broader economic and social situation and life chances) not least through a traditional male breadwinner model set against defamilialization and masculinization of women as they engage in work; (2) ironically light of ideal types, attention to the proliferation and diversity of living arrangements and familial choices; and (3) the taking of Gary Becker and Talcott Parsons as points of departure and yet incorporation of casual reference to multiple equilibria, Pareto efficiency, the knowledge economy, inequality and homogamy, human capital, social investment, information failure, and the troika of family, market and government. This might be thought not so much to be completing an intellectual revolution as consolidating a counter-revolution (see also Powell and Barrientos 2011: 74).

9.4 . . .TO POLICY

But, third, what then of the policy implications of the WRA that are, for example, claimed in principle by Sharkh and Gough, not least for developing countries? On this, across the literature, there is primarily a stunning, if unobserved, silence (as opposed to identifying different policies and outcomes attached to regimes). This is for good reason despite what I suspect is, for most who contribute to the literature without a neoliberal predisposition, an inclination to favour expanded welfare provision through the state and the Scandinavian levels and forms of provision. The problem is that the WRA almost inevitably offers little by way of policy advice, for two compelling and complementary reasons. On the one hand, in welfare as in many other things (even crime and other thriller fiction these days), we all want to be Scandinavian. But either the WRA offers no advice on how to transition from one regime to another in view of lack of theory, or, what theory there is, such as appeal to power and resources, suggests that transitions are pre-empted by underlying determinants such as own history, and organization and balance of class or other forces and their corresponding politics and ethos. So, 'become like Sweden', is either unhelpful or infeasible. On the other hand, with welfare regimes as ideal types, whether grounded in underlying power and resources or not, there is little scope for the intermediate relations, processes, structures, agencies and ideational factors that influence, if not determine, policy in detail to be incorporated into the analysis. In short, the WRA essentially precludes policy considerations at the levels both of grand regime determination and (passage to) policy and outcomes in detail.

These observations are borne out to a large degree by Jensen (2011a) who highlights the extent to which the WRA has been based upon income transfers as opposed to welfare services, and how much more challenging is broadening the approach from concentration on pensions and social security. More broadly, what work there is on welfare services tends to fall into three categories: (1) programme-specific, drawing on health care, child care or education, for example; (2) typologies to assess whether services fall into welfare regimes in cross-country comparisons; and (3) attempts to gauge whether or not there are close relations between the sorts of income transfers that occur and the provision of welfare services. Whilst those under (1) tend to overlook broader influences and implications, those under (2) and (3) beg the question of why the same ideal types should prevail, or be determined by the same factors, for income transfers as for welfare services.

Jensen supports this conclusion by drawing upon the idea that a broader set of constituencies are now involved in making welfare policy than a stereotyped strengthening of labour movements and left-wing governments (and the reformist march to some form of socialism or, at least, social democracy perceived to be characteristic of the now long-since evaporated post-war boom). Moreover, this is not just different interests but differently and more narrowly focused. Indeed:

> Two points should be noted here. First, the policy development of individual welfare programmes is difficult to understand by relying on macro-level factors, such as the power of the left. Much more important is the strength of sector-level interest groups. Second, the strength of these sector-level interest groups may vary considerably from one sector to the next . . . this entails that it becomes difficult to talk of *the* welfare state in a country because the policy dynamic is likely to be very different in different welfare programmes. The within-country variation is, in other words, likely to be as great as, or greater than, the between-country variation. (Jensen 2011a: 409)

More specifically, Jensen argues that welfare services are distinct from income transfers because they involve provision, 'the production mode', that 'entails a transformation of the input (money) into an output (the actual in-kind service)'. As a result, vested interests are created in the process of provision itself and, in addition, this tends to induce both the participation of the state and more complex conflicts over the levels and forms of provision. Indeed, 'The effect of these different production modes is quite dramatic' (ibid. 410), with reference made to vested, possibly conservative, interests of those attached to the processes of provision as opposed to macro-goals and ideational factors around equality, and so on. In short, Jensen (2011a: 411) concludes: 'The welfare service component is tricky to analyse compared with the transfer component, not least because the individual services constituting this component are of such varied quality. Healthcare, education and social care are hugely different fields characterized by very different policy dynamics.'

There is much to commend in this conclusion but it suffers from being derived from a dependence upon drawing the distinction between welfare as income transfers and as services. This is not simply or primarily because there are comparable difficulties for the WRA for both, but also because that one is produced and other is not, in some sense, is insufficient in explaining why welfare provision as a whole is differentiated into whether it is services or not. State involvement, vested sectoral interests and processes of provision are equally applicable to income transfers. This is, for example, especially and increasingly obvious in the case of pensions, and more generally where public provision might involve private agencies (subcontracting the assessment for disability, housing or other benefits, for example) (see also Jensen 2011b). In short, income transfers as much as welfare services equally 'are hugely different fields characterized by very different policy dynamics'.

9.5 CONCLUDING REMARKS

From the review of the WRA, the following conclusions can be drawn:

1. The WRA was never appropriate for addressing social policy because of its failings in providing a political economy of capitalism and its implications for economic and social reproduction.
2. As a result, its empirical limitations have been exposed in failing to fit highly diverse patterns of social policy by place and programme, even within what has been an ever-expanding set of ideal types within its frame of reference.
3. Whatever its applicability in explaining social policy in the delimited context of developed countries in, or emerging from, the post-war boom, the WRA's relevance has been undermined by the transformations wrought by neoliberalism, and especially the direct and indirect, if variegated, influence of financialization on forms and content of provision and on policy-making processes and delivery.
4. Alternatives to the WRA, in both analysing social policy and proposing alternatives, require a political economy of neoliberalism, an acknowledgement of its dependence on financialization, and how these lead to variegated outcomes over time, place and programme. This might best be achieved by examining the factors underpinning individual programmes in the context of neoliberal economic and social reproduction, through attention to the housing system, the pension system, the health, education and social security systems, and so on, in their specific contexts. In the case of developing economies, this might best be achieved through combining the notion and aim of a developmental welfare state with that of a public sector system of provision.

The purpose of this chapter has not, however, been to carry this analytical and policy programme forward (Fine 2014a). Rather, it has been to speculate on how the literature on social policy does itself reflect the systemic nature of the current crisis. It has, for example, become trite to observe that, in contrast to the 1930s, there is nothing equivalent today to the Keynesian revolution in (macro)economics to inspire confidence that economic prosperity can be restored. The Keynesian revolution did not, however, underpin the post-war boom which, as suggested earlier, reflected particular forms of global, economic and social restructuring in which the state played a major role over and beyond, and outweighing, manipulation of effective demand. Indeed, it is conventional wisdom amongst scholars that the Keynesian revolution, that is, the IS/LM (investment/saving/liquidity preference/money supply) approach, has had little overlap with Keynes's own ideas (although these were themselves seriously misleading in divorcing macroeconomics from the determinants of long-run economic performance). Rather, the Keynesian revolution, whatever its dissonances with the realities of the post-war boom, did provide the frame within which corresponding policies could be discussed and promoted.

Much the same is true of the monetarist counter-revolution and its ultimate trajectory to the new consensus macroeconomics that has had as little contact with the realities of the economy (and policy), as it allowed these realities and policy-making to evolve under the smokescreen of these perspectives. In this respect, the systemic nature of the current crisis is revealed both in the helplessness with which traditional scholarship confronts it and, in contrast to the Great Depression and Keynesianism, as well as the breakdown in the post-war boom and monetarist counter-revolution, the apparent lack of any mainstream alternatives on the horizon. It follows from the historical record that systemic crisis can be reflected either in breakdown and displacement of, or inertia in, scholarly conventional wisdom.

A parallel trajectory of inertia marks the social policy literature in general and the WRA in particular in the face of the current crisis. Yet, unlike economics, it has not been discredited by its own practitioners nor in popular discourse. Whilst a product of the Keynesian and welfarist perspectives, and their confrontation with an emerging neoliberalism, it has primarily remained rooted in its original frames of reference with insufficient regard for the erosion of the corresponding conditions that prompted it. However well these themselves may have been understood, the systemic nature of the current global crisis has cruelly exposed the inabilities of the WRA to understand the variegated nature of neoliberal social policy, itself reflecting the systemic nature of the neoliberal period and its crisis of economic and social restructuring.

But possibly the most significant lesson to derive from the continuing health of the WRA through the crisis is that it is not enough for intellectual opposition to turn the tide of neoliberal policy. After all, the WRA essentially favours the return of some form of Keynesian and Scandinavian welfarism. It has no influence in practice; a depressing state of affairs for those who consider that a reformed economics, still so far off the agenda, could itself bring about major policy change in the absence of a change in the balance of social forces.

NOTES

1. This chapter draws heavily on a section of Fine (2014b).
2. I have written extensively on these and the related issues that follow: Fine (2007, 2009, 2010, 2011, 2012a, 2012b, 2013, 2014a, 2014b) and Fine and Hall (2012), for example.
3. For a pot pourri of welfare regimes: Gal (2010), MacGregor (2013), Mayes and Mustaffa (2013), Choi (2013), Kasza (2006) and Midgley and Piachaud (2013).
4. See also Gal and Greve (2010: 657), and van Hooren and Becker (2012) for hybrid varieties for child care as opposed to elderly care in Netherlands.
5. As an alternative fix to hybrids (if retaining proliferation of regimes), Hudson and Kühner (2012) add an East Asian productive regime but limit their ambitions to 'fuzzy' fits, or fuzzy set ideal type analysis (FSITA).
6. For contributions that continue to support the WRA despite their own evidence to the contrary (of various sorts), see Kuitto (2011), Kersbergen (2013), Ferragina and Seeleib-Kaiser (2011), Franzoni and Voorend (2009, 2011), Kammer et al. (2012), Gough and Sharkh (2011) and Sharkh and Gough (2010).

REFERENCES

Arts, W. and J. Gelissen (2002), 'Three Worlds of Welfare Capitalism or More? A State-of-the-Art Report', *Journal of European Social Policy*, 12(2), 137–158.

Aybars, A. and D. Tsarouhas (2010), 'Straddling Two Continents: Social Policy and Welfare Politics in Turkey', *Social Policy and Administration*, 44(6), 746–763.

Bambra, C. (2005), 'Health Status and the Worlds of Welfare', *Social Policy and Society*, 5(1), 53–62.

Bambra, C. (2007), 'Defamilisation and Welfare State Regimes: A Cluster Analysis', *International Journal of Social Welfare*, 16(4), 326–338.

Berggren, U., S. Blomberg and J. Petersson (2010), 'Traits of a Representative Welfare State: The Swedish Example', *International Journal of Social Welfare*, 19(4), 402–411.

Chang, Y. and Y. Ku (2013), 'Social Policy and its Implications to Structural Shifts: A Comparison between Taiwan and Korea in the Colonial Era', in M. Izuhara (ed.), *Handbook on East Asian Social Policy*, Cheltenham, UK and Northampton, MA, USA: Edward Elgar.

Choi, Y. (2013), 'Developmentalism and Productivism in East Asian Welfare Regimes', in M. Izuhara (ed.), *Handbook on East Asian Social Policy*, Cheltenham, UK and Northampton, MA, USA: Edward Elgar.

Esping-Andersen, G. (1990), *The Three Worlds of Welfare Capitalism*, Princeton, NJ: Princeton University Press.

Esping-Andersen, G. (1999), *Social Foundations of Postindustrial Economies*, Oxford: Oxford University Press.

Esping-Andersen, G. (2009), *The Incomplete Revolution*, Oxford: Polity Press.

Ferragina, E. and M. Seeleib-Kaiser (2011), 'Welfare Regime Debate: Past, Present, Futures?', *Policy and Politics*, 39(4), 583–611.

Fine, B. (2002), *The World of Consumption: The Cultural and Material Revisited*, London: Routledge.

Fine, B. (2007), 'Financialisation, Poverty, and Marxist Political Economy', paper prepared for Poverty and Capital Conference, 2–4 July, University of Manchester, accessed 26 February 2015 at http://eprints.soas.ac.uk/5685/.

Fine, B. (2009), 'Social Policy and the Crisis of Neo-liberalism', prepared for Conference on The Crisis of Neo-Liberalism in India: Challenges and Alternatives, Tata Institute of Social Sciences (TISS) Mumbai and International Development Economics Associates (IDEAs), 13–15 March, accessed 26 February 2015 at http://www.networkideas.org/ideasact/jan09/PDF/Fine.pdf.

Fine, B. (2010), 'Locating Financialisation', *Historical Materialism*, 18(2), 97–116.

Fine, B. (2011), 'Locating the Developmental State and Industrial and Social Policy after the Crisis', UNCTAD, *The Least Developed Countries Report 2011: The Potential Role of South–South Cooperation for Inclusive and Sustainable Development*, Background Paper no. 3, accessed 26 February 2015 at http://www.unctad.org/Sections/ldc_dir/docs/ldcr2011_Fine_en.pdf.

Fine, B. (2012a), 'Neo-liberalism in Retrospect? – It's Financialisation, Stupid', in K-S. Chang, B. Fine and L. Weiss (eds), *Developmental Politics in Transition: The Neoliberal Era and Beyond*, Basingstoke: Palgrave Macmillan.

Fine, B. (2012b), 'Financialisation and Social Policy', in P. Utting, S. Razavi and R. Buchholz (eds), *Global Crisis and Transformative Social Change*, London: Palgrave Macmillan.

Fine, B. (2013), 'Towards a Material Culture of Financialisation', Fessud Working Paper Series, no. 15, accessed 26 February 2015 at http://fessud.eu/wp-content/uploads/2013/04/Towards-a-Material-Culture-of-Financialisation-FESSUD-Working-Paper-15.pdf.

Fine, B. (2014a), 'Financialisation from a Marxist Perspective', *International Journal of Political Economy*, 42(4), 47–66.

Fine, B. (2014b), 'The Continuing Enigmas of Social Policy', prepared for the UNRISD project on Towards Universal Social Security in Emerging Economies, UNRISD Working Paper 2014–10, June, accessed 26 February 2015 at http://www.unrisd.org/Fine.

Fine, B. and D. Hall (2012), 'Terrains of Neoliberalism: Constraints and Opportunities for Alternative Models of Service Delivery', in D. McDonald and G. Ruiters (eds), *Alternatives to Privatization: Exploring Non-Commercial Service Delivery Options in the Global South*, London: Routledge and Cape Town: HSRC Press, accessed 26 February 2015 at http://www.hsrcpress.ac.za/product.php?productid=2287&freedownload=1.

Fine, B. and E. Van Waeyenberge (2013), 'A Paradigm Shift that Never Was: Justin Lin's New Structural Economics', *Competition and Change*, 17(4), 355–371; expanded version published as 'A Paradigm Shift that Never Will Be? Justin Lin's New Structural Economics', SOAS Department of Economics Working Paper Series, no. 179.

Franzoni, J. and K. Voorend (2009), 'The Role of Distributional Coalitions in Welfare Regimes: Chile, Costa Rica and El Salvador', *Social Policy and Administration*, 43(4), 364–381.

Franzoni, J. and K. Voorend (2011), 'Actors and Ideas Behind CCTs in Chile, Costa Rica and El Salvador', *Global Social Policy*, 11(2–3), 279–298.

Gal, J. (2010), 'Is There an Extended Family of Mediterranean Welfare States?', *Journal of European Social Policy*, 20(4), 283–300.

Gal, J. and B. Greve (2010), 'Editorial Introduction', *Social Policy and Administration*, 44(6), 655–657.

Gough, I. and M. Sharkh (2011), 'Financing Welfare Regimes: Mapping Heterogeneous Revenue Structures', *International Journal of Social Welfare*, 20(3), 280–291.

Greve, B. (2009), 'Editorial Introduction', *Social Policy and Administration*, 43(2), 101–104.

Hudson, J. and S. Kühner (2012), 'Analyzing the Productive and Protective Dimensions of Welfare: Looking Beyond the OECD', *Social Policy and Administration*, 46(1), 35–60.

ILO (2014), 'Building Economic Recovery, Inclusive Development and Social Justice', World Social Protection Report 2014/15, Geneva: ILO.

Izuhara, M. (2013), 'Introduction', in M. Izuhara (ed.), *Handbook on East Asian Social Policy*, Cheltenham, UK and Northampton, MA, USA: Edward Elgar.

Jawad, R. and B. Yakut-Cakar (2010), 'Religion and Social Policy in the Middle East: The (Re)Constitution of an Old–New Partnership', *Social Policy and Administration*, 44(6), 658–672.

Jensen, C. (2011a), 'The Forgotten Half: Analysing the Politics of Welfare Services', *International Journal of Social Welfare*, 20(4), 404–412.

Jensen, C. (2011b), 'Determinants of Welfare Service Provision after the Golden Age', *International Journal of Social Welfare*, 20(2), 125–134.

Kam, Y. (2012), 'The Contributions of the Health Decommodification Typologies to the Study of the East Asian Welfare Regime', *Social Policy and Administration*, 46(1), 108–128.

Kammer, A., J. Niehues and A. Peichl (2012), 'Welfare Regimes and Welfare State Outcomes in Europe', *Journal of European Social Policy*, 22(5), 455–471.

Kasza, G. (2006), *One World of Welfare: Japan in Comparative Perspective*, Ithaca, NY: Cornell University Press.

Kersbergen, K. (2013), 'What Are the Welfare State Typologies and How Are They Useful, If at All?', in B. Greve (ed.), *The Routledge Handbook of the Welfare State*, London: Routledge.

Kuitto, K. (2011), 'More Than Just Money: Patterns of Disaggregated Welfare Expenditure in the Enlarged Europe', *Journal of European Social Policy*, 21(4), 348–364.

Künzel, S. (2012), 'The Local Dimension of Active Inclusion Policy', *Journal of European Social Policy*, 22(1), 3–16.

MacGregor, S. (2013), 'Welfare: Theoretical and Analytical Paradigms', Towards Universal Social Security in Emerging Economies: Process, Institutions and Actors, UNRISD Background Paper.

Mätzke, M. and I. Ostner (2010), 'Introduction: Change and Continuity in Recent Family Policies', *Journal of European Social Policy*, 20(5), 387–398.

Mayes, D. and Z. Mustaffa (2013), 'Social Models in the Enlarged European Model', in D. Mayes and Z. Mustaffa (eds), *The Changing Welfare State In*

Europe: The Implications for Democracy, Cheltenham, UK and Northampton, MA, USA: Edward Elgar.
Midgley, J. and D. Piachaud (eds) (2013), *Social Protection, Economic Growth And Africa*, Cheltenham, UK and Northampton, MA, USA: Edward Elgar.
Ortiz, I. and M. Cummins (2013a), 'The Age of Austerity: A Review of Public Expenditures and Adjustment Measures in 181 Countries', Initiative for Policy Dialogue and the South Centre, Working Paper, March, accessed 26 February 2015 at http://policydialogue.org/files/publications/Age_of_Austerity_Ortiz_and_Cummins.pdf.
Ortiz, I. and M. Cummins (2013b), 'Austerity Measures in Developing Countries: Public Expenditure Trends and the Risks to Children and Women', *Feminist Economics*, 19(3), 55–81.
Pfeifer, M. (2012), 'Comparing Unemployment Protection and Social Assistance in 14 European Countries: Four Worlds of Protection for People of Working Age', *International Journal of Social Welfare*, 21(1), 13–25.
Powell, M. and A. Barrientos (2011), 'An Audit of the Welfare Modelling Business', *Social Policy and Administration*, 45(1), 69–84.
Saritas, S. (2013), 'Review of the Pension Provisions in the European Union Countries', Fessud Working Paper Series, no 13, accessed 26 February 2015 at http://fessud.eu/wp-content/uploads/2013/04/REVIEW-OF-THE-PENSION-PROVISION-ACROSS-THE-EUROPEAN-UNION-COUNTRIES_13.pdf.
Scruggs, L. and J. Allan (2006), 'Welfare-State Decommodification in 18 OECD Countries: A Replication and Revision', *Journal of European Social Policy*, 16(1), 55–72.
Sharkh, M. and I. Gough (2010), 'Global Welfare Regimes: A Cluster Analysis', *Global Social Policy*, 10(1), 27–58.
van Hooren, F. and U. Becker (2012), 'One Welfare State, Two Care Regimes: Understanding Developments in Child and Elderly Care Policies in the Netherlands', *Social Policy and Administration*, 46(1), 83–107.
Walker, A. and C. Wong (2013), 'Social Protection, Governance and the Dynamics of Inclusion and Exclusion in East Asia', in M. Izuhara (ed.), *Handbook on East Asian Social Policy*, Cheltenham, UK and Northampton, MA, USA: Edward Elgar.
Wendt, C. (2009), 'Mapping European Healthcare Systems: A Comparative Analysis of Financing, Service Provision and Access to Healthcare', *Journal of European Social Policy*, 19(5), 432–45.
Willemse, N. and P. de Beer (2012), 'Three Worlds of Educational Welfare States? A Comparative Study of Higher Education Systems across Welfare States', *Journal of European Social Policy*, 22(2), 105–17.
Wong, L. (2013), 'From Apartheid to Semi-Citizenship: Chinese Migrant Workers and their Challenges to Social Policy', in M. Izuhara (ed.), *Handbook on East Asian Social Policy*, Cheltenham, UK and Northampton, MA, USA: Edward Elgar.

10. The policy-based and conjunctural causes of the 2008 crisis

Turan Subasat

This chapter argues that the 2008 international crisis was primarily caused by rapidly increased balance-of-payments disequilibrium in a number of major developed countries. Theoretically speaking, the simultaneous implementation of trade and financial sector deregulation (a lethal cocktail) often leads to persistent current account imbalances. During the 1980s and 1990s, many developing countries experienced large current account problems and subsequent crises. Staring from the 2000s, current account problems were also aggravated in a number of developed countries for several conjunctural reasons. First, after the East Asian financial crisis in 1997, many developing countries pursued policies to have large current account surpluses in order to enlarge their reserves as a precaution, and invested these funds in the United States (US) and other developed countries. Second, a rapid increase in oil prices since 1998 caused large current account surpluses in the oil exporting countries and these funds were also invested in the same developed countries. The increase in global liquidity helped to form large current account deficits in many countries. Third, due to its competitive exchange rate policy and particularly after its accession to the World Trade Organization in 2001, China had large current account surpluses which were mirrored as current account deficits in many other countries. Finally, it is often argued that Germany pursued mercantilist policies, facilitated with the creation of the euro in 1999, which led to large current account surpluses in Germany and current account deficits in the other eurozone countries. As history has repeatedly demonstrated, such persistent and large current account deficits often lead to a significant rise in financial activities and create bubble economies which are bound to collapse.

The focus on current account problems (as policy-based and conjunctural factors) does not, however, mean that the systemic factors should be overlooked. On the contrary, as evident from the US and other developed countries, the systemic factors often played a fundamentally important role. I completely agree with Kotz (Chapter 2 in this volume) that the full power of Marxism to explain capitalist crises cannot be utilized unless the particular form of capitalism at a given time and place, state policies and contingent events, are taken into account. As will be argued below, the stagnant real wages were compensated by excessive lending to workers in the US which was unsustainable even if the US had no current account deficits. The US, however, went beyond compensating low wages by domestic lending and borrowed excessively from the international markets. Therefore, both systemic and policy-based sources of crisis should be considered.[1]

Some political economists (such as Mavroudeas and Paitaridis 2014; Mavroudeas 2016) consider policy-related explanations as mainstream, as such explanations presumably do not account for the deep-rooted contradictions of capitalism. Political economists, however, often supplement their crisis theories by considering specific historical events and state policies. Policy-making is deeply enrooted in class relations and directly relevant to the political economy perspectives. This chapter, therefore, rejects the rigid separation of policy-based explanations from the systemic explanations and argues that many policy-based causes are in fact also systemic. There is a need, however, to separate policy-making from policy errors. The focus on policy errors takes an accidental view of crises and implies that crises could be prevented by learning from and circumventing mistakes. Policy-making, however, involves conscious decisions based on social interactions. Policies are social constructions influenced by complex class struggles and collaborations. Therefore, they cannot be treated as policy errors. A simultaneous deregulation of trade and financial sectors, which often led to financial bubbles and crises, for example, resulted from conscious policy choices of capitalist classes to assault workers since the 1980s (see Campbell and Bakir, Chapter 7 in this volume).

This chapter first discusses four prevalent political economy approaches to the crisis. It briefly considers the explanations that focus on the domestic causes of the crisis, such as the tendency of the rate of profit to fall (TRPF). It then deals with an important argument by Wolff (2012), which focuses on the rapid expansion of credit to workers to compensate stagnant wages in the US. After considering the European Union (EU) imperialism argument by Mavroudeas and Paitaridis (2014) in the context of the EU periphery (Greece), it finally deals with the notorious financialization arguments. Section 10.2 expands on the current account disequilibrium as the main cause of the financial crisis. Section 10.3 concludes.

10.1 PREVALENT POLITICAL ECONOMY EXPLANATIONS OF THE 2008 CRISIS

This section critically reviews four selected political economy explanations of the 2008 crisis.

10.1.1 The Domestic Sources of Crisis

Most political economy explanations of the crisis revolve exclusively around the domestic sources of crisis which include the TRPF, underconsumption, overaccumulation, productive and unproductive labor, systemic devaluing of fixed capital due to technical change and financialization. These explanations focus on the contradictory structural characteristics of the capitalist mode of production within individual countries.

The TRPF, for example, anticipates a decline in profit rates in those countries that experience rapid increase in their organic composition of capital which eventually leads to crisis. The empirical validity of TRPF in the 2008 crisis has been challenged and there is no agreement on declining profit rates in the countries that experienced financial crisis.[2] Whatever the theoretical and empirical merits of the TRPF and the other theories which focus on the domestic sources of crisis, they can hardly explain a crisis that struck many countries almost simultaneously from 2008. Such international crisis must have common causes that go beyond their country-specific circumstances.[3]

A simple analogy will be useful here. The TRPF (particularly the interpretation that treats the theory as a long-run trend rather than a cyclical tendency) is similar to dying from old age, and counteracting factors are analogous to things that extend lives. While people can prolong their lives by adopting a healthy lifestyle (such as a healthy diet and physical exercise), death is inevitable nevertheless. Although separating the underlying causes (old age) from the triggers (such as a simple flu that can kill an old person) is essential, not all deaths are due to old age. Suppose that a pathologist works in a hospital and examines two or three bodies every day to identify the causes of death, which can be many. One day, the hospital receives 20 bodies, which is very unusual. A sensible way to deal with these bodies is to consider whether there is a common cause of death rather than considering their individual conditions. For example, if the pathologist is informed that they had been in the same restaurant the night before their death, considering food poisoning first would be a sensible approach. Ignoring this possibility and focusing on the individual conditions would hardly make sense. This does not mean, however, that an individual's overall heath is unimportant since perhaps only the weak and old individuals were affected badly from food poisoning and died, whereas individuals who were strong and young survived. As argued earlier, therefore, both internal and external factors need to be investigated.

In the case of the 2008 financial crisis, a few common problems can be identified in almost all countries: rapidly increasing capital inflows, trade and current account deficits, external debt, domestic credit, household debt, housing prices, and rapid decline in saving rates, and so on. Explaining the financial crisis without regard to these common problems, and focusing only on the domestic sources of the crisis, would be a mistake. This is, however, what many political economists in effect do. While most political economy literature on the financial crisis focuses on the US and Greece, it treats an international crisis as if it can be explained by exclusively focusing on domestic problems of these individual countries.

10.1.2 Stagnant Wages in the US

Despite rapidly increasing labor productivity in the US, Wolff (2012) argued, real wages have been stagnant since the 1970s. Because low wages were compensated by the increase in lending to workers, stagnation due to demand deficiency was avoided, but this rapidly created a bubble economy which was unsustainable.

This is an important argument that focuses exclusively on a domestic source of crisis which has some relevance to the financial crisis in the US. There is little doubt that the strategy to increase profit rates without causing a demand deficiency was unsustainable regardless of the current account deficits the US faced. There are, however, two major flaws with this argument. First, not all countries that experienced a decline in real wages compared to productivity increase have encountered a similar crisis. Germany, for example, also experienced a wage compression but relied on external markets (it had a trade surplus) to compensate low domestic demand caused by low wages. As a result, unemployment declined rapidly in Germany, but it increased in the US. The US, however, went beyond compensating low wages by domestic lending (financed by the extra domestic profits) and borrowed excessively from the international markets, which Wolff (2012) fails to address. Second, crisis is not specific to countries that experienced extreme wage cuts, since countries that experienced rapid wage increases also experienced financial crisis. In other words, Wolff's explanation is useful to a limited extent in the case of the US, but unhelpful to explain a crisis that is international.

10.1.3 The EU Imperialism

In addition to focusing on declining profit rates, Mavroudeas and Paitaridis (2014) emphasize external exploitation (unequal exchange) and surrendering the control of monetary, fiscal and trade policy to the EU as explanations of the loss of international competitiveness of the EU periphery (Greece). In this view the unequal exchange is evident in the declining terms of trade of the eurozone periphery relative to the core. This point was argued based on a comparison of three countries: Greece (periphery), Austria (core) and Sweden (a non-eurozone EU member). The analysis shows that while Greece (and to a lesser extent Sweden) experienced a decline in its terms of trade since joining the EU in 1981, Austria experienced an improvement. The introduction of the euro in 1999, however, did not cause any further deterioration in terms of trade for Greece and Sweden. The conclusion driven from this simple comparison is that 'the euro-core EMU [European Monetary Union] members gained from the European integration process against both the euro-periphery EMU members and euro-core non-EMU members' (Mavroudeas and Paitaridis 2014: 169).

This exercise can be criticized from a number of perspectives. First, whatever the theoretical merit of unequal exchange theory is, simple terms of trade comparisons can neither prove nor disprove it. Unequal exchange could exist even when terms of trade are improving, which could indicate a lessening of unequal exchange. Second, an observation of single factoral terms of trade can produce misleading results since it fails to account for productivity and quality changes. Third, a simple comparison of three countries is far too simplistic to tell us anything meaningful about the unequal exchanges in the EU. One could easily select alternative sets of countries to prove this argument wrong. For example, between 1960 to 2010 Austria, Finland and France (core EU countries) experienced significant deterioration in their terms of trade, while Malta, Portugal and Spain (periphery EU countries) experienced significant improvements. Fourth, unequal exchange is irrelevant to the financial crisis as it is a theory of underdevelopment but not of financial crisis. Unequal exchange at best may explain why the periphery countries in the EU have not been growing more rapidly, but tells us nothing about the financial crisis. Fifth, as opposed to the claims of Mavroudeas and Paitaridis (2014), my calculations (by using World Bank data) show that the Greek terms of trade increased significantly between 1985 and 2004, and declined slightly afterwards, probably due to higher oil prices. Sixth, Mavroudeas and Paitaridis (2014) fail to explain the crisis in the imperialist core countries. In other words, if the crisis in Greece was caused by imperialism, what caused the crisis in the EU core imperialist countries such as France?

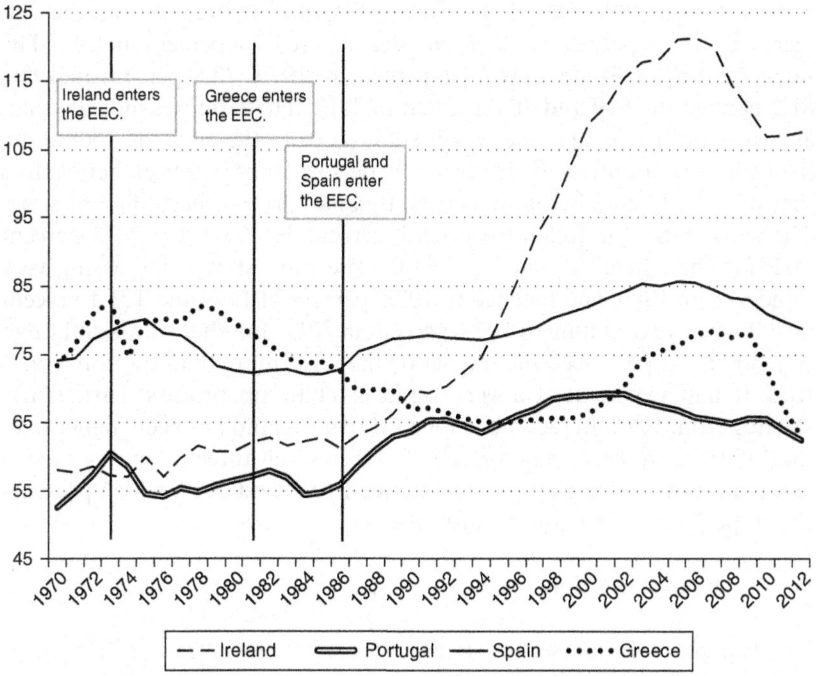

Note: The core countries are Germany, France, Belgium and the Netherlands.

Source: Author's calculation based on World Development Indicators data.

Figure 10.1 Per capita income (in constant PPP) as percentage of the euro-core countries.

Finally, the economic growth performance in periphery countries relative to the core portrays a mixed picture (see Figure 10.1). Greece's per capita income (in constant purchasing power parity, PPP) as a percentage of that of the euro-core countries (Germany, France, Belgium and the Netherlands) was 73.4 percent in 1970, and went up to 77.8 percent in 1981 when Greece entered into the European Economic Community (EEC). It declined to 65.6 percent in 1999 when Greece entered into the European Monetary Union (EMU). It went up to 78.3 percent in 2009, before declining again to 63 percent in 2012. Overall, Greece's per capita income declined against the EU core which supports the EU imperialism argument. The same figures, however, tell a different story for the other periphery countries. Portugal's per capita income as a percentage of that of the euro-core countries was 52.5 percent in 1970, which went up to

55.9 percent in 1986 when Portugal entered into the EEC. It continued to increase to 68.8 percent in 1999, and declined to 62.4 percent in 2012. The same figures for Spain were 74.1 percent in 1970, 72.8 percent in 1986, 81.2 percent in 1999 and 78.8 percent in 2012. These figures indicate that, although both Portugal and Spain suffered from the crisis of 2008 more than the core countries, their economic performance had been better than that of the EU core before the crisis. Ireland tells a rather different story. The same ratio for Ireland was 58.1 percent in 1970, and 57.3 percent in 1973 when Ireland joined the EEC. The ratio started increasing very rapidly from 1986, and reached to 102.8 percent in 1999 and 121.1 percent in 2006, before declining to 107.6 percent in 2012. In other words, although Ireland also experienced the impact of the crisis more than the core countries, it had experienced a very rapid catching-up process, particularly starting from 1986. In fact, per capita GDP in Ireland has been higher than that of the core countries since 1999. Overall, all three countries experienced a rapid catching-up process between 1970 and 2012, which provides no support for the EU imperialism thesis.

10.1.4 Financialization

The last part of this section is allocated to financialization, a popular explanation of the crisis which deserves to be taken seriously and explored carefully. I will first briefly expose the financialization arguments and then assess their relevance to the crisis. Despite its popular use, financialization is not clearly defined. Most definitions of financialization focus on the causes, consequences and the specific forms that it takes in different countries. Therefore they are not definitions per se, but descriptions of what are observed in a few selected countries that cannot be generalized. Lapavitsas (2011), for example, defines financialization as the transformation of *mature capitalist economies* with three interrelated features: first, large corporations rely less on banks and have developed their own financial capabilities; second, banks have shifted their activities toward households; and third, households have become increasingly involved in financial transactions.[4] In this view financialization represents a new stage of capitalism in which financial capital is not only increasingly autonomous from productive capital, but also dominates it as well as exploiting the households through the provision of loans and usurious activities. Financialization leads to excessive leveraging and financial bubbles which eventually collapse and cause financial crisis.

These features, however, do not constitute an unambiguous definition. Rather, they can be considered as a description of the developments of the financial sector in a narrow array of mature capitalist economies. Such a narrow description leads to overgeneralizations and fails to capture the abundant experiences of many developing and developed countries with varying characteristics (see Desai, Chapter 8 in this volume).

For example, both the US and Germany have experienced financialization but the US suffered from the financial crisis more than Germany, which implies that alternative forms of financialization may indeed lead to different outcomes.[5] Financialization per se, therefore, may not be responsible for financial crisis but the specific forms that financialization takes in different countries may better explain the incidence of financial crisis. The above definition can also hardly provide any insights regarding how and why many developing countries (that were not financialized as much as the mature capitalist economies) have experienced financial crisis since the 1980s. As it was discussed earlier, most (if not all) developing and developed countries that experienced financial crisis had large current account deficits prior to their crisis.

The failure to define financialization clearly and to separate its different configurations often leads to the failure to establish a clear link between financialization and financial crisis. While Lapavitsas provides an interesting framework for the analysis of financialization, he fails to establish an unambiguous link between financialization and financial crisis. In a series of papers, the same points have been reiterated but no clear exposition is provided regarding why financialized markets should experience financial crisis, and why some financialized markets experience financial crisis while others do not.[6]

Once a clear definition of financialization is provided, however, the causes, consequences and specific forms that it takes can be discussed, and it can be established whether and what type of financialization can be linked to financial crisis. Epstein (2005: 3) defines financialization as 'the increasing role of financial motives, financial markets, financial actors and financial institutions in the operation of the domestic and international economies'. This broad definition is useful and guides us into a definition which is even simpler: financialization is the expansion of financial services as percentage of total national income. This definition is value-free, does not attribute to it a negative or positive meaning, and allows us to consider various forms of financialization in countries depending on their own country-specific peculiarities. There is financialization, for example, as long as the financial sector is noticeably expanding, whether or not large corporations and households increasingly engage in financial transactions. The opposite is also true. Even when large corporations and households increasingly engage in financial activities, there is no financialization as long as the financial sector is not noticeably expanding.[7]

A separation of financialization from its specific forms is necessary to explain various experiences of financialization and financial crisis. Financialization has four different configurations which are vitally important for the debates over the link between financialization and financial crisis. The failure to separate these four levels often leads to overgeneralizations and misleading conclusions.

First, financialization could be a natural phenomenon (comparable to industrialization) instigated by economic progress itself. As such, financialization could simply mean a natural increase in the share of financial services in total gross domestic product (GDP). As once the share of industry increased and the share of agriculture declined in total economic activities, now the share of services (including financial services) might be increasing as economies develop. This could be due to faster productivity increase in industry and a demand shift to services. Technological changes that allow individuals and non-financial firms to increasingly engage in financial activities could also be deemed normal. Such developments could be considered as a global phenomenon occurring everywhere in the world depending on the development levels of countries. Such structural transformations, however, need not necessarily cause financial instabilities as long as financial sectors are well regulated. Although productive and unproductive labor discourse is relevant here, the historical experience shows that it cannot be used to explain financial crisis due to the reasons discussed earlier. Unproductive labor is relevant to the broader services sector and not limited to the financial services sector (see Harvey, Chapter 3 in this volume).

Second, financialization could also result from the deregulation of financial markets, particularly due to the privatization of pensions, health care, education and housing. The decline in the state provision of such services leads to the expansion of private financial services which could also be considered as global since liberalization policies have been widely adopted at varying levels. While such policies may not be in the public interest, they do not necessarily cause financial instabilities as long as they are properly regulated. The first and second types of financialization, therefore, tend to be global (that is, arising in all countries), and cannot explain an international crisis that hit some but not all countries.

Third, few countries could have a financial sector larger than the international norm. In the United Kingdom (UK) and US, for example, state policies were specifically designed to promote the financial sectors to become the financial centers of the world. Such a preference necessarily undermined their industrial sector, as specific policies were adapted to increase the international competitiveness of their financial services. Margaret Thatcher once famously said, 'we do not need manufacturing industry, we are to be a service economy'. Deindustrialization in these countries, therefore, has been very rapid. Such an expansion of the financial services, however, is not a global phenomenon and cannot be generalized. The expansion of financial services in few countries, in fact, could lead to smaller financial services sectors in other countries. Although it may not be in the interest of working classes, there is also no reason to assume that such financialization could necessarily lead to any major current account problems and cause financial crisis in these countries. While the US and UK experienced massive capital inflows and outflows for a long time, their net capital inflows (which have caused large current account deficits) remained relatively low until 1997. Financialization in these countries, therefore, is rather different than financialization in other developed and developing countries. Defining financialization based on the experiences of these countries (regardless of the specific forms that it takes in others) and generalizing their experiences is misleading. In other words, the domination of the financial sector over the real sector as a global phenomenon is nonsensical, since the financial sector feeds on the real sector. Claiming that this cannot even happen in one country, however, is equally erroneous. Theoretically speaking, few countries can stop producing manufactured goods and export only financial services. Contrary to the first and second types, the third type of financialization is not a global phenomenon, but it also need not cause financial crisis. The historical experience shows that being a financial center is irrelevant to financial crisis, which is experienced by a wide range of countries.

Fourth, deregulated financial markets could lead to overfinancialization, which is often unsustainable. Financial activities occasionally expand more than can be considered as sustainable, often due to excessive financial inflows. As it is obvious from the current account deficits in many developing and developed countries over the last few decades, such excessive influx of external funds often lead to bubbles which ultimately burst. While some of these funds could be invested in productive capacity, the financial sector needs to find alternative outlets once the productive investment opportunities are quickly exhausted, and encourages businesses and households to engage in risky and speculative types of investment. Overfinancialization is also not a global phenomenon, since not all countries can be net importers of financial resources. Overfinancialization, bubbles and crisis were experienced by many developing countries prior to the 2008 crisis, regardless of the three interrelated features of financialization. Financialization, described by Lapavitsas therefore, is neither a necessary nor a sufficient condition for financial crisis.

Financialization in the US and UK took two different forms in two separate time periods. While financialization since the 1980s was a policy choice to establish global financial centers, the overexpansion of the financial activities since 1997 resulted from excessive capital inflows.[8] The overwhelming capital inflows and the absence of external investment opportunities led the Western banks to target their own population, which proceeded to the formation of bubbles and crisis. Widespread predatory, usurious and dishonest lending practices (such as securitization) in the US, for example, should be seen in the context of this necessity. The aggressive lending policies in the US, in essence, were not dissimilar to the aggressive lending policies to developing countries during the 1970s. After two oil shocks, which caused massive increase in global liquidity, large banks targeted developing countries as suitable outlets to dump the excessive petrodollars. A similar strategy would not have worked this time since developing countries' ordeal is not yet over and they have learned a valuable lesson. Therefore large banks in the developed countries had no choice but to target their own households as new outlets.

The separation of these different types is essential to understand the true nature of financialization and its links with financial crisis. The following two examples will be indicative. First, while both the US and Germany experienced the first and second types of financialization, only the US experienced the third and fourth types of financialization and suffered from financial crisis. Moreover, Germany has not been associated with financialization. A simple search in Google Scholar shows that, while there is a rich literature on financialization in the US, there is almost none on financialization in Germany. This is not because the financial sector is small in Germany, but because it has not experienced the third and fourth types of financialization. This observation can be generalized to the countries that experienced a rapid deterioration in their current accounts and those that did not. In other words, while there is a rich financialization literature on the current account deficit countries such as Ireland, Italy, Greece and Spain, there is hardly any literature on the current account surplus countries such as Japan and China. Lapavitsas admits that there are differences between financialization in Germany and the US but provides no analytical tool to assess the causes and consequences of such differences. Another search in Google Scholar also shows that the word 'financialization' was rarely used until 1997, when excessive capital flows started (Figure 10.2). The popular use of the concept increased incrementally with the increase in current account disequilibrium in the US. These developments can hardly be considered as coincidental.

Second, the empirical evidence suggests that, increase in financial activities mostly takes the form of 'real estate; renting and business activities' (RE) rather than 'financial intermediation' (FI) which implies overfinancialization. The Organisation for Economic Co-operation and Development (OECD) provides 'value added in financial intermediation;

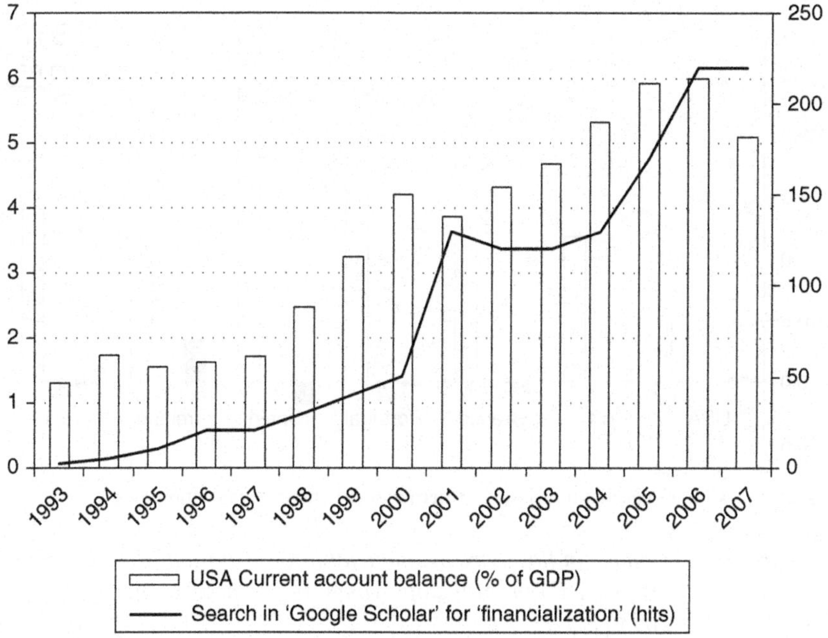

Note: To show the link between these variables clearly, the US current account balance (deficit) was converted into surplus by multiplying the figures by −1.

Sources: World Development Indicators and Google Scholar.

Figure 10.2 The US current account balance and search in Google Scholar for 'financialization'

real estate; renting and business activities' ($VA^{FI\&RE}$)[9] data which are not disaggregated. While the share of $VA^{FI\&RE}$ in the total economy increased significantly in most countries that have experienced financial crisis, it is not possible to identify whether this increase was due to an increase in 'value added in financial intermediation' (VA^{FI}) or 'value added in real estate; renting and business activities' (VA^{RE}). The International Labour Organization, however, provides disaggregated employment data for both 'financial intermediation' (L^{FI}) and 'real estate; renting and business activities' (L^{RE}).[10] Although the labor share is not a perfect substitute for the value added share, it is a reasonable proxy. The International Labour Organization data show that while the L^{RE} share in total employment increased significantly in most countries, the L^{FI} share tended to decline. Just to give an example, while in Portugal the $VA^{FI\&RE}$ increased from 19.3 percent in 2000 to 22.5 percent in 2008 (by 3.2 percent) and the $L^{FI\&RE}$

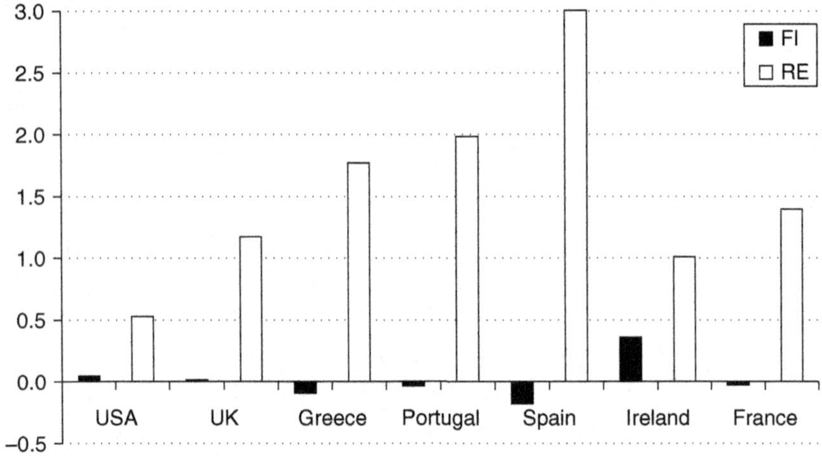

Source: Author's calculation based on International Labour Organization data.

Figure 10.3 Change in the share of financial intermediation (FI) and real estate (RE) in total employment between 2000 and 2008 (%)

share in total employment increased from 6.2 percent to 8.1 percent (by 1.9 percent), the share of L^{FI} declined from 1.9 percent to 1.8 percent (by −0.1 percent). Therefore, the increase in the share of $L^{FI\&RE}$ in total employment was due to the increase in L^{RE} which increased from 4.3 percent to 6.3 percent (by 2.0 percent). Similar trends are observed in other countries (see Figure 10.3).

In other words, a radical increase in the financialization before the crisis was largely due to the increase in RE activities rather than FI activities, which is inconsistent with the financialization thesis but in support of the overfinancialization thesis. The crisis in advanced countries was due purely to a bubble created by excessive capital inflows which encouraged RE activities and caused economic bubbles. This is also evident from the radical increase in housing prices in these countries starting from 1997. According to the OECD Housing Prices database, while real housing prices between 1997 and 2007 increased by 187 percent in Ireland, 142 percent in the UK, 117 percent in Spain, 112 percent in France, 101 percent in Greece, and 59 percent in the US, they declined in current account surplus countries, by 28 percent in Japan and 17 percent in Germany.

Although the economic bubbles were led by the housing sector and associated with a radical increase in household indebtedness in many countries, this was not always the norm. Countries experienced varieties of financial bubbles. In Portugal, for example, the real housing prices increased only by 7.5 percent between 1997 and 2007 despite the household debt to income ratio increasing by 122.7 percent. In Spain, the debt to income ratio of the non-financial corporations increased by 356 percent between 2000 and 2007, whereas the household debt to income ratio increased only by 88.6 percent.

Overfinancialization, which is evident from large current account deficits, is one of the most important causes of the recent financial crises in developed countries as well as crises in developing countries since the 1980s. The next section will investigate the causes of these large current account deficits and why they matter.

10.2 CURRENT ACCOUNT DEFICIT AS A CAUSE OF FINANCIAL CRISIS

This section deals with the policy-based explanations of the financial crisis and the focus is on current account disequilibrium. There is no agreement amongst economists regarding when a current account deficit becomes a series risk. Some economists believe that a current account deficit which allows an economy to invest more than is possible by using domestic savings is never a problem. A larger current account deficit means a higher rate of investment and economic growth, which allows the repayment of the borrowed resources without a major problem. A similar view suggests that a current account deficit in a growing economy is expected, since exports depend on other countries' economic growth whereas imports depend on own economic growth. When a country grows faster than the others, it will experience a current account deficit and become a victim of its own success.

A number of objections can be leveled against these arguments. First, the external resources could be used to expand domestic consumption, which would lead to lower domestic savings rather than higher investments.[11] In this case, the economy will not grow and servicing debt will be arduous. Second, as many financial crises since the 1980s have indicated, external resources can be used in unproductive and speculative types of investment. Finally, borrowed resources could be invested into socially and economically beneficial sectors (such as health and education) that do not generate foreign currency, which could cause problems in debt servicing.

The argument which considers current account deficit in a rapidly growing country as normal is only accurate under very restrictive assumptions. When trade and financial markets are deregulated in a country that experiences faster productivity growth in its non-tradables than its exportables, a current account deficit may indeed be predictable. This implies that economic growth is stimulated by productivity increase in the non-tradables sector, which creates extra demand for importables without increasing international competitiveness of the exportables. If this is also associated with trade and financial deregulation which allows a country to finance its trade deficit from the international financial markets, a current account deficit becomes almost inevitable. The experiences of some Asian countries (such as China and South Korea) proves that, when increase in growth is (at least partially) caused by increased competitiveness of the exportables, or trade and financial sectors are not deregulated simultaneously, rapid economic growth need not result in current account deficit.

An alternative perspective that can be taken more seriously suggests that a current account deficit that exceeds 6 percent of GDP becomes unsustainable (Milesi-Ferretti and Razin 1996). The sustainability of the current account deficit, however, cannot be judged by its size and duration. Sustainability should be judged based on whether or not the favorable conditions for debt service are created. If the external resources are effectively used in productive areas of the economy, they can be paid back without major problems, which indicates that the current account deficit is sustainable. If the external resources are used in unproductive areas, however, the current account deficit should be considered as unsustainable regardless of its size and duration. A current account deficit can be sustained for a considerable period of time by accumulating the problems and postponing the solutions, provided that the current account surplus countries are willing to finance it. Sustaining a current account deficit for a considerable period of time, however, does not mean that it is sustainable. The unsustainability of the current account deficit will sooner or later become obvious. The necessary adjustments could take the form of a soft landing or a crash. Very often, however, both current account deficit and current account surplus countries become so co-dependent on the continuation of the status quo that a progressive correction of the disequilibrium becomes unlikely. The longer the delay, the larger and the more destructive the necessary adjustment is.[12]

When capital movements are strictly controlled (foreign borrowing is not allowed), neither trade nor current account deficit can arise. Countries can import as much as they export. While trade deficit can occur for a short period of time, changes in the exchange rate equalize imports and exports in the long run. For example when GDP (particularly non-tradables) in a country grows faster (slower) than the other countries, the extra demand for importables as well as foreign currency will also grow faster (slower). The local currency will lose (gain) value which will both increase (reduce) exports and reduce (increase) the demand for imports and establish equilibrium. Since it is not possible to finance extra imports by using external financial resources, trade or current account deficits cannot form. Under a liberal financial regime where it is possible to finance extra imports by external resources, however, the exchange rate will not perform its trade-equalizing functions. If an increase in imports can be financed by external borrowing, the exchange rate will become overvalued and will not be able to establish trade equilibrium. In the same manner, financial deregulation will not lead to excessive international borrowing as long as suitable trade policies (either to curb excessive imports or to encourage exports) are adapted to achieve trade equilibrium.

The simultaneous deregulation of the finance and trade since the 1980s led to large capital flows, and caused overvalued exchange rates and unsustainable trade and current account deficits. Even the flexible exchange rate policies failed to prevent overvalued exchange rates. The frequency of bubble economies and financial crisis has increased and their damaging impacts have been aggravated. Initially financial crises were considered to result from policy mistakes and weak financial markets in developing countries. Prudent macroeconomic policies and developed financial architecture meant developed countries should be immune from financial crises. Since the 2008 crisis, however, this view has been proven wrong. The bubble economies had been forming in many developed countries since 1997, evident from their rapidly growing current account imbalances. The growth in global current account imbalances was due to a number of conjunctural reasons.

First, the financial crises experienced in many developing countries during the 1980s and 1990s encouraged them to have a more vigilant approach to financial flows and external borrowing. The financial crisis in East Asia in 1997 encouraged many countries[13] to push their exports and accumulate large precautionary foreign reserves.[14] These reserves were largely kept in the US and other developed countries. The limited global demand for these large financial resources forced banks to target households in developed countries.

Second, crude oil prices, which had declined since 1990, started rising from 1998 and this accelerated from 2002. The crude oil spot price per barrel increased fourfold from $26 in 2001 to $100 in 2008. The radical increase in crude oil prices led to large current account surpluses in oil exporting countries. These extra funds were also transferred to the US and other developed countries, which contributed to their large current account deficits. This reminds us of the oil crisis of the 1970s which subsequently caused massive external debt problems for many developing countries, particularly in Latin America.

Third, since its accession to the World Trade Organization in 2001, the

Chinese current account surplus increased significantly. China adopted a competitive exchange rate policy by fixing its currency against the US dollar, which contributed greatly to its large current account surplus. The Chinese current account surplus temporarily increased after the Asian crisis of 1997, from 0.8 percent of its GDP to 3.9 percent, and declined back to 1.3 percent in 2001. Since 2001, however, it steadily increased to 10.1 percent in 2007.

Finally, special reference has been made to the eurozone countries. The 'eurozone crisis' is essentially a current account disequilibrium explanation of the crisis in a few European countries. Krugman (2013), for example, argued that 'the creation of the euro was followed by the emergence of huge imbalances, with vast amounts of capital flowing from the core to the periphery'. Lapavitsas et al. (2012) analyzed the eurozone crisis in terms of the polarization between the core and periphery. While the core refers to Germany, France, Belgium and the Netherlands, comparisons are often made with Germany. The periphery often refers to the PIGS (Portugal, Ireland, Greece, Spain).

Lapavitsas et al. (2012) argue that the eurozone crisis is a crisis of competitiveness in an asymmetrical monetary union. In this view, the growing balance-of-payments disequilibrium between the core and periphery countries has been the main factor behind the crisis. Due to the asymmetrical functioning of the EMU, the core (periphery) countries experienced large current account surpluses (current account deficits) and capital account deficits (surpluses) from the advent of the euro. The German current account surpluses are often blamed for causing problems not only for the eurozone area but also for the world economy. Germany is accused of being obsessed with fiscal discipline, wage competitiveness and export surpluses, and adopting beggar-thy-neighbor policies. 'The result has been a structural current account surplus for Germany, mirrored by current account deficits for peripheral countries' (Lapavitsas et al. 2012: 4).

In this story, financialization played (if any) a secondary and ambiguous role as the focus is on the current account imbalances. While the standard financialization arguments are reiterated, their role is not clearly specified. Obviously, the introduction of the euro could potentially cause external imbalances and housing bubbles without the financialization of large businesses and households. Financialization, therefore, is neither necessary nor sufficient to the discussions over the eurozone crisis.

An alternative explanation of the eurozone crisis has focused on the superior growth performance of the periphery countries (Milios and Sotiropoulos 2010). In this view, the periphery countries are the victims of their own success under the monetary union, as their rapid economic growth increased their imports faster than exports which led to their external imbalances. As I argued earlier, however, this argument is only accurate under very restrictive assumptions which fail to account for increased export competitiveness due to rapid productivity increase.

10.3 CONCLUSIONS

This chapter argues that the conjunctural and policy-based factors played a more important role in the 2008 financial crisis than the systemic factors. This does not mean, however, that systemic factors (which I consider in Chapter 11 in this volume) are unimportant. While systemic factors may have played an important role in individual countries, an international crisis is unlikely to result from such factors unless a strong spillover mechanism is identified, particularly from a large country (the US) to the others. This chapter considers a number of systemic causes of crisis and argues that they are unlikely to be pertinent.

After briefly exposing the financialization arguments, this chapter argues that the related literature largely disappoints because it overgeneralizes and fails to capture the diverse experiences of many developing and developed countries with varying characteristics. This chapter defines financialization broadly as the expansion of financial services as a percentage of total national income, and identifies four levels of financialization which are instrumental to explain the diverse experiences of financialization and financial crisis. Out of four different levels of financialization, only overfinancialization, which is associated with excessive financial inflows and current account deficits, is concomitant with financial crisis. The empirical evidence suggests that the radical increase in 'financialization' before the crisis was largely due to the increase in real estate activities rather than financial intermediation activities, which is inconsistent with the financialization thesis.

This chapter concludes by arguing that overfinancialization, which is evident from large current account deficits, is the most important cause of the recent financial crises in developed and developing countries since the 1980s. The simultaneous implementation of trade and financial sector deregulation, which is considered as a lethal cocktail, often leads to persistent current account imbalances and subsequent crisis. When capital movements are strictly controlled, trade and current account deficits cannot form. And policies to ensure trade equilibrium will not lead to excessive international borrowing even under financial deregulation. The simultaneous deregulation of finance and trade, however, allows countries to borrow from international markets to support their current account deficits for a considerable period of time. The deregulation policies adopted since the

1980s led to unsustainable current account deficits and subsequent crises in many developing countries first. The growth in global current account imbalances in the 2000s, that mainly influenced the developed countries, resulted from a number of conjunctural reasons. First, the financial crises in developing countries led them to accumulate large foreign reserves as a precaution, which were largely kept in the US and other developed countries and contributed to their large current account deficits. Second, the crude oil prices increased very rapidly between 2002 and 2008 and led to large current account surpluses in oil exporting countries and deficits in others. Third, from its accession to the World Trade Organization in 2001, China experienced large current account surpluses which were mirrored as current account deficits in other countries. And finally, the introduction of the euro aggravated the current account balances between the core and periphery eurozone countries.

Such a rapid increase in current account deficits and accumulation of external debts inevitably led to overfinancializations and bubbles which were bound to collapse. That is, in effect, what happened in the US and other developed countries from 2008.

NOTES

1. To account for the systemic causes of crisis, I will develop a theoretical model in Chapter 11 in this volume by utilizing Marx's simple and expanded reproduction schemes.
2. See the debate between Harvey (Chapter 3 in this volume) and Roberts (Chapter 4 in this volume).
3. The same point has been made by Weeks (Chapter 6 in this volume) and Harvey (Chapter 3 in this volume).
4. I will not cover alternative approaches to financialization in this chapter but a good exposition of the radical approaches (Marxist, post-Keynesian and other heterodox) to financialization can be found in Lapavitsas (2011). See also Subasat (Chapter 1 in this volume) for a summary of the financialization debates in this book.
5. Although Germany was not immune from the devastating impacts of the crisis and GDP experienced a sharp decline in 2009, it recovered rapidly in contrast to the US and the other countries that experienced the financial crisis.
6. Moreover, Lapavitsas's arguments over the crisis in the US and the crisis in the eurozone do not complement each other, as his explanation on the US crisis focuses on financialization, whereas his explanation of the eurozone crisis focuses on external imbalances caused by the introduction of the euro. While he also mentions financialization in the case of eurozone countries, its role is not specified clearly and the focus is on the current account surpluses of Germany and current account deficits of the periphery countries.
7. In this view, the increase in financial activities such as credit cards, online financial transactions by households and the increase in financial activities of large corporations are not worth coining a name for, unless they increase the share of financial sector in total economic activity, since they are no more significant than the increase in household mobile telephones, internet access or international travel. Increase in such economic activities due to technological progress is normal and deserves no specific name.

8. I will investigate the causes of these capital flows in the next section.
9. $VA^{FI\&RE} = VA^{RE} + VA^{FI}$.
10. $L^{FI\&RE} = L^{RE} + L^{FI}$.
11. This was the case in the US and in most countries that experienced financial crisis.
12. The co-dependent trade relationship between the US and China is a good example. From 1979, China adopted a development strategy based on a trade surplus which financed the domestic consumption boom in the US.
13. For example Thailand, Malaysia and Indonesia as well as Argentina and Brazil. The average current account balance to GDP ratios for five years before and five years after the 1997 crisis were −5.8 and 7.7 in Thailand, −2.3 and 4.3 in Indonesia, −1.5 and 4.7 in South Korea, and −6.1 and 10.6 in Malaysia. The same figures were −3.6 and 4.7 in Argentina, and −3.6 and 1.1 for Brazil.
14. The devastating policies of the International Monetary Fund (IMF) during the 1997 crisis also played an important role.

REFERENCES

Epstein, G. (2005), 'Introduction: Financialization and the World Economy', in G. Epstein (ed.), *Financialization and the World Economy*, Cheltenham, UK and Northampton, MA, USA: Edward Elgar.

Krugman, P. (2013), 'The Harm Germany Does', *New York Times*, 1 November, accessed 17 June 2015 at http://krugman.blogs.nytimes.com/2013/11/01/the-harm-germany-does/?_r=0.

Lapavitsas, C. (2011), 'Theorising Financialization', *Work, Employment and Society*, 25(4), 611–626.

Lapavitsas et al. (2012), *Crisis in the Eurozone*, Verso: London.

Mavroudeas, S. and D. Paitaridis (2014), 'The Greek Crisis: A Dual Crisis of Overaccumulation and Imperialist Exploitation', in S. Mavroudeas (ed.), *Greek Capitalism in Crisis: Marxist Analysis*, Routledge: New York.

Milesi-Ferretti, G.M. and A. Razin (1996), 'Sustainability of Persistent Current Account Deficits', NBER Working Papers No. 5467.

Milios, J. and D. Sotiropoulos (2010), 'Crisis of Greece or Crisis of the Euro? A View from the European Periphery', *Journal of Balkan and Near Eastern Studies*, 12(3), 275–292.

Wolff, R.D. (2012), *Capitalism Hits the Fan: The Global Economic Meltdown and What To Do About It*, Chicago, IL: Haymarket Books.

11. The systemic causes of the 2008 crisis: an alternative theoretical perspective

Turan Subasat

In Chapter 10 in this volume, I focused on large and rapidly increasing current account deficits as the main (policy-based and conjunctural) cause of the 2008 crisis but also argued that the systemic causes should not be overlooked. Prior to the crisis, for example, the US economy was already unsustainable not only because of the large current account deficits but also due to the stagnant real wages which had been compensated by excessive lending to workers to offset insufficient demand. Many authors in this book argue that such a system would not have lasted long, and justifiably focus on the various forms of systemic causes of crisis.

This chapter aims to develop an alternative theoretical model based on Marx's reproduction schemes to enhance the understanding of the cyclical nature of capital accumulation and the systemic causes of crisis.[1] A particular emphasis is placed upon the distribution of income between capitalists and workers,[2] and the time gap between the production of means of production and means of consumption.

The model aims to show that even in the absence of variation in relative class power (the shares of profits and wages remain the same), problems associated with insufficient demand could lead to stagnation and crisis, since different stages of capital accumulation require different levels of wages and profits to avoid insufficient demand. The dynamics of the capital accumulation process necessitate radical changes in income distribution to maintain sufficient demand which is near impossible to achieve. When there is a large reserve army of labor (unemployment), lower wages bring about faster accumulation of capital and once the reserve army of labor declines substantially (there is labor shortage), demand deficiency starts, which requires capitalists to increase radically either their consumption or wages. Both are very difficult adjustments for capitalists. Restoring sufficient demand via large state expenditures (supported by large taxes) would equally be resisted by capitalists.

The model employs Marx's ([1894] 1978) assumptions in Volume II of *Capital* where he discusses the schemes which are admittedly restrictive. Such assumptions, however, are reasonable at that level of abstraction as long as one does not rush to move from abstract to concrete without taking a number of considerations into account. For example, the model needs to be developed to account for technological changes, international trade, international financial movements and so on. While this chapter will scratch the surface, a deeper analysis requires a more advanced model which will be developed in a separate paper.

Although the model links crisis to insufficient demand, it is not a typical underconsumptionist model where it is often argued that capitalism cannot maintain itself and needs pre-capitalist markets. While the model both complements and challenges the alternative Marxian theories of crisis, it significantly differs from them in terms of its main logic and implications.

11.1 SIMPLE AND EXPANDED REPRODUCTION

As a first step, the simple and expanded reproduction schemes are presented and their well-known conclusions are elucidated.[3] Marx divides the economy into two departments and works with the following numerical example. Department 1 produces means of production and department 2 produces means of consumption:

$$\begin{array}{ll} \text{Dept 1} & 4000C1 + 1000V1 + 1000S1 = 6000 \\ \text{Dept 2} & \underline{2000C2 + 500V2 \ + 500S2 \ = 3000} \\ & 6000C + 1500V + 1500S = 9000 \end{array}$$

There are a number of standard assumptions that govern the reproduction schemes: no technical progress (constant labor productivity across departments), commodities exchange at their values (direct prices), constant composition of capital (capital–labor ratio), constant value and price of a unit of output, constant real output, constant real and money wages, constant surplus value and value created per worker, no labor shortage (sufficient reserve army of labor), no insufficient demand, no financial system, no international lending or borrowing, and no international trade. In this simple reproduction scheme, the total value of the means of production is 6000 and the total value of the means of consumption is 3000. The value of the output of each department is divided into three parts: the value of the means of production (constant capital, C1 and C2), the value of the labor-power employed (variable capital, V1 and V2), and the surplus value created in production (S1 and

S2). The continuation of this simple reproduction requires the means of production to be available for purchase at the beginning of the production period. This, in turn, requires it to be produced in the preceding period. Values are created through the production in both departments. The workers and capitalists consume the commodities of department 2. The means of production are used in the production process. While their physical form is destroyed or transformed, their value passes to the newly generated commodities. The logic of simple production requires an equal amount of value to be produced and consumed (realized) in each circuit of capital. For uninterrupted reproduction, the total new values (variable capital and surplus value) in both departments must be spent on means of consumption. Spending by workers and capitalists in department 1 on means of consumption must equal spending by department 2 capitalists on inputs (means of production). A failure of capitalists to spend all of the surplus value on the output of department 2 would result in insufficient demand. Accordingly, department 1 uses 4000 of its own production from the previous period, sells 2000 to department 2 and buys means of consumption in return. The remaining 1000 of means of consumption are bought by workers and capitalists of department 2.

Given the assumptions and explanations above, Marx's model has two important implications that play an essential role in my model. First, increase in output (expanded reproduction) requires employing more workers. Since technology and labor productivity are constant, the only way to increase output is to employ more workers. If no new workers are available for employment, expanded reproduction is impossible and the economy is stuck in simple reproduction. Second, simple reproduction requires V1 + S1 = C2, and expanded reproduction requires V1 + S1 > C2. Here Marx recognizes that there is a time gap between the expansions in departments 1 and 2. In other words, expansion in department 2 cannot take place unless expansion in department 1 is completed. In plain language, it would be impossible to produce more means of consumption unless the means of production are expanded first. This time gap between the expansions in departments 1 and 2 explains why capitalist savings are essential for expanded reproduction.[4]

11.2 THE ESSENCE OF THE ARGUMENT

The key to my argument is the fact that there is a time gap between the expansion of the means of production and the expansion of the means of consumption. The expansion process starts with the production of more means of production (in phase 1), and the expansion of means of consumption (in phase 2) follows with a delay. In order to increase bread (representing all means of consumption) production, for example, the production of tractors (representing all means of production) must be increased first.

Assuming that technology is constant, the increase in means of production (phase 1) requires the employment of more workers. These new workers will create extra demand for means of consumption before more means of consumption can be produced (phase 2). Capitalists will have to reduce their consumption (save) in phase 1 in order for the new workers to maintain their physical existence (consume). Eventually the production of consumption goods will increase (phase 2) and the expansion process will be completed. Capitalists can now increase their consumption.

The uninterrupted expansion of production (expanded reproduction) requires the continuous expansion of employment and net savings by capitalists. The higher the net savings (that is, lower capitalist consumption) the faster the expansion. Capitalists can minimize their consumption level without causing insufficient demand so long as more workers are employed to expand production. When the economy is close to full employment[5] and labor shortage begins, however, expansion will no longer be possible (simple reproduction). Net capitalist savings will start causing insufficient demand and realization problems. In this case, capitalists will either have to increase radically their consumption or wages to avoid insufficient demand. If neither happens, insufficient demand will cause production and employment to decline (a crisis) which can help to explain the cyclical nature of capitalist production. The following numerical example will help to clarify these arguments.

11.3 A NUMERICAL EXAMPLE

Before illuminating this example, it should be noted once again that all Marx's assumptions above are employed here. The model can be made more realistic by modifying the assumptions. The production of means of consumption (say bread) requires a number of means of production (such as tractor, fertilizer, drill, and so on, to produce wheat; mill to produce flour; and oven to bake bread) to be produced first. Increasing the production of bread, therefore, starts by first producing more tractors, fertilizers, drills, mills and ovens. The time gap between these two can be very long, which has important implications.

The example in Figure 11.1 is useful to explain these implications. Let us start with simple reproduction in time period 1 (T1). Suppose that the economy has 20 units of labor, half of it (10 units) employed in the

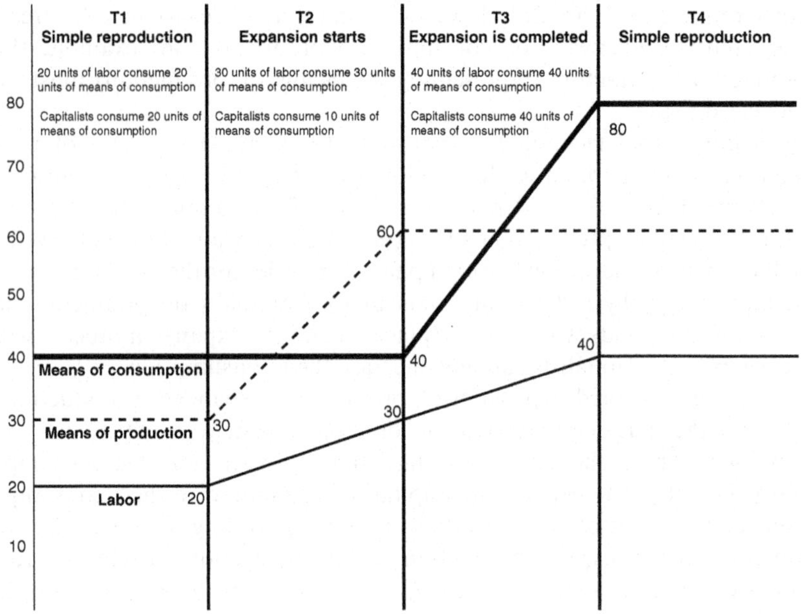

Figure 11.1 *Simple and expanded reproduction with a time gap between the production of means of consumption and means of production*

production of 30 units of means of production (in department 1), and the other half (10 units) employed in the production of 40 units of means of consumption (in department 2). It is further assumed that social reproduction requires each worker to consume 1 unit of means of consumption. This implies that 20 units of means of consumption are consumed by labor and the remaining 20 units must be consumed by the capitalists. To avoid insufficient demand, the means of consumption that are not consumed by labor must be consumed by the capitalists.

Expanded reproduction starts (in time period T2) by the doubling of means of production from 30 to 60 units. To achieve this, 10 extra units of labor must be employed in department 1, which increases the total labor from 10 to 20 units in this department and 20 to 30 units in total. Since the production of means of consumption remains constant (40 units) in T2 and 30 units of labor need 30 units of means of consumption, the amount of means of consumption left for capitalists go down from 20 to 10 units. This is because the newly employed 10 units of labor create extra demand for 10 units of means of consumption before the production of means of consumption can be increased. This implies that if capitalists are unwilling to reduce their consumption, the expansion process cannot start and the economy is stuck in simple reproduction.

The expanded reproduction is completed in T3, when the 60 units of means of production (produced in T2) and 10 more extra units of labor are employed in department 2 to increase the production of means of consumption from 40 to 80. The units of labor employed in department 2 go up from 10 to 20 and the total units of labor in both departments go up from 30 to 40. Now that 40 units of labor consume 40 units of means of consumption, the remaining 40 units of means of consumption must be consumed by capitalists. In T4 the economy goes back to simple reproduction where everything (labor, means of production and means of consumption) is doubled and the expansion process is completed.

What do we learn from this simple example, which admittedly does not depict an accurate picture of the real-life economics? The first and most important lesson is that capitalists' consumption plays a crucial role for the stability of the system. If it is too high during the expanded reproduction, capital accumulation will be very slow; and if it is too low during the simple reproduction, there will be insufficient demand, leading to the stagnation or even collapse of the economy. The second lesson is that if the economy follows the path depicted above (that is, simple reproduction – expanded reproduction – simple reproduction) capitalists' consumption will have to follow a rather erratic pattern (moving up and down) to maintain sufficient demand, which will be rather unpleasant for them. Alternatively they can reduce or increase wages (and thus profits), which will be equally unpleasant for labor. Third, if capitalists are unwilling to make such radical changes to their consumption or wages, the economy will experience insufficient demand. Production will decline until it matches demand, and unemployment will increase. Once there is a large enough reserve army of labor, the accumulation process will start again.

Luckily for capitalists, however, accumulation is a continuous process, where (although there is still a time gap between them) both the means of production and means of consumption unremittingly expand. In other words, capital accumulation does not intermittently move from simple reproduction to expanded reproduction and simple production again. Even the long-lasting expansion processes, however, will inevitably end up in simple reproduction once the economy experiences labor shortage.

As discussed earlier, uninterrupted expansion requires the continuous expansion of employment and savings by capitalists. Provided that extra workers are employed to expand production (who create demand for means of consumption), capitalists can reduce their consumption without triggering insufficient demand. Theoretically speaking, capitalists can reduce their consumption to zero without causing demand deficiency so long as they employ more workers to compensate for the absence of their demand. Capital accumulation will be very rapid and continue for a considerable period of time without facing any major demand problems. In other words, so long as the economy is expanding, capitalists' consumption will only affect the speed of accumulation but have no negative impact on demand.

This type of accumulation, however, cannot continue forever and the economy has to end up in simple reproduction once there are no more workers left to employ. This is because, given the assumptions Marx made, capital accumulation depends on the employment of new workers, and the economy has a limited number of workers. Once the reserve army of labor declines substantially, the economy will stagnate (simple reproduction) but stagnation is unlikely to be the end-point. If capitalists fail to increase their consumption or wages radically to reverse insufficient demand, production and employment will plunge and the economy will experience a crisis until the excess production is eliminated. Once sufficient numbers of workers become unemployed, the capital accumulation process can start once again.

11.4 IMPLICATIONS OF THE MODEL

The implications of the model can be investigated on three levels: first, given the rigid assumptions of the model; second, with the introduction of productivity change, international trade, international finance and foreign direct investment (FDI) into the model; and third, in terms of its interaction with the other Marxian theories.

Even with the restraining assumptions above, the model is a valuable device to reveal a number of interesting points regarding the nature of capital accumulation and crisis. The first and most notable proposition of the model is that crisis should follow a period of rapid capital accumulation and increased employment, an expectation that is often supported by actual experience.

Second, the model suggests that no uniform factoral distribution of income will serve the economy well at all times. The same income distribution can bring superior growth at one time but stagnation at another, depending on the stage of capital accumulation. The economy will grow faster with low wages before full employment. If wages remain low after full employment is reached (simple reproduction), however, the economy will experience insufficient demand and stagnation. If wages remain low and capitalists are unwilling to increase their consumption to offset insufficient demand, rapid increase in unemployment and crisis will prevail.

Third, the model also implies that decline in production due to insufficient demand is a regular occurrence which cannot be easily rectified by state policies. Once the reserve army of labor declines substantially, the insufficient demand becomes so significant that filling the demand gap by the state, which requires significant increases in the level of taxes and consumption expenditures, becomes near impossible.[6] Capitalists would rigorously resist rapid tax increases, which would radically reduce their net profits. Likewise, expansionary fiscal and monetary policies to stimulate investment would be ineffective in resolving the problem, since the underlying cause is insufficient demand for means of consumption.[7]

Fourth, the model can help to explain the different patterns of capital accumulation in developed and developing countries and the trap that many middle-income countries experience. Lewis's dual-sector model suggests that low-income countries typically have a large (surplus) population in the agricultural sector and smaller employment in the manufacturing sector. If carefully designed industrial policies lead to an expansion of the manufacturing sector, the expanded reproduction could continue for a considerable period of time by withdrawing the surplus population from the agricultural sector to the manufacturing sector. This expansion could be resource-driven (based on labor and capital) without needing innovation and high productivity. This development pattern could explain the long-lasting development experiences of many countries (such as Mexico, South Africa, Indonesia, Thailand and Brazil) that eventually experienced the middle-income trap when they failed to move to a more technology-based development. Such a growth pattern is unavailable to the high-income countries with typically smaller agricultural sectors. The model could also explain why income distribution tends to be better in high-income countries and why worsening income distribution causes more problems for them.

The above outcomes will be altered somewhat when technological changes, international trade, international finance and FDI are introduced into the model. While a detailed investigation of these results requires a more sophisticated model, which I aim to develop in a separate article, it is only possible to scratch the surface in this chapter.

Technological changes would impact the model in a number of complex ways depending on whether they take place uniformly in both departments, have impact on the exploitation and unemployment rates, and whether the economy is under simple or expanded reproduction. Whether or not productivity increases uniformly in both departments is unimportant under expanded reproduction. If productivity increases in one of the departments faster than in the other, the department that experiences the faster productivity increase would create less demand for new workers, and more workers would be employed in the department that experiences the slower productivity increase. If wages fall behind the productivity increase and the exploitation rate rises, capitalists would have larger resources to expand production faster by employing more labor. The same is true if capitalists do not increase their consumption proportionally to the increase in production. An increase in productivity, however, is likely to cause some unemployment, particularly in the rapid productivity sectors. In this case, the change in total unemployment will be determined by these contradictory tendencies. A non-uniform productivity increase under simple reproduction would lead to more unemployment in the department that experiences the faster productivity increase. If wages lag behind the productivity increase, the exploitation rate rises; and if capitalists' consumption fails to increase rapidly, insufficient demand will be aggravated and the decline in employment will be faster. The net impact on the total means of consumption will be determined by the decline in employment and the increase in productivity.

The introduction of international trade and capital flows into the model would extensively complicate the picture as the story would change significantly depending on the trade theory adopted. Assuming that international trade plays a neutral role,[8] the outcome would vary depending on whether trade is balanced and the economy operates under simple or expanded reproduction. A balanced trade would have no significant impact on the implications of the model under simple or expanded reproduction. Capital accumulation (and disaccumulation) would continue as described above. A persistent trade surplus (deficit), which implies that the country is a net international lender (borrower), under expanded reproduction (where the economy is not demand-constrained) would reduce (increase) financial resources available for domestic capital accumulation and slow down (stimulate) the economy. Under simple reproduction, a trade surplus would become an important source of external demand, particularly if capitalists are unable to increase their consumption, unwilling to increase wages, and resist tax increases. A trade surplus, however, at best can keep the economy steady but cannot permanently resolve the problem. A trade deficit under simple reproduction would reduce the demand for domestic products further and aggravate the crisis.

Assuming that it plays a neutral role,[9] capital accumulation would be faster (slower) with extra (lesser) resources associated with inward (outward) FDI under expanded reproduction. Under simple reproduction, while inward FDI would only replace (crowd out) domestic production, outward FDI would cause a temporary increase in unemployment and stimulate domestic investment.

The model both complements and challenges the alternative Marxian theories depending on whether the economy operates under simple or expanded reproduction. It should be noted at the outset that a detailed coverage of the debates over the alternative Marxian theories is beyond the scope of this chapter. The basic assumptions of the model are kept intact to facilitate a simpler exposition of the following discussions.

A standard Marxian underconsumption theory suggests that workers cannot generate sufficient demand for means of consumption since their consumption constitutes only a portion of the total net income.[10] The remaining means of consumption must be consumed by capitalists, which creates a dilemma. If they spend all their profits to purchase means of consumption, they will have no capital to expand investment; and if they spend a portion of their income to expand capital, however, there will be insufficient demand for means of consumption. The theory claims that capitalism has an inherent tendency to expand means of consumption faster than the demand for them. Brewer (1984: 122), for example, suggests that 'while capitalists try to buy more means of production (to expand production) and less consumer goods, the result will be a surplus of unsaleable consumer goods'. The same point was made by Rosa Luxembourg ([1913] 2003: 319):

> It goes without saying that if the capitalists of Department I relatively restrict their consumption for purposes of accumulation, there will be a proportionately greater unsaleable residue of consumer goods in Department II; and thus it becomes more and more impossible to enlarge the constant capital . . . If the capitalists in Department I relatively restrict their consumption, the capitalists of Department II must relatively expand their personal consumption in proportion. The assumption of accelerated accumulation in Department I would then have to be supplemented by that of retarded accumulation in Department II.

She claims, therefore, that 'expanded reproduction is algebraically possible but socially impossible' (Shaikh 1978: 228) and that capitalism is incapable of self-expansion and needs the non-capitalist world to grow.

While my model is primarily concerned with insufficient demand, it is obvious from the above explanations that it is not a typical underconsumptionist model. Unlike such models, expanded reproduction is logically possible due to the time gap between the expansion of means of production and means of consumption. The model implies that neither too-low wages nor too-low capitalist consumption will always cause insufficient demand (underconsumption) so long as there are available workers to expand production. The expansion process can successfully continue and insufficient demand arises only when the reserve army of labor declines substantially. Therefore, while Shaikh (1978: 231) correctly points out that in Marx's view 'capitalists are driven to accumulate as rapidly as possible, so that self-expanding reproduction . . . is the normal tendency of the system', this does not necessarily imply that 'the limits to the accumulation process do not arise from an insufficiency of demand'.

While underconsumption means low levels of production due to insufficient demand, overproduction implies unsold commodities and the piling up of idle use values. Weeks (Chapter 6 in this volume) suggests that overproduction refers to overproduction of means of production, since overproduction is impossible when commodities are produced directly for consumption. The disproportionality theory was one of the leading Marxist theories of crisis prior to World War I (Kuhn 1979), which focused on the imbalances between the two departments of production when one department experiences overproduction compared to the other. In a sense, therefore, overproduction and disproportionality can be considered as sister theories. The disproportionality often results from the unplanned and anarchic nature of market economies. Bellofiore (Chapter 15 in this volume) argues, however, that such mismatches are resolved due to rapid price-and-quantity adjustments and a more organized form of capitalism. Assuming that demand for means of production depends on demand for means of consumption, a point supported by Marx,[11] a systemic and long-lasting overproduction is unlikely.[12]

In my model, disproportionality (overproduction) between the sectors is unlikely to be a source of concern as long as the economy is expanding. This is because a temporary overproduction in any of the sectors can quickly be resolved by slowing down expansion in that sector while continuing expansion in the other until the correct balance between these two sectors is established. Under simple reproduction, however, overproduction of means of production (disproportionality) requires a large portion of the workers to move from department 1 to department 2. In other words, production in department 1 would have to decline and that in department 2 would have to increase. In this case, disaccumulation in department 1 would be associated with accumulation in department 2, leaving the total accumulation unaltered. Obviously this process would not be pain-free.

The profit squeeze theory suggests that as the economy gets closer to full employment, increase in wages may squeeze profits and cause a crisis.[13] Profit squeeze in my model is relevant only under expanded reproduction where excessive wage increases could slow down or even stop capital accumulation. As opposed to the profit squeeze argument, however, high wages could in fact act as a stabilizer and delay crisis by increasing demand under simple reproduction. Decline in the reserve army of labor, increase in wages and decline in profits may indeed be associated with crisis. This does not, however, imply that crisis is caused by profit squeeze. Under simple reproduction, profits are bound to decline due to insufficient demand regardless of wage increases.

The interaction between the tendency of the rate of profit to fall (TRPF) theory and my model would be very similar to the profit squeeze theory. If technological changes lead to increase in the organic composition of capital and decline in the rate of profit (an issue extensively debated in this book), the story presented above regarding the impacts of productivity increase would slightly be modified to account for the decline in profit rates. Capital accumulation would be slower under expanded reproduction due to lesser reinvestable profits. Decline in profit rates, however, would help the economy by increasing demand from workers under simple reproduction.

The moral depreciation of fixed capital refers to the failure to recapture the value of fixed means of production due to the development of new and superior machines that undermine the profitability of the old (Weeks Chapter 6 in this volume). It should be noted that problems associated with the moral depreciation could only result from very rapid, large and unpredictable technological changes. If productivity changes are predictable, the economic life of fixed means of production is shorter than their physical life, and capitalists can calculate their depreciation accordingly.[14] As long as capitalists can estimate the economic life of fixed means of production accurately, they can generate sufficient funds to replace them. If the moral depreciation is mild, firms that work with the old fixed means of production can continue operating with a smaller profit margin. In other words, not all moral depreciation, due to technological changes, would lead to capitalist crisis.

If technological changes are so rapid, large and unpredictable as to cause major depreciation of fixed means of production, the impact would be equivalent to their (partial or complete) physical destruction and would require their (partial or complete) replacement. The first impact of such technological changes under both simple and expanded reproduction would be similar. Initially, the adaptation of the new technologies by some firms would lead to an increase in the production of means of consumption and a decline in prices. The other firms (that lag behind the technological developments) would experience depreciation in their old fixed means of production. Some of these firms are likely to leave the market, which would cause unemployment and decline in the availability of means of consumption (a crisis) under simple reproduction. Once these firms are eliminated, capital accumulation would start again, unemployment would decline and there would be a major increase in the availability of means of consumption. Under expanded reproduction, however, the net impact would depend on the contradictory interactions between the forces of accumulation, productivity increase and destruction of capital. The accumulation process would temporarily slow down, stop or even be reversed (crisis). After some firms leave the market, capital accumulation would continue as before.

11.5 CONCLUSIONS

What are the advantages of this model, and how is it relevant to the 2008 crisis? It would be too ambitious, at this level of abstraction, to move from abstract to concrete and establish a direct link between the model and the 2008 crisis. For this, as it was stated earlier, a more sophisticated version of the model is required. This does not, however, mean that in its current form the model is less relevant to the 2008 crisis compared to the other Marxian theories, and that it has nothing meaningful to say about it.

A brief review of the relevant literature reveals that the other systemic theories of crisis also often fail to move from abstract to concrete in an unambiguous way, and exhibit weaknesses in terms of providing empirical evidence. Rather than establishing an explicit causal link between the alternative Marxian theories and the crisis, many scholars prefer to detach the immediate triggers of the crisis from their systemic underlying causes that may have played a determining role in the background. Freeman (Chapter 5 in this volume), for example, suggests that attempts to establish a direct link between the TRPF and crisis signifies a major confusion since the TRPF worsens all the other contradictions of capitalism and causes crisis indirectly. In his view, while Marx offered a theory of crisis based on the TRPF, he did not reduce the theory into a mechanism. Weeks (Chapter 6 in this volume) uses the moral depreciation of capital theory to expose the systemic nature of the 2008 crisis. Rather than establishing a direct link between this theory and the crisis, he shows that amongst the many disruptions in the accumulation process between 1929 and 2013 only two episodes qualify as crises in terms of being systemic or severe: the Great Depression of the 1930s and the 2008 crisis. Clearly, the identification of the 2008 crisis as systemic does not prove that it resulted from the moral depreciation of capital. I am not criticizing these papers for not establishing a direct causal link between the theories they endorse and the crisis, but arguing that the lack of a direct link is neither unusual nor to be considered as a major weakness.

It is worth stating once again that the above arguments are very sensitive to the assumptions made over international trade, finance and capital movements. The results would change significantly once instabilities associated with the financial sector and problems associated with free trade are integrated into the model. Although the problems of financialization are extensively discussed in this book and in the relevant literature, problems associated with international trade and capital movements are largely overlooked. In other words, although a more sophisticated version of my model is admittedly required to see the real impact of trade and finance, the alternative Marxian theories also often fail to integrate these issues into their arguments.

An important advantage of my model is that it could be developed into a fuller version by extending the reproduction schemes in two ways: first, introducing the depreciation of fixed means of production explicitly into the model proves to be a source of considerable insight; and second, disaggregating means of production into fixed and circulating components is essential to generate the categories of net saving and net investment, which are instrumental to demonstrate the general nature of capital accumulation. Once these concepts are clarified, a useful Marxian theoretical framework can be formulated to challenge the mainstream (both neoclassical and Keynesian) models.

The following points could be made regarding the relevance of the model to the 2008 crisis. While both the US and Germany experienced wage compressions, they adopted different strategies to avoid insufficient demand. In the case of the US, underconsumption manifested itself as overaccumulation since the US capitalists designed a clever yet short-term plan to delay crisis.[15] Rather than increasing wages, they promoted household debt to offset insufficient demand, which was inevitably unsustainable. Unemployment declined from 6 percent in 2003 to 4.6 percent in 2007, right before the crisis, but it increased to 9.6 percent in 2010 which is consistent with the expectations of my model. The large trade deficits in the US under simple reproduction may have reduced the demand further and aggravated the crisis. Insufficient demand in Germany was lessened by large trade surpluses which may have helped to avoid job losses and modified the decline in economic growth rates. This policy helped to reduce unemployment in Germany from 11.1 percent in 2005 to 5.5 percent in 2012, but it was not sufficient to evade a crisis where the GDP declined by 5.6 percent in 2009. Although large and increasing trade surpluses may have helped the German economy, in line with the expectations of the model, they were insufficient to resolve the problem. Overall growth performance has not been superior in Germany to that in the US over the last decade, but the decline in growth has been much more notable in the US than in Germany.

The model and above discussions regarding trade, capital flows and FDI could help to explain the global nature of capitalist crisis. Economies under simple reproduction would have incentives to have a trade surplus, and send capital and FDI to other countries, which will stimulate faster capital accumulation under expanded reproduction. Eventually, however, these countries will also face simple reproduction (stagnation) which may lead to a simultaneous (or global) crisis. This could also help us to understand the so-called eurozone crisis. The European periphery (Greece, Spain, Ireland and Portugal) may have benefited from receiving capital from the center (particularly Germany) as long as their economy was expanding, but once the periphery experienced stagnation (simple reproduction), the continuation of the trade deficit and capital inflows may have only worsened their problems.[16]

NOTES

1. The validity and usefulness of the reproduction schemes is questioned by some Marxian economists who consider the schemes as inappropriate tools to analyze the dynamics of capital accumulation and crisis (Fine 2012: 449). Reproduction schemes, for instance, are often criticized for ignoring the importance of money. Others, however, consider them as an expedient alternative framework to challenge the neoclassical orthodoxy.
2. Class struggle and the distribution of income between workers and capitalists play an important role in many Marxian theories of crisis. If wages are too low, for example, there can be realization problems; and if too high, there can be a profit squeeze that hinders capital accumulation (see Harvey, Chapter 3 in this volume).
3. The schemes have attracted widespread attention from Marxist and non-Marxist scholars over the years (Luxemburg [1913] 2003; Morishima 1973; Koshimura 1975; Bleaney 1976; Turban 1984; Okishio 1988; Sardoni 1989; Carchedi and de Haan 1995; Reuten 1998; Trigg 2006). While many valuable contributions have been made to the schemes, they remain relatively undeveloped compared to their mainstream rivals. Morishima (1973), for example, developed the schemes by using sophisticated mathematical models. These models, however, are far too complex, not easy to comprehend and elucidate, and unviable in the analysis of many contemporary macroeconomic issues.
4. The importance of the time gap between the production of means of production and means of consumption is also recognized by the moral depreciation of capital theory (see Weeks, Chapter 6 in this volume).
5. It should be noted that Marx considered full employment as a vulgar fantasy, as capitalism has an inherent tendency 'to create and maintain a relative surplus population of workers – the reserve army of the unemployed' (Shaikh 1980: 33). Therefore I use 'full employment' here as a metaphor for a significant decline in unemployment.
6. Although lower wages would generate faster capital accumulation, the necessary adjustments (increase in wages and/or taxes) to sustain demand would also be proportionally greater under simple reproduction. If capitalists and the state fail to undertake these adjustments to increase demand, the crisis (decline in production or supply) would proportionally be larger.
7. Although this chapter does not discuss it in detail, it is clear from the above arguments that the model has important implications for the Keynesian and post-Keynesian theories. Unemployment, for example, does not always result from the lack of demand (Keynesian argument) and savings do not always result from investment (post-Keynesian argument). Unemployment results from the lack of demand only under simple reproduction, and policies to bust aggregate demand by fiscal policies are likely to fail. Although investments could bring about higher savings by increasing income, the lack of savings can be a real barrier for capital accumulation, particularly in low-income

countries. These arguments, however, do not necessarily invalidate the Keynesian theory altogether. If an economy experiences stagnation for other reasons (such as widespread pessimism) the Keynesian policies could still be relevant.

8. Free trade is likely to cause massive problems particularly for low-income countries. A detailed investigation of the impact of trade under alternative trade theories and policies requires a more advanced version of the model.
9. FDI may have positive or negative impacts depending on whether it takes the form of greenfield investment or mergers and acquisitions, and whether it establishes limited or extensive linkages with the local economy. The benefits will be limited if multinational corporations adopt transfer pricing, lower domestic savings and investment rates by repatriating their profits, import inputs from their subsidiaries in other countries rather than buying them from domestic companies, and use their economic power to influence government policies.
10. Clarke (1990: 443) argues that underconsumptionism was often rejected because it 'had become associated with a Keynesian reformist politics, which sought to overcome the crisis-tendencies of accumulation by intervention at the level of distribution and exchange, while leaving the social relations of capitalist production intact'.
11. 'As Marx pointed out, the production of constant capital is "ultimately limited" by consumption demand "for production of constant capital never takes place for its own sake, but simply because more of it is needed in those spheres of production whose products do go into individual consumption" (Marx [1867] 1977: 420)' (Desai, Chapter 8 in this volume).
12. 'The idea of capitalism as a never-ending production of producers' goods which would make the paucity of consumption demand irrelevant is largely a fantasy of many Marxist economists' (Desai, Chapter 8 in this volume).
13. Rapid wage increases could also result from class struggles.
14. For example, computers often have a shorter economic life than their physical life due to rapid but predictable technological changes that require companies to purchase new computers before the old ones become physically unusable.
15. The distinction between underconsumption and overaccumulation is often blurred. Kotz (Chapter 2 in this volume), for example, argues that an underconsumption crisis was avoided via the consumer spending promoted by household debt which led firms to invest in fixed capital to serve the rising sales volume. As evident from rapidly declining industrial capacity utilization rates, this extra capacity turned into surplus (overproduction) once the asset bubble deflated and consumer spending declined in 2008. As this story suggests, the distinction between underconsumption and overproduction is not clear-cut since an underconsumption crisis was diverted into an overproduction crisis by the policies adopted.
16. As was argued in Chapter 10 in this volume, with the exception of Greece, the 'peripheral' countries (Portugal, Spain and Ireland) in the EU experienced much faster per capita gross domestic product (GDP) growth rates than the 'core' countries from their entrance to the EU to the 2008 crisis.

REFERENCES

Bleaney, M.F. (1976), *Underconsumption Theories*, London: Lawrence & Wishart.

Brewer, A. (1984), *A Guide to Marx's Capital*, New York: Cambridge University Press.

Carchedi, G. and W. de Haan (1995), 'On the Replacement of Fixed Capital in Marx's Simple Reproduction', *History of Political Economy*, 27(3), 599–604.

Clarke, S. (1990), 'The Marxist Theory of Overaccumulation and Crisis', *Science and Society*, 54 (4): 442–467.

Fine, B. (2012), 'Revisiting Rosa Luxemburg's Political Economy', *Critique: Journal of Socialist Theory*, 40(3), 449–456.

Koshimura, S. (1975), *Theory of Capital Reproduction and Accumulation*, Ontario: DPG Publishing Co.

Kuhn, K. (1979), *Economics and Marxism Vol. 2*, London: Macmillan.

Luxemburg, R. ([1913] 2003), *The Accumulation of Capital*, London, UK and New York, USA: Routledge.

Marx, K. ([1867] 1977), *Capital*, Vol. I, London: Penguin.

Marx, K. ([1894] 1978), *Capital Volume 2*, Harmondsworth: Penguin.

Morishima, M. (1973), *Marx's Economics: A Dual Theory of Value and Growth*, Cambridge: Cambridge University Press.

Okishio, N. (1988), 'On Marx's Reproduction Scheme', *Kobe University Economic Review*, 34, 1–24.

Reuten, G. (1998), 'The Status of Marx's Reproduction Schemes: Conventional Logic or Dialectical Logic?', in C.J. Arthur and G. Reuten (eds), *The Circulation of Capital: Essays on Volume Two of Marx's Capital*, London: Macmillan.

Sardoni, C. (1989), 'Some Aspects of Kalecki's Theory of Profits: Its Relationship to Marx's Schemes of Reproduction', in M. Sebastiani (ed.), *Kalecki's Relevance Today*, Basingstoke: Macmillan.

Shaikh, A. (1978), 'An Introduction to the History of Crisis Theories', in Crisis Reader Editorial Collective (ed.), *US Capitalism in Crisis*, New York: URPE.

Shaikh, A. (1980), 'Foreign Trade and the Law of Value: Part II', *Science and Society*, 44(1), 27–57.

Trigg, A.B. (2006), *Marxian Reproduction Schema: Money and Aggregate Demand in a Capitalist Economy*, London, UK and New York, USA: Routledge.

Turban, M.A. (1984), 'Roman Rosdolsky's Reconsideration of the Traditional Marxist Debate on the Schemes of Reproduction on New Methodological Grounds', in S. Koropeckyj (ed.), *Selected Contributions of Ukranian Scholars to Economics*, Cambridge, MA: Harvard University Press.

PART IV

Crisis and Finance

12. Inequality, money markets and crisis

Simon Mohun[1]

Many causal factors have been identified for the crisis that erupted in 2007 following the price downturn in the United States housing market about a year earlier. There was the attempt to extend home ownership to populations previously neglected because of poverty, with mortgage debt structured so that refinancing was required after two (or three) years, in which case rising house prices would extend housing equity to these populations. There was a central bank failure to recognize and act on a bubble in house prices and, later, confusion over the relevance of moral hazard. Misaligned incentives were pervasive, including borderline fraudulent practices in loan originations; ratings agencies were paid by the creators (rather than potential purchasers) of complex and opaque securities; and extraordinarily large salaries and bonuses were paid for satisfying generic rather than unique performance criteria.[2] Not least was the complacency engendered by statistical models relying on uncorrelated risks, with a negligible tail-risk probability seemingly validated by the very weak recession of 1991, the 'great moderation' of the 1990s, and the limited impact of the dot.com bubble burst at the end of that decade.

These features (and doubtless others like them) are important. But well-meaning policies, poor regulation, misaligned incentives, fraud and banking excess are frequent historical occurrences, whereas systemic crises are not. Indeed, it seemed reasonable at the time that the United States Federal Reserve (Fed) Chairman Bernanke could testify to Congress in March 2007 (after nine months of falling house prices) that 'the problems in the subprime market were likely to be contained' (FCIC 2011: 17). Subsequently he remarked, in evidence to the Financial Crisis Inquiry Commission (FCIC), that 'Prospective subprime losses were clearly not large enough on their own to account for the magnitude of the crisis' (FCIC 2011: 27). And 'the stock market goes up and down every day more than the entire value of the subprime mortgages in the country' (FCIC 2011: 227). In fact, by the end of 2009, all impaired Alt-A and subprime mortgage-backed securities amounted to about $300 billion (securities are impaired when they have suffered realized losses or are expected to suffer realized losses imminently), whereas United States (US) gross domestic product (GDP) in 2009 was $14.4 trillion. Hence the magnitude of impaired mortgages was only about 2 per cent of GDP. Yet Bernanke could tell the FCIC:

> As a scholar of the Great Depression, I honestly believe that September and October of 2008 was the worst financial crisis in global history, including the Great Depression. If you look at the firms that came under pressure in that period . . . only one . . . was not at serious risk of failure . . . So out of . . . 13 of the most important financial institutions in the United States, 12 were at risk of failure within a period of a week or two. (FCIC 2011: 354)

So how did problems in only a small part of the financial system cause the imminent collapse of the whole financial system?

Bernanke did remark that 'what created the contagion, or one of the things that created the contagion, was that the subprime mortgages were entangled in . . . huge securitized pools' (FCIC 2011: 227). The crisis, that is, arose out of something systemic. This chapter follows a 'money view' (Grad et al. 2011; Mehrling 2011; Mehrling et al. 2013; Pozsar et al. [2010] 2012; Pozsar 2014a, 2014b) which focuses on the underlying structure (the 'plumbing') of the US financial system in order to explain the systemic nature of the financial crisis.

Two features in particular are important to this view. First, what instrument counts as 'money' for any market participant depends upon its trading at par on demand, with a credit risk attached to it determined by its proximity to government guarantees. That proximity determines that money instruments are hierarchical, and that promises to use these instruments to pay a debt depend upon their position in the hierarchy and may not therefore be realized. Second, the notion of a 'bank' is elastic, if by 'bank' is meant an institution whose assets are loans of longer-term duration than the money liabilities that fund them (a maturity transformation always subject to liquidity risk). Prior to the crisis, only a subset of such institutions had access to complete liquidity insurance provided by central bank backstops, and the remainder (with either partial or no central bank insurance), which had to purchase private insurance, have come to be called 'shadow banks'. But this terminology throws an unwarranted emphasis on 'legitimate' and 'illegitimate' banking practices, the latter described by Mehrling et al. (2013) as 'regulatory evasion in good times combined with unauthorized access to the public purse in bad times'. With the proliferation of non-bank financial intermediaries, it is better to focus more generically on the whole financial system, called here the 'neoliberal financial system' because of its basis in lightly regulated markets.

There are three difficulties that should be mentioned. First is a difficulty throughout with tenses. The crisis erupted more than seven years ago at the time of writing in early 2015. But the basic structure of the neoliberal financial system has changed little, apart from major transformations in the activities of the central bank. Hence it is difficult to know whether to describe the system in the present or the past tense. Second, the neoliberal financial system is a world system based on the dollar. Most of this chapter is couched in terms of US institutions, but these are better thought of as institutions with a world purview that happen to be based largely on the eastern seaboard of the US, although they are of course subject to the governance of wherever they operate. And third, while the elasticity of the notion of a bank has been mentioned, this creates a terminological difficulty as to whether the referent is a specific institution, or whether it is a specific function. The chapter distinguishes between a neoliberal bank that is a commercial bank and a neoliberal (investment) bank that is a dealer. Prior to 2008, specialist dealers intermediated risk but did not undertake maturity transformation, although at the same time most commercial banks had dealer desks. After 2008, all of the former investment banks that survived have become commercial banks, either through being taken over or through legal transformation.

What this chapter adds to the 'money view' is a more focused historical perspective on the evolution of the system. The large compensation packages paid in the financial sector are generally considered to be one of the proximate causes of the inequality generated by the surge in top incomes. This chapter proposes that this causal chain also works in the opposite direction: the growth in inequality at the top of the income distribution is a major cause of the growth of the neoliberal financial sector and its instabilities. This implies that, because soaring top incomes are a generic characteristic of neoliberalism, so too is the crisis of 2007–2009.

12.1 THEN AND NOW

The neoliberal financial system is a complex organism many more times removed from the real economy of production, trade and consumption than it was in the nineteenth century. This is important, because of a general but mistaken view that finance is a superimposition on the 'real' economy, an epiphenomenon or veil that must be lifted to explore the real economy. The mistake arises out of a failure to focus on the money relations of a capitalist economy. At its most abstract, it is central to how a capitalist economy works that value achieves an independent existence in money-form through its circuits. Since money is a form of debt,[3] financial circuits of debits and credits are the plumbing without which the flows of the real economy could neither function nor indeed exist. At its most concrete, the plumbing, then, describes the detail of financial circuits, and these, like everything else, evolve historically. A contrast with the nineteenth-century financial system (dominated by London banks) will help to make this clear, showing in passing how the mistaken interpretation of money as a veil could arise.

In Marx's day, firms financed production and trade by issuing bills of exchange (credit notes) with a usual term of 90 days. These were 'accepted' (guaranteed) by banks for a fee. But a bill could be also be 'discounted' (bought) by a bank at less than its face value, also for a fee, with the difference between the bill's face value and its discounted value constituting a rate of interest accruing to the bank for the remainder of the bill's term. Banks financed their discounting with cash or with bank account deposits (subject to prudential liquidity requirements), and the receiving firms spent these payments on other maturing bills. So firms managed their daily cash inflows (from sales revenues and discounted bills) and their cash outflows (for input purchases and maturing bills) through this discounting mechanism, and through it they financed the purchase of inputs in order to produce the outputs whose sale enabled the flow of repayments. In their turn, banks amassed portfolios of bills, with varieties of maturity dates and hence cash inflows, which in turn financed new discounts and hence cash outflows. Banks managed their cash inflows and outflows by adjustments in the discount rate: too many maturing bills and not enough requests for discounting, and the bank would reduce its discount rate; if the opposite, it would increase it.

If a firm experienced problems with selling its outputs, it might have to default on its accepted bills, and the accepting bank would then suffer a cash shortfall. If this could not be managed by commercial borrowings, the accepting bank would have to meet its cash shortfall by using its own resources, reducing its own cash (drawing on its reserves held at the Bank of England), or by borrowing more from the Bank (against any security that would be acceptable in normal times, but at a penal rate of interest; Bagehot [1873] 1999). With this (painfully learnt) procedure, domestic financial problems with one bank, caused by difficulties in the real economy, could be prevented from cascading through the whole delicately balanced system of cash credits and debits.

But bills of exchange accepted and discounted at London banks were also used to finance production and trade the world over, and for foreigners gold alone was an acceptable form of payment. So the Bank of England had to manage its gold inflows (from maturing international bills of exchange) and its gold outflows (from requests for new discounts) through variations in its own discount rate. If outflows exceeded inflows, the Bank could not create new gold (in contrast to its ability to create new credit domestically), and if it could not stem the imbalance (via for example loans from other central banks), it would ultimately have to suspend convertibility. This could only be avoided if foreigners would accept payment in sterling instead of gold, but the gold standard never in fact evolved into this sort of gold–sterling system.

In sum, the dominant financial asset was the bill of exchange; and problems in the production and sale of output were directly reflected in finance through imbalances in cash flows. Normally, producers and traders paid their debts with bank deposits; banks with their reserves at the Bank of England, and the Bank of England with gold, a hierarchy of money in which each level settled using the claims of entities at the next higher level. But in a crisis, only domestic or foreign cash would do, all at par on demand at rates fixed in gold.

The neoliberal world is different. The US rather than the United Kingdom (UK) is the dominant economy, so that institutionally the Federal Reserve Bank has replaced the Bank of England. The post-1945 Bretton Woods arrangements established a gold–dollar system, which in due course evolved into today's purely dollar system, after the dollar's link to gold was abandoned in 1971. But the most dramatic change is that the dominant financial asset is no longer the bill of exchange with its direct links to the finance of production and trade. Instead the dominant neoliberal financial asset is the 'sale and repurchase agreement' or 'repo', and it is undertaken purely for financial reasons.

In a repo, a borrower of cash sells a bundle of securities for $\$x$ to a lender of cash with an agreement that the cash borrower will repurchase the securities for $\$y$ after a fixed term (often overnight). The ratio $(y - x)/x$ is the repo rate, effectively a rate of interest. The value of the securities, say $\$z$, will generally be of greater value than their sale price, and the ratio $(z - y)/y$ is the 'haircut'.[4] The securities thereby act as collateral for the cash loan, and in the event that the cash borrower defaults on repayment, the cash lender owns the securities to keep or sell. During the interval in which the cash lender owns the securities, they can be used as collateral in further transactions by the cash lender. This 'rehypothecation' of collateral creates a collateral multiplier, although its size is unknown.

Whereas bills of exchange financed production and trade, and so were short-term debt collateralized by real goods, repos finance the holding of purely financial assets. The neoliberal financial system is built around repo-based money dealing activities, organized through dealers who intermediate risk: foreign exchange, duration and credit. With derivatives separating the flow of risks from the flow of funds,[5] the dealers made most of their profits through this intermediation process.[6]

In the modern hierarchy of money, as in Marx's day, each level continues to settle using the claims of entities at the next-higher level. Part of this hierarchy remains the same as in Marx's day. The central bank issues reserves, and commercial banks issue deposits. All traders in the economy settle their debts with commercial bank deposits, and commercial banks settle their debts through their central bank reserve accounts. What is different from Marx's day is what happens both above and below these parts of the hierarchy. Above, central banks settle in dollars or safe dollar-denominated assets (US Treasuries). Below, dealers issue repos, and money market mutual funds issue constant net asset value shares. Neither repos nor money market mutual fund shares can be used to settle debts, but they remain money because they can be traded on demand for a commercial bank deposit at par which can then be used for settlement of debts. At all levels of this hierarchy, the money liabilities issued by institutions are the money assets of institutions below them, which are used in turn to fund their money liabilities. Thus, as in Marx's day, commercial banks (wholesale and retail) issue deposits as money against their central bank reserves. And, not as in Marx's day, dealers issue repos as money against assets of overnight government repos with commercial (wholesale) banks; and money market mutual funds issue constant net asset value shares as money against overnight repos issued by dealers.[7]

Moreover, the money liabilities issued by institutions at each part of the hierarchy are more liquid, shorter-term and safer than their assets. All institutions have this maturity mismatch and therefore incur rollover risk, and in a crisis depend upon their stock of overnight money assets (their liquidity) and their access to secured funding (either to the central bank or to credit lines at commercial banks).

This too is hierarchical. For extra liquidity, money market mutual funds can only lend securities against cash (provided someone wants to borrow), and access credit lines from banks (provided they are maintained). Dealers can in addition borrow against their assets (provided someone will lend). Thus according to the Lehman Brothers bankruptcy report:

> Lehman funded itself through the short-term repo markets and had to borrow tens or hundreds of billions of dollars in those markets each day from counterparties to be able to open for business. Confidence was critical. The moment that repo counterparties were to lose confidence in Lehman and decline to roll over its daily funding, Lehman would be unable to fund itself and continue to operate. (cited by Gorton and Metrick 2012a)

Of course, dealers could also sell assets (provided anyone would buy), but the danger then is a fire sale, with a liquidity crisis becoming a solvency crisis. Moving up the hierarchy, retail and wholesale banks have access to the central bank as lender of last resort (subject to having sufficient assets to meet the required haircuts), and so are generally not compelled to sell assets. And the central bank can in the last resort print money.

Repos issued by dealers are at the heart of the modern market-based financial system, dealers funding around half of their assets through repo. But the overall size of the repo market is unknown. At the pre-crisis peak, gross outstanding claims were perhaps $10 trillion in the US, $10 trillion in euro markets and a further $1 trillion in the UK (cited in Gorton and Metrick 2012a). Since repos are issued to finance the holding of financial assets, the linkages to the 'real' economy are not the more or less transparent ones of Marx's day. These linkages can however be pursued further by considering the rate of profit.

12.2 THE RELEVANCE OF THE RATE OF PROFIT

A standard approach in the Marxian tradition is to relate crisis to movements in the rate of profit. A secular decline in profitability at some point generates a crisis as investment falls in response to falling profitability, and resolution of the crisis reverses the secular decline that caused it. There are well-known problems of both structure and agency in this approach, but there are also considerable empirical difficulties, and these are the focus here.

The post-1945 'golden age' of a weak form of social democracy, with its commitments to full employment, social protection, the legitimacy of trade unions and state interventions in the economy, fixed exchange rates, and heavily regulated and restricted finance, gradually undermined the conditions of its own existence. By the 1970s, an era of growth had been replaced by stagflation, itself a symptom of a stalemate in the class struggle over the future direction of the economy.[8] The stalemate was resolved at the end of the 1970s with the Fed's dramatic interest rate rise, commonly considered to initiate the era of neoliberalism. This era was one of state-sponsored attacks on trade unions and the working class more generally, combined with a celebration of global capital mobility, a sustained programme of deregulation and privatization, an ideology of free markets that emphasized state failure over market failure, a prejudice against state-financed social expenditures, and a prioritization of direct tax reductions, especially for the rich.

This systematic dismantling of the structures of the 'golden age' successfully stemmed the fall in the average rate of profit that had characterized the latter years of the 'golden age'. Evaluating the fixed capital stock at current replacement cost rather than historic cost, from its post-war peak

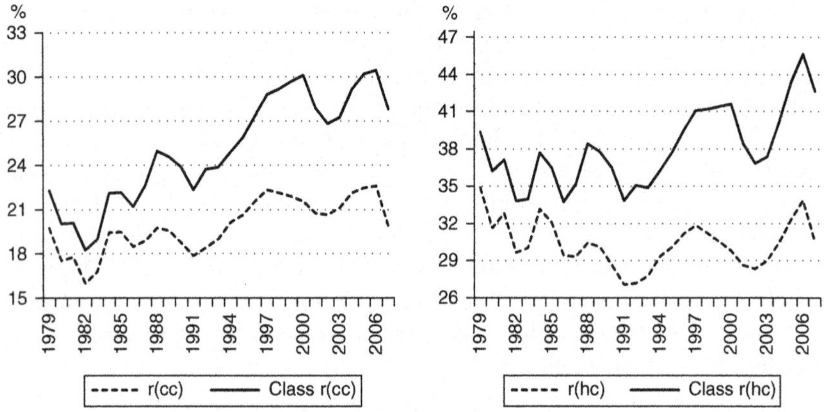

Note: The rate of profit (dotted line) is the ratio of the net operating surplus of private industries to the net non-residential private fixed capital stock of private industries (excluding inventories). The class rate of profit (solid line) is the same, except that it includes in the numerator an estimate of the employee compensation accruing to capitalists. The numerator is defined by the current year, the denominator by the December figure of the previous year.

Sources: BEA (NIPA, GPO, FAT, at http://www.bea.gov/national/index.htm#gdp) and Mohun (forthcoming).

Figure 12.1 The rate of profit in the neoliberal era, all private industries, US (left-hand panel: at current cost; right-hand panel: at historic cost)

of 27.7 per cent in 1966, the rate of profit fell to a trough of 16 per cent in 1982, followed by a fluctuating recovery to a peak of 22.6 per cent in 2006. In terms of historic cost capital stock, the pattern is different, for the neoliberal rise in the rate of profit began a decade later, from 27.1 per cent in 1991 to a peak of 33.9 per cent in 2006.

The dotted lines in Figure 12.1 show the details for the neoliberal era from 1979 to 2007. And while each rate of profit fell from 2006 over the following year (2.7 percentage points in current cost; 3.4 percentage points in historic cost), this is hardly evidence of a falling rate of profit of such severity as to imperil the system as a whole.

One of the well-documented features of the neoliberal era is the extraordinary increase in inequality as top incomes soared (Piketty and Saez 2003). Mohun (forthcoming) has used this data to estimate the total pre-tax labour and non-labour personal incomes of the capitalist class, where membership of the latter is defined by possession of sufficient non-labour income that receipt of a labour income is an option rather than a necessity. Since capitalist labour income can be treated in class terms as a form of profit, adding it to the numerator of the rate of profit defines a 'class rate of profit', shown as the solid lines in Figure 12.1. The dramatic rise in the labour income component of capitalist income thereby imports a marked and increasing upward shift to the class rate of profit in both its current cost and historic cost measures. This at least partially resolves an important puzzle of the neoliberal experience: in an era in which the working class has been comprehensively defeated, why didn't the rate of profit rise by more? One answer is that capitalists could divert profit income into their labour income packages, and the construction of a 'class rate of profit' compensates for this. And one consequence is that it makes a falling rate of profit account of the 2007–09 crisis even more implausible.

But there is a further consequence. Consider now the profit share depicted in Figure 12.2, defined as the net operating surplus of all private industries normalized by the net domestic product (NDP) of those industries.[9]

Again the dotted line is the conventionally defined measure, and the solid line adds the labour income component of capitalist personal income to the numerator. From 1980 to 2006, the neoliberal era saw an enormous 14.4 percentage points rise in the 'class profit share', well over twice the 6.5 percentage points rise in the conventionally defined profits share. Since luxury consumption can only account for a limited amount, this implies very large annual additions to amounts of cash seeking a home.

These amounts of cash have a number of different institutional manifestations. Some of them are held by global non-financial corporations, some by asset management and securities lending companies; some are the cash holdings of long-term mutual funds; some are held by insurance companies and pension funds; some are held directly by wealthy individuals, and some by hedge funds.[10] Pozsar (2011) estimates that this cash in 2007 amounted to a total of $3.8 trillion, spread across pools averaging $10 billion each, and each managed by a single central decision-maker (such as a corporate treasurer or an asset manager).

Whatever the institutional manifestation, these cash pools were (and are) generally subject to written mandates regarding cash investment policies, which govern what the cash manager can do. These mandates are conservative: safety of principal comes first, the next priority is liquidity, and only after safety and liquidity are ensured is yield considered. But bank deposits are not an option. Commercial bank deposits were only insured up to $100,000 (fixed in 1980 by the Federal Deposit Insurance Corporation, and raised to $250,000 after 2008), and safety of principal was hardly pursued by holding large uninsured bank deposits (and

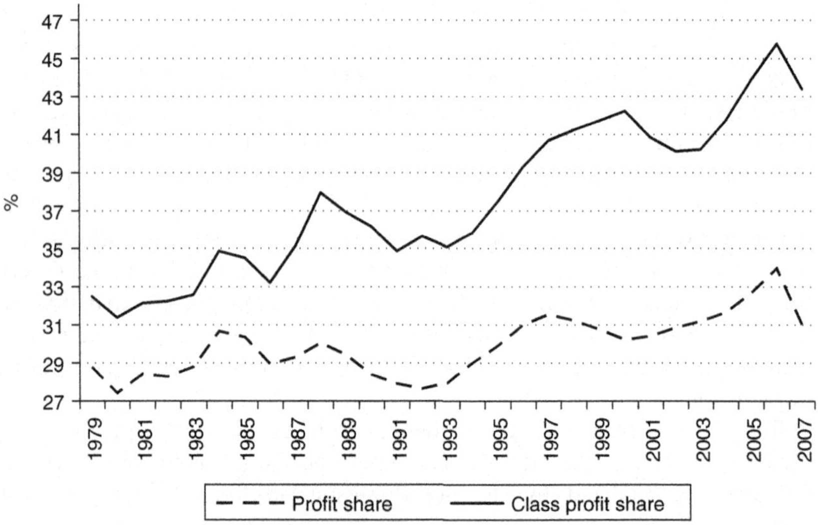

Note: Profit share (dotted line) is the ratio of net operating surplus to net domestic product, for all private industries. The class profit share adds capitalist labour income to the numerator.

Sources: BEA (NIPA, GPO, FAT, at http://www.bea.gov/national/index.htm#gdp) and Mohun (forthcoming).

Figure 12.2 Profit share of NDP in the neoliberal era, all private industries, USA

becoming an uninsured and unsecured creditor of the bank). Moreover, institutional cash pools do not want money for transactions purposes, but for liquidity, collateral management and other investment purposes, so that commercial bank deposits are not especially suitable. For non-commercial-bank deposit alternatives which were insured, the obvious choices were instruments guaranteed by the US government (Treasury and agency securities), but in the years running up to the crisis they were in short supply (by an amount estimated by Pozsar 2011 as well over $1 trillion).[11] So seeking investments in 'safe' assets for terms ranging from overnight to a year, the only possibility was to invest in privately insured, privately created instruments. This was done largely through repo.

The time path of the rate of profit is therefore central to the account of the crisis, not because it fell (since it did not), but because it rose, and in class terms rose dramatically with the huge labour income increases at the top of the personal income distribution. It is the cash pools thereby generated and their search for investment safety in repo that is central to the explanation of the crisis. To see why this is the case, it is helpful to consider the historical evolution of the neoliberal financial system.

12.3 THE EVOLUTION OF THE NEOLIBERAL FINANCIAL SYSTEM

In response to the banking collapses of the Great Depression, banks were subjected to considerable regulation. Commercial banking was separated from investment banking; there were restrictions on the formation of banks and the location of their branches; interest rates were prohibited on checking accounts and subject to a 3 per cent ceiling on deposit accounts; and there were restrictions on what borrowers could be charged. During the 'golden age', banks allegedly operated according to a 3–6–3 rule: collect deposits at 3 per cent, lend them at 6 per cent, and be on the golf course at 3pm. There is some doubt that life really was like that (Walter 2006), but whatever the case, life changed from the end of the 1970s as bank profitability came under considerable pressure.

This pressure came from two directions. The first came from the corporate loans side. Large creditworthy US corporations had always historically issued their own bonds directly (because banks were too small to fund the capital requirements of industrialization), but this process spread widely across the corporate sector in the 1980s with the development of (longer-term) 'junk bonds' and (shorter-term) 'commercial paper'.

Junk bonds were issued by corporations as high-yield, because they were below investment grade (the credit rating of the issuing corporation was BBB or below). Organized originally through underwriting at Drexel Burnham Lambert, and later at competing investment banks, junk bonds were used to finance mergers and acquisitions through leveraged buyouts: the acquirer issued a junk bond to pay for an acquisition, and then used the cash flow of the acquired firm to repay the debt over time. In contrast to junk bonds, commercial paper comprised short-term debt issued directly by the largest and most creditworthy firms. Substituting for short-term unsecured bank loans, through the 1980s it grew at an annual compound rate of 17 per cent. In terms of the impact of junk bonds and commercial paper on bank loans, Gorton and Metrick (2012b) cite studies showing that bank loans accounted for 36.6 per cent of the total credit market debt raised between 1977 and 1983, but only 18.2 per cent of the total debt raised between 1984 and 1989.

As junk bonds and commercial paper were substituted, respectively, for longer- and shorter-term bank loans in the US, the loss of business put downward pressure on bank profitability, which was further exacerbated by competition from foreign banks in the US domestic market. Gorton (1994) reports that Japanese banks in particular underpriced by more than 0.5 per cent (50 basis points) in order to enter the US domestic banking market for corporate loans, generating a loss to US banks as they were forced to respond by reducing their lending rates.

The second pressure on profitability came from the deposits side. Because of their interest rate ceilings, banks started losing deposits to money market mutual funds from the late 1970s. When the ceilings were removed, banks were then forced to devote considerable resources to price rather than non-price competition for (both wholesale and retail) deposits with money market mutual funds, which was expensive (Gorton 1994; Gorton and Metrick 2012b). The result of these pressures was sharply falling profitability, illustrated in Figure 12.3 in which the rate of profit in banking is normalized to that of all private industries.

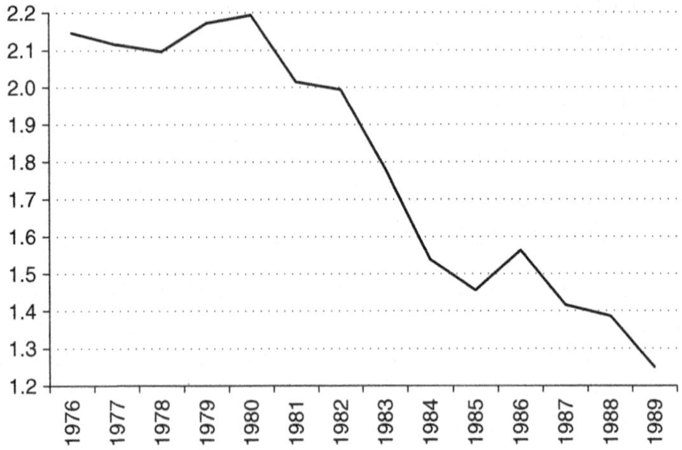

Note: Rate of profit defined for banking as the ratio of the gross operating surplus for banking (SIC 1972 and 1987) to the non-residential private fixed capital stock for NAICS 5210 (Federal Reserve Banks) and 5220 (Credit intermediation and related activities). Data limitations preclude excluding Federal Reserve Banks from the ratio, using only SIC or only NAICS data, and using net rather than gross data. SIC is the Standard Industrial Classification (https://www.osha.gov/pls/imis/sic_manual.html); NAICS is the North American Industrial Classification System (http://www.census.gov/eos/www/naics/).

Source: BEA (NIPA, GPO, FAT).

Figure 12.3 Rate of profit in banking as a proportion of the rate of profit in all private industries, US, 1976–89

Because of this steep relative fall in banking profitability, capital left the commercial banking industry for more profitable unregulated bank-like activities, and under this pressure commercial banking was restructured in order to compete more effectively. This restructuring used new developments in information and communications technology to enable market processes to be applied to the division of labour within a bank, so that its traditional loan-making process was broken into its constituent parts, each part becoming a separate market operation. The traditional pre-neoliberal bank originated and approved loans, held them (and their associated credit risks) to maturity, funded them with shorter-term deposits, and made money on the interest rate spread. By contrast, the neoliberal bank was a financial holding company, comprising both a bank (which partly continued to originate loans but also purchased them from specialized loan originators) and a network of subsidiaries (engaged in asset management and dealing, competing with the pre-crisis investment banks). The purpose of this network of subsidiaries was to securitize and distribute the loans via 'special purpose vehicles' (and to retain some of the loans for investment purposes). The only involvement of the bank in this was through the loans and credit guarantees it made to its subsidiaries. Compared with its non-neoliberal predecessor, the neoliberal bank thereby offloaded its credit risks and substituted market risk, earning its money through fees rather than interest rate spread.

Securitization was the central element in this transformation. Banks used special purpose vehicles to hold pools of loans off-balance sheet, and to sell investment-grade securities (typically tranched according to seniority, thereby catering to demands for different amounts of risk) which were backed by the income flows accruing to these pools. The revenues obtained from the sale of the securities created then financed the purchase of the loan pools themselves. The loan pools were formed primarily out of mortgage loans, automobile loans, student debt and credit card receivables, and the corresponding securities were generically called 'asset-backed securities'; those based on mortgages were 'mortgage–backed securities', divided into residential mortgage-backed securities and commercial mortgage-backed securities.[12] If asset-backed securities themselves were tranched and securitized, the resulting security was called a 'collateralized debt obligation'. And collateralized debt obligations in turn could be tranched and securitized, creating collateralized debt obligation squared securities, and so on.

This transformation to neoliberal market-based banking took time to be effected. Noting that much banking deregulation in fact amounted to a validation of trends already being pursued by market participants, legislation in 1980 and 1982 removed interest rate ceilings, allowing banks to compete with money market funds for deposits; intra-state branching restrictions were relaxed by the banks themselves through the 1980s; 1994 legislation removed inter-state branching restrictions; and in 1999 the legal requirement that investment and commercial banking be separate was repealed. On securitization, financial engineering took time in the 1980s to resolve such issues as early repayments of mortgage debt. And not until 1997 did J.P. Morgan introduce the Broad Index Secured Trust Offering which was the precursor for producing collateralized debt obligations from credit derivatives. Finally for repo, the first Global Master Repurchase Agreement was published in 1992, and revised in 1995 and 2000.

The complexity of neoliberal banking created opacity, but the fundamentals are that the securitization process bundles loans and resells them, funding its operations through repo. In April 2011, outstanding securitized assets in the US amounted to some $11 trillion, substantially more than the total of all outstanding marketable US Treasury securities (Gorton and Metrick 2012b).

If securitization could supply asset-backed securities in such volume, it was only because there was a demand. This demand came from the private cash investors described above.[13] Pozsar (2014a) calls them 'institutional cash pools . . . managed by cash portfolio managers whose mandate is "do not lose"'. Wholesale cash deposits are uninsured, and so are always invested in better credit risk instruments that are interest-earning. As described above, these latter are found in repo.

If cash portfolio managers are invested in repo (either directly or through money market mutual funds), then counterparties must post investment-grade collateral. The counterparties are risk portfolio managers, which are vehicles (such as hedge funds and absolute return funds) that use leverage to 'beat the benchmark'. They require cash in order to fund levered fixed-income positions, to post as collateral in shorting, and to provide margins in derivatives trades. And they get the cash by posting investment-grade securities in repo.

So risk portfolio managers use repo to supply securities and demand cash. Their assets are asset-backed securities and the swaps with which they actively pursue risk, and their liabilities in addition to their equity are the cash obtained from reverse repos. Cash portfolio managers use repo to demand securities and supply cash. Their assets are the money market instruments used in repo, and their liabilities (in addition to their equity) are the swaps (foreign exchange, interest rate and credit default) that they accept to minimize risk (currency, duration and credit). In this manner, the rapidly growing cash pools drove the securitization process.

In the middle are the dealers. As money dealers, their liabilities interface with the asset side of cash portfolio managers as they repo asset-backed securities as collateral for cash, and their assets interface with the liabilities side of risk portfolio managers as they reverse repo collateralized cash loans; this dual interface makes the markets that establish the price of funding. And as risk dealers, their balance sheet on both sides comprises swaps, interfacing on one side with cash portfolio managers seeking safety, and on the other with risk portfolio managers seeking risk; and this dual interface makes the markets that establish the price of risk. Thus the dealers were (and are) at the heart of the process, interfacing between cash portfolio managers and risk portfolio managers.[14]

In principle, dealers[15] operate matched books: identical long and short positions so that price risk is eliminated. But in practice dealers have to take the opposite side of any trade any customer wants, by virtue of their dealing function, without immediately being able to make an offsetting trade. So dealers must take inventory positions (whether long or short) and, in consequence of their exposure to price risk, must make buying and selling prices according to their inventory positions. For example, suppose cash pools increase in size, so that there is an increased demand for securities in repo. Dealers respond by running down inventories, and to restore their position must increase their buy price of securities, reducing their yield and risk premia, in order to prompt increasing supply of securities through the securitization process.[16]

The flows of money are huge. As of the second quarter of 2012, according to Pozsar (2014b), more than $3 trillion was placed with dealers by cash portfolio managers; the dealers lent on $2.5 trillion, and used the remainder to finance their securities' inventory positions.

12.4 CRISIS IN THE NEOLIBERAL FINANCIAL SYSTEM

In pre-neoliberal commercial banking, banks had to hold a fraction of their deposits as reserves, and in the last resort could borrow from the central bank. In neoliberal banking, when banks engage in repo transactions to borrow money, they are forced to keep a fraction of their assets as reserves via the repo haircut mechanism. And the transactions are 'insured' via the collateralization process.

Once subprime mortgages were impaired (through falling house prices), this affected all institutions holding securitized mortgages on their balance sheets, but the location and size of exposure to subprime risks was unknown. This immediately had an impact in inter-bank markets as the value of collateral used in repo began to fall. And as soon as questions about dealer stability were raised, so that cash portfolio managers might have to sell the securities they were holding for the cash they were supplying (and sell at whatever market prices they could get), repo rates and haircuts were raised across all private assets. Gorton and Metrick (2012a) describe how this amounted to a run on the dealers: with a repo market of $10 trillion and haircuts of zero, dealers can borrow $10 trillion against equivalent asset-backed securities collateral; with haircuts of 20 per cent, banks are $2 trillion short, and no financial system could survive a drain of that amount.

Suppose the demand for securities falls. Then dealers' inventories rise, and they reduce the buy price of securities to restore their inventory position. But that can prompt questions about the fundamental value of the securities used as collateral, so that the reduced price does not call forth an equilibrating reduction of supply, but rather prompts further haircuts, draining liquidity from dealers and hence risk portfolio managers and forcing deleveraging.[17] Once money markets cease to fund capital markets, the neoliberal financial system faces meltdown.

Hence large-scale deleveraging was forced on the dealers, and just as cash portfolio managers ran on the dealers, dealers ran on the risk portfolio managers, the levered portfolio managers in pursuit of yield.[18] This evaporation of liquidity bankrupted dealers, some of the hedge funds and, but for state bailouts, the commercial banks.

12.5 CONCLUSION

What then was, and remains, destabilizing is the growth of cash portfolio managers, fueled by the neoliberal growth in top incomes. In policy terms, this suggests that unless the issue of soaring top incomes is addressed, the neoliberal financial system remains crisis-prone. But it is not clear just how this issue could be addressed within the framework of neoliberalism. The 1920s saw similar growth of top incomes followed by financial crisis, and that was only resolved by the complete transformation of capitalism via the New Deal and war-time planning into the weak form of social democracy that facilitated the 'golden age'. That historical parallel suggests that only a major transformation of neoliberalism will do.

The second issue prompted by this chapter is the irrelevance of much Marxist theorizing to the financial system. Crises are breaks in the circuit of capital, but those breaks always occur in the markets for short-term debt, and when liquidity evaporates there are hugely damaging consequences that cascade through financial circuits and into the real economy. What then is required is much more attention to precisely how money markets work, because without their financing there are no capital markets and hence no real economy.

NOTES

1. Many thanks to Sue Himmelweit for helpful comments and discussion. The usual disclaimer applies.
2. In 2006, the labour compensation packages of the chief executive officers of leading investment banks were: Citigroup $25.98m, Bank of America $27.87m, Bear Stearns $33.85m, Lehman Brothers $40.5m, Morgan Stanley $41.41m, Merrill Lynch $48m and Goldman Sachs $54.72m.
3. In the United Kingdom, for example, about 97 per cent of all money is created by the commercial banking system as bank deposits (a liability of the banks). Only about 3 per cent of money is notes and coins issued by the Bank of England (a liability of the central bank).
4. A reverse repo is exactly the same transaction from the point of view of the seller of cash.
5. Duration risk through interest rate swaps, foreign exchange risk on liquidity needs in different currencies through currency swaps, and credit risk through credit default swaps.
6. On the important insurance mechanism of credit default swaps, see Stulz (2010).
7. See Pozsar (2014a, 2014b) for a more detailed elaboration of the hierarchy, using the distinctions between government repos and private repos, banker-dealers' government trading desks and their private credit trading desks, and government-only money market funds and prime money funds. The post-crisis arrangements are now different, since dealers and money market funds currently (early 2015) have access to reserve accounts at the Fed.
8. Mohun (2014) shows this stagnation in terms of an essentially flat rate of exploitation through the 1970s, in marked contrast to what came later.
9. Current cost and historic cost distinctions are irrelevant to the profit share.
10. Some is also held by the public sector: central banks smooth exchange rates and make domestic monetary system interventions; and municipalities manage cash receipts prior to their expenditure.
11. Partly because so many of them are held overseas, a consequence of both generally US balance-of-payments deficits, and specifically the determination of South and East Asian countries to insure against a repetition of the currency crises of the late 1990s.
12. Commercial paper too is securitized, as asset-backed commercial paper (ABCP). ABCP conduits have portfolio managers who make active (although rule-bound) decisions, and must mark portfolios (daily or weekly) to prevailing market prices, which then determines their borrowing ability. In contrast, special purpose vehicles are passive robots that follow predetermined rules; they have no physical location and no employees.
13. Plus the cash necessary for the public sector management of foreign exchange reserves and local government.
14. See Duffie (2010). Commercial banks were also involved although they tended to use other sources of funding than repo.
15. *Qua* dealers rather than proprietary traders.
16. Turner (Financial Services Authority 2009) describes the falls in yield over a 20-year period.
17. See Brunnermeier (2009) for descriptions of how initial shocks are amplified if funding becomes problematic. Leveraged investors are forced to retrench, but this leads to more losses and higher haircuts, which makes the funding problem worse. See also Krishnamurthy (2010).

18. This is oversimplified, because it ignores the run on asset-backed commercial paper in 2007 and 2008. See Kacperczyk and Schnabl (2010) for details.

REFERENCES

Bagehot, W. ([1873] 1999), *Lombard Street: A Description of the Money Market*, New York, USA and London, UK: Wiley.

Brunnermeier, M.K. (2009), 'Deciphering the Liquidity and Credit Crunch 2007–2008', *Journal of Economic Perspectives*, 23(1), 77–100.

Duffie, D. (2010), 'The Failure Mechanics of Dealer Banks', *Journal of Economic Perspectives*, 24(1), 51–72.

FCIC (2011), 'The Financial Crisis Inquiry Report', Final Report of the National Commission on the Causes of the Financial and Economic Crisis in the United States, Washington, DC: Government Printing Office.

Financial Services Authority (2009), 'The Turner Review: A Regulatory Response to the Global Banking Crisis', London: Financial Services Authority.

Gorton, G. (1994), 'Bank Regulation When "Banks" and "Banking" Are Not the Same', *Oxford Review of Economic Policy*, 10(4), 106–119.

Gorton, G. and A. Metrick (2012a), 'Securitized Banking and the Run on Repo', *Journal of Financial Economics*, 104(3), 425–451.

Gorton, G. and A. Metrick (2012b), 'Securitization', in G. Constantinides, M. Harris and R. Stulz (eds), *Handbook of the Economics of Finance*, Amsterdam: North-Holland.

Grad, D., P. Mehrling and D.H. Nelson (2011), 'The Evolution of Last-Resort Operations in the Global Credit Crisis', available at http://ssrn.com/abstract=2232347 (accessed 23 April 2014).

Kacperczyk, M. and P. Schnabl (2010), 'When Safe Proved Risky: Commercial Paper during the Financial Crisis of 2007–9', *Journal of Economic Perspectives*, 24(1), 29–50.

Krishnamurthy, A. (2010), 'How Debt Markets have Malfunctioned in the Crisis', *Journal of Economic Perspectives*, 24(1), 3–28.

Mehrling, P. (2011), *The New Lombard Street, How the Fed Became the Dealer of Last Resort*, Princeton, NJ: Princeton University Press.

Mehrling, P., Z. Pozsar, J. Sweeney and D.H. Neilson (2013), 'Bagehot was a Shadow Banker: Shadow Banking, Central Banking, and the Future of Global Finance', accessed 23 February 2015 at http://ssrn.com/abstract=2232016.

Mohun, S. (2014), 'Unproductive Labor in the US Economy 1964–2010', *Review of Radical Political Economics*, 46(3), 355–379.

Mohun, S. (forthcoming), 'Class Structure and the US Personal Income Distribution, 1918–2012', *Metroeconomica*.

Piketty, T. and E. Saez (2003), 'Income Inequality in the United States, 1913–1998', *Quarterly Journal of Economics*, 118(1), 1–39; tables and figures updated to 2013 in Excel format, January 2015, available at http://eml.berkeley.edu/~saez/.

Pozsar, Z. (2011), 'Institutional Cash Pools and the Triffin Dilemma of the US Banking System'. Working Paper WP 11/190, International Monetary Fund.

Pozsar, Z. (2014a), 'Shadow Banking: The Money View', Working Paper 14-04, Office for Financial Research, US Treasury.

Pozsar, Z. (2014b), 'How the Financial System Works', Appendix to 'Shadow

Banking: The Money View', Working Paper 14-04, Office of Financial Research, US Treasury.

Pozsar, Z. et al. ([2010] 2012), 'Shadow Banking', Staff Report No. 458, Federal Reserve Bank of New York, revised 2012.

Stulz, R.M. (2010), 'Credit Default Swaps and the Credit Crisis', *Journal of Economic Perspectives*, 24(1), 73–92.

Walter, J.R. (2006), 'The 3-6-3 Rule: An Urban Myth?', *Federal Reserve Bank of Richmond Economic Quarterly*, 92(1), 51–78.

13. The crisis of finance and the crisis of accumulation: it was not a 'Lehman Brothers moment'

Jan Toporowski

The financial crisis since 2008 has been analysed by critics of finance as a crisis of deregulation, financialization, neoliberalism and speculation (most notably by Duménil and Lévy 2011; see also Turner 2009; Phillips 2014). There was indeed in 2008 a crisis of liquidity in money and capital markets (Nesvetailova 2010). But crisis incidents in the financial markets cannot be understood without a serious analysis of how capitalism functions, integrating the theory of production with distribution, and the financing of capital accumulation. Most authors who undertake such a critique have done so by adding a dimension of debt to theories of capitalist production and distribution. Debt is then supposed to exacerbate the contradictions of capitalism by offering new forms of financial accumulation and burdening income with usurious debt payment obligations, a new 'regime of accumulation' commonly called 'financialization' or 'financialized capitalism' (Duménil and Lévy 2011; Lapavitsas 2013). In general this literature integrates finance into capitalist production and distribution as debt that has to be financed out of income. This chapter attempts a more complex analysis of finance, showing how long-term finance changes the functioning of capitalist enterprises and through that the functioning of the capitalist economy and its crises. Such an analysis of finance in capitalism requires not just the incorporation of corporate finance into the analysis of capitalism, but also the identification of debt structures, the processes by which balance sheets are modified and kept liquid, and the effects of this on capitalist institutions.

These considerations then point to the dynamics of the present crisis, that lay behind the incidents in the financial markets that are commonly used in the political economy literature to describe the present crisis. The chapter argues that the present crisis was initiated in the summer of 2008 by non-financial corporations that had become over-reliant on short-term borrowing to finance merger and takeover activity. The squeeze on the liquidity of non-financial corporations obliged them to reduce fixed investment. This reduction in investment transmitted the crisis to the rest of the economy. It was this reduction that has seriously impaired the ability of economies to support debt structures.

13.1 LONG-TERM FINANCE AND THE CRITIQUE OF POLITICAL ECONOMY

Political economy is not received economic wisdom, a set of doctrines that either must be true or frame research, because like Schumpeter's 'vision' it is necessary to have a theoretical starting point in any study of society. In Marxian terms it is an understanding of how capitalist production and distribution determine the way in which capitalism has evolved, combined with a systematic criticism of economic ideas and policy.[1] Marx's political economy is based on a theory of value. Volume II of *Capital* was supposed to show how value is realized. The volume is subtitled *The Process of the Circulation of Capital*. This process is what we now call the circular flow of income which represents the income flows that Marx described in the schemes of reproduction laid out in this volume. However, he was not satisfied with the draft he had written and intended to revise it (see Kowalik 2014: Appendix I). In particular, he showed in the volume a scheme of simple reproduction (reproduction without any increase in production, or of the capital stock), but he did not complete the exposition of expanded reproduction (Marx 1974a: Chapters XX and XXI). The question of the conditions for realization was to be taken up by Rosa Luxemburg in her *Accumulation of Capital* (Luxemburg 1921). In his book on Luxemburg's theory, Tadeusz Kowalik argues that Kalecki's theory of the business cycle solves the problem of value realization that eluded Marx and Luxemburg (Kowalik 2014).

Since the writing of *Capital*, a radical change occurred in the functioning of the capitalist economy. Legislation from the 1860s onwards eased the establishment of joint stock companies and led to the proliferation of markets for long-term debt and shares in capitalist enterprises in the advanced capitalist countries. This transformed capitalism from its 'classic' form in the mid-nineteenth century, in which capitalist enterprises were owned and controlled by individual capitalists and their more or less active partners, into its modern, twentieth-century form dominated by large joint-stock companies (Kindleberger 1993).[2]

This change had two consequences of radical importance for the stability of capitalism. In the first place, large capitalist enterprises with access to capital (long-term debt and equity) markets were able to 'fund' their long-term industrial assets with bonds, or equity. This reduced their vulnerability to credit shortages. Before this change in financing, the 'classic' capitalist enterprise was typically financed with the owner's capital. But as mechanization of production proceeded, there was an incessant need for additional capital that was usually met by short-term bank borrowing that had to be rolled over during the lifetime of the productive capital equipment that it was financing (see Dobb 1967; Niebyl 1946; Kindleberger 1993). If banks became reluctant to lend, the capitalist entrepreneur (Marx's 'functioning' capitalist) would be unable to roll over and, faced with a squeeze on his liquidity, his company could fail. This is the financial crisis that is typical of 'classic' capitalism.

The emergence of long-term debt markets allowed the capitalist entrepreneurs to refinance their short-term bank borrowing with long-term bonds. This virtually eliminated the vulnerability of the capitalist to a bank credit squeeze (see Hilferding 1981). At the same time, the capitalist entrepreneur had to ensure that the company now had sufficient liquid reserves to make interest and dividend payments on long-term debts, or equity. In addition, the company's managers had to make sure that the holders of the bonds or shares were not embarrassed by the drying-up of liquidity in the markets for bonds or shares: such a drying-up makes it difficult to sell a bond or share for a good price. The owner of bonds or shares whose market is illiquid is condemned to holding it until prices improve, with only a cash flow in the form of interest or dividends. Hence companies are obliged to hold excess capital that is turned over in restructuring their financing.

In the financial markets, financial innovation takes place to provide liquidity for the long-term securities: a whole range of new banking and financial institutions financing holdings of long-term securities with short-term borrowing. Early on, economists such as Withers (1917) and Hobson (1924) noted the shift in the basis of credit from commodity production and exchange to long-term securities. Such 'layering' of credit (lending in order to buy debt instruments) then constitutes proliferation of debt that is nowadays referred to as 'financialization' (because debt stocks rise faster than real economic activity) but is really a way in which the financial system keeps the market for long-term securities liquid. The analysis of the unstable liquidity in the capital markets was addressed in the first half of the twentieth century in the work of Thorstein Veblen (1904) and John Maynard Keynes (1936), and in the second half of the twentieth century by Hyman Minsky (1986). Minsky (1986) demonstrated the need for capitalist firms to maintain a certain level of investment expenditure in order to realize profits and make payments on their debts.

The second major change attendant upon the expansion of long-term finance was the rise of monopoly capital. Companies could now expand far more expeditiously by buying their competitors' long-term debts or shares, rather than entering into the precarious business of taking their competitors' business away by more effective selling in markets. The trusts and monopolies that dominated capitalism by the end of the nineteenth century were the creation of the capital markets rather than, as Alfred Marshall believed, the results of either 'natural' or political monopolies or increasing returns to scale. For Rudolf Hilferding (1981), the link with the capital markets forms the essence of monopoly capital. Hilferding (1981) first put forward an explanation of the new capitalist instability, caused by the interplay between monopoly and competitive segments in the capitalist economy. This was a theme that was to be later systematically investigated by Michał Kalecki (1932, 1967), who thought that he was addressing the Rosa Luxemburg's and Mikhail Tugan-Baranovsky's respective explanations of the conditions under which value is realized in the capitalist economy, but was really engaged in a critique of Hilferding's conclusion that cartelization stabilizes capitalism. In the second half of the twentieth century, the analysis of monopoly capital came to be associated with Paul Sweezy (see in particular Magdoff and Sweezy 1987).

13.2 FINANCE AND THE CRITIQUE OF POLITICAL ECONOMY SINCE THE TWENTIETH CENTURY

Following Alfred Marshall, mainstream economic theory dispensed with a theory of value and regressed into a theory of the firm in which profits are merely a margin over costs of production. That margin is given 'naturally' (because it is so obvious in a profitable enterprise) by capital productivity. In this way both the question of value and its realization disappear from neoclassical economics. In neoclassical economics, monetary theory is determined in the 'sphere of commodity circulation' by the exchange relation, with interest rates determined in a market for 'saving' or 'savings' (unspent income). With the widespread acceptance since the 1970s of 'micro-foundations' as a necessary methodological principle, the capitalist firm and its financing disappear from the mainstream narrative, replaced by exchange of surplus commodities between households, so that production and exchange are the results of household decisions. Finance is transformed into household decisions on savings portfolios, and corporate finance has been reduced to the choice of financing for household-based firms, and their 'information' and principal–agent problems, as if a century and a half of financial development and innovation had simply not happened (see Shabani and Toporowski 2015).

Outside the mainstream, post-Keynesianism, perhaps the only modern school of thought in economics that has taken finance seriously, proceeds in general using flow of funds sectoral balances, into which fiscal policy (the original 'Keynesian' policy) may be fitted conveniently as a balance between the private sector net accumulation of assets (saving minus investment) and the trade balance (e.g., Palley 2010). The strength of the post-Keynesian approach, apart from its integration of finance into its monetary analysis, lies in its theory of aggregate demand laying down the conditions under which value is realized. However, this is not integrated with any theory of value or production and the theory of distribution is usually treated as an optional supplement to the theory of aggregate output and employment.

Money has always been central to post-Keynesian macroeconomics. In the policy disputes with monetarists since the 1960s, this interest in money has become a preoccupation with monetary endogeneity and the operation of bank credit as money. This has often been to the neglect of long-term finance and its functions in capitalism, to the point where Keynes's insistence on the importance of the long-term rate of interest is rarely observed. Post-Keynesian interest in income distribution has revived in recent years with attempts to integrate Kalecki's theory into a more classic theory of distribution (Bhaduri and Marglin 1990). As the title of one of the papers in this genre suggests, this results in being 'Keynesian in the short-run and classical in the long run' (Duménil and Lévy 1999), and therefore departs further from a credit understanding of finance. Precisely because it is not integrated with the theory of value or production, and the finance required for it, this analysis cultivates a political economy of distribution, rather than an understanding of capitalism and the role of capital accumulation.

With the exception of Paul Sweezy and his followers, Marxist political economy in the second half of the twentieth century has engaged in a critique of Keynesian theory, for its lack of a theory of production and value. This critique then indicates the theory of value as the distinctive feature of Marxian political economy. An increasingly narrow focus on the law of value as the analytical core of Marxism has largely excluded from Marxian political economy consideration of the conditions for the realization of value. While the 'regulationist' and 'social structure of accumulation' schools of Marxist theory have accommodated into their analysis the state as the organ determining the conditions for the realization of value, Marxists in general have not followed up on the work of Rosa Luxemburg and Rudolf Hilferding to analyse the conditions for the realization of value that emerge directly from capitalist relations of production, those conditions being the accumulation of capital and its financing. The result, among most Marxists, has been retrogression to a political economy of capitalism that would have been familiar to Ricardian socialists who reduced capitalism to a theory of capitalist production and a labour theory of value. Key factors in the crisis are supposed to be not so much problems in production (which are supposed to have been eliminated by the weakening of organized labour from the 1980s onwards) but a combination of state policies of neoliberalism, deregulation and speculation. In the absence of any broader analysis of the conditions for the realization of value, most Marxists have joined the post-Keynesian wage-led growth theorists to the underconsumptionist conclusion, originally advanced by the Ricardian socialists, that if there is a realization problem in capitalism, the problem arises because workers are not paid the full value of their labour.

The high visibility afforded to finance in recent years by its extravagance, in the years before the financial crisis of 2008, and its apparent position as the crucible of crises since that year, has highlighted the inadequacy of theories that see the economy as either a set of household exchanges, or a set of sectoral flows of funds, or merely a theory of value and production, with an accompanying state operating monetary and fiscal policy. Theories of financialization have been advanced to incorporate the large amount of debt transactions into theories of household exchanges, or sectoral flows, or theories of value and production (e.g., Duménil and Lévy 2011; Lapavitsas 2013). However, without an analysis of the conditions for the realization of value, those conditions being principally the accumulation of capital and its financing, theories of financialization cannot provide an adequate account of the corporate finance that lies at the heart of the capitalist economy (Toporowski 2012). The remainder of this chapter gives an account of the corporate finance, rather than the dramas of finance houses, that set off the present depression in Europe.

13.3 THE CRISIS OF ACCUMULATION

For the reasons explained above, corporate finance has been largely overlooked in explanations of the 2008 crisis. The neglect of corporate finance is a casualty of the dismissal of the firm as the key economic decision-maker in the economy. Hence the part played by corporate finances of large corporations has not really been considered as central to the macroeconomic analysis of the financial crisis.[3]

In examining the role of corporate finance in the financial crisis, or indeed in any economic conjuncture, a distinction needs to be made between non-financial business corporations and small and medium-sized enterprises. The defining feature of business corporations is that their corporate treasurers have access to the full range of financial markets, from banks, through capital markets, right up to derivatives markets. At the extreme, in the case of multinational corporations, they have access to financial markets in all parts of the world where they are not excluded by capital controls (as in China or India). This allows such corporations to take full advantage of long-term debt markets to stabilize their financing costs, for example through the issue of shares on which payments and repayments, in the form of dividends and share buy-backs, are at the discretion of the management, rather than determined by inflexible financial contracts. Long-term obligations like this also avoid the need to roll over debt.

At the other extreme are small and medium-sized enterprises that constitute Hilferding's competitive segment of capitalist enterprises. These enterprises usually operate with finance borrowed from a bank, finance that is usually of a limited term, payments on which are contractually determined. Access to a limited range of other financial services, for example leasing or foreign currency, is usually obtained through a given bank. In many countries (most notably in Germany) there exists a stratum of local banks specifically designated to provide financial services to small and medium-sized firms. This limited access to financial services by smaller companies, sometimes referred to as a 'financing gap', is the subject of a large literature, and policies to encourage venture capital and capital market-like facilities.[4] Although this is not the place to give any comprehensive treatment of the topic, it is commonly forgotten in the discussion that the amount of risk capital in an economy at any one time is limited by the size and structure of the liabilities of long-term investment institutions (Toporowski 2010). The provision of unlimited capital to all enterprises would require a massive inflation of the capital and long-term debt markets that, without a corresponding inflation of intermediary institutions to maintain the liquidity in those markets, would increase financial instability well beyond anything that has been experienced so far in the capitalist world. In effect, the restriction on access to the capital market is a stabilizing factor in an otherwise unstable financial system.

Apart from access to the capital market, there is another economic distinction to be made between corporations and small and medium-sized enterprises. This is that, despite the existence in some countries of an important segment of medium-sized enterprises that engage in fixed capital investment and even technological innovation, in general it may be said that in virtually all capitalist countries, large industrial corporations account for the vast bulk of fixed business investment. Since such investment is the key private sector determinant of the business cycle, it is usually this (rather than government policy) that creates a given macroeconomic conjuncture of boom or recession. This is further explained below. Nevertheless, also in virtually all capitalist countries, it is the small and medium-sized enterprises that account for the majority of non-agricultural private sector employment. Thus, in the private sector, it is large corporations that through their investment (or capital accumulation) determine aggregate demand and employment (or the realization of value), but small and medium-sized enterprises that actually employ most workers in the private sector. This provides a framework for understanding how the present economic crisis was created in the sphere of corporate finance.

The key mechanism was described in a report in the Business section of *The Economist* on 13 December 2008 ('Riding the rollercoaster', pp. 73–74) revealing the key relationship between debt, capital market inflation and investment in the economy. The report reviewed the accounts of the six largest industrial multinational companies. These companies had incurred net debts of $136 billion. The usual Keynesian, Austrian, Fisher and Minsky analysis of the business cycle would suggest that this arose because of those companies' enthusiasm for fixed capital investment. In fact, the report states, four-fifths of this debt was spent on mergers and acquisitions, driving the leverage ratio (ratio of net debt to equity) of these companies to an average of 2.6 (4.4 in the case of the acquisition-hungry Cemex, 4.0 in the case of Lafarge, and 3.5 in the case of Tata Steel).

With borrowing at an unsustainable level, what could the companies do? 'Raising equity is tricky since investors had been sucked dry by capital-hungry banks' (confirmation that the supply of equity is not as elastic as theory would suggest; see Toporowski 2010). Nor would asset sales generate much cash inflow: 'disposals could occur only at miserly prices, if at all, because most potential buyers have no access to funds themselves' (*The Economist*, op. cit.). The report concludes by identifying the mechanism that appears to the companies, and the author of the report, the most effective way of cutting their debt:

> [I]n the fight to survive, the biggest weapons are cuts in production and capital spending. ArcelorMittal has led the way on the former with a reduction of output by one third that even its chairman, Lakshmi Mittal, calls 'very aggressive'. The cuts to investment plans are as dramatic: ArcelorMittal, Lafarge and Cemex have sliced their budgets for next year by between one-third and one-half, and on December 10th Rio (Tinto) cut its planned capital expenditure in 2009 from $9 billion to $4 billion. Xstrata has yet to announce its plans, but a 50% reduction is possible. [In the event, Xstrata cut its planned capital expenditure by $3bn, leaving capital expenditure of $3.2bn.]

The report concluded that these expenditure cuts 'would mean a $15bn boost in annual cash flow – equivalent to about 18 months' worth of interest costs . . . It is a glimmer of hope during these bleakest of times.' One may forgive a journalist for failing to see beyond the balance sheet that a corporation is trying to repair. But those familiar with the analysis of Fisher, Keynes, Kalecki, Minsky and Steindl know that this way of dealing with excess debt is the mechanism of economic depression in a finance capitalist economy: large corporations are foolish to suppose that their cash flow, or sales revenue, would stay unchanged if they reduce their investment on the scale done by those corporations in 2008.

Subsequent reports of the debt problems of large companies (that is, companies with access to the capital markets) have confirmed that it is not their fixed capital investments, but their capital market operations that have driven those companies into difficulties. A report on Tata Motors, promoting its latest venture in car production in India ('The Tata Nano, The new people's car – Why the Nano alone cannot solve mounting problems of its maker', *The Economist*, 26 March 2009) could not overlook the financial difficulties of this branch of the Tata empire. The report revealed that Tata Motors had a financial deficit that was expected to be at least $3.4 billion in 2009. 'About $1.4bn of that is in the form of short-term loans raised for working capital'. The remaining '$2bn relates to the bridging loan taken out last year [that is, in 2008] to finance its $2.3bn purchase of Jaguar Land Rover (JLR), a British premium carmaker, which must be either repaid or refinanced in June (2009)'. At the end of 2008, 'an attempt to raise $885m through a rights issue ended up with Tata Sons, the group holding company, taking up 61% of the ordinary shares' (*The Economist*, ibid.). In other words, the capital market was unable to provide most of the equity capital that the company needed.

Perhaps the most curious relationship between a large company and the capital markets is that of General Electric. This relationship is curious not only because it reveals so much about how large corporations use financial markets, but also because it demonstrates the willingness of management experts and economists to accept the claims of business leaders made charismatic by the financial boom. Under Jack Welch, its chief executive from 1981 to 2001, General Electric was supposed to be managed in accordance with profit targets requiring quarterly increases in those profits. These were enforced by management techniques that bewitched the business press and the prestigious *Harvard Business Review*. Another recent report revealed that these profit increases were in fact largely due to the financial operations of General Electric's financial subsidiary GE Capital ('General Electric: Losing its Magic Touch', *The Economist*, 19 March 2009). GE Capital had been set up in 1932 as the General Electric Contracts Corporation to assist in financing the company's industrial activities. However, by the 1980s, GE Capital was in effect operating like a bank, raising funds through bond issues and commercial paper to invest in various financial assets. During the period of financial market inflation, GE Capital became a useful source of additional profits: if General Electric was due to miss its profit target, GE Capital would sell financial assets to generate the profits required. It was not the much-touted efficient management of industrial resources that made General Electric so profitable, but the operations of its banking subsidiary GE Capital in the 'shadow banking system'.

In 2008, General Electric was plunged into difficulties when GE Capital found itself unable to roll over commercial paper due for repayment, and holding assets that could not be sold except at a loss. As a bank, GE Capital benefited from United States (US) government measures to support banking. However, the company lost its valuable AAA credit rating, which was cut in March 2009 to AA+, and was forced to cut its quarterly dividend by two-thirds, the first time the dividend had been reduced since 1938. General Electric was forced to raise $15 billion of new capital from a consortium that included Warren Buffett's Berkshire Hathaway (ibid.).

Overall, the Organisation for Economic Co-operation and Development (OECD) data show a decline in fixed capital investment in plant and machinery in the countries most exposed to the financial crisis between 2007 and 2012, of 23 per cent in the United Kingdom (UK), 15 per cent in the USA (a low-investment economy) and 18 per cent in the European Monetary Union. It is this decline in investment, rather than any fall in the consumption of indebted households (household consumption fell by 5 per cent during this period in the UK, and actually rose in the USA and the euro area), that has caused the so-called 'Great Recession' in Europe and North America.

13.4 CONCLUSION

The analysis of the recent financial crisis and its subsequent macroeconomic impact cannot be separated from a critique of political economy in the form of an analysis of how capitalism has evolved in the twentieth century, and a critique of economic theory and policy. A critique of political economy derived from an understanding of the law of value and the conditions for its realization indicates that the financial crisis is rooted in the balance sheet problems of capitalist corporations rather than in the incidents of banking at that time. It was not the failure of Lehman Brothers that 'caused' the crisis from 2008, but the failure of investment (capital accumulation) upon which capitalism depends for the realization of value.

ACKNOWLEDGEMENT

I am grateful to Turan Subasat, John Weeks, Riccardo Bellofiore, Joseph Halevi and Simon Mohun for helpful suggestions in the development of this chapter. Any remaining errors are my own.

NOTES

1. See Marx's Preface to the first German edition of Volume I of *Capital*, or his Preface to *A Contribution to the Critique of Political Economy* (Marx 1938, 1970).
2. Engels tried to incorporate this shift towards long-term financing into Marx's *Capital* with a short chapter on the stock market that he added to Volume III of *Capital* (Engels, 'Supplement to Capital Volume Three', Marx 1974b). But this did not go beyond deprecating the speculation in that market, in terms that are common currency in modern, superficial critiques of finance.
3. A rare exception here is the study of Cemex given in Vargas y Albino Luna (2012).
4. The cult of capital markets has been notable in the European Union under the Lisbon Agenda (see Frangakis 2009).

REFERENCES

Bhaduri, A. and S. Marglin (1990), 'Unemployment and the Real Wage: The Economic Basis for Contesting Political Ideologies', *Cambridge Journal of Economics*, 14(4), 375–393.

Dobb, M. (1967), *Papers on Capitalism, Development and Planning*, London: Routledge and Kegan Paul.

Duménil, G. and D. Lévy (1999), 'Being Keynesian in the Short Term and Classical in the Long Term: The Traverse to Classical Long-Term Equilibrium', *Manchester School*, 67(6), 648–716.

Duménil, G. and D. Lévy (2011), *The Crisis of Neoliberalism*, Cambridge, MA: Harvard University Press.

Frangakis, M. (2009), 'EU Financial Market Integration Policy', in J. Grahl (ed.), *Global Finance and Social Europe*, Cheltenham, UK and Northampton, MA, USA: Edward Elgar.

Hilferding, R. (1981), *Finance Capital: a Study of the Latest Phase of Capitalist Development*, London: Routledge and Kegan Paul.

Hobson, J.A. (1924), *Gold Prices and Wages: An Examination of the Quantity Theory*, London: Methuen and Co.

Kalecki, M. (1932), 'The Influence of Cartelization on the Business Cycle', in J. Osiatyński (ed.), *Michał Kalecki Collected Works Volume I Capitalism Business Cycles and Full Employment*, Oxford: Clarendon Press.

Kalecki, M. (1967), 'The Problem of Effective Demand with Tugan-Baranovsky and Rosa Luxemburg', in J. Osiatyński (ed.), *Michał Kalecki Collected Works Volume II Capitalism: Economic Dynamics*, Oxford: Clarendon Press.

Keynes, J.M. (1936), *The General Theory of Employment, Interest and Money*, London: Macmillan.

Kindleberger, C.P. (1993), *A Financial History of Western Europe*, New York: Oxford University Press.
Kowalik, T. (2014), *Rosa Luxemburg. Theory of Accumulation and Imperialism*, Basingstoke: Palgrave.
Lapavitsas, C. (2013), *Profiting without Producing: How Finance Exploits us All*, London: Verso Books.
Luxemburg, R. (1921), *Die Akkumulation des Kapitals Ein Beitrag zur őkonomischen Erklärung des Imperialismus*, Berlin: Frankes Verlag.
Magdoff, H. and P.M. Sweezy (1987), *Stagnation and the Financial Explosion*, New York: Monthly Review Press.
Marx, K.H. (1938), *Capital – A Critical Analysis of Capitalist Production*, London: George Allen & Unwin.
Marx, K.H. (1970), *A Contribution to the Critique of Political Economy*, New York: International Publishers.
Marx, K.H. (1974a), *Capital – A Critique of Political Economy Volume II The Process of Circulation of Capital*, London: Lawrence & Wishart.
Marx, K.H. (1974b), *Capital – A Critique of Political Economy Volume III The Process of Capitalist Production as a Whole*, London: Lawrence & Wishart.
Minsky, H.P. (1986), *Stabilizing an Unstable Economy*, New Haven, CT: Yale University Press.
Nesvetailova, A. (2010), *Financial Alchemy in Crisis: The Great Liquidity Illusion*, London: Pluto Press.
Niebyl, K.H. (1946), *Studies in the Classical Theories of Money*, New York: Columbia University Press.
Palley, T.I. (2010), 'America's Exhausted Paradigm: Macroeconomic Causes of the Financial Crisis and Great Recession', Washington, DC: New America Foundation.
Phillips, T. (ed.) (2014), *Europe on the Brink, Debt, Crisis and Dissent in the European Periphery*, London: Zed Books.
Shabani, M. and J. Toporowski (2015), 'A Nobel Prize for the Empirical Analysis of Assets Prices', *Review of Political Economy*, 27(1), 62–85.
Toporowski, J. (2010), 'A Theory of Capital Rationing', Working Papers No. 166, Department of Economics, School of Oriental and African Studies, University of London, September.
Toporowski, J. (2012), 'Neologism as Theoretical Innovation in Economics: The case of "Financialisation"', Working Papers No. 171, Department of Economics, School of Oriental and African Studies, University of London, March.
Turner, G. (2009), *No Way to Run an Economy – Why the System Failed and How to Put It Right*, London: Pluto Press.
Vargas y Albino Luna, G. (2012), 'El papel de la incertidumbre en la crise de Cemex', *Economía Informa*, Enero–Febrero, 372, 34–50.
Veblen, T. (1904), *Theory of Business Enterprise*, New York: Charles Scribner's Sons.
Withers, H. (1917), 'Lombard Street To-day', in W. Bagehot (ed.), *Lombard Street A Description of the Money Market*, London: John Murray.

14. Contradictions of capital accumulation in the age of financialization

Özgür Orhangazi

The 2008 US financial crisis and the ensuing 'Great Recession' has brought increased interest in the transformation of the financial structures since the 1980s and in the changing relationship between the financial sector and the rest of the economy. The term 'financialization', which in its broadest sense refers to the increase in the size and significance of the financial sector, has gained widespread use. Financialization has involved a number of changes that have taken place in the relationship between financial markets and institutions and the non-financial sector, especially the non-financial corporations (NFCs). On the one hand, NFCs came under more intense pressure from financial markets and institutions and their decision-making process has increasingly been reshaped to conform to the demands of finance; and on the other hand, NFCs themselves have increasingly got involved in financial investments (Orhangazi 2008a).

As such, financialization of the US economy and its crisis led to renewed interest in Marxian analyses of money and finance and of the structural transformations that have taken place since the early 1980s. Despite differences in usage, the concept of financialization in this literature has two common implications: first, it implies that a structural change has taken place, within which finance has played a central role; and second, this change has had (at least potentially) negative consequences for the economy. In this chapter, while critically engaging with some of this literature, I present two broad arguments. First, financialization can be understood as an inherent tendency within capitalism, and historically this tendency has manifested itself in different forms. Second, the relationship between finance and the productive accumulation process is a complex and contradictory one and Marxian theorizations of financialization need to take these complexities and contradictions into account. In other words, financial and real sides of the economy should not be taken in abstraction from each other but rather as forming a contradictory unity. This argument runs against some Keynesian arguments that see finance simply impinging upon the real economy, as well as some Marxian arguments where finance is presented only as an afterthought where determination runs only from the real side to the financial. In this regard, some of the arguments here partly follow from Orhangazi (2011), where I argued that the relationship between the real and financial sides of the economy has become increasingly more complicated and contradictory. Therefore, presenting the rise of finance as some external force impinging on the economy is a simplification that ignores other structural problems originating in the economy and fails to give a complete explanation of the rise of finance and its relation to the rest of the economy. Likewise, presenting financialization simply as a response to accumulation problems in the non-financial parts of the economy also amounts to an oversimplification.

The rest of the chapter is organized as follows. In section 14.1, I present the argument that financialization is an inherent tendency within capitalism and acquired a new form under neoliberalism. Hence, I argue, the common theme found in some Marxian approaches that financialization is simply a response to the problems in the real sector falls short of explaining the complexities of the era of financialization. In section 14.2, I argue that in Marxian economic theory finance plays a contradictory role within capitalism, and that financialization further intensified these contradictions. Section 14.3 concludes with a brief overview of the arguments presented.

14.1 THE ROOTS OF FINANCIALIZATION

Historically, the separation of ownership and management in capitalist firms can be seen as a first step towards financialization. Through this separation, reached at the stage of corporate capitalism, the owner ceases to be a direct proprietor of productive capital. The owner's relationship to productive capital is financialized as productive capital now 'appears as commodified financial capital and the revenue generated by corporate productive capital appears to the capitalists, qua rentier, as a stream of financial payments' (Pineault 2001: 35). As such, financialization can be seen as an inherent tendency of the capitalist accumulation process. The transformation of ownership from direct ownership of productive capital to ownership of financial securities, in a way, allows the capitalist to escape risks built into the productive capital accumulation process, and not to be stuck in a productive investment. A productive capitalist enterprise always faces risks due to competition, especially in the introduction of new technologies and new products. Capital struggles to escape these risks through various methods. Monopolization and/or securing state protection of the investment can help the capitalist to curtail these risks to a certain degree. Shifting capital from the productive sphere to the financial sphere is another way of avoiding these risks. Kotz (2011) argues that this is one of the reasons why Rockefellers, for example, shifted their fortune born in oil to finance and real estate as the capital in their bank – Chase Manhattan Bank – was not tied to any particular form of productive capital. However, banking still involves risks, especially when it involves lending money to productive enterprises. Capital may acquire more safety through holding and dealing in marketable securities as this approaches to the ideal form in which the form of capital can be changed instantly when risks increase. That way, the risks of new products and processes is borne mostly by workers, while capital remains safe (Kotz 2011). This then creates an underlying tendency in capitalism towards financialization; that is, towards an increased role for financial markets, institutions and motives in the operation of the economy.

The financialization tendency has manifested itself in various forms throughout capitalism's history. The rise of 'finance capital' in the early twentieth century is one example. Hilferding ([1910] 1985) argued that under modern capitalism competition was replaced by a process of concentration and centralization of capital that led to the creation of cartels and trusts. This process brought banks and industrial capitalists together as finance capital, a close integration of the financial capital of banks with industrial capital in which banks acquired a dominant position and representatives of banks joined the boards of corporations, reflecting direct control. This integration emerged as a result of the increased reliance of large monopolistic corporations on banks to finance their investments. Finance capital was not only economically important but also socially and politically powerful, as it pushed governments to implement policies that would protect it domestically while supporting it internationally in efforts towards global expansion (Orhangazi 2011). In the case of the United States (US), major banks led by J.P. Morgan controlled most of the US industry at the beginning of the twentieth century (Kotz 1978: 24–39). They aimed to prevent destructive competition as well as financial speculation. In this set-up, financial institutions were oriented towards developing the real sector and preventing excess competition there. There were, of course, financial speculators such as Jay Gould, but the main structure of finance was oriented towards controlling and developing the real sectors. However, by the 1920s new financial centers arose outside New York, challenging the power of New York banks, while large corporations such as the Ford Motor Company emerged outside the control of bankers. This era saw the rise of more financial speculators, such as the Van Sweringen brothers of Cleveland and Samuel Insull of Chicago (Kotz 1978), as unregulated markets allowed them and some of the old financiers to engage in speculative activities. The 1920s were characterized by a succession of two forms of financialization: the earlier system of finance capital based on a close relationship between finance and industry, aiming to develop industry through elimination of destructive competition, gave way to the rise of financial speculation where financial actors prioritized pure financial profits independently of the health of the non-financial sector.

Following the Great Depression and World War II, a new institutional set-up emerged, in which finance was strictly regulated and made subservient to the needs of productive capital accumulation (Kotz 2011; Orhangazi 2008a: Chapter 3). In this period, this tendency toward financialization was held in check by institutional arrangements, which were ultimately a reflection of the relative power of various classes and groups at the time. However, once neoliberalism began gaining strength, barriers to the expansion of finance were removed.[1] In fact, financial institutions had already been getting around regulations through financial innovations, and the pressure exerted by them coupled with neoliberal policies led to a rapid wave of financial deregulation and liberalization after 1980. Financialization this time emerged as part of a regime shift from the regulated economy of the post-war era to the neoliberal regime. Hence, financialization should be considered as part of a wide range of developments in the post-1980 era including the shift in the US economy towards off-shoring and its transformation into a service and rentier economy (Harvey 2003). It is clear that a shift from patient financial markets that seek long-term growth to impatient financial markets that raise financial costs forces NFCs to pay larger shares of their income to financial markets, and changed managerial incentives and shortened planning horizons of NFCs have occurred (Crotty 2005). These changes took place in the context of neoliberal restructuring. While financialization has deeper roots that are not necessarily related to neoliberalism, financial deregulation and liberalization policies in the neoliberal era furthered financialization tendencies (Kotz 2011).

The role of the state in this process is important and there are different arguments regarding the role of the state policies in the financialization process. While it is clear that the state played a facilitating role in the rise and spread of financialization, Magdoff and Sweezy (1987) argue that this was due to the belief that financial expansion would help to sustain economic growth. Panitch and Gindin (2012) argue that the US state actively promoted financialization as it involved 'Americanization of finance' and contributed to the strengthening and universalization of US power. Krippner (2011), on the other hand, argues that while financialization allowed the state to avoid a number of dilemmas that policy-makers faced, it was not a purposeful outcome but rather an unintentional outcome of policies attempting to solve other problems.

In the Marxian literature on financialization we find a common narrative that sees financialization as emerging in response to the troubles in the non-financial capital accumulation process. In its general formulation, the argument runs as follows. Beginning in the 1970s, the sphere of production has been characterized by low profitability, and faced with low profitability in the production process capital shifted to the financial realm in search of higher profits. While this shift provided temporary relief, the underlying problems in the production side of the economy remained and kept reasserting themselves in the form of crises of different magnitudes, and the crisis that began with the collapse of the US financial sector in 2008 is a resurfacing of the underlying crisis. There are a number of variants of this general argument. For example, Arrighi (1994), who was one of the first scholars to use the concept of financialization, argued that the expansion of finance as an epochal change was part of the latest long wave of capitalism. Arrighi's argument that financialization signals a transition from one accumulation regime on a world scale to another is based on Braudel's thesis that the stages of financial expansions are a sign of the maturity of major capitalist developments (Braudel 1984). In this long wave approach, each long cycle of capitalism involves, first, an increase in material production followed by a crisis of overaccumulation; and second, a financial expansion cycle. Financialization, then, is an outcome of two inherent tendencies within capitalism: overaccumulation of capital, and competition among states for mobile capital. The overaccumulation of capital is reflected as an exhaustion of profitable investment opportunities in the real sectors of the economy, which is usually accompanied by increasing product market competition. The turn towards financial expansion worsens the weaknesses in the real economy and has negative implications for real capital accumulation.

A somehow similar argument was put forward by the *Monthly Review* approach, which sees financialization as a response to the 1970s' crisis, though from a completely different theoretical vantage point (e.g. Foster and Magdoff 2009). According to this approach, the mature state of capitalism is dominated by monopolies, that create a continuously expanding surplus value whose absorption becomes the main problem and leads to wasteful activities, sales effort, increased military expenditures and so on. By the 1970s the surplus absorption problem led to a crisis and capital began looking for a safe haven in the speculative activities of finance. Hence, financialization is an outcome of the search for a sphere for the absorption of surplus that could not find profitable investment opportunities in the real sector with the exhaustion of the post-World War II stimulants to demand, such as post-war reconstruction, automobilization, the military–industrial complex, and so on. Both Arrighi and the *Monthly Review* approach agree that financialization is triggered by overaccumulation problems, though overaccumulation is a result of increased competition in the former, and increased monopolization in the latter.

Brenner (2009) argues that there has been a chronic overcapacity problem in production since the 1970s, mainly due to increased international competition, that has lowered the profit rates. This led to a 'permanent and latent' crisis in advanced economies whose actualization has been prevented by the financial expansion. Harman (2010) and Callinicos (2010) make similar arguments to the effect that overaccumulation is a chronic condition of contemporary capitalism, and financialization with its credit expansion serves to counteract the stagnation tendencies and create periods of booms. However, once the credit expansion comes to an end, stagnation is manifested. Harvey (2003) argues that overaccumulation of capital leads to shrinkage of profitable investment opportunities and hence requires a temporal and spatial reshuffling of the processes of production and accumulation. Overaccumulation requires a redirection of capital into more profitable places and/or postponement of investments. Financialization helps this 'spatio-temporal fix' by redirecting capital flows from one space to another. Financialization brings a 'financial fix' as capital is directed towards the realm of finance in search of profits. However, Harvey also takes into consideration a number of other factors effective in the rise of financialization, especially the role of changing accumulation patterns, institutional changes and neoliberal policies, stressing that political decisions have been effective in the drive towards financialization through financial market liberalization and deregulation (Harvey 2005).

These approaches to financialization attempt to seek structural causes for the rise of financialization as they treat it as a general response to a profitability crisis. The emphasis on the causation running from the production sphere to the financial sphere is perhaps partly due to the fact that often these analyses, either explicitly or implicitly, attempt to build themselves against the Keynesian approaches that see the financial expansion as essentially caused by the financial liberalization and deregulation policies. Furthermore, historically, Marxian theorization presumed the primacy of real capital accumulation over financial factors. While these analyses do not deny the role of the institutional changes, they rather present them as a structural necessity of the underlying problems in the production side of the economy. In effect, they present a one-way causation between the real and financial realms of the economy, through which the financial sphere is determined by the real accumulation process. This provides an incomplete picture of the financialization process and ignores the structural changes that take place in the non-financial sector due to changes in financial structures and practices (see section 14.2 below).

Another problem with the overaccumulation thesis has to do with its high level of abstraction. Capital is treated as a singular entity; various divisions and differentiations within capital are mostly ignored in the search for structural explanations of the origins of financialization. However, the search for a structural explanation often prevents a thorough understanding of the choices and behaviors of the different economic and political actors that were involved in this process. For example, if the (non-financial) capital running into stagnation was escaping from real activities to financial activities, then the economic reasons and motivations of different capitals within the real sector need to be explained clearly. In other words, if 'non-financial capital has indeed been seeking escape from stagnation by engaging in the speculative activities of finance, it follows that industrialists, merchants, and bankers must have had economic reasons to change their conduct, which have to be specified accordingly' (Lapavitsas 2013: 17–18).

The underlying claim that capitalism has been in a permanent (but latent) overaccumulation crisis since the 1970s is another critical issue with the overaccumulation thesis. Seeing the more than three decades between the 1970s and 2008 as a period of crisis rather empties the concept of crisis from any analytical meaning. It is clear that the rate of economic growth has been relatively lower in the post-1980 era compared with the 'golden age' years in the US and many other economies. However, this period has also witnessed strong recovery in the profitability of the US non-financial corporate sector, reasons for which need to be explained.[2] Furthermore, capitalism sustained growth through new centers of accumulation especially in China and other East Asian countries; production has been transformed through new technologies, especially in information and telecommunications, and so on. Dynamic accumulation in many other parts of the world is not explained, as much is invested in the notion that the normal state of contemporary capitalism is stagnation in the absence of state intervention and financial expansion.

Perhaps a more important problem with these approaches originates from the lack of theorization of financial profits. As the financial sector is not analyzed but treated as a black box without an analysis of its own logic of accumulation, these approaches fail to explain how financial profits can be higher at a time when profitability in the real sector is falling. This analytical problem is further aggravated with the actual timing of low profitability in the real sector and the rise of financialization. Financialization took off in earnest in the 1990s, after profitability of the NFCs began recovering.[3]

14.2 FINANCIALIZATION AND DYNAMICS OF ACCUMULATION

In this section, I argue that financialization should be understood in terms of its contradictory nature and that the relationship between real capital accumulation and the financial sector is inherently complex and contradictory. This is an argument inherent in Marxian economic theory, in sharp contrast with mainstream theory. In mainstream economic and financial theory, the role of the financial sector is simply to serve the needs of the economy. In the standard model, markets and economies are portrayed as inherently stable, and macroeconomic models study only stable states that are affected by external shocks. Financial markets provide essential services to the economy, such as providing liquidity, mobilizing and pooling savings, and allocating funds to investment. They gather, process and disseminate information possessed by different agents in the economy and hence provide services of screening and monitoring, risk management, diversification and hedging. According to these models, as financial markets perform these functions, the prices of financial assets are supposed to reflect their fundamental values in the real economy. Financial markets, therefore, increase the allocative efficiency of the system (Dowd 1996).[4]

Marxian economic theory, however, portrays capitalism as an inherently unstable system. The primary driving force of capitalism is the accumulation of capital, and capital accumulation systematically creates contradictions resulting in crises. The sources of instability and crises can be found in different parts of the accumulation process itself. In very simplified terms, capital accumulation takes place in three stages. The first stage involves the purchase of capital, labor and other inputs; the second stage is the production process; and the third stage is the sale of products. At the beginning of the process, money capital is invested with the expectation of a profit to be realized at the end of the process. Therefore, accumulation is closely associated with the rate of profit, which depends on conditions at different stages of the accumulation process. Potentially, problems at any point could have destabilizing effects for the whole system, and various scholars point out different potential problems at different stages of the process.[5] For instance, conditions of the labor market could generate instability in the first stage of accumulation. A decline in the rate of unemployment (reserve army of labor) and/or increased bargaining power of labor could lead to an increase in wages and/or to a reduction in workplace discipline. If the productivity growth falls behind the wage growth, a decline in the share and rate of profit would be observed, leading to a decline in the pace of accumulation. The second stage of accumulation involves potential contradictions in terms of the organization of production, choice of technology, supervision of the labor process, and labor productivity. For example, competition among firms results in adoption of the most efficient technology, but when all the firms follow the same route an increase in their capital outlays could lead to a decline in profitability. Labor-saving technical change leads to an increase in the capital–labor ratio and hence creates a tendency for a secular decline in the rate of profit. In the third stage of the process, both the level and the composition of aggregate demand as well as the distribution of income among classes are important variables that would affect realization of the surplus value and hence profitability and accumulation. For example, a high unemployment rate and/or low wages could increase profitability, but at the same time could lead to a shortfall in aggregate demand or to disproportionality among the supply and demand of different sectors, which then would lead to a failure of realization of surplus value (Orhangazi 2011).

Within this rich literature, most of Marxian economic theorization focused on the real components of the accumulation process without paying much attention to the financial side. Sweezy (1997) warned that Marxian approaches failed to take finance seriously because of a one-sided conceptualization of the accumulation process:

> Basically, I think the answer is that its conceptualization of the capital accumulation process is one-sided and incomplete. In the established tradition of both mainstream and Marxian economics, we treated capital accumulation as being essentially a matter of adding to the stock of existing capital goods. But in reality this is only one aspect of the problem. Accumulation is also a matter of adding to the stock of financial assets. The two aspects are of course interrelated, but the nature of this interrelation is problematic to say the least. The traditional way of handling the problem has been in effect to assume it away: for example, buying stocks and bonds (two of the simpler forms of financial assets) is assumed to be merely an indirect way of buying real capital goods. This is hardly ever true, and it can be totally misleading. (Sweezy 1997: 56–57)

It should still be noted, however, that while mostly emphasizing the real sector roots of capitalist instability, Marxian economic theory also points out the contradictory and often destabilizing role of finance. Financial markets and institutions support capital accumulation by mobilizing large amounts of money capital, and allow accumulation to take place at a faster rate and a larger scale than otherwise possible. However, finance can also exacerbate capitalist instability, which can originate either in the financial realm or in the real sector. When there are favorable conditions for accumulation, investment expands rapidly, leading firms to use more credit. The pace and scale of expansion at this stage would depend on the amount of financial capital invested in capital accumulation. These expansions endogenously create disturbances in the financial or real side of the economy. An adverse development in the real side of the economy could turn into a crisis and collapse, if it leads to or is accompanied by troubles in the financial markets. Likewise, a disturbance originating in the financial sector can spread to the real side of the economy by disrupting the accumulation process. An overextended and fragile system can turn what might have been a mild downturn into a financial crisis (Harvey 1982; Crotty 1986; Orhangazi 2011). Hence, the relationship between the financial and real sides of the economy forms a contradictory unity where finance not only provides the necessary means for accumulation but also may exacerbate periodic disturbances in the economy that can originate either in the financial or the non-financial side of the economy. In other words, finance plays a dual role by sustaining the accumulation of capital and at the same time undermining it. Finance capital is both an important and dominating accelerator of the accumulation process and a destabilizer. The credit system allows the accumulation process to take place at a faster pace and on an expanded scale that would otherwise not be attainable. When the conditions are favorable and investment expands rapidly, the resulting increase in confidence levels leads firms to make use of greater amounts of credit, while the creditors make more loans, some of which are increasingly riskier. The pace and the scale of the expansion then depend on the amount of financial capital thrown into accumulation. However, these expansions prepare their own ends as they endogenously produce either financial or real problems within the economy. Crotty (1986: 68) underlined that:

> adverse nonfinancial developments which would have caused only a mild and temporary hesitation in an ongoing expansion in the absence of an oversensitive financial environment can generate a crisis and collapse in its presence. Moreover, semiautonomous disturbances in the financial sector can themselves initiate a crisis if the system is oversensitive. And an overextended, oversensitive financial system can turn what might have been a mild downturn into a financial panic and depression.

14.2.1 Financialization of the NFCs

In short, in Marxian economic theory, finance is an integral part of the accumulation process and should be understood with its contradictory role. Seen from this perspective, financialization of the NFCs has led to a number of complex and contradictory transformations. First, financialization meant increased involvement of the NFCs in financial investments, which contributed to NFC profitability on two levels. Its direct contribution was through the financial incomes derived from the financial operations. The involvement of NFCs in financial activities was partly due to the hedging needs of the corporations in an increasingly volatile financial environment, while shareholder pressure forced them to generate short-term returns. Initially, a large portion of these financial activities were oriented towards extending credit to their own consumers and thus helping sales, a second way through which financialization contributed to NFC profitability. Furthermore, credit expansion and asset price appreciations indirectly contributed to NFC profitability through their positive effect on aggregate demand. Proceeds from financial activities contributed to the profits of the corporations and most likely kept firms that were otherwise not profitable in business for an extended period of time, and high financial profits contributed to prolonged excess capacity problems in certain industries, notably the automobile industry. Financial expansions had another impact on the accumulation by artificially increasing demand and hence leading to overinvestment in certain sectors (Kotz 2011). However, increased financial investments of NFCs also show the contradictory effects of financialization over accumulation as the promise of higher returns in the financial markets, together with shareholder pressure for short-term returns, put a downward pressure on investment in real capital stock (Orhangazi 2008b).

Although explicit control of banks over corporations is not observed in this era, there is a complicated relationship between the financial and real sides of the economy as a result of the transformations that took place in the financialization era. The rise of the institutional investors and the so-called shareholder revolution brought a change in the ownership structure of the corporations and in the demands of the owners from the corporations, signaling a shift from 'managerial capitalism' towards 'shareholder capitalism'. As a result of the prominence of the interests of creditors and shareholders, the behavior of the NFCs was now increasingly determined by the demands of the financial sector, implying indirect dominance of financial sector over the non-financial sector. While financial capital does not directly dominate industrial capital, the alliance of the interests of the managers with that of shareholders led to the dominance of financial interests in the economy. Financialization has thus been characterized by the primacy of the financial logic over the productive capital accumulation. An indicator of this is the introduction of financial criteria for the NFCs. One result of this shift is observed in increased payments by the NFCs to the financial markets and a change in the management perspective towards short-termist strategies. A number of works in the literature show that this change is associated with decreased investment by the NFCs (Orhangazi 2008b; Davis 2013). In a way, this aspect of financialization has created a tendency working against the overinvestment, excess capacity problems: in terms of the dynamics of investment, when we consider the pressure of the financial imperatives on the NFCs to increase short-term profitability, certain types of investment projects with longer time horizons are discouraged. It is not a coincidence that waves of plant closures and downsizing occurred as a result of pressure from financial markets. However, at the same time, periods of financial expansions and bubbles led to excess investment in different sectors, including high-technology, luxurious office buildings and, more recently, housing. Hence, the overall impact of financialization on capital accumulation seems to be contradictory.

As a side note, post-Keynesian theorizations of financialization have certain similarities with some of these arguments as they see the process mainly emanating from the removal of regulations. According to this approach, the rise of rentiers has strengthened the financial sector at the expense of the productive sectors of the economy. The dominance of finance is partly responsible for the poor performance of investment and output in advanced capitalist economies (e.g. Stockhammer 2004). There are different versions of the post-Keynesian approach, as well. For example, Palley's (2013) account of financialization sees the process as a response to the demand deficiency problem created by neoliberal policies and the financial deregulation by expanding credit and through financial innovations. The reluctance of some Marxian theorists to acknowledge the potential negative effects of financialization on the productive sphere seems to originate from the hesitancy to agree with reformist Keynesian policies aiming to constrain the negative effects of financialization on the real economy. Therefore, in positioning themselves against reformist Keynesian approaches, Marxian theorizations sometimes miss the dialectical and contradictory relationship between the financial and real sides of the economy.

14.2.2 Globalization of Production

Both aspects of the financialization of the NFCs are directly related to the changing global patterns of capital accumulation, which involved the breaking-up of production processes and their relocation in different parts of the world depending on cost and market considerations. The combination of increased product market competition and financial market pressure – the 'neoliberal paradox' (Crotty 2005) – forced NFC managers to look for ways to reduce costs. NFC management chose to focus on 'core competence' and sought to subcontract remaining operations. In this way, they reduced domestic investment needs and managed to meet shareholder demands. The result of this process was the shift of sources of profits from domestic output markets to foreign input markets. This shift has contributed to the maintenance of high profit rates and a high share of profits in national income in industrialized countries. While offshoring helped cost reduction and boosted profits, it also reduced the need for corporations to invest as they turned over production to contractors (Milberg 2008; Milberg and Winkler 2013). While increasing profitability satisfied shareholder demands, the reduced need for investment allowed the NFCs to distribute more to the shareholders and/or to invest in financial assets. As manufacturing operations declined in core countries, this process allowed NFCs to distribute a larger share of their revenues to financial markets. The reduction in investment needs also allowed them to directly delve into financial investments. As financialization created greater incentives for cost-reducing and flexibility-enhancing offshore production by US lead firms, the sustainability of this set-up was enhanced by the successful utilization of global value chains. Financialization further encouraged restructuring of production, and this was critical in sustaining the financialization trends of the post-1980 era.

14.2.3 Labor

Financialization in conjunction with globalization has been a significant contributor to the worsening of the condition of labor. In the post-1980 US economy, average real earnings declined until the mid-1990s; while they slowly increased after this point they never recovered back to the highs reached in the early 1970s. Various factors have been cited for the wage stagnation. Relocation of production to lower-cost sites put US workers in direct competition with the global reserve army of labor, whose size grew immensely with the increased participation of China in world industrial production. Meanwhile, the domestic balance of power moved against labor. Declining power of labor organizations and deunionization were coupled with the decline of the social wage through cuts in or eliminations of social programs such as guaranteed retirement pensions, unemployment benefits and so on. Flexible labor markets involved widespread use of temporary and contingent workers, which led to decreased job security, bargaining power and declining wages (Rosenberg 2010). In terms of economic policy, a shift from full employment targeting of the 'golden age' to inflation targeting and a reduction in social programs which brought down the social wage decreased the bargaining power of labor. Financialization contributed to this trend in various ways. Financial market pressures intensified exploitation by cutting wages and worsening working conditions, together with mass firings as a result of downsizing. The shareholder value maximization dictum was often invoked to promote the downsizing of the firms' workforces. Takeovers facilitated by financial markets have been effective in breaking labor contracts and forcing wages down. The 2000s witnessed a wave of leveraged takeovers undertaken by private equity funds. These private equity funds took over firms, restructured them and sold them back. In the process of restructuring, many jobs, health and retirement benefits, and similar commitments to employees were eliminated in order to enhance the resale value of the firm (Orhangazi 2008c). Hence, finance has effectively contributed to the overall stagnation of wages, and redirecting income from labor to finance has been a hallmark of the financialization process (Duménil and Lévy 2004). When taken together, financialization and global value chains led firms to shift their labor policies from 'long-term, full-time employment with the provision of health insurance and pension benefits' to 'reducing costs by hiring younger workers, with less tenure and fewer benefits' (Milberg and Winkler 2013: 24).[6]

While financialization contributed significantly to undermining the income of labor, it also provided a solution to it, albeit a temporary and contradictory one. Two dynamics supported household consumption in this era: increasing household indebtedness, and the wealth effect created through the rising asset prices. Faced with stagnating wages, households relied more than ever on borrowing in order to maintain their purchasing power. In the face of stagnating wages, households kept increasing their consumption by increased participation in the labor force, by working longer hours and finally by borrowing (Wolff 2010). While the households spent a declining share of their incomes on consumer goods, thanks to the impact of cheaper imported products, increased medical, education and insurance expenses pushed households to borrow in order to maintain their standard of living (Warren 2007). Credit became central in providing the means to continuing expansion of consumption despite stagnant wages (Barba and Pivetti 2009). Furthermore, rising asset prices allowed the creation of a wealth effect, which acted as an important mechanism in maintaining the purchasing power of the households and supporting consumption. Speculative asset bubbles allowed households to increase the debt-financing of their expenses by allowing them to use their houses and other assets as collateral.

14.3 CONCLUDING REMARKS

Financialization of the US economy led to contradictory outcomes for the capital accumulation process. It has changed the behavior of the NFCs, leading to increased financial investment, while an increasing portion of their earnings were transferred to the financial markets. This process went hand in hand with the rise of global value chains, which decreased domestic investment needs, increased profits and allowed the NFCs to continue financial investments and allocate a large portion of their earnings to the financial markets, while contributing to uneven development globally through the rise of new centers of accumulation. At the same time, it contributed to the worsening of the conditions of labor and increased inequality, while credit expansions and asset bubbles added to aggregate demand in a period when other factors pushed the aggregate demand down. Historically there have been a number of periods of financialization. Novel features of the current period have been the acceleration of the speed of circulation of financial capital and the decline in financial transaction costs, which have been effective in the emergence of speculative bubbles followed by busts. By forcing the NFCs to move capital accumulation and productive processes to new geographical locations with lower costs, financialization has contributed to both uneven economic development and inequality by driving wages down. In Harvey's (2014: 178) terms, 'The merchants and rentiers as well as the financiers are repositioned as the arbiters of capital accumulation relative to industrial capital'. However:

> There is, in all of this, a deep irony. Historically, industrial capital waged a mighty struggle to free itself from the chains of the landlords who extracted rent, the usurious financiers and the merchants who looked to rob or buy cheap and sell dear in unevenly constructed markets. Twenty-first-century capitalism seems to be busy weaving a net of constraints in which the rentiers, the merchants, the media and communications moguls and, above all, the financers ruthlessly squeeze the lifeblood out of productive industrial capital, to say nothing of the workers employed. It is not that industrial capital disappears. It has merely become subservient to capital in its other more fantastic and virulent forms. (Harvey 2014: 179)

Hence, developing a full understanding of the financialization process with its complex and contradictory features, allows us to make better sense of the crisis as well as the state of the world economy.

NOTES

1. Fine (Chapter 9 in this volume) notes that 'neoliberalism does signify a separate stage of development, one that is marked by the heavy and increasing role of finance in both economic and social restructuring. This is reflected most obviously in the phenomenal rise of financial markets themselves and also their influence on how economic restructuring takes place, together with the increasing role of finance in social reproduction, not least with privatisation of public services, and so on . . . this signifies that financialization is at the heart of neoliberalism, and is what has sustained it over three decades (as opposed to

temporary and contingent interventions on behalf of finance). Neoliberalism promotes financialization, and financialization impacts directly and indirectly on economic and social restructuring and reproduction.' (p.160, this volume.)

2. Shaikh (2011) explores the role of financialization in this recovery of profitability and finds that both cheap financing and finance's contribution to aggregate demand contributed to the recovery in profitability.
3. See Pollin (1996), Orhangazi (2008a) and Levina (2014) for a discussion of the sources of financial profits.
4. Crotty (2013) provides a thorough critique of the mainstream financial theories. He shows that the theory of 'efficient financial markets' is a fairy tale based on grossly unrealistic assumptions, and argues that this theory was a significant contributor to the crisis as it helped to justify the financial deregulation process.
5. See Itoh and Lapavitsas (1999: 126) for a brief review of how different Marxian economists stressed one or the other crisis tendency.
6. See Campbell and Bakır (Chapter 7 in this volume) for a look at the relationship between financialization and labor.

REFERENCES

Arrighi, G. (1994), *The Long Twentieth Century: Money, Power, and the Origins of our Times*, London: Verso.

Barba, A. and M. Pivetti (2009), 'Rising Household Debt: Its Causes and Macroeconomic Implications – A Long Period Analysis', *Cambridge Journal of Economics*, 33(1), 113–137.

Braudel, F. (1984), *Civilization and Capitalism*, New York: Harper & Row.

Brenner, R. (2009), 'What is Good for Goldman Sachs is Good for America: The Origins of the Present Crisis', Center for Social Theory and Comparative History, Paper 2009–11.

Callinicos, A. (2010), *Bonfire of Illusions: The Twin Crises of the Liberal World*, Cambridge: Polity Press.

Crotty, J. (1986), 'Marx, Keynes and Minsky on the Instability of the Capitalist Growth Process and the Nature of Government Economic Policy', in D. Bramhall and S. Helburn (eds), *Marx, Keynes, and Schumpeter: A Centenary Celebration of Dissent*, Armonk, NY: ME Sharpe.

Crotty, J. (2005), 'The Neoliberal Paradox: The Impact of Destructive Market Competition and Modern Financial Markets on Nonfinancial Corporation Performance in the Neoliberal Era', in G.A. Epstein (ed.), *Financialization and the World Economy*, Cheltenham, UK and Northampton, MA, USA: Edward Elgar.

Crotty, J. (2013), 'The Realism of Assumptions Does Matter: Why Keynes–Minsky Theory must Replace Efficient Market Theory as the Guide to Financial Regulation Policy', in M.H. Wolfson and G.A. Epstein (eds), *The Handbook of the Political Economy of Financial Crises*, Oxford: Oxford University Press.

Davis, L. (2013), 'Financialization and the Nonfinancial Corporation: An Investigation of Firm-Level Investment Behavior in the US, 1971–2011', University of Massachusetts Economics Department Working Paper 2013-08.

Dowd, K. (1996), 'The Case for Financial Laissez-Faire', *Economic Journal*, 436, 679–687.

Duménil, G. and D. Lévy (2004), *Capital Resurgent: Roots of the Neoliberal Revolution*, Harvard, MA: Harvard University Press.

Foster, J.B. and F. Magdoff (2009), *The Great Financial Crisis: Causes and Consequences*, New York: Monthly Review Press.

Harman, C. (2010), *Zombie Capitalism: Global Crisis and the Relevance of Marx*, London: Bookmarks.

Harvey, D. (1982), *Limits to Capital*, New York: Verso.

Harvey, D. (2003), *New Imperialism*, Oxford: Oxford University Press.

Harvey, D. (2005), *A Brief History of Neoliberalism*, Oxford: Oxford University Press.

Harvey, D. (2014), *Seventeen Contradictions and the End of Capitalism*, Oxford: Oxford University Press.

Hilferding, R. ([1910] 1985), *Finance Capital: A Study of the Latest Phase of Capitalist Development*, London, UK and Boston, MA, USA: Routledge & Kegan Paul.

Itoh, M. and C. Lapavitsas (1999), *Political Economy of Money and Finance*, London: Macmillan.

Kotz, D. (1978), *Bank Control of Large Corporations in the United States*, Berkeley and Los Angeles, CA: University of California Press.

Kotz, D. (2011), 'Financialization and Neoliberalism', in Gary Teeple and Stephen McBride (eds), *Relations of Global Power: Neoliberal Order and Disorder*, Toronto: University of Toronto Press.

Krippner, G. (2011), *Capitalizing on Crisis: The Political Origins of the Rise of Finance*, Cambridge, MA: Harvard University Press.

Lapavitsas, C. (2013), *Profiting Without Producing: How Finance Exploits Us All*, London, UK and New York, USA: Verso.

Levina, I. (2014), 'A Puzzling Rise in Financial Profits and the Role of Capital Gain-Like Revenues', Political Economy Research Institute Working Paper 347.

Magdoff, H. and P.M. Sweezy (1987), *Stagnation and Financial Explosion*, New York: Monthly Review Press.

Milberg, W. (2008), 'Shifting Sources and Uses of Profits: Sustaining US Financialization with Global Value Chains', *Economy and Society*, 37(3), 420–451.

Milberg, W. and D. Winkler (2013), *Outsourcing Economics: Global Value Chains in Capitalist Development*, Cambridge: Cambridge University Press.

Orhangazi, O. (2008a), *Financialization of the US Economy*, Cheltenham, UK and Northampton, MA, USA: Edward Elgar.

Orhangazi, O. (2008b), 'Financialization and Capital Accumulation in the Non-Financial Corporate Sector: A Theoretical and Empirical Investigation on the US Economy, 1973–2003', *Cambridge Journal of Economics*, 32(6), 863–886.

Orhangazi, O. (2008c), 'Wall Street vs. the labor movement', *New Labor Forum*, 17(1), 101–107.

Orhangazi, O. (2011), 'Financial' vs. 'Real': An Overview of the Contradictory Role and Place of Finance in the Modern Economy', *Research in Political Economy*, 27, 121–148.

Palley, T. (2013), *Financialization: The Economics of Finance Capital Domination*, Basingstoke: Palgrave Macmillan.

Pantitch, L. and S. Gindin (2012), *The Making of Global Capitalism: The Political Economy of American Empire*, London, UK and New York, USA: Verso.

Pineault, E. 2001, 'Finance Capital and the Institutional Foundations of Capitalist

Finance: Theoretical Elements from Marx to Minsky', unpublished paper, Ecole des Hautes en Sciences Sociales, Paris.
Pollin, R. (1996), 'Contemporary Economic Stagnation in World Historical Perspective', *New Left Review*, September–October, 109–118.
Rosenberg, S. (2010), 'Labor in Contemporary Social Structure of Accumulation', in T. McDonough, M. Reich and D.M. Kotz (eds), *Contemporary Capitalism and its Crises*, Cambridge: Cambridge University Press.
Shaikh, A. (2011), 'The First Great Depression of the 21st Century', in L. Panitch, G. Albo and V. Chibber (eds), *The Crisis this Time: Socialist Register 2011*, London: Merlin Press.
Stockhammer, E. (2004), 'Financialization and the Slowdown of Accumulation', *Cambridge Journal of Economics*, 28, 719–741.
Sweezy, P.M. (1997), 'More (or Less) on Globalization', *Monthly Review*, 49(4), 1–4.
Warren, E. (2007), 'The New Economics of the Middle Class: Why Making Ends Meet has Gotten Harder', Testimony before Senate Finance Committee, 10 May.
Wolff, R. (2010), *Capitalism Hits the Fan*, Northampton, MA: Olive Branch Press.

15. Which crisis, of which capitalism? A Marxian and financial Keynesian interpretation of neoliberalism and the great recession

Riccardo Bellofiore

This chapter argues that Marxian theory together with financial Keynesianism may contribute to understanding the current 'great' capitalist crisis. Both, however, need some revision in light of changing capitalist reality. In section 15.1, I will present some considerations about the Marxian theory of crisis. In section 15.2, I will do the same with some interesting developments within financial Keynesianism (Graziani 2003; Minsky [1975] 2008a, [1986] 2008b). My perspective is that financial Keynesianism must be incorporated within Marxian theory. Marxian theory and financial Keynesianism must be reread in a long-run perspective of the capitalist dynamics. This will help to resolve internal difficulties of the theories.

Marxian theory and financial Keynesianism are peculiar in that they are, so to speak, historically determined: both need to be historicized, taking into account the changes in social and economic theory, as well as the metamorphosis of capitalist reality. Marx taught us that capital has a fetish-character, and that it is constituted through human action. Thus we need to pay attention to 'objective' developments and to the dynamics of class struggle.

Capital develops through internal dynamics (though this is never separated from politics or state intervention). Each crisis erupts because of the contradictions inherent in the factors explaining the prosperity. Minsky went back to Schumpeter to look at capitalism through a stages approach: this is also my perspective rereading Marx. Each 'great' crisis of capitalism goes along with a crisis in economic theory. That is why a revival of Keynes or Sraffa, which is asked by many heterodox economists, is not enough. Effective demand failures and distributional conflict are of course present, but in completely different historical, social and economic conditions than nowadays. For the same reason we cannot just repeat Marx, Graziani or Minsky.

This is the reason why, in section 15.3, I will discuss the idiosyncratic features of neoliberalism. In this section I shall refer to the interpretations of neoliberalism which see it not as a resurrection of laissez-faire but as a politically managed configuration of capitalism. In section 15.4, I shall show that neoliberalism was a kind of paradoxical financial and privatized Keynesianism, a money manager capitalism built upon a 'concentration without centralization' of capital, new forms of corporate governance, a new kind of aggressive competition, capital market inflation, 'manic' savers leading to indebted consumption, and a new active economic policy. It was a capitalist configuration which presented itself under the appearance of a 'new' capitalism.

During the Great Moderation workers' exploitation was deepened, effective demand was fueled internally and disequilibria were seen as stabilizing. The reality, however, was the opposite: a compressed instability, nurturing that inner unsustainability which eventually exploded in the first decade of the new millennium. In section 15.5, I shall briefly discuss the global and European crises.

The Great Recession was not due to the global (trade) imbalances, government debts or the ill-designed Euro in the case of European crisis. These crises cannot be overcome without a revolution, either 'from above' or 'from below': without a new political and institutional configuration, and a new economic policy. It is here that a radicalized version of Minsky's version of the socialization of investment may turn out to be an essential economic policy element even for a Marxian left.

15.1 MARX AND THE CRISIS

The dialectics of circularity of capital as a 'subject' and 'fetish' (the Hegelian moment in Marx) versus the linearity of exploitation within the labor process traversed by class struggle (the anti-Hegelian moment in Marx) are crucial to understanding the current global crisis on the background of Marx's theory of crisis. Crisis is for Marx the necessary explosion, and at the same time the temporary solution, of the contradictions of capitalist accumulation. Capitalism is a monetary economy of production where commodity exchange is universalized. Money detaches sales from subsequent expenditures, and supply may not find outlets because of hoarding. In most of the three volumes of *Capital*, Marx assumes that commodities are sold at their social values (in Volumes I and II) or at their prices of production (in Volume III). Moreover, Marx's schemes of reproduction in Volume II show that a growth path independent of the level of consumption demand is an abstract possibility, dependent on some 'balance' between intersectoral trades. Though equilibrium is a chance, the fortuitous occurrence of a separation between buying and selling explains only the possibility of crises. Marx is arguing for the necessity of crises, and he traces it back to the capitalist class relation itself.[1]

The first argument about crisis is found in the general law of capital accumulation at the end of *Capital*, Volume I. With a constant composition of capital, an increase of the value invested sooner or later exhausts the supply of labor-power, tightening the labor market. Wage rises exceed the dynamics of labor's productive power. Profits are squeezed, accumulation and labor demand slow down, while labor-saving methods of production are introduced. With a given capital, mechanization reduces the share of variable capital. To produce the same output fewer workers are needed, and they are replaced by machines. The effect on employment of a rise in the rate of accumulation depends on the increase in the size of capital, but also on the change in its composition, and it can go either way: employment may increase or decrease. The pace and the structure of the accumulation of capital, which is the independent variable, vary through the cycle, to reproduce an industrial reserve army of potential workers ready to be included in the valorization process, and exerting a downward pressure on wages, which is the dependent variable.

This argument for the profit squeeze in the cycle, however, is not the main line in Marx's crisis theory. Capitalist accumulation is boosted by relative surplus value extraction, ensuring an increase of the productive power of labor. Workers' real wages and the share of surplus value may both grow as long as a higher workers' consumption is expressed into a decreasing value of labor power. Mechanization is not just a reaction to distributive struggles, it is first of all an autonomous capital push to control living labor: a powerful lever to regulate both the exchange value and the use value of labor-power. It nevertheless creates a difficulty, because it is a force which relatively removes workers from the point of production. When the technical composition of capital (the material ratio of means of production to workers) goes up, this factor contributes to the expulsion of workers; but living labor is the exclusive source of value and surplus value. If this is reflected in a rise in the value composition of capital (the ratio of the value of the elements of constant capital over the value of the elements of variable capital), the rate of profit tends to fall. Some authors have extended this tendential fall of the rate of profit from an argument about the cyclical dynamics of capital to an explanation for so-called long waves; others prolong the thesis into a theory arguing for a secular downward trend in profitability.

In the end a rise in the rate of surplus value could not counteract the negative sway on the rate of profit of a higher (value) composition of capital. The strongest case is the reference to an absolute limit to the surplus labor that may be pumped out from a given population. If variable capital tends to zero, surplus value exhausts the new value exhibiting in money the total social working day. The composition of capital is now the reciprocal of the maximum rate of profit, which in its turn acts as the ceiling for the actual rate of profit. The numerator of the maximum rate of profit meets a ceiling in the living labor extracted from workers, while the continuing increase of its denominator pushes it down. At the ruling prices, individual capitalists are forced to introduce more capital-intensive techniques, lowering unit costs and gaining temporary extra profits, even though the longer-run effects of their behavior force a devaluation of commodities and depress the average rate of profit.

This argument downplays the possible effects of technical change through the devaluation of all commodities, including the elements of constant capital. It cannot be excluded a priori that the devaluation of the elements of constant capital might be strong enough to raise the maximum rate of profit. A parallel criticism is that – since the actual rate of profit is related not only negatively to the composition of capital but also positively to the rate of exploitation – the upsurge in the rate of surplus value could outweigh the increase in the composition of capital. It must however be considered that Marx's law is stated with reference to the rise in the organic, and not the value composition of capital. The latter fully reflects the revolution in the prices of the elements of constant and of the elements of variable capital produced by mechanization, whereas the former measures inputs at the prices before the introduction of the new techniques. The organic composition of capital thus cannot but reflect the movement of the technical composition.

If the rate of surplus value goes up and counteracts the tendency of the rate of profit to fall, it is more and more likely that the system will stumble upon a third type of crisis, a realization crisis. The Marxist debate took two different paths on this. One side stressed disproportionalities, that is, sectoral imbalances between supply and demand, due to the unplanned nature of market economies: the unevenness of capitalist development may degenerate into a 'general glut' of commodities. However, this difficulty is overcome thanks to price and quantity adjustments and/or a more organized form of capitalism (Hilferding's position). The other side of the debate is sometimes wrongly labeled as underconsumptionist. It maintained that the decrease in the wage share within the new value translates into a decrease in effective demand (Kautsky's position).

A more sophisticated version is the one by Rosa Luxemburg: net investments are unable to make up for decreasing consumption, since long-term profitability of new machine goods depends on future outlets, and these latter are less and less predictable. Effective demand failures originate from a fall in investments. Joan Robinson (1972) and Michał Kalecki ([1967] 1971) clarified that this is an approach based on underinvestment, not underconsumption (this can be best appreciated reading the recently translated book by Tadeusz Kowalik 2014 on Rosa Luxemburg). When the 'external' factors mitigating the insufficiency of demand – mainly, net exports to non-capitalist areas – are exhausted, and when capitalism is entirely globalized, the tendency to the final breakdown materializes.

Kalecki ([1967] 1971) objected that the insufficiency of effective demand may be solved by what he dubbed 'domestic' exports, such as governments' budget deficits financed by the injection of new money. A similar role may be played by the unproductive consumption coming from 'third persons' drawing their incomes from deductions from total surplus value, as in Baran and Sweezy (1966). To be compatible with a smooth accumulation of capital, these solutions call for the continuation of the pressure on living labor. The pressure will be more intense if, as Paul Mattick (1969) thought, the Keynes–Kalecki way out means an increase in production, but not capitalist production (that is, a decrease of the share of productive workers in the economy). In this event, the profit squeeze may come directly from struggles in capitalist labor processes.

It is here that the re-reading of Marxian crisis theory built upon the dialectics between circularity of capital and linearity of exploitation comes in. We may read the tendential fall in the rate of profit as a meta-theory of crises, incorporating within it the different kind of crises which can be derived from *Capital*, and we may extend it into an historical narrative of the evolution of capitalism. The tendential fall in the rate of profit due to a rising value composition of capital was going on during the late nineteenth-century Great Depression. Fordism and Taylorism gave way to a rise in the rate of exploitation. This counteracted the tendency for the rate of profit to fall, but strengthened the tendency for the relative wage to fall, and created the conditions for a realization crisis: the Great Crash of the 1930s. The so-called 'golden age' of capitalism which followed was predicated on a higher pressure on productive workers to obtain enough living labor and higher surplus labor. This opened the way to workers' struggle in capitalist labor processes and a new, great social crisis of capitalist accumulation, located inside the immediate valorization process: a key factor of the Great Stagflation of the 1970s. Capitalist restructuring was opening a new capitalist phase, so-called neoliberalism.

15.2 THE CIRCUIT THEORY OF MONEY AND FINANCIAL INSTABILITY

The crisis of actually existing Keynesianism opened what Joan Robinson (1972) called the second crisis of economic theory (the first was related to the Great Crash of the 1930s). As she wrote, the issue was clearly no more about the aggregate level of production and employment but about the composition of output: for whom and what to produce. Workers' struggles put in question how to produce, and showed in practice the truth of the labor theory of value: the new value added depends on the (potentially antagonistic) extraction of living labor from the living bearers of labor-power. In fact, Joan Robinson faulted the Keynesians too, and even discerned some ambiguity in the same *General Theory*. On the same line, Hyman Minsky ([1975] 2008a) wrote that Keynesianism has been based on a 'bastard' economic policy synthesis leading to social and ecological disasters. Kalecki ([1967] 1971) saw the reasons for demise of Keynesianism better than the others. The crisis of capitalism in the 1960s and 1970s questioned the consensus in macroeconomic theory which was built too much on aggregated models where money did not matter and class conflict was ignored.

After the 1970s economic policies as well as capitalism moved to another stage. It was a structural morphological metamorphosis associated with changes in banking, finance and (private and public) debt. In my view, the entire so-called heterodoxy was lagging behind a proper understanding of what was going on: neo-Ricardianism and post-Keynesianism, but also Marxism. The reason was partly that the monetary aspects of Marx were not developed (among the few exceptions, Suzanne de Brunhoff's writings stands out). Moreover, sections in Volume III were left at the stage of drafts, where we read more Engels than Marx. These drafts were not only contradictory, but also depicted a capitalist economy which was not fully developed and financially sophisticated. For some critical economists, including myself, it was more interesting to look at Schumpeter or Keynes before *The General Theory* (particularly, *The Treatise on Money*), both influenced by Wicksell, as the political economists of the twentieth century. The critique of political economy had to rediscover itself as a macro-monetary labor theory of value and to fully mature as a monetary theory of capitalist production. That was the intellectual project of the first circuit theory of money, undertaken especially by Graziani and Parguez who developed an approach referring to the cycle of money capital in Volume II and to interest-bearing capital in Volume III. Credit-money was essential to capitalist accumulation, first of all as (banking) finance to production, the 'command' of the firm sector over workers' labor. A parallel development was Minsky's financial instability hypothesis, where the stress was on finance to fund capitalist investment in the longer term. These theoretical developments cannot be explored in depth here but their relevance and the need to update them will briefly be discussed.[2]

For monetary circuitists, capitalism is a sequence of concatenated phases opened by the creation of purchasing power by banks. Money is neither a commodity nor bilateral credit, it is rather a credit instrument in a triangular transaction, allowing the payer to finally settle payment obligations with the payee by means of promises to pay from a third agent; nowadays, a bank. Monetary payments for inputs are made prior to production and the selling of output on the commodity market. The differential access to money as purchasing power sets up asymmetries of power among social agents and this differential access is the principal factor determining the real structure of the economy.

The simplest circuit model takes place in a closed economy without the state where the basic agents are the commercial banking sector (the central bank is initially ignored), firms and households (workers). The monetary circuit is made up of three phases. First, the banking system creates purchasing power *ex nihilo*, enabling firms to cover their current costs of production (the wage bill). Loans make deposits, with the banking system meeting no ceiling in the creation of money (a view connected to post-Keynesian horizontalism). Production begins, according to the autonomous decisions of entrepreneurs concerning the level and allocation of employment (and, thereby, the size and composition of real output). Workers choose how to divide money income between consumption and savings. Savings may be spent in the financial market, buying securities issued by firms, or be kept as money balances. The approach highlights the relationship (of functionality as well as of contradiction) between industrial and banking capital.

The role of the stock exchange is to allow firms to recover the leakages from workers' expenditure due to savings, and get back the initial finance anticipated. If, on the other hand, savings add bank deposits to past liquid balances, firms remain indebted to banks: the permanence of a money stock signals an equivalent credit of households with the banking sector. If the state or a foreign sector is included, there can be inflows of money for firms which are 'free' from the payment of interests to banks. The circuitist scheme was able to highlight the way capitalist firms were, first (in the 1970s), able to rationalize and restructure the labor process going into bank debts; and then (beginning with the 1980s) could disintermediate thanks to growing public deficits. Financialization – that is, favoring financial to productive placements – was possible because of growing disequilibria in balance sheets, with agents incurring losses willing to go in debt towards non-banking agents possessing liquid holdings. Financialization was the consequence of the combination of government deficits plus credit squeeze.

Hyman Minsky's contribution is an extension of Keynes, combining an investment theory of the business cycle with a financial theory of investment. In his financial instability hypothesis, in a period of 'tranquil' growth and 'robust' finance, firms' and banks' liability structures spontaneously give way to fragility. Capitalism as a complex financial structure is a production of money by means of money, as in circuitism. Availability and terms of financial agreements govern investment which brings about gross profits that, in turn, feed back into the financial structure. Finance is needed to produce current output, to buy new capital goods, and, more generally, to own capital assets. Production of investment goods, however, is special as their construction time spans across many periods and their returns flow from an uncertain future, and so they need to be funded through a longer-term external finance.

Positions in capital assets require long-term finance, a combination of internal and external funds. They may be financed by intermediaries other than banks, or directly by savers, through instruments whose liquidity is subject to their convertibility into bank money. Like commercial banks, financial intermediaries are profit-seeking agents, which constantly try to extend credits, financing new positions. In prosperity economic units lower their margins of safety, their liability structures embody a higher degree of risk, while the money (and finance) supply becomes infinitely elastic. In a complex financial system, investment may also be financed through portfolio adjustment, reducing balance sheet liquidity and causing a rise in the price of capital assets. If a restrictive monetary policy actually wants to constrain the larger, effective, quantity of money, the central bank must determine a dramatic compression in reserves, and this usually happens when the boom is already well under way.

When the economy is financially robust, most agents are in a hedge-financing position. The validation of outstanding debts and risky projects fosters euphoric growth, developing into boom, and then a bubble. A rising debt–equity ratio is associated with higher short-term financing of fixed capital and long-term financial assets. As more and more of the financing of investment – both production and demand – comes about through external debts, and since firms increasingly enter speculative and Ponzi positions, the demand for finance becomes almost inflexible in the course of the cycle. When 'something happens' and the supply of finance is constrained by more prudent bank attitudes or tougher restrictive actions from the central bank, with a sudden, severe and unexpected increase in the cost of financing, the crisis breaks out. A recursive negative spiral gets going. Debt-deflation and financial turbulence strike the real economy, curbing income growth and bringing about mass unemployment.

In an economy with a small public sector and without a lender of last resort, the lower turning point will occur only after monetary contraction and bankruptcies restore 'robust' finance. In the Great Crash this meant a huge debt deflation and a highway to hell. The successive Keynesian big government and the central bank as lender of last resort sustain gross profits (which are positively related to government budget deficits) and support the liability structure (thanks to the higher cash inflows helping to meet cash commitments, and to the refinancing and reserves helping to prevent banks' and financial intermediaries' bankruptcy). 'Keynesian' economic policies are however unable to abolish the fundamental processes leading to instability; what they can and must do is to repress and counteract the most harmful ills, and to make sure that 'it' does not happen again.

15.3 NEOLIBERALISM AS AN ACTIVE POLITICAL CONFIGURATION OF CAPITALISM

After the Volcker–Thatcher–Reagan counter-revolution, capitalism turned out to be quite different than expected by Marxists or post-Keynesians – even by the sophisticated versions I depicted before.[3] Although Minsky's financial instability hypothesis (FIH) (whatever its theoretical shortcomings, which I do not discuss here) may have contributed to the understanding of some of the limits of Keynesianism and its collapse, and although monetary circuitism was able to look at capitalist crisis as a process of restructuring and rationalization (in both cases forcefully stressing the role of money and finance), the capitalism which was taking shape was novel on many grounds, and required a new understanding. The issue to be dealt with is about the kind of capitalism constructed during the 1970s and 1980s, and which went into crisis in 2007–08 – neoliberalism –which is too often reduced to a resurgence of classical laissez-faire and to an incarnation of neoclassical mainstream theory. More satisfying answeres are most easily found in the discourse of political scientists or sociologists.

The first reading of neoliberalism is the one recently proposed by Wolfgang Streeck (2013). Streeck begins his narrative in the late 1960s and the 1970s. It is a Kalecki-inspired view, where the re-emerging capital–labor antagonism (in distribution and within the labor processes of valorization) and the consequent tendency to a crisis were contrasted with 'buying time' through money. The capitalist class, in the Great Stagflation decade, mounted a successful resistance against the conditions it had to accept after 1945 in order to remain politically acceptable when challenged by an alternative economic and social system. This authentic 'capital strike' was a symptom of a legitimation crisis leading to a 'long goodbye' of capitalism from democracy, under the new capitalist configuration of neoliberalism.

After 1980, the neoliberal counter-revolution was marked by a rise in public debt and a curtailment of social and democratic demands. The tax cuts to 'starve the beast' paradoxically turned the beast itself, the state, into a permanent debtor, forcing it to restrain social expenditures and obey the dictates of the financial markets (first dominated by government bonds, afterwards by stocks, later on by housing). Against citizens, the original constituency, the fundamental constituency, became the creditor class, which demanded a rising value-appreciation of their savings, that is, of their other assets. This led first to crisis at the periphery, but more and more the financial crises spread to the center. Crisis itself became the main instrument for the international financial elite to conquer political power through their delegates. This was followed by a consolidation phase, where the state, public and social sphere were transformed so as to meet the financial markets' expectations. Governments have to pay the creditor class before protecting citizens. In what are the weakest (though intriguing) pages of his book, Streeck sees in the euro the paradigmatic example of this dynamic. The single currency is made the culprit of everything, and the argument turns into a too-easy appeal to popular insurgence.

The second perspective on neoliberalism is Philip Mirowski's (2013) *Never Let a Serious Crisis Go To Waste*. Contrary to classical liberal doctrine, neoliberalism knows well that the conditions for the existence of the 'good society' must be constructed and that they will not come about naturally. The same German ordoliberalism argues that competition needs to be directly organized by the state, by embedding the 'free' market into other social institutions. It is a biopolitical configuration which argues that bodies must be 'made' responsive to market signals (the reference here is to Foucault's notion of 'governmentality'). The neoliberal project is not at all willing to destroy the state; rather, it powerfully redefines its shape and functions. This is what Jamie Peck called a kind of 'regulation-in-denial', where marketization of government functions is presented as a shrinking of the state. The corporations can do no wrong, and monopolistic positions are due to the misguided activities of the state or political pressures. The inequality of economic resources and political rights is a necessary (permanent) feature of the ideal market system, and the repressive powers of the state must be strengthened, since the poor have so little to lose.

In a nutshell, neoliberalism has nothing to do with classical liberalism, nor laissez-faire. It is, rather, a constructivist, state-driven project creating, rather than registering, an allegedly 'natural' equilibrium respecting individual preferences. It is the opposite. 'Biopolitically', neoliberalism constructs the same individuals corresponding to the presumed human nature actually imposed from above.

On the background provided by Streeck (2013) and Mirowski (2013), it cannot come as a surprise that the third reading of neoliberalism which I suggest was put forward by Colin Crouch (2011) after the crisis, for example in his book *The Strange Non-Death of Neoliberalism*. Crouch provocatively defines neoliberalism as 'privatized Keynesianism'. The term was anticipated in some of my writings with Halevi. I think that with a different meaning it also appeared in the 1970s. Financial innovations facilitated consumer debt, either backed by collateral or completely unsecured. The system was a market-generated functional equivalent of government demand management and sustained consumption by separating purchasing power from individual labor income. Borrowing was undertaken by individuals themselves on the basis of property mortgages or credit card ratings largely divorced from the labor market situation.

15.4 THE ASCENT AND COLLAPSE OF PRIVATIZED KEYNESIANISM

The Great Moderation of the late twentieth century, leading to the Great Recession of the early 2000s, originates in capital's reaction to the 1960s and 1970s crisis within the capital–labor social relation. The 'real subsumption of labor to finance' – that is, the subordinated integration of households into the stock exchange market, and their going deeper and deeper into bank indebtedness – is one side of the coin. The 'deconstruction' of labor is the other: a new corporate governance leading to a 'centralization without concentration'. Mergers and acquisitions rendered capital more centralized. The centralization process did not typically lead to highly integrated companies (though China may be an exception). Contrariwise, productive networks based on the outsourcing of upstream production activities, and made up of many small and medium-sized enterprises, have been set up. The result was the disappearance of an increasingly homogeneous working class and its replacement by a precarious and fragmented working class. 'Financialization' and 'casualization' eroded the strength of labor against capital, once again leading to a dramatic increase in exploitation and the rate of surplus value.

Minsky (see Whalen 1997) aptly defined this new capitalist phase as 'money manager capitalism'. It must be read as a constellation of capital where traumatized workers went hand in hand with 'manic' savers and indebted consumers. The attack on labor in the labor market and the labor process made the Phillips curve horizontal: full employment of a precarious job force was now possible, without the risk of inflation in the goods market (inflation came back after a while, but from oil, raw materials and commodities). Unemployment penetrated into the employed labor force through the spreading of part-time, casual and informal occupations. Meanwhile the continuous appreciation of accumulated savings was leading to a fall in saving relative to income, with the propensity to save eventually becoming negative. Pension and institutional funds nurtured capital market inflation which was *ex post* hedging corporations' balance sheets, at least for a while. As Toporowski (2010) remarks, the middle classes were sedated by escalating property values and found an illusory security from uncertainty.

The model of banking was no longer 'originate to hold', but 'originate to distribute': banks sought to maximize their fees and commissions by issuing and managing assets in off-balance-sheet affiliate structures. In this context, bankers had no interest in credit evaluation, which was now provided by rating agencies. In the Anglo-Saxon type of capitalism, with the public sector trying to reduce its deficits everywhere, the household sector became a net borrower, and the non-financial business sector a net lender. Household saving behavior was helping to overcome the stagnationist tendency, but banks were losing their best customers, while the financial system was increasingly characterized by an intrinsic (though hidden) instability. Financial innovations won the day: they reduced risk individually, but increased it globally (an example being subprime lending).

This new configuration of capitalism was made possible by a new role of the central bank in managing the creation of liquidity so that the continuous increase in asset values could continue undisturbed. The central bank also assured the viability of the shadow banking system and financial intermediaries. Through Greenspan, quantitative monetarism stepped down, being replaced by a policy where money was made available in unlimited amounts at any interest rate established by the central bank. The money supply became flat, and was finally recognized as endogenous even within the mainstream. It was an eminently political management of effective demand, manipulating indebted consumption as the pillar of autonomous demand; that is one reason why I labeled it 'privatized Keynesianism'.

Competitive deflation, capital asset inflation and the increasingly leveraged position of households and financial companies were complementary elements of a perverse mechanism where real growth was doped by toxic finance. Labor as an activity, too, was affected. There was a shift from procedures and norms defined *a priori* in a stable organizational and technological context – production as a plan to be implemented – to a performance checked *a posteriori*. Different fragments of the production cycle were considered as independent firms. In the 1980s the main form taken by this process was outsourcing as externalization; in the 1990s, the qualitative novelty was in-house outsourcing. Nowadays, it is modules and networks.

Being based on burgeoning private debt, this 'new' capitalism was unsustainable and collapsed first with the dot.com crisis. Households risked turning from the 'manic' to the 'depressive' phase as savers, reducing consumption to reduce their debt exposure. The risk was avoided with a return to military Keynesianism (after September 11th) and then to a revised form of the asset bubble-driven privatized Keynesianism. This second bubble phase ended rather quickly. The new monetary policy was unable to make ends meet in conditions of inflation, because of a surge in prices of oil and raw materials. Although capital asset prices were not considered a problem – and wage inflation was not on the agenda – commodities price inflation worried the Federal Reserve (Fed) and other central banks, and from 2004, the Fed began to increase interest rates such that by 2005, United States (US) house prices softened. The proliferation of subprime mortgages, with the enticement of poor households to enter the financial swamp, was an attempt to keep the real estate bubble inflating by any means. The hope that the increase in borrowing costs could be offset by a further rise in asset values, thereby expanding the value of the collateral used in loan applications, faded away. The widespread view that opaque securitization packages would efficiently distribute risk, and that the emerging countries' savings would cover the deficits of the United States, Britain, Australia and Spain, were revealed to be a double deception. This time the 'depressive' phase was irresistible, and the economy fell into the biggest crisis since the Great Crash.

15.5 EUROPEAN TRANSFORMATIONS

For some European countries a neo-mercantilist approach, together with a process of industrial restructuring, was the way to manage the effective demand constraint through a current account surplus in the balance of payments. The surplus accrued to Germany and its satellites (among them, the Netherlands, Belgium, Austria, Switzerland, Denmark and the Scandinavian countries). The profits resulting from this position of advantage were invested abroad along two different paths: into US 'toxic' finance; but also in Europe, fostering the existing financial and real imbalances. For European (especially French and German) banks and finance the Treasury bonds of the European periphery played a role similar to subprime loans in the US between 1999 and 2008. The European neo-mercantilist model was soon put under severe stress as the US and Southern European export markets collapsed between mid-2007 and mid-2008. After a brief Keynesian interlude between late 2008 and early 2009, the turning of private debt into public debt led to pressure to cut public expenditures. The spread of austerity and the domino effects after the Greek crisis beginning in 2010 brought into the open the fallacies in the institutional design of the euro. These fallacies were not only the arbitrary ceilings to government deficits and the debt to gross domestic product (GDP) ratio, but also the rules denying the European Central Bank (ECB) the possibility to buy government bonds. The system had no mechanism for eliminating excessive debt in the economy.

The multi-speed dynamics of Europe are well known by now, and can be grasped through a Luxemburg–Kalecki vision. Net exports were the driving force in the core (Germany and the satellites), with the resulting profits invested abroad. The insertion of Europe in the 'new' capitalism's financial world meant that these investments found their way into toxic finance. Within the single currency, the Treasury bonds of the European periphery played a role for European banks and finance (especially, French and German) similar to that of US subprime loans. Germany, like the rest of Northern Europe, had a historical need to export to Southern Europe, where it realized the largest part of its profits. Trade deficits in France, Italy, Spain, Portugal and Greece were crucial to Germany's competitiveness. They also held down the nominal valuation of Germany's currency, the euro (compared with what it would have been under the Deutsche Mark, or with a euro restricted to the net exporters). Moreover the single currency deepened a competitive deflation – not just because of wage repression, but also due to the increase in the productive power of labor – and thus a real devaluation. German economic strength is due to a specialization in advanced machinery and high-quality manufacturing, and not just wage deflation.

Before the Great Recession, European trade imbalances were not considered to be a binding constraint, nor was there any urgent concern about government finances. In fact, where real-estate bubbles did not spur growth (as they did in Spain and Ireland), government deficits were implicitly seen to be essential counterweights to the stagnationist tendency springing from the German economic policy approach. The drama about sovereign debt is ill-posed even today, if one looks at other countries such as the US, United Kingdom (UK) or Japan.

Another misunderstanding is that global imbalances within the eurozone ought to be a problem for the European Monetary Union (EMU). The liabilities of the national central banks relative to the ECB are not constrained, and they are charged the main official rate. These imbalances, which are quite natural in large economic areas like Europe (and the eurozone) can in principle continue indefinitely. This is the other side of the coin of a mechanism like the EMU unifying the former national currencies into a single currency: a 'normal' balance of payments crisis is not possible, irrespective of real imbalances (on all this, see Bellofiore et al. 2015). This of course does not negate the real dramatic consequences of intra-EMU current account imbalances, without proper interventions, and that they can indirectly constitute a threat to the single currency.

It is necessary to go deeper into the structural industrial and financial dimensions to understand the European transformations, and the current crisis. The origin, as anticipated, was the actual implementation of Kalecki's prophecy of a capital strike when an actual reduction of the mass and share of profits resulted from the success of labor struggles, as happened in the late 1960s and early 1970s. The rollback strategy – initiated in the mid-1970s, largely achieved in the 1980s, accelerated and sharpened after the fall of the Berlin Wall in 1989 – led to the weakening of the working class, an outcome achieved also through new productive networks; and to the progressive enfeebling of the national trade unions in the European Union (EU) countries. This was strongly instrumental in setting up a highly fragmented labor market. The progressive freedom of circulation of capitals and not of workers in the Eastern European countries was also the way to realize what Sinn nicknamed the 'German Bazaar economy'. The German economic matrix went into a deep transformation from the mid-1990s, with an eastward enlargement and outsourcing, as compared to the quantitative narrowing and qualitative degradation of the productive base in Southern Europe. The geography of German trade was consequently altered, with China and the neighboring Eastern European countries (more and more integrated into the value-chain) becoming crucial partners. Germany appears to have profited from the above-mentioned hidden relative undervaluation of the euro, on external markets; but it also gained on the production costs side from the open devaluation of the currencies of the Eastern European countries against the euro.

Together with this transnational productive integration, financial integration has been a new powerful lever of change. The exposure to liberalized financial markets started before the introduction of the single currency and had major impacts on the way European economies are structured today. Financial integration was pursued at least from the early 2000s, leading to a common capital market and a common market in financial services. Cross-border mergers and acquisitions:

> have effectively integrated the balance sheets of the respective national banking systems in the European Union. As a result, banks in all countries of the European Union are exposed to risks in other countries, in the sense that they

> have assets or subsidiaries in other countries or, at the very least, that they have liabilities to the European Central Bank. (Toporowski 2013)

Exiting the euro, and even reflationary policies, do not seem to go to the heart of the matter. The former option would likely turn out badly not only because the exchange rate that would help the needs of trade may lead to worsening balance sheets, but also because the most important factors in nurturing disequilibria in the deficit countries are structural. They have to do with the way Germany has constructed a transnational network of production. The German matrix of production nowadays goes beyond national borders. More generally, the geography of trade has changed in Europe, and this affects the output composition and import content of different countries, currently giving way to an impoverishment of the ties among peripheral nations, and so on. Reflationary policies may well profit Eastern Europe and China, and only marginally Southern Europe and Ireland.

15.6 REVISIONS

Capitalism has moved on, and so must Marxian theory. After the 1970s, it was urgent to put back at the center of the critique of political economy its constitutive monetary aspects; but this could not be done effectively without a confrontation with the great monetary heretics of the twentieth century, Schumpeter and Keynes (and their ancestor, Wicksell). This was the key contribution by Minsky, and Graziani and Parguez, which should be connected with a Luxemburg–Kalecki underinvestment perspective – as it was. But this is not enough: the full understanding of neoliberalism and its crisis requires a further critical development.

Monetary circuitism has to be revised; and in fact it has been, by circuitist authors themselves. One reason is that the monetary circuit itself changed its working in the late twentieth century. At center stage there is now the link between banks and financial intermediaries and households. As Seccareccia (2012) writes, 'the practical disappearance of household saving and the ever growing household indebtedness has fueled the expansion of speculative derivatives because of the demand arising from the growing savings of the non-financial corporate sector'. Money enters through a different channel, though Graziani is right in saying that this is finance to production in disguise.

Also, the financial instability hypothesis had to be looked at with fresh eyes: when money manager capitalism worked in high gear the mounting leverage came from private debt, but this had to do with consumption, not investment. The process was in fact for a long while stabilizing, not destabilizing. At the same time, Minsky proposed a stage approach to capitalism which is the financial counterpart of the historical re-reading of Marxian accumulation and crisis theory that I proposed at the beginning of this chapter (on this, see Bellofiore 2014).

Minsky focused on US capitalism. Commercial capitalism (since, more or less, the seventeenth century) is the first stage, progressively turning into industrial capitalism (more and more relevant in the second half of the eighteenth century and the first half of the nineteenth century). Merchant banks and commercial banks financed goods in transit, inventories and goods in process. Business owners based their acquisition of capital assets on self-financing in commercial capitalism, while industrial capitalism in the US saw the emergence of wild-cat financing. During the nineteenth century, however, a new form of capitalism was in the making: finance capitalism. Long-term investments in heavy infrastructures (railroads, mills and fixed capital) may require the involvement of the state and/or adventurous financing. In the financial capitalism stage the financiers were mainly investment bankers and big corporations; the large shareholders dominated over firm managers. In Europe, and especially in Germany, this era was the background for Hilferding's *Finanz-Kapital.*

Finance capitalism collapsed in the Great Crash, due to both financial (Fisher's debt-deflation) and real causes (the Luxemburg–Kalecki realization crisis). The next stage was managerial capitalism as the outgrowth of World War II. Household and business debts were low, and external financing ultimately involved 'big government'. Managerial capitalism was characterized by high profits, high investments, massive *ex ante* fiscal deficits, neutralized by growth until the mid-1960s and 1970s. In this period power shifted from large shareholders to corporate managers. The upshot was a capitalism of big corporations, large banks and financial institutions, and new intermediaries like mutual and pension funds. The economic process became more and more dominated by money managers who had as a target the 'valorization of capital' (the appreciation of the investments of the holders of their liabilities, including households). Under managerial capitalism employers offered pension plans to workers, and financial institutions started to aggressively manage retirement funds and other assets held by organizations and households. Institutional investors became the new masters of the economy. Funds bought equity from highly leveraged buyout non-financial businesses. According to Minsky, it was these funds' behavior which made business management highly sensitive to stock market evaluations, and transformed American capitalism into a socially predatory form. As I suggested before, such alterations affected corporate governance, favoring the institution of a network or modular productive system far from the system of the vertically integrated big factory but also from that of the traditional small or medium-sized firm. The new configuration pushed forward a policy of downsizing and of variable costs compression, which jeopardized employment conditions, so that employment became discontinuous and precarious.

Minsky's money manager capitalism accurately describes the financial determinants of what I have called the 'real subsumption of labor to finance' and 'centralization without concentration', terms giving a historicized and class meaning to what nowadays is labeled with the void terminology of 'financialization'. The rate at which money flowed from funds to financial markets enabled non-financial firms to issue shares more cheaply, the returns of which increasingly depended upon speculative gains. This process gave way to an overcapitalization of productive enterprises.[4] The next efforts should be to develop from here a financial theory of accumulation.

Real subsumption of labor to finance, together with centralization without concentration, meant a powerful systemic answer to the Social Crisis of the 1960s and 1970s, and dismantled the conditions which in those decades made social (and workers') struggles so effective. They went so far as to alter time and space as conditions of valorization: they impacted directly on the process of production, generating longer working hours, extracting greater effort from workers, and forcing an increase in the labor supply provided by families; they deconstructed the working class, which was 'lost in space' (the Marxian side of the story of money manager capitalism, if you wish) (see Bellofiore and Vertova 2006).

The challenge is not only to go deeper in the inquiry about the integration of finance with production and accumulation, but also to map the connections with the dynamics of the capitalist labor process and the working conditions; something which cannot be delegated to a separate sociological dimension, or taken as exhaustively analyzed in Marx. This is the heart of Marxian critical political economy.

15.7 SUMMARY AND CONCLUSIONS

The collapse of neoliberalism is the breakdown of privatized Keynesianism; that is, of a capitalist process ultimately driven by a politically governed indebted consumption. By definition, the driving power of demand and hence production cannot be, on a global scale, net exports. It is unlikely that it will be private investments. Sooner or later, it has to be government expenditure in deficit, monetarily financed by the central bank. But reflationary policies are not the simple way out that Keynesians think. For Minsky – already in the 1970s – a better solution would rather be a policy of 'socialization' of investments (through public 'productive' expenditure), of employment (the state as 'employer of last resort'), and of banking and finance (promotions of small and medium-sized firms). Minsky went far beyond Keynesianism in reinventing the New Deal.

There is no such thing as economic development not based on prior debt. Recent decades have confirmed that *ex post* government deficits are the condition for the net creation of income in the private sector. However, as Parguez (2014) insists, we should not forget that there are 'bad' and 'good' deficits. 'Bad' deficits are the non-planned result of the tendency to stagnation, of shock therapies, of deflationary policies, of the unsustainability of toxic finance, and so on. By contrast, 'good' deficits are planned *ex ante* deficits. Their aim is to build up, and improve, a stock of productive resources. They are a means for the production of wealth: a long-run investment in tangible goods (infrastructure, green conversion, alternative forms of transport, and so on) and intangible goods (health, education, research, and so on). Gender-balanced and nature-friendly approaches are intrinsic to this policy. Welfare itself has to be transformed from supplying nominal subsidies, to direct intervention 'in kind' as part of a wider horizon of 'planning'.

A deficit spending of this type immediately raises the government debt to GDP ratio, but the subsequent growth in the denominator will make this jump only temporary. Such an intervention may have positive effects from a capitalist point of view; those effects which fascinate post-Keynesian economists. It supports the real economy from the demand side, stabilizes the financial sector by providing sound financial assets, and increases the productivity in the system. This kind of intervention can – and must – be part of a class-oriented left-wing 'minimum programme'. It yields not a stable model of a new capitalism, but rather an 'imbalance': an uneven terrain where the issue of overcoming capitalism in the end has to be dealt with.

A related argument about Europe: the European crisis is the crisis of neo-mercantilism and a faulty institutional structure of the single currency. Here too it is clear that reflationary policies are insufficient. In the last 15–20 years the European economy has gone through a deep financial and industrial transformation. Eurozone countries share the same payment system. There is nothing unusual in internal imbalances: they are absorbed by the banking system, and do not lead to problems for the single currency. Balance sheets of banks and intermediaries are integrated, and the public debt is managed on the bond market. Germany has spread its industrial and trade network, so that increases in demand will be transmitted to a transnational value chain located in Eastern and Central Europe. The European economy needs expansionary policies together with credit, industrial and regional policies. Coordinated government deficits, financed by the ECB, should be targeted on innovation, material and immaterial infrastructures, and to directly provide employment. A 'big push' is needed from the state.

The point is that nothing like this can be a capitalist project today. In fact, it looks too much like some kind of socialism. Only a deepening of the crisis and the construction of a transnational social movement against capital could open some space in a new direction. Capitalist crisis means, as always, the collapse of a particular phase of capitalist accumulation; and at the same time, the painful restoration of profitability through crisis itself. It may be the transition to a new stage of capitalism if complemented by appropriate, 'new' economic policies.

We are far from seeing a light at the end of the tunnel, and the risk is that the latter may prove to be an oncoming train. If the crisis has the traits underlined here, current capitalism involves a permanent attack on labor and social reproduction. A progressive way out cannot be divorced from a deep change in social relations, and social struggles from below.

NOTES

1. For the discourse on crisis developed here see Bellofiore (2011), and the references there. On the falling rate of profit I agree with David Harvey's Chapter 3 in this volume.
2. See Bellofiore (2013), and the references in that article.
3. On neoliberalism and its crisis, and for references, see Bellofiore and Vertova (2014). This should be complemented with the arguments that David Kotz and Özgür Orhangazi develop in Chapters 2 and 14, respectively, in this book.
4. See Chapter 13 by Toporowski in this volume. For a different take on financialization, see Simon Mohun's Chapter 12 in this volume.

REFERENCES

Baran, P.A. and P.M. Sweezy (1966), *Monopoly Capital*, New York: Monthly Review Press.

Bellofiore, R. (2011), 'Crisis Theory and the Great Recession: A Personal Journey, from Marx to Minsky', P. Zarembka and R. Desai (eds), *Revitalizing Marxist Theory for Today's Capitalism, Research in Political Economy*, 27, Bingley, UK: Emerald Group Publishing, 81–120.

Bellofiore, R. (2013), 'Endogenous Money, Financial Keynesianism and Beyond', *Review of Keynesian Economics*, 1(2), 153–170.

Bellofiore, R. (2014), 'The Socialization of Investment, from Keynes to Minsky and Beyond', Levy Economics Institute of Bard College, WP no. 822, December.

Bellofiore R., F. Garibaldo and M. Mortagua (2015), 'A Credit-Money and Structural Perspective on the European Crisis: Why Exiting the Euro is the Answer to the Wrong Question', *Review of Keynesian Economics*, 3(4), 471–490.

Bellofiore R. and G. Vertova (2006), 'Lost in Space? The Geographical and Political Dimension of Uneven Capitalist Development', in Giovanna Vertova (ed.), *The Changing Economic Geography of Globalization*, London: Routledge.

Bellofiore R. and G. Vertova (2014), *The Great Recession and the Contradictions of Contemporary Capitalism*, Cheltenham UK and Northampton, MA, USA: Edward Elgar Publishing.

Crouch, C. (2011), *The Strange Non-Death of Neoliberalism*, Cambridge: Polity Press

Graziani, A. (2003), *The Monetary Theory of Production*, Cambridge: Cambridge University Press.

Kalecki, M. ([1967] 1971), 'The Problem of Effective Demand in Tugan-Baranovsky and Rosa Luxemburg', reprinted in M. Kalecki (1971), *Selected Essays on the Dynamics of the Capitalist Economy 1933–1970*, Cambridge: Cambridge University Press.

Kowalik, T. (2014), *Rosa Luxemburg: Theory of Accumulation and Imperialism*, Palgrave Macmillan.

Mattick, P. (1969), *Marx and Keynes – The Limits of the Mixed Economy*, Boston, MA: Porter Sargent.

Minsky, H.P. ([1975] 2008a), *John Maynard Keynes*, New York: McGraw Hill.

Minsky, H.P. ([1986] 2008b), *Stabilizing an Unstable Economy*, New York: McGraw Hill.

Mirowski, P. (2013), *Never Let a Serious Crisis Go To Waste*, London: Verso.

Parguez, A. (2014), 'The True Rules of a Good Management of Public Finance: An Explanation of the Fatal Eurozone Crisis', in R. Bellofiore and G. Vertova (2014), *The Great Recession and the Contradictions of Contemporary Capitalism*, Cheltenham, UK and Northampton, MA, USA: Edward Elgar Publishing.

Robinson, J. (1972), 'The Second Crisis of Economic Theory', *American Economic Review*, 62(May), 1–9.

Seccareccia, M. (2012), 'Financialization and the Transformation of Commercial Banking: Understanding the Recent Canadian Experience Before and During the International Financial Crisis', *Journal of Post Keynesian Economics*, 35(2), 277–300.

Streeck, W. (2013), *Gekaufte Zeit. Die vertagte Krise des demokratischen Kapitalismus*, Berlin: Suhrkamp Verlag.

Toporowski J. (2010), 'The Wisdom of Property and the Politics of the Middle Class', *Monthly Review*, 62(4), 10–15.

Toporowski, J. (2013), 'International Credit, Financial Integration and the Euro', *Cambridge Journal of Economics*, 37(3), 571–584.

Whalen, C.J. (1997), 'Money-Manager Capitalism and the End of Shared Prosperity', *Journal of Economic Issues*, 31(2), 517–525.

16. The contested nature of financialization in emerging capitalist economies

Annina Kaltenbrunner and Elif Karacimen[1]

Finance has always played an important role in the circulation and accumulation of capital. In the current phase of capitalism this role has further deepened and broadened. The distinctive characteristics of the current era in relation to finance have been captured by the notion of financialization. The crisis that erupted in the US economy in 2008 and then spread to the rest of the world economy has led to a surge of interest in financialization. This is so because the specific characteristics of the crisis originated from the financialized character of the advanced capitalist economies over the last few decades.

Why advanced capitalist countries have financialized is still open to debate. One strand of explanation traces this back to the stagnation of late capitalism. Starting with the seminal work of Magdoff and Sweezy (1972), these accounts locate financialization in the falling rate of profit, largely due to increased monopolization and intercapitalist competition. The consequent repression of wages and slowdown in investment resulted in a contraction of demand, temporarily offset by 'demand management' policies. During that time, debt levels surged and a series of financial activities served for the continuation of the system (Magdoff and Sweezy 1972, 1987; Arrighi 1994; Brenner 2004; Foster and Magdoff 2008). Other authors emphasize the determining role of government policies which have unleashed the forces of finance and have led to an unprecedented increase in financial markets and financial actors. The growth in financial systems, in turn, had negative implications for real capital accumulation (and contributed to the falling rate of profit) through 'crowding-out' effects, increasing payments to financial markets, shortening the planning horizon, and augmenting uncertainty about the cost of future external funds in the face of financial market volatility (Boyer 2000; Aglietta and Breton 2001; Duménil and Lévy 2004; Stockhammer 2004; Crotty 2005; Orhangazi 2008).

The above approaches represent juxtaposing views of financialization, whose drivers are located in either productive sectors (whose developments trigger changes in the financial sphere) or the policy and financial sphere which then has repercussions on capital accumulation. This chapter suggests that although it is important to build the analysis on problems in the 'real' economy, one should not ignore the interactions between the 'real' and finance (Hilferding and Bottomore 1990; Lapavitsas 2010; Ashman and Fine 2013). Instead of a dichotomous understanding of finance and the productive sector, financialization should be approached through the identification of historically new patterns and needs in the symbiotic relationship between the financial system and different agents of society. While new financial practices arose to meet these new needs, many innovations in finance have promoted restructuring of the production system itself (Albo et al. 2010). In other words, finance is not something simply positioned on production. There is a causal relation between real accumulation and finance even if real accumulation sets the principles for the latter (Lapavitsas 2010). This symbiotic interpretation of financialization is important to reveal the contradictory role of finance in capital accumulation: while finance creates the conditions for capital accumulation, it also lays the seeds for its instability. Finance is crucial to strengthen the power and expansion of the capitalist class. It offers the opportunities for speculative activities, which can be reinvested to expand capital accumulation. It is, however, these same speculative activities which can affect capitalists' business negatively, for instance through crowding-out effects, new risks and uncertainties, and the occurrence of financial crises.

If one acknowledges the contradictory role of finance in capital accumulation, the analytical focus shifts to identifying the conditions under which finance takes what role. These conditions include the specific historical and institutional trajectories of national processes of capital accumulation, the structural real sector configurations and the specific forms finance takes itself. This shifting analytical focus not only helps to shed light on the roots of the financialization process itself, but also provides insights into the new dynamics and forms finance presents depending on the context under consideration, its functions and dysfunctions for capital accumulation, and the roots of financial crises. This also means that, as pointed out by Fine (2013), rather than analysing capital accumulation at the aggregate level attention has to be paid to how capital is accumulated and the potential productive restructuring which takes place as a result of financialization. For example, whereas investment might fall (or indeed continue to grow) at the aggregate level, the dynamics might differ fundamentally according to firm size, sector, openness and so on.

It is in this context that this study looks into the financialization of emerging capitalist economies (ECEs). Despite the richness of debates concerning the roots of the 2008 crisis, its relation to financialization and its implications for capital accumulation, there has hitherto been little attempt to assess the changing dynamics of finance in ECEs. Those authors who have done so, have noted that financialization processes in ECEs are closely related to and intensified with their integration into the world economy (Painceira 2011; Correa et al. 2012; Levy-Orlik 2012; Kaltenbrunner and Painceira 2013; Powell 2013; Karacimen 2014). Although we agree with this view, we argue, in line with our view of finance set out above, that it is important not to take financialization as a typical process that each country will follow, but as a dynamic one that is shaped by and interacts with the specific capital accumulation process and institutional and historical features of each country (Doucette and Seo 2011; Ashman and Fine 2013). This also includes accounting for countries' specific financial market structures which will influence how financialization manifests itself and interacts with the 'real' economy. Moreover, our analysis underscores the contradictory nature of finance. On the one hand, increased international integration created new opportunities for capitalists in these economies which have allowed them to expand their business and supported capital accumulation. On the other hand, the increased articulation with domestic and international financial markets brought new risks and historically novel financial needs, which have distracted from real investment and led to the restructuring of production. This includes the vulnerability to financial crises emanating in the financial systems of core capitalist countries. Although the global financial crisis of 2007–08 started in the United States (US), it had strong repercussions on ECEs. Financialized and globally integrated countries were hit hardest by the initial financial turmoil. However, in line with the variegated nature of financialization postulated in this chapter, the specific channels and repercussions of the crisis depended on the nature of domestic capital accumulation and financial structure in each country (ODI 2008; IDS 2008; ECB 2010).

To make these points, we place particular emphasis on the changing asset and liability structures of non-financial corporations (NFCs) as institutions reflecting fundamental or structural changes in capitalism (Michell and Toporowski 2014). Arguably, NFCs also constitute the main link between financial system changes and capital accumulation. We draw on evidence from a wide range of different ECEs to underline the contextual and contradictory nature of financialization processes. It is important to note, though, that our chapter is primarily conceptual, and aims at highlighting the variegated and complex nature and implications of financialization. Future research will complement this analysis with detailed, comparative case studies to further illustrate our points.

Following this introduction, section 16.1 gives a brief overview of the beginnings of financialization of ECEs to set the background for a detailed discussion of the recent financialization of NFCs in section 16.2. Section 16.3 concludes.

16.1 FINANCIALIZATION IN EMERGING CAPITALIST ECONOMIES

16.1.1 The 1980s and 1990s: The Beginnings of Financialization

Any deliberate attempt to characterize the changes in the financing behavior of NFCs in ECEs over the last decade necessitates looking at the financialization of those economies from a historical perspective. Compared to core capitalist countries, financialization of ECEs is relatively recent. Its beginnings are frequently rooted in the resolution of the Latin American debt crisis and the Brady Plan in close connection with these countries' nascent integration into the international financial markets in the 1980s (Pauly 2003; Painceira 2008; Vasudevan 2009; Mahmud 2010). The steep rise in US interest rates in 1978–79 precipitated widespread default among ECEs. After a few unsuccessful attempts to solve debt-related problems, the 1989 Brady Plan introduced a new strategy to manage these countries' external debt: negotiations between private creditors and debtor countries to instigate a shift from debt rescheduling to debt relief.

The Brady Plan had three important implications for the financialization of ECEs. First, it played a crucial role in creating sovereign debt markets. These markets are an important element of early financialization processes where alternative financial assets are not available yet. While a part of the debt reductions was funded via loans from international financial institutions, the rest was rescheduled into Brady Bonds.[2] The sale of these bonds in the secondary markets was thought to allow diversification of sovereign risk away from private creditors to international capital markets by introducing ECE sovereign bonds as international portfolio assets (Vasudevan 2009). Second, the Brady Plan increased the dependency of ECEs on international capital markets for their financing needs and created the necessity for widespread capital account liberalization. While for the banks the restructuring worked well, as it allowed them to remove the debt from their balance sheets and free up assets for other uses (Mahmud 2010), the plan failed to reduce debt to sustainable levels (Sachs 1989). Finally, debt negotiations under the Brady Plan strengthened the role of international financial institutions (Pauly 2003). Debt restructuring negotiations occurred within the context of International Monetary Fund (IMF) standby agreements which conditioned any debt reductions on policy adjustment programmes and market-oriented reforms (also known as the Washington Consensus). These reforms included, prominently, the liberalization of financial markets, both domestically and internationally, such as the liberalization of interest rates, the privatization of banks, the removal of the state from the banking system, and capital account liberalization. The theoretical underpinnings of the financial liberalization argument were based on the seminal work by McKinnon (1973) and Shaw (1973). In this view, the end to 'financial repression' should increase domestic savings (through higher interest rates), investments, and the overall efficiency of these investments through higher allocative efficiency and competition. In a similar vein, capital account liberalization would allow savings to be pooled and allocated efficiently throughout the world by equalizing the rate of return globally (Akyüz 1993). Moreover, international capital mobility was thought to allow countries to tidy over liquidity shortfalls and thus smooth consumption over time.

Although facilitated by the Brady Plan and instituted by international organizations, it is important to note that these financial liberalization measures strongly reflected the changing needs and demands of domestic capital to integrate into the world economy. In many ECEs the inward-oriented model of import substitution had reached its limits by the 1980s due to the constraints imposed by the domestic market. Although trade and financial liberalization accelerated the process, Katz (2001) shows in the case of Latin America that the gradual transformation of new patterns of production specialization was already under way in the 1970s. Latin American countries significantly increased their demand for foreign capital, long before the implementation of structural reforms actually began. At the same time, the inadequate resolution of the debt crisis required ECEs to generate the necessary foreign exchange to meet their foreign obligations. As a result, export-oriented models of capital accumulation became increasingly widespread. The opening to the world market and the need to compete internationally created new demands by domestic capital on the financial system to fund operations, acquire working capital in different currencies, and hedge exchange rate and interest rate risk.

As a result of these financial liberalization measures, the early 1990s were marked by a remarkable rise in capital flows to ECEs. While this created opportunities for some NFCs, as will be discussed below, rather than increasing resources for investment, liberalization measures generally led to increasing volatility and instability, persistently high interest rates and extreme disruption in foreign exchange markets. External financial liberalization eased both the financial operations of non-residents in national markets and residents' acquisition of assets and liabilities denominated in foreign currencies (Akyüz 1993). In this new environment, exchange rates became just another asset price open to speculation (Ertürk 2003). At the same time, the abundance of foreign capital encouraged the appreciation of domestic currencies, resulting in a significant deterioration of current accounts and making these countries even more dependent on volatile capital flows.

These conditions encouraged financial and speculative activities in domestic markets (Akyüz 1993). Banks, and to a lesser extent large domestic companies, started to borrow on international financial markets and invest in domestic (very often unproductive) assets, such as real estate, construction and/or indeed financial assets. These arbitrage operations were further stimulated by the high domestic interest rates, which resulted in extensive carry trade operations, mostly in domestic public debt. As far as the sovereign debt market was concerned, the situation led to increased involvement of private investors in domestic capital markets. Financial institutions, especially commercial banks, became major agents in government debt markets, increasingly crowding out funds for real investments. At the same time, higher exchange rate and interest rate volatility increased the risk of international operations, rising domestic agents' precautionary holding of financial assets.

Thus, accompanied by domestic financial liberalization measures, the opening up of capital accounts and increased international integration deepened the 'domestic financialization' in these countries by articulating them into the international markets and creating new risks and opportunities which fostered financial market involvement by domestic agents. Again, however, while these policy changes were important drivers, demands of financial and non-financial economic agents for extra funding and investment opportunities abroad also played a crucial role in this process. Increased access to (international) financial markets allowed domestic capital to expand their operations, both domestically and internationally. Indeed, it was during this time that selected ECE companies first started to become international players and were able to take advantage of the global market and compete internationally (Hiratuka and Sarti 2011; Ozturk 2011). According to data from the United Nations Conference on Trade and Development (UNCTAD) the stock of outward foreign direct investment from ECEs increased from a little more than US$70 billion in 1980 to nearly US$400 billion in 1996. The leading ECE capital exporters were Hong Kong, Taiwan, Brazil, Singapore, South Africa and China (UNCTAD 2014). The increased availability of finance was a crucial element in this expansion. The wave of capital flows ended suddenly with the Asian Crisis of 1997–98. As a result, between 1997 and 2001, many ECEs experienced sudden capital outflows leading to severe financial crises with dramatic domestic impacts in terms of contractions in demand, declines in growth rates and rises in unemployment. The policies implemented in the aftermath of these crises, the next section shows, contributed substantially to further deepen domestic financialization processes in these countries.

16.1.2 The 2000s and Beyond: Deepening Financialization

The 2000s saw a further push to financial liberalization and opening to cross-border capital flows. In addition, ECEs adopted new policies that benefited from the financial expansion in the world market. Inflation targeting, reserve accumulation and central bank independence became the key monetary tools. Moreover, ECEs were urged to float their exchange rates to avoid inappropriate government intervention and allow an efficient allocation of resources.

As to the first policy change, high inflation is a major threat to stability and to the earnings of the financial sector as they lead to erosion in the real value of financial wealth. Moreover, inflation targeting regimes offer a high degree of transparency and credibility important for financial sector decisions. This is further supported by central bank independence which ought to remove monetary policy decisions from the erratic influences of government policies. At the same time, holding foreign exchange reserves became regarded as an important tool to prevent sudden capital outflows and to reduce exchange rate instability. As detailed by Painceira (2008, 2012) reserve accumulation has two adverse effects on ECEs. First, it generates a sustained capital transfer from emerging to core capitalist economies, as ECEs pay high returns on their liabilities, that are the capital flows received, but earn very little return on their assets (mostly short-term US Treasury securities given the US dollar's role as world money).[3] Second, the necessity of sterilizing the excess liquidity to prevent inflationary pressures provides a large amount of short-term debt securities to the domestic banking system (BIS 2007).[4] This not only leads to an increase in domestic public debt (indeed, throughout the early 2000s there was a remarkable growth in domestic bond markets in ECEs) but also allows banks to expand their own balance sheets, contributing to the growing size of domestic financial systems.[5] Finally, floating exchange rate regimes created new opportunities and risks for economic actors and contributed to the increased size and complexity of financial markets. In the case of domestic currency investments funded on international financial markets (by either domestic or international players), the exchange rate becomes a crucial part of domestic returns (Kaltenbrunner 2014). Thus, whereas exchange rate speculation was imminent at the moment of speculative attacks in the 1990s, it became a permanent feature of operations in the 2000s. At the same time, the large swing and increased volatility of exchange rates created new risks for (domestic) economic actors, requiring increased hedging operations; and again, tighter links to financial markets.

As a result of these policy changes, capital flows to ECEs reached unprecedented levels and domestic financial markets grew rapidly in the 2000s. As to the former, private financial flows surged from an average of US$487 billion in 2003–05 to more than US$1500 billion in 2007, to contract to less than US$500 billion again in 2009 due to the global crisis. In addition, the nature of these capital flows changed. As Kaltenbrunner and Painceira (2015) show, rather than bank lending or foreign currency sovereign debt flows, private capital flows were increasingly directed towards (short-term) domestic currency assets, such as domestic currency bonds, equities and even more complex assets such as derivatives. In relation to domestic financial markets, ECEs' share of global debt market capitalization increased from just above 5 per cent in 2000 to more than 15 per cent in 2010 (Black Rock 2010). As set out above, a large share of these securities were held by domestic financial institutions, which acquired high profits by lending governments the funds they obtained from domestic and international financial markets. At the same time, the share of emerging markets in global stock market capitalization increased from below 10 per cent in 2000 to nearly 30 per cent in 2010 (Black Rock 2010). In some countries, such as Brazil, Poland, South Korea and Mexico, derivatives market activity reached unprecedented levels (BIS 2010). Similar to their activities in the domestic public bond market, banks could borrow cheaply on offshore financial markets and invest in these new domestic asset classes.[6]

Thus, in the 2000s, policy changes and the unprecedented size and changing nature of capital flows fostered domestic financialization processes in ECEs. Along with the deepening role of finance, these included major changes in the behavior of financial institutions, NFCs and households and their relations to each other.[7] This generalization though should not lead one to ignore the specific experiences of each country and the domestic imperatives that played a pivotal role in shaping ECEs' financialization processes. Global forces and the risks and opportunities created by international economic integration were important factors for the financialization process of ECEs. However, it was the demand by domestic capital and the specific nature of domestic capital accumulation which fundamentally shaped the drivers and manifestations of these changes taking place.[8] This meant that financialization had complex implications for the level and structure of capital accumulation, with repercussions differing among the capitalist class. Moreover, it led to varying repercussions of the international financial crisis. To make these points more clearly, the next section analyses the significant changes in the operational and financial activities of NFCs in ECEs over the last decade.

16.2 THE FINANCIALIZATION OF NON-FINANCIAL CORPORATIONS IN EMERGING CAPITALIST ECONOMIES

The balance sheet characteristics of NFCs and their relations with domestic and international financial markets have changed over recent years. On the asset side, ECE companies have increasingly invested in short-term financial assets (Demir 2008, 2009a, 2009b; Araujo et al. 2012; Levy-Orlik 2012; Seo et al. 2012; Powell 2013). On the liability side, recent years have seen a shift from bank lending to borrowing from open markets, frequently offshore and in foreign currency (World Bank 2007; IMF 2014).

As discussed for the 1980s and 1990s, while the international integration and the policy changes described in the previous section were crucial drivers of these financialization processes, they also reflect important structural changes in domestic production and the needs and push of domestic capital for further expansion. The productive integration of ECE firms in the world economy initiated in the 1990s accelerated markedly in the 2000s. According to UNCTAD the share of developing countries' foreign direct investment (FDI) outflows increased from 5 per cent in 1990 to 30 per cent in 2012. The total outstanding stock of outward FDI reached nearly US$4 trillion in 2013, more than 13 times its level in 1996 (UNCTAD 2014). NFCs from ECEs have become key players in international trade and investment. China, Hong Kong, Korea, Mexico, Singapore and Chile have taken their places among the 20 largest FDI investors globally (UNCTAD 2013).

While this has created new scope for export-led expansion and the international allocation of resources, it has also opened up novel sources of funding. Corporate sector borrowing from international markets became a major characteristic of the global integration of ECEs in the 2000s. This includes both borrowing from foreign banks and, most recently, from global bond markets, in particular from Eurobond and US dollar bond markets (World Bank 2007; IMF 2014). In addition, large NFCs have started to fund themselves on domestic bond and stock markets, frequently substituting for bank lending.[9] Building on a unique data set, Celik et al. (2015) put forward that between 2000 and 2013, the total amount of money raised through bond issues by companies from ECEs increased by almost 15 times, reaching US$467 billion. These new sources of funding have played a paramount role in the international expansion of NFCs. At the same time, Hiratuka and Sarti (2011) note the example of Brazil, where a large share of recent FDI outflows was driven by ECE firms' strategy to become 'global players', which boosted their stock market valuation and capacity to leverage in financial and capital markets abroad.

Despite these general trends, specific domestic imperatives and circumstances have led to different manifestations of these processes. For example, the most impressive growth in domestic corporate bond markets has been seen in Malaysia, Thailand and Chile. As of 2010, the outstanding bond issuance was 36 per cent, 18 per cent and 15 per cent of GDP, respectively, in these countries, compared to an average of 10–15 per cent in core capitalist economies (World Economic Forum 2012). In other cases, such as Turkey, loans from foreign banks and foreign branches of domestic banks have become the major international financing avenues for NFCs (Karacimen 2014). Further, looking into the experiences of each country shows that social and cultural factors played a role in counterbalancing the move towards financialization. For instance, in the case of Malaysia, while there has been a notable increase in corporate bond issuance in the post-1997–98 crisis era, there has been also a parallel rise in Islamic finance, a development which could be seen as a move away from the market-driven logic of credit expansion (Rethel 2010).

These differences, in turn, fundamentally shaped the impact of the international financial crisis on ECEs. In general, trade has been the most important channel through which the recession following the global crisis has been transmitted globally. ECEs were affected differently according to the contribution of exports to their growth in comparison to domestic demand (Akyüz 2014). However, as indicated in the introduction, countries with more sophisticated and integrated financial systems were affected worse by the outbreak of the subprime crisis (ODI 2008). The channels differed though. For example, whereas selected firms in Mexico, Brazil and Poland faced substantial losses from speculative derivatives operations (see below), firms and households in selected Eastern European countries (for example, Estonia and Latvia) faced multiplying debt burdens due to the high volume of foreign currency loans and sharp depreciations in their currencies (ECB 2010).

Finally, in line with the contradictory nature of finance postulated in this chapter, it is important to note that while the financialization processes described above were crucial to support the international expansion of large ECE capital, these changes have also increased the susceptibility of domestic NFCs to financial risk, created new financial needs, and opened new sources of financial speculation; all with important implications for the level and structure of capital accumulation. On the one hand, financial liberalization has increased the range of opportunities for NFCs to take advantage of high returns in financial markets.[10] On the other hand, the increasingly global networks and access to (international) financial markets has required ECE NFCs to operate in different currency and financial markets to hedge their operations, which frequently became speculative as firms' financial expertise increased (Farhi and Borghi 2009). Corporate bond issuances and offshore bank borrowing have largely been in foreign currency, which have led to a significant rise in foreign currency debt. According to the IMF, foreign currency borrowing by emerging and developing economies increased by 50 per cent between 2007 and 2012 (IMF 2013), causing concerns about international interest rate hikes or currency depreciation (Correa et al. 2012) and hedging demands by NFCs. The increase in bond issuance has also contributed to a rise in debt–equity ratio and hence higher corporate leverage ratios (IMF 2013). Indeed, several studies present evidence that, similar to NFCs from core countries, NFCs in ECEs have substantially increased their holding of cash and very liquid short-term financial assets, for both speculative and hedging purposes (Kalinowski and Cho 2009; Correa et al. 2012; Karwowski 2012; Bacchetta and Benhima 2013; Powell 2013). For the same reasons, NFCs have increasingly engaged in derivative activities. For example, Rossi Junior (2011) and Farhi and Borghi (2009) discuss the widespread use and strong losses of NFCs in the international financial crisis in Brazil, Mexico, South Korea, Hong Kong and China as a result of their speculative exposures to derivatives. In another study, analysing data for Argentina, Brazil, Chile, Mexico and Venezuela during the turbulent period 2000–02, Gatopoulos and Loubergé (2013) suggest that derivative markets were effective tools for hedging for firms in these countries.[11]

Demir (2008) shows for Mexico, Argentina and Turkey that these financial operations have had detrimental implications for capital accumulation as domestic NFCs substituted real for financial investments. At the same time, he presents evidence that in certain instances NFCs could use the increased possibility to generate profits through financial investments to fund real investment projects in the face of volatile growth, macroeconomic uncertainty, high interest rates and restricted alternative financing opportunities. In Turkey, for example, past profits from financial investments provided additional funds to support new fixed investment, even if the net economic effect of increasing financial assets in the portfolios of NFCs was found to be mixed (Demir 2007). However even if the aggregate level of investment remains unaffected, these financialization processes might have important implications for the structure and nature of capital accumulation (Fine 2013). For example, the higher risk and uncertainty due to financial market exposure might lead to a shift of firm investment towards short-term (less risky) and higher-yielding operations, such as construction, real estate and or/services, leading to an important restructuring of the economy. Correa et al. (2012) observe some of these outcomes in the Mexican case. Brazil, in turn, has experienced a continuing process of 'reprimarization' of its economy as firms have invested in highly profitable primary resources, such as commodities and mining and /or natural resource-based manufacturing such as food, metal, paper and cellulose (Hiratuka and Sarti 2011; Ministry for Development, Industry and Trade 2013). Several ECEs have experienced a shift away from employment-intensive production, such as textiles, as NFCs have attempted to cut costs and increase profitability (Hiratuka and Sarti 2011; Ergüneş 2012).

On the level of market structure, increased access to finance might be used by large capital to engage in mergers and acquisitions, rather than greenfield investment, leading to a centralization and monopolization of the market. Hiratuka and Sarti (2011) show that the majority of the internationalization strategies of Brazilian NFCs in the region were dominated by mergers and acquisitions rather than by newly set-up production plants. Finally, financialization processes described above are not homogenous among different types of NFCs, depending on sector, international openness and size (Correa et al. 2012; Levy-Orlik 2012; Powell 2013). As to the latter, evidence shows that large firms are more able to profit from more developed financial markets, due to their easier access, expertise and resources available. Moreover, small and medium-sized enterprises (SMEs) traditionally depend more on bank financing which might be impaired as banks turn to households, resulting in an overall reduction of available finance for SMEs (Pollard 2003; Rethel 2010). This bifurcation of the NFC sector potentially has important repercussions on the quality of the growth performance, employment and wealth distribution.

16.3 CONCLUSIONS

This chapter has highlighted the symbiotic and contradictory nature of finance and financialization. It has tried to make this point by first showing financialization processes of ECEs more generally and then discussing in more detail the financialization of NFCs over recent years based on existing literature. The focus on NFCs was justified by the unique position of these economic agents in the process of capital accumulation. The chapter argues that financialization processes and their manifestations depend distinctly on the specific country, sector and business structures. At the same time, the rising importance of finance has had a complex and two-way relationship with capital accumulation. In the case of ECEs, on the one hand, the increased availability and diversity of finance has allowed large NFCs to expand globally. On the other hand, this internationalization and the rising importance of finance have created new risks and opportunities for NFCs which have lowered their incentive for fixed investment and/or led to an important restructuring of production processes. One such risk includes the stronger spillover from financial crises in core capitalist countries, as evidenced by the impact of the global financial crisis on ECEs. Again, evidence shows that this impact has not been homogenous, with different sectors and different firms affected in various ways.

This argument has two important implications. The first is methodological. If financialization is a complex, nationally distinct process shaped by specific historical, institutional and spatial characteristics, uncovering these characteristics has to be the analytical core of the research process. This, in turn, calls for comparative case study research rather than aggregate analyses. The second implication is analytical. If the relationship between money capital and productive capital is complex, then a clear dichotomous and negative relationship between the 'financial' and the 'real' cannot be drawn. Analytical interest should thus lie in the nature of capital accumulation and the resulting implications for income distribution, poverty and indeed class conflict. As mentioned in the introduction, this chapter has set out the conceptual framework to analyse financialization in ECEs. Future research will conduct detailed case studies to uncover the specific historical, institutional and spatial factors which shape: (1) the manifestations and nature of financialization of NFCs in ECEs; and (2) its contradictory relation to capital accumulation.

NOTES

1. In preparing this chapter we benefited from an exchange of ideas with Jeff Powell, Juan Pablo Painceira and Paulo dos Santos, and for this we would like to thank them.
2. The conversion of debt to equity in the form of tradable bonds was the key element of the Brady Plan. See Ünal et al. (1993) for a detailed explanation of how the plan worked.
3. Despite the large capital inflows to developing countries in the 2000s, reserve accumulation led to net capital flows from developing to developed countries (Painceira 2012).
4. Obviously, there are exceptions to this general pattern. While the issuance of central bank securities was an important tool for sterilization in many ECEs (BIS 2007), the Turkish Central Bank did not do this unless it was inevitable. This was because as government securities were already in circulation, the Central Bank debt instrument would have offered an alternative to Treasury securities and caused a potential fragmentation in the secondary markets. Hence, in contrast to other ECEs, in Turkey, which already

had a large government securities market, the last decade was marked by a shrinking volume of government securities held in domestic banks (Karacimen 2014).

5. Sterilization had led to an increase in government debt securities that could be presented as collateral. From December 1999 to June 2010, for a set of larger emerging economies, the issuance of government debt securities rose from around $1 trillion to $5 trillion (Moreno 2011). The detailed country data are provided on the Bank for International Settlements (BIS) website (www.bis.org/statistics/secstats.htm).
6. As shown by Kaltenbrunner and Painceira (2015), the returns of these new asset classes, such as equities and derivatives, are often constituted by capital gains which can further increase financial instability.
7. It is now well established that a particular dimension of financialization is the remarkable rise in household assets and liabilities. Banks in ECEs have increasingly engaged in consumption, mortgage and auto loans provision. This was very much related to their need for alternative sources of funding in response to NFCs' turn to alternative sources, leading to a remarkable growth in household credit, albeit from a low base (IMF 2006; Kalinowski and Cho 2009; Karacimen 2014).
8. According to Saad-Filho (2007), monetary policies of the 2000s aimed at fulfilling the requirements of domestic capital by promoting the integration between domestic and international capital through capital flows which require a stable macroeconomic environment.
9. It should be noted though that although large corporations have moved from banks to open markets, banks remain an important source of funding in many ECEs.
10. An opportunity which is arguably even stronger in ECEs, given their persistent high return differential to advanced capitalist economies.
11. The evidence regarding the usage of derivatives for hedging and speculative purposes is mixed. However, from a political economic perspective, the dominance of the speculation motivation is obvious. Otherwise it is impossible to explain the size of the derivatives market, the turnover of which is several times that of world gross domestic product and world trade (Lindo 2013).

REFERENCES

Aglietta, M. and R. Breton (2001), 'Financial Systems, Corporate Control and Capital Accumulation', *Economy and Society*, 30(4), 433–466.

Akyüz, Y. (1993), *Financial Liberalization: The Key Issues*, Geneva: United Nations Conference on Trade and Development.

Akyüz, Y. (2014), *Liberalisation, Financial Instability and Economic Development*, New York, USA and London, UK: Anthem Press.

Albo, G., S. Gindin and L. Panitch (2010), *In and Out of Crisis*, Oakland, CA: PM Press.

Araujo, E., M. Bruno and D. Pimentel (2012), 'Financialisation against Industrialisation: A Regulationist Approach to the Brazilian Paradox', *Revue de la Regulation*, accessed 20 January 2015 at http://regulation.revues.org/9604.

Arrighi, G. (1994), *The Long Twentieth Century: Money, Power, and the Origins of our Times*, New York: Verso.

Ashman, S. and B. Fine (2013), 'Neo-liberalism, Varieties of Capitalism, and the Shifting Countours of South Africa's Financial System', *Transformation: Critical Perspectives on Southern Africa*, 81–82, 144–178.

Bacchetta, P. and K. Benhima (2013), 'The Demand for Liquid Assets, Corporate Saving, and International Capital Flows', mimeo.

Bank for International Settlements (BIS) (2007), 'Financial Stability and Local

Currency Bond Markets', Committee on the Global Financial System (CGFS) Paper 28.
Bank for International Settlements (BIS) (2010), 'Statistical Appendix – Derivatives Markets', *BIS Quarterly Review*, March, http://www.bis.org/publ/qtrpdf/r_qt1003.htm.
Black Rock (2010), 'The Growing Importance of Emerging Markets', March.
Boyer, R. (2000), 'Is a Finance-Led Growth Regime a Viable Alternative to Fordism? A Preliminary Analysis', *Economy and Society*, 29(1), 111–145.
Brenner, R. (2004), 'New Boom or New Bubble', *New Left Review*, 25, 57–102.
Celik, S., G. Demirtas and M. Isaksson (2015), 'Corporate Bonds, Bondholders and Corporate Governance', OECD Corporate Governance Working Papers, No. 16, Paris: OECD Publishing. DOI: http://dx.doi.org/10.1787/5js69lj4hvnw-en.
Correa, E., G. Vidal and W. Marshall (2012), 'Financialization in Mexico: Trajectory and Limits', *Journal of Post Keynesian Economics*, 35(2), 255–275.
Crotty, J. (2005), 'The Neoliberal Paradox: The Impact of Destructive Product Market Competition and "Modern" Financial Markets on Nonfinancial Corporation Performance in the Neoliberal Era', in G. Epstein (ed.), *Financialization and the World Economy*, Cheltenham, UK and Northampton, MA, USA: Edward Elgar.
Demir, F. (2007), 'The Rise of Rentier Capitalism and the Financialization of Real Sectors in Developing Countries', *Review of Radical Political Economics*, 39(3), 351–359.
Demir, F. (2008), 'Financial Liberalization, Private Investment and Portfolio Choice: Financialization of Real Sectors in Emerging Markets', *Journal of Development Economics*, 88(2), 314–324.
Demir, F. (2009a), 'Capital Market Imperfections and Financialisation of Real Sectors in Emerging Markets: Private Investment and Cash Flow Relationship Revisited', *World Development*, 37(5), 953–964.
Demir, F. (2009b), 'Volatility of Short-term Capital Flows and Private Investment in Emerging Markets', *Journal of Development Studies*, 45(5), 672–692.
Doucette, J. and B. Seo (2011), 'Limits to Financialization? Locating Financialization within East Asian Exportist Economies', Discussion Paper No. 21, Hitotsubashi University Invited Fellows Program, Hitotsubashi University, Tokyo.
Duménil, G. and D. Lévy (2004), *Capital Resurgent: Roots of the Neoliberal Revolution*, Cambridge, MA: Harvard University Press.
Ergüneş, Nuray (2012), 'Global Integration of Middle-Income Developing Countries in the Era of Financialization: The Case of Turkey', in C. Lapavitsas (ed.), *Financialisation in Crisis*, Boston, MA: Brill.
Ertürk, I. (2003), 'Governance or Financialisation: The Turkish Case', *Competition and Change*, 7(4), 185–204.
European Central Bank (ECB) (2010), 'The Impact of the Financial Crisis on the Central and Eastern European Countries', *ECB Monthly Bulletin*, July, 85–96.
Farhi, M. and R.A.Z. Borghi (2009), 'Operações com Derivativos Financeiros das Corporações de Economias Emergentes no Ciclo Recente', *Estudos Avançados*, 23(66), 169–188.
Fine, B. (2013), 'Financialization from a Marxist Perspective', *International Journal of Political Economy*, 42(4), 47–66.
Foster, J.B. and F. Magdoff (2008), 'Financial Implosion and Stagnation', *Monthly Review*, 60(7), 1–29.
Gatopoulos, G. and H. Loubergé (2013), 'Combined use of Foreign Debt and

Currency Derivatives under the Threat of Currency Crises: The Case of Latin American Firms', *Journal of International Money and Finance*, 35, 54–75.
Hilferding, R. and T.B. Bottomore (1990), *Finance Capital: A Study in the Latest Phase of Capitalist Development*, London: Routledge.
Hiratuka, C. and F. Sarti (2011), 'Investimento Direto e Internationalizacao de Empresa Brasileiras no Periodo Recente', Ipea Texto para Discussao, 1610, April.
Institute of Development Studies (IDS) (2008), 'Voices from the South: The Impact of the Financial Crisis on Developing Countries', *Institute of Development Studies*, November, http://www.ids.ac.uk/files/Voices_from_the_South_Report.pdf.
International Monetary Fund (IMF) (2006), *Global Financial Stability Report*, April.
International Monetary Fund (IMF) (2013), *Global Financial Stability Report*, April.
International Monetary Fund (IMF) (2014), 'Making the Transition from Liquidity to Growth Driven Markets', *Global Financial Stability Report*, April.
Kalinowski, T. and H. Cho (2009), 'The Political Economy of Financial Liberalization in South Korea: State, Big Business, and Foreign Investors', *Asian Survey*, 49(2), 221–242.
Kaltenbrunner, A. (2014), 'Financial Integration and Exchange Rate Determination: A Brazilian Case Study', *International Review of Applied Economics*, 29(2), 129–149.
Kaltenbrunner, A. and J.P. Painceira (2013), 'International and Domestic Financialisation in Middle Income Countries: The Brazilian Case', Paper presented at the 1st FESSUD Conference, Amsterdam.
Kaltenbrunner, A. and J.P. Painceira (2015), 'Developing Countries' Changing Nature of Financial Integration and New Forms of External Vulnerability: The Brazilian Experience', *Cambridge Journal of Economics*, 39(5), 1281–1306.
Karacimen, E. (2014), 'Financialization in Turkey: The Case of Consumer Debt', *Journal of Balkan and Near Eastern Studies*, 16(2), 161–180.
Karwowski, E. (2012), 'Financial Operations of South African Listed Firms: Growth and Financial Stability in an Emerging Market Setting', Conferencia international do ieSe, Mozambique, September.
Katz, Jorge (2001), 'Structural Reforms, Productivity and Technological Change in Latin America', Libros de la Cepal 64, Santiago: Economic Commission for Latin America and the Caribbean (ECLAC), http://repositorio.cepal.org/bitstream/handle/11362/2277/S2001905_en.pdf;jsessionid=38CCEEA56988D64B5E7D31D4225D94FB?sequence=1.
Lapavitsas, C. (2010), 'Financialisation and Capitalist Accumulation: Structural Accounts of the Crisis of 2007–9', Research on Money and Finance Discussion Papers, no. 16, accessed 4 January 2015 at http://www.researchonmoneyandfinance.org/images/discussion_papers/RMF-16-Lapavitsas.pdf.
Levy-Orlik, N. (2012), 'Effects of Financialization on the Structure of Production and Nonfinancial Private Enterprises: The Case of Mexico', *Journal of Post Keynesian Economics*, 35(2), 235–254.
Lindo, D. (2013), 'Political Economy of Financial Derivatives: A Theoretical Analysis of the Evolution of Banking and Its Role in Derivatives Markets', PhD Dissertation, University of London.

Magdoff, H. and P. Sweezy (1972), *The Dynamics of US Capitalism*, New York: Monthly Review Press.
Magdoff, H. and P.M. Sweezy (1987), 'Capitalism and the Distribution of Income and Wealth', *Monthly Review*, 39(5), 1–16.
Mahmud, T. (2010), 'Is It Greek or Déjà vu All Over Again? Neoliberalism and Winners and Losers of International Debt Crises', *Loyola University of Chicago Law Journal*, 42(4), 629–712.
McKinnon, R.I. (1973), *Money and Capital in Economic Development*, Washington, DC: Brookings Institution Press.
Michell, J. and J. Toporowski (2014), 'Critical Observations on Financialization and the Financial Process', *International Journal of Political Economy*, 42(4), 67–82.
Ministry for Development, Industry and Trade (MDIC) (2013), 'International Trade Statistics', accessed 5 March 2015 at http://www.desenvolvimento.gov.br//sitio/interna/interna.php?area=5&menu=608.
Moreno, R. (2011), 'Foreign Exchange Market Intervention in EMEs', BIS papers no. 57(12).
Orhangazi, O. (2008), 'Financialization and Capital Accumulation in the Non-financial Corporate Sector: A Theoretical and Empirical Investigation of the US Economy, 1973–2004', *Cambridge Journal of Economics*, 32, 863–886.
Overseas Development Institute (ODI) (2008), 'The Global Financial Crisis and Developing Countries', Background Note, October.
Ozturk, O. (2011), 'Global Crisis and Late Development: Internationalization of Turkish Finance Capital', in İ. Siriner, F. Morady, J. Mika, M. Aydın, Ş.A. Koç, H. Kapucu and E. Doğan (eds), *Political Economy, Crisis and Development*, London: IJOPEC.
Painceira, J.P. (2008), 'Developing Countries in the Era of Financialisation: From Deficit Accumulation to Reserve Accumulation', in C. Lapavitsas (ed.), *Financialisation in Crisis*, Leiden: Brill.
Painceira, J.P. (2011), 'Central Banking in Middle Income Countries in the Course of Financialisation: A Study with Special Reference to Brazil and Korea', PhD Dissertation, University of London.
Painceira, J.P. (2012), 'Financialisation, Reserve Accumulation, and Central Banking in Emerging Economies: Banks in Brazil and Korea', Research on Money and Finance Discussion Papers no. 38, accessed 7 February 2015 at http://www.researchonmoneyandfinance.org/index.php/publication/discussion-papers.
Pauly, L.W. (2003), 'New Therapies from Contemporary Money Doctors: The Evolution of Structural Conditionality in the Bretton Woods Institutions', in M Flandreau (ed.), *Money Doctors: The Experience of International Financial Advising, 1850–2000*, London: Routledge.
Pollard, J.S. (2003), 'Small Firm Finance and Economic Geography', *Journal of Economic Geography*, 3(4), 429–452.
Powell, J. (2013), 'Subordinate Financialisation: a Study of Mexico and its Non-Financial Corporations', PhD Dissertation, SOAS, University of London.
Rethel, L. (2010), 'Financialisation and the Malaysian Political Economy', *Globalizations*, 7(4), 489–506.
Rossi Junior, J.L. (2011), 'Hedge or Speculation? Evidence of the Use of Derivatives by Brazilian Firms during the Financial Crisis', Insper Working Paper, 243.
Saad-Filho, A. (2007), 'Monetary Policy in the Neoliberal Transition: A Political Economy Review of Keynesianism, Monetarism and Inflation Targeting', in

R. Albritton, R. Jessop and R. Westra (eds), *Political Economy and Global Capitalism: The 21st Century, Present and Future*, London: Anthem Press.
Sachs, J. (1989), 'Making the Brady Plan Work', *Foreign Affairs*, 68(3), 87–104.
Seo, H.J., H.S. Kim and Y.C. Kim (2012), 'Financialization and the Slowdown in Korean Firms' R&D Investment', *Asian Economic Papers*, 11(3), 35–49.
Shaw, E. (1973), *Financial Deepening in Economic Growth*, New York: Oxford University Press.
Stockhammer, E. (2004), 'Financialisation and the Slowdown of Accumulation', *Cambridge Journal of Economics*, 28(5), 719–741.
Ünal, H., A. Demirgüç-Kunt and K. Leung (1993), 'The Brady Plan, 1989 Mexican Debt-Reduction Agreement, and Bank Stock Returns in United States and Japan', *Journal of Money, Credit and Banking*, 25(3), 410–429.
UNCTAD (2013), *World Investment Report 2013*, New York: United Nations.
UNCTAD (2014), 'Foreign Direct Investment Statistics Flows and Stocks', interactive database.
Vasudevan, R. (2009), 'Dollar Hegemony, Financialization, and the Credit Crisis', *Review of Radical Political Economics*, 41(3), 291–304.
World Bank (2007), *Global Development Finance*, World Bank: Washington, DC.
World Economic Forum (2012), Redefining the Emerging Market Opportunity: Driving Growth through Financial Services Innovation, Geneva: World Economic Forum.

PART V

The Crisis Unfolds

17. The Greek crisis: structural or conjunctural?

Stavros D. Mavroudeas

The Greek crisis is one of the major episodes that followed the 2007–08 global crisis. Several economic traditions compete in explaining it. This chapter reviews the alternative explanations of the Greek crisis from the standpoint of Marxism. It follows the 'circuit of capital perspective' (Fine and Harris 1979) in maintaining that the production sphere is the dominant one, and those of circulation and distribution follow. This causality involves feedback relations also. The main argument of the chapter regarding economic crises is that all major and protracted crises necessarily have a gearing in this dominant sphere. This does not deny the existence of crises that stem from the other spheres. However, these crises are expected to have lesser impact.

The terminology employed is the following. Structural explanations attribute the crisis mainly to the structure of the economy and, consequently, focus on long-term processes. They are subdivided as: (1) deep structural or systemic explanations (attributing the crisis to factors that lay at the heart of the capitalist system); and (2) weak structural explanations (attributing the crisis to middle-range historically specific factors). This classification does not imply that systemic causes do not take a historically concrete expression. Rather, it implies that systemic relations are mediated through intermediate processes and are ultimately expressed in concrete expressions. On the contrary, weak structural explanations reject or remain agnostic regarding essential relations and focus on intermediate middle-range processes.[1] Conjunctural explanations attribute it to faulty economic policies and focus on short-term processes.

There are three main groups of alternative explanations: mainstream, radical and Marxist. Mainstream explanations stem mainly from the 'new consensus macroeconomics' that represents the current fusion of practical neoliberalism with conservative Keynesianism and dominates governmental and international organizations. They have a very weak crisis theory. Neoclassical theory assumes that capitalism is inherently stable. Destabilization occurs only when some agents act irresponsibly by not following the prudent behaviour inscribed in the system. Therefore, a crisis cannot have deep structural causes but derives from faulty conjunctural forces. New Keynesian theory, on the other hand, has dropped Keynesianism's possibility theory of crisis and has – implicitly or explicitly – adopted the systemic crisis-free view of neoclassicism. Thus, for new Keynesianism as well, crises stem mainly from policy errors. Both streams can recognize weak structural causes as the mid-term consolidation of these erroneous policies.

Consequently, mainstream explanations consider the Greek crisis as: (1) a predominantly conjunctural one (stemming from nationally specific policy errors); and (2) independent of the global economic crisis (which is considered as a purely financial one). They are subdivided into three main currents. This chapter criticizes the mainstream explanations for failing to appreciate the structural character of the Greek crisis and for putting the blame for the crisis and the burden for its resolution on labour.

Radical explanations follow the radical political economy tradition. This current has a variegated view of crisis theory. It recognizes the structurally crisis-prone nature of capitalism. But when it comes to the specific analysis of a crisis it opts for middle-range, historically specific causes rather than systemic ones. This current also involves a wide range of variations. Post-Keynesian analyses seldom differ from the rest by insisting on the typical Keynesian lack of adequate demand. Other perspectives emphasize mid-term institutional factors. In general, radical approaches attribute both the global 2007–08 crisis and the Greek crisis to some intermediate factor – usually neoliberalism and the European Monetary Union (EMU) – but not to capitalism's systemic contradictions. Moreover, radical explanations of both the 2007–08 global crisis and the Greek crisis usually adopt the 'financialization thesis'.[2]

The radical camp views the Greek crisis as a blend of conjunctural and structural causes. It argues that the Greek crisis is the product of policy deficiencies (the dominance of neoliberal financialization policies) which might have turned to structural weaknesses (the emergence of a neoliberal financialized stage of capitalism). This approach relates Greece to the global economic crisis but mainly externally, and also agrees in principle with the orthodox view that the latter is a purely financial crisis. Radical explanations are criticized for failing to comprehend the deep structural nature of the Greek crisis and for resorting to inadequate conjunctural and weak structural explanations. Consequently, they resort to incoherent policy proposals.

Marxist explanations constitute the third group. Marxism rightfully claims the more developed theory of crisis than any other economic tradition. For Marxism, economic crisis is neither an accidental anomaly nor a chance outcome of capitalism's modus operandi, but an expression of its inherent contradictions. Marxist analysis focuses on capitalism's fundamental contradiction and secondary contradictions, and studies them through labour value theory's toolbox. There continues to be heated debate within Marxism regarding the fundamental crisis mechanism. However, all streams attribute to the profit motive the main role: a crisis (whatever its causal mechanism) should lead to a fall in profitability. Indeed, this is the major difference between Marxist and radical macroeconomic models. Following from these theses, for Marxism, every major economic crisis is necessarily geared in the fundamental relations of the capitalist mode of production, and particularly in the dominant sphere of the circuit of capital. This does not exclude cases of crises caused by problems in the sphere of circulation or distribution, but it considers them as an exception. In particular, crises caused by instabilities in the financial system do exist but they must be related – even *ex post* – to the production sphere. Moreover, such crises cannot be either major or protracted.

Marxist explanations argue that the Greek crisis is part of the 2007–08 global crisis. Both are expressions of capitalism's deep structural tendencies, particularly the tendency of the rate of profit to fall (TRPF). These structural crisis tendencies are being aggravated by Greek capitalism's subordinate position within the European imperialist bloc and the existence of relations of imperialist economic exploitation (that is, broad unequal exchange and strategic inferiority between the euro-core and the euro-periphery economies). Hence financialization and neoliberalism are considered to be conjunctural by-products of these deep structural tendencies. Thus, Marxist analyses propose strong structural explanations. This chapter argues that Marxist explanations grasp better the deep structural dimensions of the Greek crisis and its roots in the sphere of real accumulation.

17.1 MAINSTREAM EXPLANATIONS

Mainstream theory utterly failed to foresee the Greek crisis.[3] When the crisis erupted, its initial reaction was to formulate an austerity policy response in the form of the European Union–European Central Bank–International Monetary Fund (EU–ECB–IMF) Economic Adjustment Programme (EAP). A theoretical explanation was offered only *ex post*, thus justifying criticisms that mainstream analyses serve simply as legitimizers of pro-capital policies.

As already argued, mainstream explanations by nature emphasize conjunctural factors. The initial mainstream justifications of the 1st EAP focused almost exclusively on such factors, such as the argument that Greece is inherently profligate. There was only fleeting reference to some structural problems (for example, low competitiveness, business unfriendliness caused by excessive regulation).[4] But the emphasis of the programme and the public discourse supporting it was on conjunctural factors, and especially the supposedly big and well-paid public sector. This was done for political reasons, as the dominant class wanted to divide private and public employees. However, as soon as the 1st EAP started failing utterly on its milestones, austerity measures had to expand to the private sector as well. Then the structural dimension was unearthed by pointing to the falling competitiveness. This led, in the 2nd EAP,[5] to an emphasis on structural reforms engulfing the whole of the Greek economy.

17.1.1 A Greek 'Disease'

This is the first mainstream explanation which was voiced by EU and Greek governmental bodies that signed the EAPs. It maintains that Greece is a special type of economy which is prone to fiscal deficits financed through borrowing (which created large external debts), and falling competitiveness. It argues that these deficiencies were caused by particular Greek national characteristics, that is, it is a Greek 'disease'. Therefore, it emphasizes mainly policy errors and recognizes structural deficiencies only as a consequence of these nationally specific policy errors.

The initial version stressed only the first problem. It maintained that Greece is characterized by low productivity, high wages and a big public sector. The focus was on the public sector, which was branded as clientelist, with high wages and low productivity and a limited ability to collect taxes. Consequently, fiscal deficits are accumulated which are financed through foreign loans (as EMU-facilitated low interest rates) resulting in a widening external debt (expressed in a deteriorating current account). Additionally, Greece violated the EMU provisions by forfeiting statistical data. With the advent of the 2007–08 crisis international financial markets started scrutinizing fiscal deficits and external debts. Consequently, the unsustainability of the Greek debt was discovered and the Greek crisis erupted.

However, as soon as the 1st EAP started failing, the problem of competitiveness was put forward. It was argued that not only the public but also the private sector is characterized by low productivity, high wages and rigid labour market regulation, culminating in falling competitiveness. Consequently, the current account worsened not only because of public borrowing but also because of diminishing exports and increasing imports. High wages fuelled consumption, which was directed towards imports, since domestically produced goods were uncompetitive.

The Greek 'disease' lost credibility when other EMU economies went into crisis. The initial defence was to attribute the expansion of the problem to contagion from Greece. This was a weak argument since it neglected the significantly different characteristics of the other economies (for example, Ireland and its predominantly banking crisis). This newer version led to collectively branding these countries as prone to fiscal and banking profligacy: instead of a Greek, a South 'disease' was discovered (e.g. ECB 2012; Panetta 2011). However, as the EU's crisis expanded beyond the PIGS countries (Portugal, Ireland, Greece, Spain) and started touching Italy and even euro-core countries (for example, Belgium, the Netherlands and France), the popularity of the South 'disease' explanation receded.

The analytical foundation of the Greek 'disease' explanation hinges upon the twin deficits hypothesis (TDH) which contends that in a country with a fiscal and a current account deficit the causality runs from the former to the latter. The falling competiveness operates as a separate channel that aggravates the current account deficit. The outcome is a debt crisis.

17.1.2 The EMU is not an Optimal Currency Area (OCA)

The second mainstream explanation supports that the Greek 'disease' is aggravated by the EMU's structural deficiencies. Because the EMU is an unsustainable non-optimal currency area (OCA), it is prone to asymmetric shocks that exacerbate national 'diseases'. Thus, the Greek crisis is caused by both national conjunctural factors and European structural problems. This explanation is voiced mainly by Anglo-Saxon commentators either neoliberal (e.g. Feldstein 2010) or neo-Keynesian (e.g. Krugman 2012). While sharing the fiscal profligacy argument of the first explanation (and the TDH), this explanation recognizes a rather weak structural cause: the non-OCA character of the EMU.

17.1.3 National Disease Exacerbated by EMU Deficiencies that Can Be Rectified

The third mainstream explanation attributes the Greek crisis to the combination of national policy errors (high fiscal deficits and debt) with problems caused by the EMU's incomplete architecture. Nevertheless, it maintains that these problems can be solved by deepening the EU's economic and political unification. This explanation is expressed mainly by European analysts who are in favour of European unification but have ideological (Keynesian) and/or practical reservations regarding the actual process of the European integration (e.g. De Grauwe 2010; Lane 2012).

The EMU's incompleteness is attributed to the existence of a North–South dichotomy which leads to trade and current account imbalances that destabilize it. There are two main variants of the EMU's current account imbalances argument. The first is mainstream and is offered by Blanchard and Giavazzi (2002), who argue that EMU economies have different savings rates (the poorer countries have lower savings rates) and different growth rates (less developed countries have higher growth rates). As a result of these differentials and within a supposedly convergence process (reinforced by the EMU), funds flow from richer countries to poorer ones, resulting in current account deficits for the latter. This was branded as 'good imbalances' that supported the convergence process and would ultimately be smoothened as this convergence process proceeded. After the onset of the crisis, the proponents of this variant abruptly changed position and the 'good imbalances' became 'bad'. This time it was the fiscal profligacy of poorer countries that led to increased external borrowing and caused unsustainable current account deficits (Jaumotte and Sodsriwiboom 2010). This mainstream variant of the current account imbalances argument is compatible with the TDH.

There is a second variant of the current account imbalances argument proposed by the EMU's post-Keynesian criticizers (e.g. Botta 2012). It argues that the EMU's structure causes real exchange rate differentials, making the North more competitive at the expense of the South. Thus, euro-core economies acquire trade surpluses against euro-periphery trade deficits. This is reflected in the current account deficits of the latter. In this variant the TDH is rejected and instead current account deficits are posited as the cause of fiscal deficits (e.g. Nikiforos et al. 2014). The more combative versions of this second variant argue that the EMU is a neo-mercantilist structure where the North exploits the South. This argument is even more pronounced in the more radical post-Keynesian financialization analyses.

The first variant of the current account imbalances argument has been taken up by the aforementioned mainstream theorists who do not ascribe to the 'financialization' thesis but aim to rectify the EMU by making it more unified (e.g. Merler and Pisani-Ferry 2012). The usual add-ons are fiscal and banking union.

This third mainstream perspective has also serious deficiencies. First, it offers only a 'weak' structural explanation as it discerns structural problems only in the sphere of circulation. It agrees with the second mainstream explanation with regard to the EMU's problems pointed out by the OCA theory. But it believes that a more economically and politically unified EU can overcome these problems. In this belief it departs from the harder versions of the second explanation which believes that an economic and political unification of the EU similar to that of the US is impossible. This is the second major problem of this perspective. Its political and economic voluntarism goes against historical wisdom. Europe has been the main ground where capitalism was born on the basis of the nation-state, and national political and economic identities are deeply entrenched. This makes a politically and economically unified Europe a utopia.

17.1.4 Mainstream's Shortcomings

Mainstream explanations, irrespective of their differences, ultimately understand the internal causes of the Greek crisis through the TDH lens. Wages are posited as the factor triggering both the fiscal and the current account deficits. It is argued that Greek (nominal) unit labour costs increased faster than those of the other European countries. Thus they worsened both the budget deficit and the current account deficit (e.g. EC 2010: 3).

This argument is highly problematic for a number of reasons. First, there is an extensive literature disputing whether (nominal) unit labour costs are a convincing measure of competitiveness. Second, the Kaldor paradox shows that competitiveness is not an exclusive virtue of low wages. Competitiveness depends not only on costs and especially wage costs (cost competitiveness), but mainly on qualitative factors (structural competitiveness). Third, contrary to the assertions of the EU and the Greek government, Greek wages have been constantly lagging behind productivity increases. Furthermore, Greek productivity increased faster than that of Germany, for example. Thus, Greek real unit labour costs (that is, the wage share in the product) have been falling continuously for several decades. Fourth, restoring competitiveness by decreasing wages presupposes that competitors will keep their wages stable or, at least, will reduce them less. However, this race to the bottom is a universal trend, at least for the countries in restructuring programmes. Thus, any cost competitiveness gains are short-lived and precarious.

But mainstream explanations of the Greek crisis have also wider problems. First, they totally underestimate the significance of the 2007–08 global crisis. This is unanimously considered as a mere financial crisis without origins in the sphere of real accumulation. However, if this crisis is as significant and lengthy as it appears to be, it must surely have some basis in the main economic sphere. Second, they consider the Greek crisis as independent of this global crisis. Before the onset of the Greek crisis, they maintained that Greece was insulated from the global crisis. They argued that the latter had only an exogenous impact on the Greek economy by worsening the international economic environment and promoting pessimism about sovereign debts. This has now been proven to be erroneous, as even mainstream analyses recognize. Third, the TDH's applicability for Greece is disputed. For example, Katrakilidis and Trachanas (2011) argued that while the TDH is confirmed for the pre-accession to the EMU period (1960–80), it is rejected for the post-accession period (1981–2007). For the latter period the opposite holds: the current account deficit caused increasing fiscal deficit. For these reasons, mainstream explanations fail to appreciate the fundamental structural dimensions of the Greek crisis and relegate it to policy errors and/or to weak structural deficiencies.

17.2 RADICAL EXPLANATIONS

While there are various versions, the radical explanations are dominated by the financialization thesis.[6] There exist some other versions. Stathakis (2010) argues that the Greek crisis is a mainly fiscal one but it was caused by Greek capital's notorious tax evasion and cronyism. While the latter is certainly true, it cannot account for either the severity or the length of the crisis. This is a problem for all explanations that view the Greek crisis as simply a debt crisis. Mainstream explanations have faced this problem and for this reason they have slowly discovered a weak structural dimension (in the problem of competitiveness). Laskos and Tsakalotos (2012) supplemented Stathakis's analysis with the EMU's trade imbalances argument and also the problem of inequality (that is supposed to cause a covert underconsumption). The underconsumptionist explanation does not fit to empirical data as the period preceding the onset of the crisis was characterized by a spectacular growth of consumption.

Three main financialization explanations have been proposed.

17.2.1 Financial Expropriation

Lapavitsas et al. (2010a, 2010b) argue that the Greek crisis is a debt crisis caused by financialized capitalism and the EMU. Financialization caused the 2007–08 crisis through leverage that created unsustainable bubbles. This is not a Marxian profitability crisis but simply a financial crisis. The world crisis affected the EMU's fragile foundations (because it is not an OCA) by aggravating the trade imbalances that stem from its neo-mercantilism. Lapavitsas et al. portray this neo-mercantilism as an inverted image of the mainstream argument about falling competitiveness. Mainstream theory argues that Greek relative wage increases led to a falling competitiveness. Lapavitsas et al. accept that competitiveness depends solely on wages. They argue that the euro-core pressurized wages more and thus acquired a permanent competitive advantage against the euro-periphery. This is the mainstream argument in reverse: the cause of the problem is the overprudent North and not the profligate South.

Thus, the eurozone was polarized between a trade-surplus North and a trade-deficit South. This imbalance was accommodated during the pre-crisis period by the North lending to the South (for the latter to buy its products). The 2007–08 crisis disrupted this structure as international financial markets questioned the creditworthiness of the South's sovereign debts and the eurozone's crisis began. Lapavitsas's policy proposal is 'Grexit' because the EMU is unrectifiable.

Lapavitsas's explanation does not pay any attention to the production sphere and to the profit rate. Consequently, he does not recognize any process of imperialist exploitation between the North and the South (in the Marxist and not the neo-mercantilist sense). Moreover, he accepts uncritically the mainstream argument that competitiveness depends mainly on wages. Furthermore his financialization argument is not supported by the Greek data (see Mavroudeas 2014). Lapavitsas's policy suggestions are also problematic. If the Greek crisis is simply a debt crisis then it may be solved not by exiting the EMU but by making it a full OCA by unifying it fiscally and politically. If the crisis is something more profound and has to do with the production sphere then exiting the EMU and remaining within the Common Market will not suffice. A full exit from the EU is required.

17.2.2 Financialization and Class Struggle

Contrary to Lapavitsas et al., Milios and Sotiropoulos (2010) argue that it was high indebtedness that led to falling competitiveness. The EMU bundles together countries with very different growth and profitability rates. Hence, it fomented high borrowing by the euro-periphery countries because they have higher profit rates which attract capital from the euro-core. This trend was augmented since the EMU allowed euro-periphery countries to borrow at low interest rates. Foreign loans boosted the euro-periphery's domestic demand, therefore giving rise to increasing inflation and deteriorating competitiveness. Milios and Sotiropoulos reject the North–South divide as a simplistic dependency argument. For them foreign loans were not a theft but a normal phenomenon that boosted growth. On this point they agree with the pre-crisis mainstream arguments that the EU helped Greece's development: they both consider the pre-crisis current account deficits to be 'good' imbalances. Greater growth opportunities and expectations of faster productivity growth justified elevated levels of fixed investment relative to the pool of domestic savings; hence the need for a current account deficit. Thus, Milios and

Sotiropoulos implicitly accept the mainstream convergence thesis. But the reality of the Greek economy proved to be different. The sustained current account deficit did not finance investment in productive assets but was used to buy the euro-core's imported goods. Thus Greece's productive structure, instead of being developed, was actually eroded. As a corollary Greece, instead of converging with the EU, actually – after a period of convergence – started to diverge.

Then Milios and Sotiropoulos introduce financialization. They argue that because modern capitalism is financialized, it leads to extreme leveraging and financial bubbles. The 2007–08 crisis (which they too understand as a financial one) transformed the euro-periphery's current account deficits, until then considered as a scourge. The markets questioned their sustainability. This obliged states to rapidly increase fiscal deficits in order to save failing businesses. This led to the collapse of the more vulnerable economies of the EU.

For Milios and Sotiropoulos, the EMU played only a peripheral role in this affair. Despite conceding that the EMU is not an OCA and that it is a neoliberal project, they do not envisage Grexit, but the EU's progressive restructuring.

17.2.3 Minskian Inflation and Disinflation

Argitis (2012) proposes a Minskian financialization explanation. He argues that Greek capitalism traditionally had:

1. a weak and obsolete technological structure;
2. a structurally weak competitiveness (because of its weak and obsolete technological structure) causing chronic and significant current account deficits (as it imported a significant portion of intermediate goods);
3. extensive cronyism between private businesses and the state (resembling the Minskian notion of the 'strong state').

The state (with its central bank) managed the inflation–disinflation process (by using the fiscal deficits more as a redistributive tool than as an anticyclical one) in order to bolster capitalist profitability. This structure was disrupted by Greece's accession into the EMU and was not substituted by another equally functional one. After entering into the EMU, the 'strong state' remained but lost the control of its central bank (as the Bank of Greece followed the ECB). Consequently, debt management became dysfunctional and the increase of financial leverage (financialization) became necessary as a new growth engine. This increased capitalism's inherent instability (as Minsky's financial instability hypothesis suggests). Then the 2007–08 crisis (which for Minskians was caused by the neoliberal policy that dethroned stabilizing Keynesian policies and increased financial instability) derailed the already unstable Greek capitalism. The 'strong state' without a strong central bank could not manage and control the debt and inflation–disinflation process. Hence, the Greek crisis erupted.

The Minskian theory, which has been rightfully criticized as phenomenological, focuses excessively on finance and neglects the real economy. It has also been criticized for having a very narrow understanding of the role of fiscal and monetary policy, derived from Minsky's problematic conception of the role of monopolies.

Regarding Greece, the Minskian explanation has serious problems. The most significant one is that the Greek crisis was not caused by excessive private debt. On the contrary, this is small compared to the more developed Western economies. Thus, it cannot be convincingly argued that the Greek problem was born from the inflation–disinflation circle of private debt. For this reason Argitis (2012) leaves aside the typical mechanism of the financial instability hypothesis and sticks more to Minsky's (1986) previous work on the significance of the political and institutional framework for securing the stabilization of the financial system. His central argument is that the disintegration of the 'strong state, strong central bank' pair led to the inability to functionally manage the inflation–disinflation process. However, this argument is disputable for the following reasons. First, it unwarrantedly assumes that the policy of the Bank of Greece was always accommodative during the post-dictatorship period, while in several cases the monetary policy was not relaxed in economic slowdowns. Second, it equally unjustifiably implies that, after accession to the EMU and the loss of independent monetary and exchange rate policy, the government and the Bank of Greece lost any ability to exert discrete policies. This is not entirely true: national authorities retained some policy instruments despite losing overall control. Finally, if Argitis's explanation is correct, then the obvious policy suggestion is Grexit. But this is something that he rejects.

17.2.4 The Problems of Financialization

Apart from their analytical problems, the financialization explanations of the Greek crisis face serious empirical problems. One can distinguish two versions of the financialization argument. The first version can be branded as 'strong financialization': Greek capitalism is financialized. The second version can be branded as 'weak financialization': Greek capitalism is not yet financialized, but financialization is imported from the external environment (the world economy).

The 'strong financialization' argument requires that two crucial conduits exist in the Greek economy. First, the private sector should be financialized. That means that capital markets dominate the financial system and have established their hegemony over its other pillar (the banking sector) which has been assimilated by them and follows their modus operandi. Second, for those financialization theories maintaining that finance exploits the workers directly and independently from productive capital (e.g. Lapavitsas), the indebtedness of private households should be very high.

Several studies have shown that the degree of financialization of both the public and the private sector in Greece is strikingly low, which is explicable. Traditionally the Greek stock exchange has been small and played a minimal role in the Greek economy, as Greek capitalism was and has remained a bank-based one. The Greek stock exchange was promoted aggressively by government policies in the late 1990s and had a meteoric growth for a few years. Then it crashed in 1999, it had a limited recovery and then collapsed with the crisis.[7] Moreover, public and social entities (like the pension funds) had no or limited exposure to the stock exchange and the new financial products.

The second conduit has similar empirical problems. Private households' indebtedness is strikingly low compared to the West. It was traditionally low in Greece, began to increase after the accession to the EMU (growing very rapidly but never reaching Western levels) and collapsed with the crisis. This pattern derives from Greece's post-war development. The middle strata, but also increasing segments of the peasants and the workers, had the ability and the culture to save. This changed with the EMU when the savings ratio collapsed and households started amassing debts. The covert increase of inflation in mass consumption goods eroded the purchasing power of all these classes. To sustain their living standards, and induced by the relatively low interest rates and the aggressive marketing policies of the banking sector, households turned to debt. This explains the very high growth rate of households' debt. However, this process remained significantly weaker than in Western economies and was terminated abruptly by the eruption of the Greek crisis.

The almost obvious empirical failure of the 'strong financialization' argument leads many of its proponents to the soft version: financialization was imported into Greece through the international environment. This argument is very weak. Apart from generalities about the global financial crisis there is no robust proof on how financialization was imported into the Greek economy. To conclude, the financialization explanations of the Greek crisis have a weak structural emphasis in not considering the problems in the production sphere. For this reason they fail to account adequately for the Greek case.

17.3 MARXIST EXPLANATIONS

All the above explanations, despite their different viewpoints and policy proposals, share a crucial analytical feature: they do not attribute the crisis to the internal logic of the system. They attribute it either to policy errors or to weak structural factors pertaining mainly to the sphere of exchange. In contrast, Marxist political economy offers a strong structural explanation of the Greek crisis by attributing its fundamental causes to problems grounded in the sphere of production.

The main analytical differentiae specificae of the Marxist explanations is their use of labour value theory and the focus upon the profit rate. On this basis they test whether the hypothesis of the classical Marxist crisis theory is applicable in the Greek case. Marxism argues that a major crisis must be grounded in the sphere of production and expressed in a secular fall of the profit rate which then is transmitted in the rest of the circuit of capital. The results of tests of the Marxist explanations verify the above-mentioned thesis.

Three main Marxist explanations have been proposed. The first version emphasizes the role of the TRPF in generating the crisis. This version adopts the productive–unproductive labour distinction in its empirical investigation. The second version focuses upon the evolution of the profit rate and also discerns a falling profitability trend. But it also recognizes other causes (apart from the TRPF) of this falling profitability. This version does not employ the productive–unproductive labour distinction in its empirical investigation. The third version also recognizes the TRPF as the systemic cause of the crisis, but in addition it emphasizes the problem of imperialist exploitation within the EU. This version also employs the productive–unproductive labour distinction in its empirical investigation.

Regarding their policy suggestions, Marxist explanations agree that a long-term transitional programme aimed at the creation of a socialist economy is required. They also concur that the crucial intermediate anchor of such a programme is Greece's disengagement from the EU (and not simply from the EMU). Disengagement from the EU would enable the creation of a self-contained economy serving the people's interests and able to democratically plan the long-term structural transformations required in order to restructure the Greek productive system.

17.3.1 A TRPF Crisis

Maniatis and Passas (2014) estimate – following Shaikh and Tonak (1994) – the main Marxian variables for the post-war period (1958–2009). They discern several different phases of capital accumulation. Then, they verify that both the Marxian and the net rate of profit started falling before the 1973 crisis. It is shown that this falling profitability trend is caused by the increase of the organic composition of capital.

The phases of capital accumulation preceding the current crisis laid the ground for it. The first phase (1958 to mid-1970s) is the 'golden age' of Greek capitalism: high profit rates (despite a slightly falling trend) caused high rates of capital accumulation and output growth, significant increases in productivity growth and increases in the real wage for productive workers and workers in general, even with a rising rate of surplus-value. The second period is that of the stagflation crisis (1973–85). The significant increase in the organic composition of capital (OCC) during the 'golden age', combined with the fall in the rate of surplus-value and the profit share as a result of successful labour struggles after the fall of the military dictatorship, produced a sharp fall in profitability, negatively affecting investment, output growth, productivity, real wage growth and employment.

The third phase, neoliberalism, started in 1986 and accelerated after 1991, led to a dramatic increase in labour exploitation. However, the resultant recovery in profitability was not coupled with a sufficient devalorization of capital and a significant decrease of unproductive labour. These requirements were not politically feasible at that time. Hence, the neoliberal period brought only a partial recovery of the profit rate, which resulted in a low rate of investment activity, output growth and, most importantly, productivity growth. Even the anaemic output growth during this period was achieved through the indirect impact of the financial bubbles which were created mostly by the expansionary monetary policies. Those bubbles, first in the stock exchange market and then in the real estate sector, created significant wealth effects for the households stimulating consumption demand, which was the only source of growth during the neoliberal period as low profitability held investment activity down. The bubbles burst and the crisis erupted in 2009 only two years after the crisis in the major capitalist economies. Fundamentally, the crisis resurfaced due to the low profitability of capital, a result of capital overaccumulation caused by the rising OCC. This rise could no longer be offset by increases in the rate of surplus-value or by some kind of expansive fiscal or monetary policy.

17.3.2 Causes of the Greek Profitability Crisis

Economakis et al.'s (2014) study of the Greek economy for the period 1960–2012 distinguishes four basic phases. The first is the 'golden era', 1960–73. During this the profit rate increased markedly, achieving the best results for the whole 1960–2012 period and peaking in 1973. This increased profitability is explained by the low OCC. While wages increased during that phase they lagged behind labour productivity increases, leading a decreasing labour share. The 1973 crisis ended this 'golden age'.

During the next phase, 1974–85, profitability declined as labour struggles intensified after the dictatorship's fall. Also the increasing OCC produced a falling profitability trend. This trend ended in 1985, when neoliberal policies were adopted.

The 1986–2006 phase of neoliberalism exhibited a weak profitability recovery; well below the 'golden age' levels. OCC decreased insignificantly because of the insufficient capital destruction during the crisis.

During the last phase of crisis, 2007–12, profitability fell rapidly to the lowest levels for the entire 1960–2012 period as it was accompanied by the OCC's dramatic increase.

From this study several conclusions can be drawn. First, the Greek crisis is essentially a competitiveness crisis. Second, the deep depression that followed the EAP's austerity policies led to a sharp decline in profitability, because of the ensuing demand fall. However, this underconsumption is only the form of appearance of the non-viability of Greek capitalism's productive model.

17.3.3 A Dual Crisis of Overaccumulation and Imperialist Exploitation

Mavroudeas and Paitaridis (2014b) also argue that the TRPF is the fundamental cause for both the 1973 and the 2007–08 crises. The empirical methodology used is similar to that of Maniatis and Passas (2014), with two differences. First, the agricultural sector is considered as capitalist. Second, the consumption of fixed capital of the unproductive trade and royalties sectors and the intermediate inputs of the royalties sector (so long as their value flows from the sphere of production) are included in the Marxian value added. The distinction between productive and unproductive labour is also employed. A crucial feature of this Marxist explanation is the importance placed upon the 'external' dimension. It is argued that Greek capitalism is a middle-range capitalism with limited imperialist abilities. It continuously strives to exploit other areas and at the same time is exploited by more developed capitalist economies.

Three main post-World War II periods are discerned: The 'golden age' (1960–73), the capitalist restructuring era (1973–85) and the neoliberal era (1985–2009). The 'golden age' (1960–73) exhibited remarkable profitability, strong growth and increased competitiveness, leading to ascendance within the international division of labour. However, this Greek 'golden age' differed substantially from the Western one as it did not include a developed welfare state and was based on the suppression of workers' rights. Moreover, it had a significant imperialist component as Greek capitals expanded, particularly in the Mediterranean area and the Middle East. The global 1973 crisis (a TRPF crisis according to Shaikh and Tonak 1994) put an end to this era in Greece too. Before the crisis the rate of surplus-value started slowing down whereas the OCC started increasing rapidly. This caused a falling profitability trend that reduced investment and ushered in a long period of anaemic performance. Moreover, the 1973 crisis coincided with the fall of the dictatorship and the resurgence of the labour movement. In order to defuse popular radicalism Greek capitalism resorted to pro-labour Keynesian income redistribution policies. Hence, Greece 'decoupled' from the West because it adopted Keynesian policies later and at a period when the West turned to neoliberalism. This hampered profitability further. Thus the post-dictatorship governments employed policies trying to combine: (1) growth (which was slowing down due to global economic crisis); and (2) managed pro-labour income redistribution, but in a manner not dramatically detrimental to capitalist profitability.

At the same time Greek capital made the strategic choice to become a full member of the European Economic Community (EEC) in 1981. The reasons behind this choice were: (1) to secure the system from popular radicalism; (2) to push through capitalist restructuring with the help of the EEC; and (3) to upgrade Greek capitalism from a middle-range imperialism to a partner in one of the major imperialist blocs. This contemporary 'Big Idea' of Greek capitalism was fraught with risks from its very beginning.

The post-dictatorship progressive Keynesian policies failed to resolve the crisis and to bolster profitability because they applied the successful post-war recipes in totally different socio-economic conditions. Post-war growth-boosting Keynesianism was successful because the war had devalorized the previously overaccumulated capitals. This was not the case with the 1973 crisis, as capitals remained critically overaccumulated in the aftermath of the crisis. Therefore, as soon as the post-dictatorship popular radicalism was checked, Greek capital abandoned progressive Keynesian policies and turned to capitalist restructuring policies.

In the beginning, conservative Keynesian restructuring policies (anticyclical demand-led growth policies but without pro-labour income redistribution) were employed. At the same time Greece's accession into the EEC removed trade protectionism and dealt a severe blow to Greek capital's competitiveness against the more developed EEC economies. The conservative Keynesian policies had limited results as they failed to adequately suppress wages and devalorize overaccumulated capitals.

They were succeeded by the already dominant in the West neoliberal restructuring policies (formally introduced in 1990). As Greek capitalist restructuring was already lagging significantly, Greek neoliberal policies almost bypassed monetarism (closed economy neoliberalism) and directly espoused open economy neoliberalism. The EEC and EU directives played a crucial role in this. The neoliberal agenda (opening of the economy, privatizations, curtailing the welfare system, tax reforms benefiting the wealthy, deregulation of labour market and the financial system, and so on) guided all the subsequent governments. Neoliberal restructuring policies bolstered, more forcefully than their conservative Keynesian predecessors, labour exploitation which was expressed in the increase of the rate of surplus-value. Of particular significance was the marked increase of the actual work-time from the mid-1990s and onwards, which reinvigorated the extraction of absolute surplus-value, after a considerable dormancy period.

Concurrently, the Eastern Bloc's disintegration opened a new area of opportunities for Greek capital, particularly in the Balkans. Taking advantage of its geographical proximity and EU membership, it penetrated into these countries, reaping imperialist extra-profits. Moreover, the massive migration to Greece from these (and later from others as well) countries facilitated the depression of wages (especially in certain sectors, for example, construction) and the expansion of flexible working relations.

Greece's 2001 accession in the EMU complicated the situation further. Greek capitalism attempted decisively to upgrade its position within the international division of labour by participating in the upper tier of European integration. But this strategic choice was risky since the severe constraints on national monetary, industrial and trade policies further weakened Greek competitiveness vis-à-vis the euro-core countries which were characterized by productive superiority. In the beginning, these problems were ameliorated by securing – thanks to the euro – cheap credit that promoted an artificial growth. This was boosted further by the organization of the 2004 Athens Olympic Games whose overpriced works bolstered Greek (and Western) capitals' profitability but at the same time worsened fiscal deficit. Essentially, whenever capital accumulation faltered the Greek state stepped in and, directly or indirectly, subsidized it. The ballooning fiscal deficit was manageable because of the cheap foreign loans and Greece's high growth rates.

Moreover, Greek capitalism followed the international trend of aggressively employing fictitious capital expansion. Cheap credit was boosted by the euro's low interest rates. The stock market became, for a short period, a significant source of enterprise finance. Private consumption was artificially boosted via cheap personal credit offered by the banks, which increased private debt. However, as already argued before, Greek capital's leverage operations and the private debt were significantly smaller than those of its Western counterparts. All these unsustainable and conjunctural factors led to an 'artificial boom' period that was accompanied by a steep increase of unproductive activities (particularly around finance and trade) which internally eroded profitability's foundations.

To sum up, the period 1985–2007 was marked by capitalist restructuring waves which strove to reverse the falling profitability and the overaccumulation of capital. These waves reinvigorated the TRPF's counteracting forces by: (1) increasing the rate of surplus-value; (2) reducing the value of labour-power; (3) reducing the value of constant capital; (4) reducing turnover time; (5) increasing foreign trade; and (6) reaping imperialist extra-profits from abroad. They were only partially successful as profitability never reached the level achieved in the beginning of its fall. Moreover, overaccumulation persisted as Greek capitalism shied away from the deep and painful devalorization required. Thus the fundamental problems remained. The fictitious capital operations and the 'artificial growth' only postponed their eruption and at the same time augmented them.

The 2007–08 crisis abruptly ended this euphoria. The 'artificial boom' collapsed and the profitability crisis lurking behind resurfaced. The financialization *deus ex machina* postponed the crisis but, at the same time, amplified further the problem of overaccumulation. As soon as productive capital's profitability – under the auspices of which surplus-value (and thus total profit) is generated – started eroding, the crisis re-emerged in all its glory. Financialization gave only a temporary respite to the crisis of profitability but at a very high cost. It increased significantly the portion of surplus-value extracted by productive capital but accruing to money capital. This aggravated further the falling profitability of productive capital and set the whole house on fire. Additionally, imperialist extra-profits collapsed as the Balkan economies entered recession, and competition with other stronger imperialisms was aggravated. Also, the global financial collapse ended cheap credit. Thus, Greek capitalism abruptly fell into crisis.

This crisis is characterized as a dual crisis of overaccumulation (caused by the TRPF) and imperialist exploitation that traumatized Greek capital's profitability and productive structure. This dual crisis took the form of the twin deficits (fiscal and current account deficit). The fiscal deficit was augmented because the state rushed to subsidize the private sector. The current account deficit was already worsening because of the falling competitiveness of Greek capital vis-à-vis its EU competitors. Then each reciprocally worsened the other. That is, contrary to the mainstream TDH, both deficits are expressions of Greek capitalism's falling profitability.

17.4 CONCLUSIONS

The length and the severity of the Greek crisis led mainstream analyses to start talking about the need for a structural change of the Greek economy. This quest began with the problem of falling competitiveness and evolved into reports and talks about a radical sectoral overhauling of the economy. However, till now, these efforts have not produced anything significant apart from loquacious reiterations of the current failed sectoral structure of the Greek economy. These reiterations more reflect vested interests rather than a true search for a viable alternative. Mainstream analyses have failed to diagnose the deep structural nature of the Greek crisis and their patchy efforts to cover the gap are inconclusive. This inability stems both from the vested capitalist interests behind them but also from the deficiencies of their analytical perspective.

Radical explanations of the Greek crisis do not perform much better since they shy away from recognizing the deep structural character of the Greek crisis and remain mesmerized by middle-range factors. They pin their hopes on an – either consensual or confrontational – overturn of the EU's neoliberal policies and structures. Thus, they fail to understand why neoliberalism became the currently dominant form of capitalist management, when and how it might be superseded, and who will benefit from this. Moreover, their infatuation with financialization and the EMU does not help them to understand the deep roots of the crisis in the production sphere. Consequently, they say even less than mainstream analyses about the why and the how of a radical productive restructuring of the Greek economy.

On the contrary, the Marxist approach exhibits a far better grasp of the Greek crisis. Its main merit is that it offers a deep structural explanation founded in the production sphere, and a long-term analysis that surpasses the myopic perspectives of the other approaches. However, despite its analytical superiority, the main unfulfilled task for Marxist analysis is to outline a coherent and realistic programme for exiting the crisis that will benefit the subaltern classes and form a bridge towards a socialist future. The necessity of such a transitional programme is the most pressing task for Marxism today in Greece.

NOTES

1. Mavroudeas (2012) offers a critique of middle-range approaches.
2. 'Financialization' argues that modern capitalism has changed radically because the finance dominates the whole circuit of capital and thus the sphere of circulation becomes the dominant one.

3 For a broader analysis of the mainstream explanations see Mavroudeas and Paitaridis (2014a).
4. EC (2010: 6) attributed the Greek crisis to: (a) persistent fiscal and external imbalances that led to a significant increase in government and external debt; and (b) rigid product and labour markets.
5. EC (2012: 9) attributed the Greek crisis to: (a) unsustainable fiscal policies, partly hidden by unreliable statistics and temporarily high revenues; (b) rigid labour and product markets; and (c) loss of competitiveness and rising external debt.
6. For a more extensive critique of the financialization explanations see Mavroudeas (2014).
7. The Athens Stock Exchange General Index lingered around 1000 points till the mid-1990s. Then it hiked to above 4000 points, only to collapse to below 2000 points before 2005. Then it hiked again to above 4000 points till the beginning of the Greek crisis. Subsequently, it collapsed to below 1000 points.

REFERENCES

Argitis G. (2012), *Bankruptcy and Economic Crisis: Failure and Breakdown of the Greek Model of Capitalism*, Athens: Alexandreia (in Greek).
Blanchard, O. and F. Giavazzi (2002), 'Current Account Deficits in the Euro Area: The End of the Feldstein–Horioka Puzzle?', Brookings Papers on Economic Activity no. 32(2).
Botta, A. (2012), 'Conflicting Claims in the Eurozone? Austerity's Myopic Logic and the Need for a European Federal Union in a Post-Keynesian Eurozone Center–Periphery Model', Levy Institute Working Paper no. 740.
De Grauwe, P. (2010), 'The Greek Crisis and the Future of the Eurozone', EuroIntelligence policy brief, March.
EC (2010), 'The Economic Adjustment Programme for Greece', European Economy, Occasional Papers no. 61.
EC (2012), 'The Second Economic Adjustment Programme for Greece', European Economy, Occasional Papers no. 94.
ECB (2012), 'A Fiscal Compact for a Stronger Economic and Monetary Union', *ECB Monthly Bulletin*, 93(May), 1–16.
Economakis, G., G. Androulakis and M. Markaki (2014), 'Profitability and Crisis in the Greek Economy (1960–2012): An Investigation', in S. Mavroudeas (ed.), *Greek Capitalism in Crisis: Marxist Analyses*, London: Routledge.
Feldstein, M. (2010), 'Let Greece Take a Holiday from the Eurozone', *Financial Times*, 17 February.
Fine, B. and L. Harris (1979), *Rereading Capital*, London: Macmillan.
Jaumotte, F. and P. Sodsriwiboon (2010), 'Current Account Imbalances in the Southern Euro Area', IMF Working Paper no.10/139.
Katrakilidis, C. and E. Trachanas (2011), 'Has the Accession of Greece in the EU Influenced the Dynamics of the Country's 'Twin Deficits'? An Empirical Investigation', *European Research Studies*, 14(1), 45–54.
Krugman, P. (2012), *End This Depression Now*, New York: W.W. Norton & Co.
Lane, P. (2012), 'The European Sovereign Debt Crisis', *Journal of Economic Perspectives*, 26(3), 49–58.
Lapavitsas C., A. Kaltenbrunner, G. Lambrinidis, D. Lindo, J. Meadway, J. Michell, J.P. Painceira, E. Pires, J. Powell, A. Stenfors and N. Teles (2010a), 'The Eurozone

Between Austerity and Default', Research on Money and Finance, Occasional Report.

Lapavitsas, C., A. Kaltenbrunner, D. Lindo, J. Michell, J.P. Painceira, E. Pires, J. Powell, A. Stenfors and N. Teles (2010b), 'Eurozone in Crisis: Beggar Thyself and Thy Neighbour', Research on Money and Finance, Occasional Report.

Laskos, C. and E. Tsakalotos (2012), 'No Return: Capitalist Crises, Social Needs, Socialism', Athens: KψM (in Greek).

Maniatis, T. and C. Passas (2014), 'The Law of the Falling Rate of Profit in the Post-war Greek Economy', in S. Mavroudeas (ed.), *Greek Capitalism in Crisis: Marxist Analyses*, London: Routledge.

Mavroudeas, S. (2012), *The Limits of Regulation: A Critical Analysis of Capitalist Development*, Cheltenham, UK and Northampton, MA, USA: Edward Elgar.

Mavroudeas, S. (2014), '"Financialization" and the Greek Case', in S. Mavroudeas (ed.), *Greek Capitalism in Crisis: Marxist Analyses*, London: Routledge.

Mavroudeas, S. and D. Paitaridis (2014a), 'Mainstream Accounts of the Greek Crisis: More Heat Than Light?', in S. Mavroudeas (ed.), *Greek Capitalism in Crisis: Marxist Analyses*, London: Routledge.

Mavroudeas, S. and D. Paitaridis (2014b), 'The Greek Crisis: A Dual Crisis of Overaccumulation and Imperialist Exploitation', in S. Mavroudeas (ed.), *Greek Capitalism in Crisis: Marxist Analyses*, London: Routledge.

Merler, S. and J. Pisani-Ferry (2012), 'Sudden Stops in the Euro Area', Bruegel Policy Contribution 2012/06, http://bruegel.org/2012/03/sudden-stopsinthe-euro-area-2/.

Milios, J. and D. Sotiropoulos (2010), 'Crisis of Greece or Crisis of the Euro? A View from the European Periphery', *Journal of Balkan and Near Eastern Studies*, 12(3), 223–240.

Minsky H. (1986), *Stabilizing an Unstable Economy*, New York: McGraw-Hill.

Nikiforos, M., L. Carvalho and C. Schoder (2014), '"Twin Deficits" in Greece: In Search of Causality', IMK Working Paper, no. 143, December.

Panetta, F. (2011), 'Life in the Eurozone With or Without Sovereign Default?', in F. Allen, E. Carletti and G. Corsetti (eds), *Life in the Eurozone With or Without Sovereign Default?*, Philadelphia, PA: FIC Press.

Shaikh, A. and A. Tonak (1994), *Measuring the Wealth of Nations: The Political Economy of National Accounts*, New York: Cambridge University Press.

Stathakis, G. (2010), 'The Fiscal Crisis of the Greek Economy', paper presented at 1st IIPPE conference, 10–12 September, University of Crete.

18. Greece, global fault-lines and the disintegrative logics of Germany's primacy in Europe

Vassilis K. Fouskas

In February 1947, and in front of a group of prominent senators and General George Marshall himself, Undersecretary of State Dean Acheson gave a passionate speech explaining why the United States (US) must intervene in Greece, which was at the time ravaged by a bloody civil war between communist and nationalist forces:

> If Greece fell like apples in a barrel infected by one rotten one, the corruption of Greece would infect Iran and all to the East. It would also carry infection to Africa through Asia Minor and Egypt, and to Europe through Italy and France, already threatened by the strongest Communist parties. (Chase 1999: 166)

Acheson's unusual call opened the way for the Marshall Plan for the reconstruction of Europe. Greece was Acheson's template of European crisis, and fixing Greece meant fixing Europe.

Since 2009, Greece and Europe have been bleeding. As in 1947, Greece is worst of all. The country's gross domestic product (GDP) has contracted by 25 per cent, unemployment has shot up to 30 per cent, and youth unemployment is currently around 60 per cent (Fouskas and Dimoulas 2013). Class polarization is visible and the political system born after the fall of the Colonels in 1974 has effectively collapsed. In October 2011, then Greek Socialist PM, George Papandreou, made an unusual international call for help and threatened to submit the country's membership of the European Union (EU) to a referendum. Yet no analogous plea since Acheson was made by a US official or any other ally. There was no America to help and there was no Marshall Aid, only International Monetary Fund (IMF) and European Central Bank (ECB) loans with usurious interest rates. So, what happened? Have Europe or Greece lost their significance for the United States? The answer cannot be positive. The US needs Europe today more than ever, especially vis-à-vis the Ukrainian and Middle Eastern contingencies. But, then, what is the problem? I argue that the United States today is no longer the credit power it was in the 1940s and 1950s and that there is a slow and protracted, yet visible and pronounced power-shift to China and other emerging capitalist economies. This relative decline of Euro-Atlantic economies is the result of the neoliberal financialization that those economies have pursued since the 1970s in order to reverse the over-accumulation crisis of the time. Herein lies the main reason why there is no Marshall Plan on the table today, not just for Europe but for tiny Greece.

This contribution identifies two problematic arguments about the origins of the Greek crisis. It also identifies one good argument that nevertheless needs some important qualifications. The first problematic argument comes from the creditor powers and their intellectuals, arguing that the crisis is fiscal (Pagoulatos and Triantopoulos 2009; Darvas et al., 2011). Roughly speaking, this means that the propensity of European states to spend overexceeds their capacity and ability to collect revenues. This is the so-called 'state profligacy' argument that puts the blame squarely on domestic factors and, by and large, the people. The second argument with which this contribution has serious problems is that this is a crisis of EU treaties and the euro as a form of world money, and that if we fix the treaties, then the problem will be solved (Arestis and Sawyer 2010). Finally, there is a third group of scholars and practitioners who have posed the most germane argument. In the words of Martin Wolf, chief economics commentator of the *Financial Times* and celebrated financial journalist, 'this is a typical balance of payments *cum* financial crisis and the fact that Greece was the first into trouble gave weight to the view that the crisis was fiscal' (Wolf 2013). Other writers, from either Marxian or heterodox perspectives, argue essentially the same (Lapavitsas et al. 2010; Stockhammer 2013; Lapavitsas 2013).

However, none of these arguments, including the third one, focus on the historical and geopolitical origins of the Greek crisis, identifying the agencies and actors behind it. And none of the arguments presented above places the crisis in a truly global context. I argue that the present crisis is a symptom of a wider, global systemic crisis bound up with the crisis of neoliberal financialization and a slow and protracted, yet steady and observable, power-shift to Asia and other emerging capitalist economies. These are processes that necessitate a 'global fault-lines' approach. 'Global fault-lines' is a novel, holistic framework of analysis in international relations and political economy that encompasses all analytical instances of the social in a macro-historical and macro-political manner. Instead of breaking up the Hegelian–Marxist totality into various epistemic instances designating causes and effects, it accepts the relative autonomy of those instances from each other as co-constitutive variables of the totality, without determination 'in the last analysis' (Fouskas and Gökay 2012).

I will thus first look into the issue of the power-shift to Asia from a global fault-lines perspective. Then I will concentrate on the Greek debt crisis as such, by way of combining historical and contemporary perspectives, thus viewing it as a symptom of those global structural forces and shifts. This chapter will reveal that peripheral social formations such as Greece, as well as their economic and political crises, are best analysed and understood by connecting the instances of political economy and geopolitics; in other words, a global fault-lines approach is rather necessary.

18.1 CRISIS IN THE EURO-ATLANTIC CORE AND THE POWER-SHIFT TO ASIA

The provenance of the financial crisis which hit the Anglo-Saxon economies in summer 2007 can be traced back to the 1970s. This was the decade of two oil-shocks, stagflation and collapse of profitability in the real economic sector and, fundamentally, President Nixon's decision to get rid of the gold fetter (Gowan 1999; Brenner 2003). The end of the gold–dollar parity and of fixed exchange rates unleashed financialization in historically unprecedented ways (Glyn 2007; Aglietta 2008; Fine 2010; Duncan 2012): credit and financial flows expanded exponentially; this process was accompanied by massive growth in the volume of global trade and foreign direct investment (FDI), including portfolio investment, asset management activity, mergers and acquisitions, and extreme speculation in currency and derivatives markets. Oil trade has been peculiarly dollarized (Fouskas and Gökay 2005). What is hiding behind the term 'globalization' is in fact a process of extreme financialization, that is, activity of unfettered and uncommitted capital, capital which is not conducive to real commodity production (Fouskas and Dimoulas 2012; Wolfson and Epstein 2013) and sustainable economic development. In the indebted West today, the real economic sector has receded, giving way to fictitious capital activity, speculative arbitrage, services and consumption, all of which are prone to boom-and-bust cycles, consumer indebtedness and extreme volatility and risk. Financial capital and generalized indebtedness have permeated the daily life of Western citizenship.

The second massive transformation of social and political relations, the sister-tendency of financialization, goes under the name of neoliberalism. This term, primarily, applies to the domestic environment of the state. For some, overcoming stagflation and the fiscal crisis of the state in the 1970s entailed the following: the welfare state must be retrenched; labour markets, banks and finance should be deregulated; and state enterprises should be privatized. By 'deregulation' is meant moving those agencies from state to private ownership and, in the case of labour unions, freeing them from state protection. This did not mean an end of state interference, inasmuch as the neoliberal state has moved to 'regulation via legislation' (Sassoon 1996). Neoliberal regimes of financial accumulation are almost entirely based on a set of complex regulations advanced by the legislative branch of the bourgeois state (Lapavitsas 2013). In this context, by the early 1980s, state elites, whether on the left or the right, abandoned Keynesianism, giving way to supply-side economics.

Essentially, neoliberalism and financialization were the responses of the West to the profitability crisis in the 1970s. Yet the failure of this strategy to restore profitability and growth rates has been spectacular; in addition, it has failed to arrest the slow and protracted decline of the Western core as a whole. This slow decline of the core goes hand in glove with the complex – and debatable for some scholars – ascendance of China and other emerging economies, especially after the end of the Cold War. China dominates the world market in rare earth elements (a class of minerals that are essential for electronics and computers) and has become the second-largest economy in the world: it overtook Japan in February 2011. China has become the engine driving the recovery of other Asian economies from the recessions of the 1990s. In September 2013 the British Chancellor of the Exchequer, George Osborne, rolled out the red carpet for Chinese banks looking to expand in London, making the City a significant Chinese offshore banking centre. China has already captured a large share of Africa's oil and minerals market and dominates the textiles industry in Latin America. China and India produce a combined total of more than half a million engineering and science graduates per year. The respective number for the US is 60000. Although financialized and integrated into a global economy in which the dollar remains the key reserve currency, the real economic output of the so-called BRICS countries (Brazil, Russia, India, China, South Africa) is healthy and their debt levels are very low (Fouskas and Dimoulas 2013: 136). Financialization increased the global debt in the time span of a decade (2002–12) in every country except China, India, Brazil, Russia and South Africa. But where do Europe and Greece figure in all this?

During the 'golden age of capitalism' of the 1950s and 1960s (Hobsbawm 1995), Germany reasserted itself as Europe's economic powerhouse. As Robert Brenner and others have argued, it was mainly competition from German and Japanese capitals that drove the downward spiral of the rate of profit in the Anglo-Saxon world (Brenner 2006; Busch 1978). Germany drove the process of European integration, outflanking France, something which was already pointed out in the late 1960s by such scholars as Nicos Poulantzas and Christian Palloix in France, and Elmar Altvater in

West Germany (Poulantzas 1974; Palloix 1975). Soon, however, problems appeared. How was the tension to be reconciled between 'deepening' and 'widening', that is, pushing for more capitalist integration in the direction of a (federal) United States of Europe, and enlarging in consecutive steps (from six countries in 1957 to 27 countries in 2010)? How could the pronounced developmental gap between the core and the periphery be bridged? With a customs union at hand since the Treaty of Rome, and prompted by the monetary instability of the late 1960s, the Europeans pushed for monetary integration with the Werner Report of 1970. It came to naught due to American pressure, yet many in Europe at the time believed that Europe's economic space represented an 'optimal currency area' – as Robert Mundell put it in a celebrated article in 1961 – an ideal regional economy almost perfect for monetary integration (Mundell 1961). This indeed was the view that more or less dominated Europe's policy-making establishment until the breakout of the current crisis. The concern was to eliminate currency crises, exchange rate instability and risk.

This is the first fallacy, namely that uneven and deeply asymmetrical levels of economic development across Europe could be bridged by putting all currencies into the same hat and then, miraculously, levelling out uneven development and structural fault-lines by pulling the rabbit out of the hat: the euro, a currency lacking the political and fiscal support of a state. The second fallacy is called financialization. From the 1980s onwards the dominant forces behind the processes of deepening and widening were other than Keynesian; they were deeply pro-monetarist, mercantilist forces: 'Europe has been Hayek-jacked'. The emphasis, also because of pressure from the United Kingdom (UK) and the US, was on widening rather than deepening. Neoliberalism and financialization suited Germany very well, but one should not confuse the German model with the Anglo-Saxon one. German banks do not operate in the same way as British or US banks (Lapavitsas 2013). The Anglo-American model is driven by consumption and debt; the German model by an anti-inflationary, export-led growth regime. These differences are very significant. From the Single European Act of 1986 to the Maastricht Treaty of 1991, and from the Growth and Stability Pact of 1997 to the launch of the euro in 1999 and after, the process of European integration has been subjected to a neo-mercantilist bias emanating from a relentless German strategy of export-led growth and wage suppression. The monetarist character of the Maastricht criteria was the result of this type of German discipline. From the mid-1990s onwards, and in order to increase profitability and price competitiveness, Germany put enormous downward pressure on wages (Stockhammer 2013).

Low wages, coupled with the institutional capacity of the German state and the dynamism of its real economic sector, magnified the existing gap between core and periphery. As we shall see, the introduction of the European Monetary Union (EMU) in 1999 exacerbated the asymmetries and monetary imbalances across Europe. Thus, when the global financial crisis trickled down to the eurozone via the banking sector – German and European banks had bought 40 per cent of American collateralized debt obligations and other toxic assets – the disintegrative tendencies of the EU multiplied overnight. Greece has been and remains the weak link in Europe's and the globe's financialization chain. This is no accident.

18.2 THE GREEK DEBT CRISIS

Greece has never been a solvent state. It always had a balance-of-payments problem (Fouskas and Dimoulas 2013; Freris 1986). From its foundation in 1830 to the present day, the country has almost uninterruptedly been insolvent. Note that Greece became a state 30 years ahead of Italy and 40 years ahead of Germany. But this was a geopolitical accident, rather than a process of ethnic homogenization led by a robust industrial bourgeoisie. The UK and France wanted to check, deter and even block Russia's position and expansion in the Eastern Mediterranean, and Egypt's penetration of the Ottoman Empire through Crete and the Peloponnese. Greece was perceived as having a significant strategic value for the West, a value that outstripped the country's real economic assets.

Even before the foundation of the Greek state, the Greek elites fighting the Ottomans had declared bankruptcy. They could not finance their struggle against the Turks. Greek elites mortgaged their future land as a collateralized debt obligation for the foreign loans received. The origins of debt were political and geostrategic, rather than economic. This is Greece's DNA: a dependent, subaltern state in the periphery of the imperial West that always lags behind the economically and technologically advanced capitalist core. Yet, because of its position on the map, the country has always had significant geostrategic value. This is the country's major fault-line, which is quite challenging to map out.

I have argued earlier that the German model of growth differs from the Anglo-American one. The former is based on a relentless pursuit of export-led growth and anti-inflation bias, whereas the latter is based on consumption and debt-driven growth. These are the two major templates across the EU, although there are more complex cases, such as that of Italy for example (Sassoon 1986; Fouskas 1998). Greece, potentially, offers a third template against which other periphery capitalisms within the eurozone and beyond might be measured.

I would endeavour to call this template 'subaltern financialization'. Countries of the periphery recycle the financial surpluses of the core, especially of Germany, increasing their indebtedness, all the while sustaining Germany's monetarist supremacy in EMU conditions and Germany's competitiveness vis-à-vis Asian and US capitals. Greece's economic and technological progress has always lagged behind the developed core, presenting a chronic balance-of-payments problem. This is a structural-historical problem. But one must also be able to identify the agency perspective here. If a country imports more than it exports, then the deficit country has an overdeveloped layer of the population, which are the big import consortia that some scholars, such as Andre Gunder Frank and Nicos Poulantzas, called *comprador bourgeoisie* (Poulantzas 1974; Frank 1972). Frank's case studies in the 1960s and 1970s concerned Latin America, but my research indicates that this, *mutatis mutandis*, is also the case with Greece. The *comprador* element has been the dominant social class in Greece. During most parts of the nineteenth and twentieth centuries, it overwhelmed a weak capitalist industrial sector and determined decision-making and corrupt practices at the state-bureaucratic level. But this element was in cahoots not just with the Greek government, but also with foreign powers and big business upon which their welfare and *comprador* profits had been dependent. This is precisely what makes Greece a dependent, subaltern country in the global division of labour. But Greece has also been a laggard from a different perspective. During the 'golden age of capitalism' in the 1950s and 1960s, the Western societies experienced high wages, low inflation, almost full employment and sustained welfare and growth. Yet Greece saw nothing of this. Under the domineering influence of Xenophon Zolotas, the policy of its central bank was monetarist, supply-side economics prevailed, and large sections of the population were excluded from political participation due to a crackdown on the communist left in the wake of the civil war. When liberal democracy was restored in 1974 after seven years of dictatorship, the right-wing government led by Constantine Karamanlis launched a Keynesian programme that clashed head on with what was already under way, although still not a dominant feature of Western political economies: the international trend of neoliberal financialization, that is, the global unleashing of money, credit and privatization processes. The same Keynesian policy of aggregate demand expansion was pursued by Karamanlis's socialist successor to power in the 1980s, Andreas Papandreou. Whereas everywhere in Europe and the West supply-side economics became the norm – not even socialist France under Mitterrand could fight neoliberalism, as the failure of the Keynesian experiment of 1981–83 has shown – Greece kept expanding its public sector, augmenting its borrowing requirement.

One important source of the Greek debt today lies in the failure of Papandreou's Cabinets to arrest the country's current account deficit by two consecutive devaluations of the drachma in the 1980s. Another is the massive domestic and external borrowing through which Greece's welfare state and nepotistic appointments in the public sector were financed (Fouskas 1997). It could be called 'Keynesianism à la Greca'. Greece entered the constellation of neoliberal financialization in the mid-1990s, that is, at least 15 years later than most countries of the core, and after the collapse of communism on its northern borders. Many at the time rushed to argue that Greece had lost its geostrategic significance for the West, and the country could plunge into debt and go bankrupt.

This prediction was wrong. Greece was very useful in the overall scheme of things, both for the North Atlantic Treaty Organization's (NATO) and the EU's processes of eastward enlargements. As Greece entered neoliberal financialization in the second half of the 1990s under the neoliberal 'modernization' agenda of Costas Simitis, the Panhellenic Socialist Movement (PASOK) Prime Minister from 1996 to 2004, it became a significant launching pad for the financialization of the Balkans and the Near East, with its banks playing a major role in these two adjacent regions (Fouskas and Dimoulas 2013, 151ff.). But was this Greek imperialism in the region? This is very doubtful. The Greek banking sector was and is completely dominated by foreign assets. More than 82 per cent of the shares of 'Greek' banks are owned by foreign individuals, insurance funds and other EU banks. Only 15 per cent are owned by Greek interests (Union of Greek Banks 2011; Michalopoulos 2012). Therefore, the neoliberal financialization of Greece from the second half of the 1990s onwards served the work of core capitals and states of Europe, and above all served Germany's expansion agenda to Eastern Europe. This is what we can call subaltern financialization, and which is closely connected to geopolitics and international security. At the same time, the profile of the Greek *comprador* entrepreneur has changed: in the main, they now borrow heavily, taking advantage of favourable interest rate regimes in order not just to finance the import of real commodities but also, importantly, to mediate in importing fictitious commodities. Greece's financialization is completely subordinate to the speculative activity emanating from the core. Greece registered high growth rates in the early 2000s, but this growth was debt-driven, that is, based on borrowing and consumption. Within the Monetary Union, which it joined in 2001, Greece and other periphery countries became more and more uncompetitive in the face of Germany's economic engine. The current eurozone crisis is a balance-of-payments crisis, although in the case of Greece, we also need to factor in its fiscal problem.

It is necessary to go a step further. The perceived geopolitical and geostrategic importance of Greece by NATO and the EU is reflected in the structure of the country's defence budget over the years. This needs to be singled out of the general political economy calculations, because it is directly connected to geopolitics and geostrategy, as well as the perceived strategic value of the country for global imperial interests.

In 2009, defence expenditure in Greece was more than 3.3 per cent of GDP, as opposed to 2.4 per cent for France, 2.7 per cent for Britain, 2 per cent for Portugal, 1.4 per cent for Germany, 1.3 per cent for Spain and 4.7 per cent for the US. Between 2005 and 2009 the purchase of 26 F-16 fighter aircraft from the US and 25 Mirage-2000s from France represented 38 per cent of the total import volume of the country (Tolios 2011: 67–68; SIPRI 2012). Greece bought all this hard gear not with cash, but with issuing of debt. In Greece there is no such thing as a military–industrial complex, but a *comprador*–military complex, hence the deeply subordinate position of the country in international political economy.

18.3 CONCLUDING REMARKS

A few conclusions can now be drawn. I have argued that we can understand neither the financial crisis nor the eurozone crisis if we fail to embrace a historical perspective and bring in geopolitics and security as co-constitutive variables of the overall analysis. The stagflation of the 1970s and the closing of the 'gold window' by President Nixon, as Joanne Gowa (1983) put it, is the key to understanding the unleashing of neoliberal financialization. This process has been driven by the great financial centres of New York and London and has transformed both the external and domestic environments of the capitalist state via boom-and-bust cycles, extreme financial engineering moving further away from the real economic sector. The dollarization of the oil industry and massive improvement in defence technology, and technology and innovation in general, are responsible for the defeat of communism and the spread of what came to be called globalization. This template is based on consumption and a debt-driven growth. However, it has failed to restore profitability in the real economic sector and, significantly, it has failed to arrest the slow, complex and protracted decline of Western economies as a whole, a decline that has been unfolding since the Vietnam War. Our world today is multipolar rather than unipolar.

Regionalization may be seen as an answer to Anglo-American-led neoliberal financialization. Indeed, under the leadership of Germany, Europe has managed to achieve a customs union and a currency union and became ambitious about eastward and southward expansion. But the introduction of the EMU exacerbated the pre-existing developmental gap between core and periphery, further sacrificing the industrial and agricultural capacity of the periphery on the altar of the success of Germany's model of neoliberal financialization. This is a neo-mercantilist model of low inflation, low wages and high export growth, what I called the second template. The model was operational as long as Germany could recycle its trade and financial surpluses across the eurozone, increasing of course the debt of the periphery. This is a type of financial capital circuit and everything goes well as long as nasty crises are kept at bay. But German and European banks were exposed to Anglo-American financialization. When the global financial crisis hit the German banks, spreading the crisis to the periphery, the recycling of surpluses was interrupted and Germany began exporting to other periphery states not just cars, but also severe austerity. This is where we are at the moment.

Greece is simply a tiny little pawn in this gigantic historical picture. Her financialization was completely subordinate to the interests of the core. But in the era of neoliberal financialization and interdependency, its bargaining power can increase as a result of the crisis. Greece owed and owes large amounts of money to its creditors. This could potentially have made her very powerful during the negotiations of 2010–12. When George Papandreou in October 2011 threatened to bring matters to a referendum, financial markets stalled. No one really knew exactly who held the mass quantities of Greek debt. At some point, Greece was on the front page of the *Financial Times* almost daily. For instance, if Greece had been pushed to an official default and exit from the eurozone, or if it had gone for a debtor-led default and exit in 2010–11, then pension funds in the United States holding Greek debt would have been unable to pay their pensioners, not to mention the possible knock-on effect that an official Greek default would have had on the European project, whatever that project is. Financial globalization makes things very complicated. Today, of course, thanks to the official agreements that Greece's pre-Syriza cabinets have signed with the creditors, the bulk of the Greek debt is held by public institutions and banks. Under conditions of monetary union, this means that it falls on the Greek people to pay the debt for which it bears no substantial responsibility. Thus, the left-wing Syriza party which rose to power in January 2015 is locked into the agreements made by the previous centre-right cabinets with the troika (the IMF, ECB and the EU), and having no control of monetary policy, it is bound to accept the constraints imposed by Germany and the financial establishment that dominates the EU. Only an independent monetary policy and a new central bank issuing its own currency and controlling interest and exchange rates is in a position to create the necessary conditions for pro-Keynesian, pro-welfare policies in

Greece. The same goes for the rest of the European states, especially those of the periphery.

As heterodox and post-Keynesian political economists have argued, the Greek and European crisis is not a fiscal crisis but rather and primarily a balance-of-payments crisis caused by the recklessness of external and domestic elites. But in this chapter I have moved beyond this thesis to look at the agency and geostrategic dimensions of the crisis in a macro-historical perspective. I have called the domestic elites a *comprador* class which has not just repeatedly failed to catch up with the core, but also has led the country to its current malaise. Whether importing real commodities (for example, German BMWs), or fictitious commodities (for example, AIG insurance), these idiosyncratic elites do not serve the cause of sustainable economic development and growth, let alone of catching up with the Western core. German-imposed austerity on Greece and Europe is decimating the middle classes. This is especially pronounced in Greece where party politics has become polarized, even if this is asymmetrical and the political system founded after the fall of the Colonels in 1974 is disintegrating.

More than 4000 people have committed suicide since 2010; there are street clinics in operation and barter has become widespread; the University of Athens recently suspended its operation for a few months due to lack of resources and administrative support personnel; the PASOK–New Democracy (PASOK-ND) government used to rule by decree, and we do not know how the Syriza government, despite its good intentions, could rule any better if it keeps insisting on avoiding the most important step, which is a negotiated exit or, failing this, a debtor-led default and exit from the eurozone. The far-right, neo-Nazi Golden Dawn party, meanwhile, is making headway. Similar racist parties everywhere in Europe, from Hungary and Italy, to England and France, pose a serious threat to liberal democracy and bourgeois values. One should wonder if the German Chancellor is proud of all this.

REFERENCES

Aglietta, M. (2008), 'Understanding the Structured Credit Crisis', *La Lettre du CEPII*, 275, Paris: Centre d'Etudes Prospectives et d'Informations Internationales.

Arestis, P. and M. Sawyer (2010), 'The Problems of the Economic and Monetary Union', *Journal of Economic Analysis*, 1(1), 1–15.

Brenner, R. (2003), *The Boom and the Bubble: The US in the World Economy*, London: Verso.

Brenner, R. (2006), *The Economics of Global Turbulence*, London: Verso.

Busch, K. (1978), *Die Krise der Europäischen Gemeinschaft*, Hamburg: Europaische Verlagsanstalt.
Chase, James (1999), *Acheson. The Secretary of State that Created the American World*, New York: St Martin's Press.
Darvas, Z. et al. (2011), 'A Comprehensive Approach to the Euro-Area Debt Crisis', Brussels: Bruegel, accessed 16 January 2013 at https://ideas.repec.org/p/mkg/wpaper/1101.html.
Duncan, R. (2012), 'A New Global Depression', *New Left Review*, 77, 1–21.
Fine, B. (2010), 'Locating Financialisation', *Historical Materialism*, 18, 97–116.
Fouskas, V.K. (1997), 'The Left and the Crisis of the Third Hellenic Republic, 1989–1997', in D. Sassoon (ed.), *Looking Left*, London: I.B. Tauris.
Fouskas, V.K. (1998), *Italy, Europe, the Left: The Transformation of Italian Communism and the European Imperative*, Aldershot: Ashgate.
Fouskas, V.K. and C. Dimoulas (2012), 'The Greek Workshop of Debt and the Failure of the European Project', *Journal of Balkan and Near Eastern Studies*, 14(1), 1–33.
Fouskas, V.K. and C. Dimoulas (2013), *Greece, Financialization and the EU. The Political Economy of Debt and Destruction*, New York, USA and London, UK: Palgrave Macmillan.
Fouskas, V.K. and B. Gökay (2005), *The New American Imperialism: Bush's War on Terror and Blood for Oil*, Westport, CT: Praeger.
Fouskas, V.K. and B. Gökay (2012), *The Fall of the US Empire. Global Fault-lines and the Shifting Imperial Order*, London: Pluto Press.
Frank, A.G. (1972), *Lumpenbourgeoisie, Lumpendevelopment*, New York: Monthly Review Press.
Freris, A. (1986), *The Greek Economy in the 20th Century*, London, UK and Sydney, Australia: Croom Helm.
Glyn, A. (2007), *Capitalism Unleashed*, Oxford: Oxford University Press.
Gowa, J. (1983), *Closing the Gold Window. Domestic Politics and the End of Bretton Woods*, New York: Ithaca.
Gowan, P. (1999), *The Global Gamble. Washington's Faustian Bid for World Dominance*, London: Verso.
Hobsbawm, E. (1995), *Age of Extremes*, London: Abacus.
Lapavitsas, C. (2013), *Profiting without Producing. How Finance Exploits us All*, London: Verso.
Lapavitsas, C. et al. (2010), 'Euro-zone Crisis: Beggar Thyself and Thy Neighbour', *Journal of Balkan and Near Eastern Studies*, 2(4), 330–368.
Michalopoulos, G. (2012), *Financing Greek Banks during the Crisis*, Athens: Alpha Bank.
Mundell, R. (1961), 'A Theory of Optimum Currency Area', *American Economic Review*, 51(4), 657–665.
Pagoulatos, G. and C. Triantopoulos (2009), 'The Return of the Greek Patient: Greece and the 2008 Global Financial Crisis', *South European Society and Politics*, 14(1), 45–58.
Palloix, C. (1975), *L' internationalisation du capital*, Paris: F. Masperó.
Poulantzas, N. (1974), *Les classes sociales dans le capitalism aujourd'hui*, Paris: F. Masperó.
Sassoon, D. (1986), *Contemporary Italy*, London: Longman.
Sassoon, D. (1996), *One Hundred Years of Socialism*, London: I.B. Tauris.
SIPRI (2012), SIPRI website, www.sipri.org (accessed 3 December 2013).

Stockhammer, E. (2013), 'Financialization and the Global Economy', in H.M. Wolfson and G.A. Epstein (eds), *The Political Economy of Financial Crises*, Oxford: Oxford University Press.

Tolios, Y. (2011), *Crisis, 'Odious' Debt and Violation of Payments*, Athens: Topos (in Greek).

Union of Greek Banks (2011), *The Greek Banking System*, Athens: UGB.

Wolf, M. (2013), 'The Toxic Legacy of the Greek Crisis', *Financial Times*, 18 June.

Wolfson, M.H. and A.G. Epstein (eds), *The Political Economy of Financial Crises*, Oxford: Oxford University Press.

19. Conclusions

John Weeks

Towards the end of 2007 the United States (US) economy suffered a wave of financial instability that would intensify and in 2008 result in the most severe contraction of aggregate output since the 1930s. The gathering economic disaster in the United States quickly spread to Europe and Japan. While a few predicted that the US 'boom' of the late 1990s and into the 2000s would at some point come to a crashing halt, it is doubtful that even modern-day Cassandras anticipated the disaster that unfolded.

The contributors to this book have discussed, analysed and debated the causes and consequences of the great contraction. Appearances suggest that the world economy has entered a sustained if slow and long-delayed recovery. Stagnation persisted for many advanced capitalist countries and spread to the middle-income countries including the cliché-ridden BRICS countries (Brazil, Russia, India, China, South Africa).

This prolonged global stagnation has manifested itself most obviously among the eurozone countries, whose collective performance since 2008 has been inferior to that of not only the United States and the United Kingdom, but also long-floundering Japan. An issue raised in this book is whether the behaviour of each country and region represents individual recessions derivative from the collapse of the US economy, or a generalized, global phenomenon.

Whether the post-2008 economic environment reflects a series of local contractions adding to a global downturn, or a global contraction successively manifested as local downturns, is closely related to whether we have lived through a 'crisis of capitalism'. All the authors agree that the end of the 2000s brought forth a 'crisis of capital' in almost every advanced country. Taken together, the richness of the contributions derives from differences in interpretation of causality.

In the past, Marxist debates over the cause of severe economic contractions revolved around three approaches. The so-called 'profit squeeze' hypothesis attracted many supporters in the 1960s and 1970s. According to this hypothesis, economic contractions result from the success of the working class in the distributional struggle. Whatever might be the theoretical strengths and weaknesses of this causal mechanism, the sharply rising profit share in almost every advanced country over the last 30 years prompts authors to reject this mechanism. A second line of argument focuses on inadequacy of aggregate demand due to the failure of private investment to match private saving (sometimes inaccurately called 'underconsumption').

In this context closely related themes run through this volume, indicating both agreement and differences both across chapters and in the wider community of Marxist scholars. Perhaps the most obvious tension arises from the term 'neoliberalism', its conceptual status and its role in the emergence of the global crisis. The uses of the concept fall into three categories. First, the term can refer to a set of policies introduced by and in the interest of capital in its struggle to weaken the economic and political power of the working class, and/or multi-class progressive social movements. Second, and a variation on the first, neoliberalism is a policy specific to the interests of financial capital and, therefore, creates the policy environment for the financialization of economic life, as well as making a change in the nature of accumulation.

A third approach among the authors in this volume rejects the interpretation that neoliberalism is a policy, viewing it as a more profound and transformative phenomenon that cannot be reversed by changes in a policy framework. While few in this book or in the wider community of Marxian scholars consider neoliberalism as a new mode of production, this third approach considers it to signal a different stage of capitalist development in that it alters the capitalist social structure or social formation. This formulation implies that the potential to reverse the neoliberal trend through existing bourgeois democratic institutions is extremely limited.

Closely linked to neoliberalism in all three approaches is its anti-democratic nature. This manifests itself on several levels. In the sphere of economic policy, neoliberal ideology justified removing the basic instruments of economic management from democratic accountability. Concretely, this involves: (1) 'independence' of central banks to 'insulate' them from political 'interference'; (2) legislative or even constitutional mandates for balanced budgets (most extreme among the countries of the European Union); and (3) so-called floating exchange rates, to eliminate the principal instrument for short-term management of the external balance. Taken together, this 'decommissioning' of macroeconomic policy liberates financial capital to manage the economy without democratic constraint.

The more fundamental anti-democratic nature of neoliberalism is manifested in its assault on trade unions throughout the globe, and especially in the United States, the United Kingdom and in several countries of the eurozone. Several chapters analyse this in the US context, linking it to the rising power of finance. In some chapters the attack on the organizations of the working class is viewed more narrowly as primarily an attempt to raise profits. We find no disagreement with the conclusion that the decline of trade union influence in the working class and in politics is an integral part of neoliberalism.

A theme with the strongest consensus in this book and among Marxists more generally is that capitalist economies have an inherent tendency to instability varying from mild fluctuations to severe crises. It is doubtful that any Marxist would disagree with that conclusion. For decades neoclassical economics has denied this instability, what Keynesians called the 'business' or 'trade cycle'.

The reader finds considerably less agreement on the cause of the instability and, therefore, its nature. Almost by definition, during every contraction of a capitalist economy we initially observe a fall in total profits and the rate of profit. However, establishing the causal link from profits to instability has vexed Marxists for more than a century. The chapters in this book provide analytical and empirical examples of substantially different interpretations of the profit–instability interaction.

The differences have several dimensions, and the authors consider one of the more vexing: measurement. As is made clear in several chapters, in capitalism we do not 'get what we see'. On the contrary, social and economic relations in capitalist society are distorted and frequently hidden by the act of exchange. This is especially true for profits. Marx famously wrote to Engels that one of the two best points in his book was 'the treatment of surplus value independently of its particular forms as profits, interest, ground rent, etc'. By this Marx meant that exchange generates an observed or exoteric form (profit of enterprises) derivative from an esoteric or hidden form (surplus value). The majority opinion among the authors, though not a consensus, is that instability and crises result from changes in the esoteric form, surplus-value. Because surplus-value cannot be directly observed, it is not surprising that controversy rages over how to measure it. The different measures used in this book provide insight into each author's analytical method.

Closely related to the measurement of profit is its division between capital of enterprise and financial capital. The theoretical basis of the productive and unproductive labour dichotomy is not explicitly pursued in this volume. However, a consensus exists across the chapters that financial capital is unproductive in the strict sense that the labour it employs does not create value, and therefore does not generate surplus-value.

The argument that finance is unproductive lies at the heart of discussions of financialization, another major theme in this volume. However one might define this concept, we have unanimity that the 2007–08 crisis of capital in the advanced countries was a financial collapse. For this reason several chapters explore the intricacies of financial capital. Out of this discussion comes the conclusion that policy changes reduced the constraints on financial capital in its parasitic appropriation of surplus-value. Whatever the causal mechanism authors use to explain the crisis, all agree that financialization made the collapse more extreme. By extension comes the theme that the growing dominance of finance in part explains the slowness of recovery.

One of the strengths of the volume is the near absence of causality mechanisms that rely on economic variables only. Of the many characteristics that distinguish Marxian analysis from neoclassical economics is the inseparable interaction of the forces and relations of production. Quite strong is the theme that the global crisis cannot be understood without reference to changes in the relations between capital and labour. Too often, Marxian analysis has tended to consider capitalism from a purely economic perspective, stressing perceived inherent and mechanical processes without reference to social relations. The chapters in this book do not take that reductionist approach.

Often critics accuse Marxists of two major analytical transgressions: (1) packaging what are essentially mainstream arguments in the language of *Capital*; and (2) retreating to the safety of purely theoretical formulations in order to disguise an inability to treat the concrete, 'reality'. The authors in this book refute both accusations. The reader will find no 'Marxology' here; that is, construction of faux arguments by extensive quotations from *Capital* and other works by Marx. The authors' success in applying aspects of the analytical framework derivative from Marx is demonstrated in both the arguments themselves and their variety.

Cynics might dismiss this variety and differences as evidence of the absence of a core framework from which to derive rigorous analysis. The truth is quite the contrary. The monolithic pedantry of mainstream economics serves a disciplining role, because those who move outside it find themselves marginalized and even expelled from the profession. By contrast, the differences among those writing in the Marxian tradition demonstrate openness to new ideas and tolerance for dissent. To put it simply, the neoclassical economists are the rigid ideologues, while Marxists thrive on theoretical differences. That is a central message of this book.

Index